THE IMMIGRANT HERITAGE OF AMERICA SERIES

Cecyle S. Neidle, Editor

Zion In America

The Jewish Experience from Colonial Times to the Present

By Henry L. Feingold

Twayne Publishers, Inc. :: New York

Library of Congress Cataloging in Publication Data

Feingold, Henry L   1931–
    Zion in America; the Jewish experience from colonial times to
the present.

    (The Immigrant heritage of America series)
    Bibliography: p. 343.
    1. Jews in the United States—History.   2. Judaism—United
States.   I. Title.
E184.J5F377   917.3'06'924   74-3239
ISBN 0-8057-3298-5

MANUFACTURED IN THE UNITED STATES OF AMERICA

Contents

Preface

THIS BOOK AIMS TO FURNISH THE GENERAL READER AND THE BEGINNING student with a clear, concise, and at the same time, scholarly historical synthesis of the American Jewish experience. An increase in the number of courses in the field in our colleges and universities indicates a noteworthy growth of interest in the field. Some of this newfound enthusiasm is undoubtedly attributable to the general interest in things ethnic. I do not find such motivation illegitimate and hope that in some way this book satisfies that interest. But I am also aware that the field of American Jewish history antedates the general interest in ethnic history. The American Jewish Historical Society was organized in 1892 and has since that time attracted many serious scholars.

The original insights and formulations which are contained in this work are derived from a fresh view of the published original and secondary sources rather than the unearthing of new material. Those familiar with the field will not fail to recognize ideas whose origin can be traced to historians like Jacob Marcus, Bertram Korn, Hyman Grinstein, Rudolf Glanz, and many others. It is these men who have produced the indispensable monographic building blocks on which any synthesis must stand. I think I have read virtually everything they have written and naturally in the process I have reshaped much of what they have said to fit into my own historical perspective. Recognition of their contribution, except where I quote them directly, is confined to the bibliography found at the end of the book. Severe space limitations compelled me to employ an abbreviated form of footnoting. Notes are confined to direct quotations and statistics and to the inclusion of additional data which do not fit into the flow of the narrative.

To state that American Jewish history begins in September, 1654, is neither technically nor conceptually true. To begin at the beginning, we must go back to the mid-fifteenth century to examine life in the Iberian and Polish havens, for it was events in these communities which impinge directly on our story. That means that the history of American Jewry is actually over four centuries old. The fact that it is a comparatively long story that must be told in a limited number of words has compelled me to remain on the surface where I might have wanted to penetrate in depth, and to omit certain elements of American Jewish history entirely. There are many such areas in the narrative which the practiced eye will recognize so that I do not need to enumerate them. I am most conscious of the omission of the entire cultural dimension, the Yiddish theater and press, and particularly the remarkable Jewish intellectual nexus centered in New York City. American Jewish history seems denuded without them. But to do these areas any sort of justice would have required an additional volume.

The sheer length of American Jewish history makes periodization especially important. It not only lends shape to the narrative but also helps delineate events. I have adopted the fourfold periodization scheme first suggested by Jacob Marcus but have modified it to make room for events, especially in the area of foreign policy and the development of the Jewish labor movement, which do not readily seem to fit into Marcus's conception.[1]

A word is in order regarding the suppositions which have shaped my thinking about American Jewish history. In their uprooting, transplantation, and acculturation experience, American Jewry has much in common with other ethnic groups. But there exists a sharp divergence in the nature and the terms of the Jewish transaction with the host country. Jews are more successful in America and at the same time retain a higher degree of group consciousness. The abundant evidence of their comparatively greater achievements in business, the professions, or in cultural pursuits, can be dismissed. For most people these things are a matter of taste. Who is to say that the contributions of a good farmer or miner are less worthy than those of an accountant or businessman? But in their group achievement, the richness of their self-help organizational infrastructure, the establishment of a unique Jewish labor movement, their political behavior, which resembles nothing so much as the behavior of an enlightened patrician aristocracy, and lastly, their amazingly rapid rise to middle-class rank—these are not matters of taste. It is "making it" in terms set down by the American culture. I call this phenomenon American Jewish exceptionalism. By this I mean not only that American Jewry produces an elite group of achievers who have had, in every period of its history, a formidable impact on the nation. That is self-evident. I mean also that within the framework of American ethnic history and world Jewish history, American Jewry is a unique group.

Characterizing a group as exceptional, even if it is a relatively value-free judgment, is fraught with danger for the historian. The general

---

1. J. R. Marcus, "The Periodization of American Jewish History," in J. R. Marcus, *Studies in American Jewish History* (Cincinnati, 1969).

reader may be tempted to dismiss the work as boastful while the professional historian will suspect that the author has not been able to muster sufficient detachment from his subject to attain objectivity. The filiopietism of early writings on American ethnic history, filled, as it was, with apologies for real or imagined shortcomings, lends credence to these suspicions. I have tried to avoid these pitfalls while at the same time not underplaying the singular character of American Jewish achievement.

Strictly speaking, comparison of American Jewry with other immigrant groups, even if it were desirable, is not possible. It is something like comparing apples and oranges. While American Jewry shares some of the characteristics of other immigrant groups and has undergone a similar reshaping by the host culture, it is not merely another immigrant-ethnic group at all. Mordecai Kaplan, the founder of the Reconstructionist movement, once classified Judaism as a separate civilization. It contained, to be sure, some ethnic elements but these were superimposed on a religious culture fashioned by thousands of years of distinctive history. Basically, it is the nature of the Jewish historical experience which differentiates American Jews from other ethnic groups in America. When the Italian or Irish immigrant left his homeland he also stepped out of its history. Denuded of his own culture and history, he was more prepared to embrace the new. The process of Americanization would take generations to complete but in the end it was achieved. Today the real American-Irish cannot fully fathom what Bernadette Devlin is getting excited about, nor is the American of Italian ancestry slandered by the term Mafia. They no longer are able to identify fully with the original culture. To the degree that the Jewish immigrant from Europe was also a Spaniard, German, Russian or Pole, that transformation also occurred to him, albeit not on the same terms, since he was never permitted to be a member of these national communities. In the case of the German-Jewish immigration of the nineteenth century and to some extent of the East European immigration of the nineteenth and twentieth, Jewish immigrants came as part of a larger wave of immigration. But they came for reasons that had something to do with their Jewishness. There was in most Jewish immigrants a feeling of belonging to a separate people which, rather than being a product of a specific territory, was internalized. It was a national culture of the spirit and for that reason it could not be so readily abandoned. Whether from Iberia, Central Europe, or Eastern Europe, the Jewish immigrant remained a part of his own distinctive civilization and therefore could not be reshaped as rapidly or completely. Their accommodation to the new country would be qualitatively different from other immigrant groups.

What we see in America is the interaction of two distinct historical traditions, both infinitely malleable. Rather than the typical model of the host nation relentlessly imposing its culture on a group of historically denuded immigrants ready to be remolded, we have in the case of America and its Jews a cultural transaction in which each takes something from the other. The sheer size and power of the host culture has, to be sure, made this transaction an unequal one, but it is not outlandish to suggest that, at least in a cultural sense, America has to some small degree also been Judaized.

The existence of an independent Jewish historico-cultural tradition poses certain problems for the historian of American Jewry. He has the alternative, for example, of viewing the Jewish experience in America as an episode in the flow of Jewish history. A decade ago, one Jewish historian compared the American Jewish experience with that of other Jewish communities in the western hemisphere with suggestive, although tentative, conclusions.[2] On the other hand, the Jewish experience can be viewed from the perspective of American history in which it has been ensconced for more than four centuries and with whose citizens it shares a common fate. I view American Jewry as being delicately suspended between these two pulls. On the one hand, it is beckoned fully to integrate with the mainstream of American life; on the other, it retains its identity and connection with K'lal Yisrael, that persistent and mysterious force which binds Jews together wherever they may be. Today that pull is illustrated by the continued impact of secularism and embourgeoisement on the American Jewish community while at the same time its connection with the state of Israel, which symbolizes the ongoingness of the Jewish historical tradition, has never been stronger.

Still other complications are encountered in viewing American Jewry in its American context. Jewish exceptionalism is acted out in a national community which in its organizational principle is itself exceptional. Unlike other nations in which Jews have found a haven, America, rather than being an organic community, is a political contrivance, invented during the Age of Reason. It has no millennia of history behind it and has absorbed millions of the world's unwanted people. Because of these circumstances it possesses a highly plastic culture which makes the task of national definition problematic. Since no one is able to say with any degree of certainty what an American is, a great deal of time and energy is devoted to discovering what he is not. One does not find in the parliament of France or England a special committee to root out un-French or un-English activities as one does in America. Organic nations know instinctively who and what belong. The Jews of fifteenth-century

---

2. Moshe Davis, "Centres of Jewry in the Western Hemisphere: A Comparative Approach," The Jewish Journal of Sociology, vol. V, No. 1 (June 1963).

Iberia, the Jews of twentieth-century Germany, the Algerians in France, and the Hindus in Britain today share one experience. They have been made aware that, secular laws notwithstanding, a centrifugal force keeps them apart from the body of the nation. This country, on the other hand, employs a centripetal force to draw its disparate elements into the national community. It is not employed consistently as any black man in America will tell you. But to the extent that other hyphenates have won access to the levers of power it has worked, perhaps not so much by dint of the process of democracy as by the size of the gross national product. For Jews, historically conditioned to apartness, this pressure toward ingathering presents both a prospect and a problem. They know all too well what they must do to survive in a hostile environment but hardly anything at all about how to cope with a benevolent one which seeks to absorb them.

In truth no Jewish community has ever faced this precise problem before. What was only a promise in Moorish Spain or in sixteenth-century Holland appears rapidly to be becoming a reality in the United States. One does best by viewing the historic odyssey of American Jewry as an entirely new chapter in the long history of Judaism. What I have presented in these pages is the story of a unique and exceptional people placed in an equally unique and exceptional milieu. Despite the many parallels one can draw to previous experiences in Jewish history, the circumstances are unprecedented. No Jewry has ever been on this path before. There are few guideposts to help us understand this page in Jewish history. It is not that we lack first-rate historians in the field. One need only peruse the bibliography to note that they are numerous. But the field still awaits a Simon Dubnow to show us the way. That a community of six million Jews which ranks in importance with the Jews of East Europe or of Iberia and even of ancient Israel itself should not yet have produced one, is a source of puzzlement. Perhaps in some way this brief book will ignite a spark of interest that will finally bring such a seminal historical mind to the field of American Jewish history. I offer it, with all its shortcomings, in that light.

Two grants, one by the Memorial Foundation for Jewish Culture, and the other, a Summer grant by the City University Research Foundation, helped me to complete this book. Dr. Cecyle Neidle, the editor of the series of which this book is part, went over each chapter with a practiced editorial eye and reminded me once again how crucial is the relationship between syntax and meaning. Myrna Engelmeyer of the Baruch College History Department, read the manuscript in its entirety and by the adroit juxtaposition of a phrase here and the insertion of a word there brought out new rich meaning in the narrative which surely would otherwise have remained buried. Needless to add, such imperfections as remain, errors of conceptualization and fact, are the author's.

HENRY L. FEINGOLD

Ludlow, Vermont

Zion in America

CHAPTER I

Old World Background

WHEN THE JEWISH EXPERIENCE IN AMERICA IS COMPARED WITH JEWISH experience in other nations its uniqueness stands out in bold relief. One finds no evidence of expulsions or officially sanctioned pogroms and relatively few instances of restrictions and prohibitions and the numerous other travesties to which Jewish history is traditionally heir. Indeed when Louis Brandeis suggested, a generation ago, that "Jewish spirit and ideals" were never more in consonance with the "noblest aspirations" of the host country than they were between America and its Jews he was pointing out the existence of a reciprocity of interest which others have noted in that area where Jewish and American history intersect.[1] Each party has reaped advantage from the existence of the other.

That reciprocity is evident throughout the more than three centuries of the American Jewish experience, but particularly so in the relationship between the "discovery" of the New World and the Jewish condition in Europe which is the subject of this first chapter. We note that at the juncture in Jewish history when the Iberian and later the Polish haven, in which Jews had found some measure of security, became untenable, their desperate need for a new refuge was realized. They were, of course, not the only group in Europe which would benefit from the discovery of America but few other groups played such an active role in the commercial activities and the development of the nautical technology which allowed it to come to pass.

In September, 1654, the bark *St. Charles* weighed anchor in the spacious harbor of the port of New Amsterdam and discharged twenty-three bedraggled passengers. They were Sephardic Jews (stemming from the Iberian peninsula) from the former Dutch colony of Recife which had been recaptured by the Portuguese in January of that year. There was little in their meager belongings to suggest that these Jews had once belonged to a thriving community. Now they stood virtually penniless on the pier, unable to square accounts with Jacques la Motte, the Captain of the *St. Charles*. Only after much argument was the grasping La Motte grudgingly satisfied with holding three of their group as security against the outstanding debt. It was not an auspicious beginning in a land that would one day become the principal hope for Jewish refuge and resettlement.

Behind the arrival of these refugees lay a long history of misfortune which began with the dispersion of Iberia's Jewish community. The Jews who lived in Spain and Portugal once considered themselves fortunate. Under the enlightened rule of the Moors, who consolidated their conquest of the peninsula in 711, the Jews thrived and even experienced a kind of "golden age" in their exile. They were able to make significant contributions to science, culture and commerce. Many became highly regarded court physicians and advisers, while others made their mark as highly skilled artisans. Not forgetting their Judaic faith, they honed sharp a special talent for interpreting Jewish law and developing its philosophical underpinnings.

The idyllic situation in which Jews found themselves under Moorish hegemony changed markedly in the thirteenth century. Divided among themselves, the Moors proved unable to withstand the Christian onslaught from the north. By the year 1212 only the kingdom of Granada in the southeastern part of the peninsula remained in their hands. Now subject to the whims of the less cosmopolitan princes in the Christian part of Spain, the position of the Jews began to deteriorate. At the behest of the indigenous merchant class, priests and certain hostile officials of the court, the activities of Jewish traders were curtailed. Jewish artisans and small merchants too began to feel the effects of unfavorable regulations. By the end of the century their once secure economic and cultural position had been replaced by uncertainty and widespread impoverishment.

Had Christian hostility been merely directed against the commercial activities of the Jews they might have been able to endure it. But it was made of more volatile stuff. In its ascendancy the Catholic Church of Spain could boast of possessing more than its share of militancy and passion. Years of struggle with Islam had generated an unmatched crusading zeal and a suspicion of all non-Christians. The memory of the favored position of the Jews under the Moslems could not fail to rankle the aroused Christian masses who had been taught by their priests that the Jews had betrayed and helped crucify their Lord. As if to compound the felony the Jews of Spain subbornly rejected Christ and the Christian faith.

Ironically the high priorities given by Spaniards to the soldierly virtues allowed some Jews to continue to play an important role in administering the kingdom. A nominal conversion to Christianity allowed many Jews to exercise the administrative and commercial talents they appeared to possess in such abundance. For generations after the decline of Moorish power Spanish princes maintained this mutually profitable liaison with this experienced cadre of administrators and businessmen called New Christians, conversos or Marranos.[2] Marranos and Jews continued to fill the critical posts that maintained the economy and the state. Some Marranos were able to enter the innermost core of the Church and state hierarchy by means of intermarriage. A liaison with a Christian prince through a highly placed Marrano or court-Jew often gave the local Jewish community a modicum of security.

But their position remained at best a precarious one since not even conversion proved sufficient to allay the hostility of the masses. Suspicion regarding the sincerity of the conversion proved relatively easy to arouse and princes were not above deflecting hostility directed against themselves to the Marrano tax farmer. On Ash Wednesday in 1391, for example, popular hostility against Jews was skillfully played upon by the monk Ferrand Martínez and by Archbishop Paul of Burgos, who was himself a convert. As a result, a bloody massacre of Jews occurred in Seville. Hundreds of Jews were slaughtered while others were forcibly converted or sold into slavery. A bloody riot in Toledo in 1449 was sparked by popular resentment against a special border defense tax of one million Maravedis paid to a Marrano tax collector. The suspicion that the Marrano conversions were not sincere had, in a minority of cases, some basis in fact. Some Marranos continued to practice in secret Judaic rituals such as lighting candles on Friday nights. Moreover, the high rate of recidivism among them was common knowledge.

It was to counteract such reversion that the tribunal of the Inquisition, which had been in existence in Aragon since the thirteenth century, was brought to Castile in 1480. Established by the Church to counteract heresy, the tribunal soon found a fertile field for its activities among the Marranos. But Ferdinand, whose maternal grandmother was rumored to have been a Jewess, had no reason to welcome the Inquisition.[3] The tribunal's jurisdiction was not controlled by the crown and its power to confiscate property could serve to enrich the Church at the expense of the crown. However, that possible disadvantage was balanced by the opportunity the Inquisition offered to weaken dissident nobles, especially among the Castilians, where the proportion of Marranos was particularly high. Agitation by the militant clergy to impose the Inquisition proved nigh impossible to withstand. Thus in 1480 the persistent pressure brought to bear by Tomás de Torquemeda, the queen's confessor, was rewarded with success. The Inquisition was institutionalized in Seville.

That served as signal to many Marranos to seek refuge in Portugal and in Spain's far-flung empire. By the turn of the fifteenth century a royal edict prohibited them from settling in the new colonies. Marrano emigration was once again permitted after the death of Isabella but in 1518, when Charles became king, it was halted again. Four years thereafter a trickle of Marrano emigration to the colonies reappeared, this time strictly regulated by the royal administration. By the end of the sixteenth century Marranos developed an alternate route to escape the clutches of the Inquisition. They fled to the Netherlands which between 1565 and 1609 waged an often bitter struggle for independence from Spain and therefore welcomed these talented, frequently wealthy, Spanish dissidents.

By 1593 Amsterdam, the thriving capital city of the Netherlands, was well on its way to becoming the "new Jerusalem." Once free of the coercive religious edicts of Spain, many Marranos lost little time in reasserting, often with a special passion, their original Jewish faith. Under Dutch hegemony the Marranos began to trickle into New World Dutch colonies like Recife which had been wrested from the Portuguese in 1620. In the colonies there frequently occurred a reunification with their coreligionists who had earlier chosen a more direct route to Spanish America.

But even in the New World their new-found security often proved to be short-lived. In 1516 the Inquisition was established in the West Indies and soon after moved to the mainland where it began to take its toll. An *auto da fé* in Lima in 1639 claimed among its victims eleven Marranos. Many others met the same fate in the next decades.[4]

Only a small proportion of Iberia's Jews, usually of high station, chose conversion and resettlement over suffering and living out their lives as a pariah group. The misfortunes visited upon these Jews gave rise to visions of redemption in which the New World came to play a prominent part. In 1650, for example, Menasseh Ben Israel, a prominent rabbi living in Amsterdam whose later negotiations with Oliver Cromwell gained unofficial access to England for Jews, saw the New World as a place where Jewish grievances and suffering would be redressed. In his work, *The Hope of Israel*, Ben Israel linked the Jews directly to the New World by accepting at face value the numerous stories then circulating that the Indians were, in fact, the ten lost tribes of Israel. For Jews, and some Christians as well, this could only mean that the biblical injunction which spoke of dispersing the Jews to the farthest corners of the earth had come to pass and that therefore the coming of the Messiah, or his second coming, was imminent.[5] Indeed this was probably the background for the success Sabbatai Zevi, the false Messiah, gained in attracting a number of followers in the Netherlands in 1648. An incidental byplay of such imaginings was the awakening of an enthusiasm for a New World haven for the long-suffering Jewish people. Indeed, barely twenty-two years after the Dutch had established themselves in Bahia in 1620, Jewish settlers arrived to establish a community in Recife.

Technically speaking, Jews did not suffer the agonies of the Inquisition. These were reserved for professing Christians who had gone astray with such heresies as Judaizing, practicing Judaism in secret. Nevertheless, the stiff-necked resistance of Jews to voluntary conversion to Christianity became a continuous source of rancor. It was important to convert the Jews not only for theological reasons but for practical ones as well. The existence of a viable Jewish community in Spain was related in some measure to the high degree of recidivism among the Marranos. For Catholic zealots the expulsion of the Jews from Spain seemed a logical solution. At the same time there were more practical souls who were aware that such a drastic step would create as many problems as it solved. After all, these stubborn Jewish aliens had lived in Spain longer than anyone cared to remember. They had become so deeply rooted in the society that a precipitous attempt to remove them would result in considerable social and economic dislocation.

With the final expulsion of the Moors in January, 1492, Spain was fully free to chase after the specter of religious homogeneity. Within two months a royal decree expelling those Jews who refused to convert to Catholicism was promulgated. The date set for their departure, August 1, 1492, the ninth of Av on the Hebrew calendar, was a fateful one. It was also the anniversary date of the destruction of the temple. Attempts to soften the decree by Rabbi Abraham Senior, the chief Rabbi of Spain, and Isaac Abrabanel, the principal financial adviser to the royal court, failed to dissuade the Spanish authorities from the drastic course they had chosen.

As the date set for the expulsion drew near, forlorn bands of Jews, many with carts piled high with household goods, could be observed crowding the roads leading to the port of Cadiz in the southwestern section of Spain. The aged and infirm who could not be taken on such an uncertain venture, accompanied their families as far as their strength would carry them and then crawled to the side of the road to die on the soil of their beloved Spain.[6] Others chose the option of converting to Catholicism, an act that had always been abhorrent to them. When the Jews caught their first glimpse of the sea, the traditional chanting stopped and a loud mournful invocation rent the air. Let the Lord part the sea and lead the children of Israel to a new Promised Land, as He had done during the exodus from Egypt.

But no such miracle occurred, at least no miracle that the 150,000 Jews about to be exiled could perceive. Painfully they resettled themselves in the Moslem states of North Africa. Some went to Palestine, others to Genoa, Salonika, and the more remote area of the Crimea. They could not know that on the day following their departure, Columbus, unable to use the port of Cadiz because it was too crowded with Jews, would set sail from the nearby port of Palos to discover the very haven for which they were praying.

Several thriving Jewish communities soon adorned the Spanish, Portuguese and Dutch possessions in the New World. It would be no exaggeration to claim that some measure of the administrative brilliance and the commercial profitability of Spanish New World rule should be attributed to them.[7] Spain's loss became America's gain, a transaction which would be repeated several times during the waves of emigration from Europe in the next three centuries. Ultimately, too, it became the northern tier of colonies rather than those of Spanish America in which the long sought-for Jewish haven was founded.

It was first the tolerant rule of the Dutch in Recife which allowed the Jews to establish themselves but even then they were not totally secure from future wanderings. In 1654 the Dutch colony was retaken by the Portuguese and the Jewish settlers were compelled to flee. It was a small remnant of this dispersion which sailed into the New Amsterdam harbor on the September day in 1654.

The preponderance of Sephardic Jews in the colonies of North America was short-lived. Soon a trickle of Ashkenazic Jews, emanating from Central and Eastern Europe, appeared in the several Dutch, Swedish, and French-controlled colonies. One historian estimates that as early as 1695 the Jewish community of New York City was equally divided between Jews of Sephardic and Ashkenazic origin and the latter group was clearly in the majority by 1729, though the Sephardic religious ritual was maintained.[8] The Ashkenazic preponderance may have been even clearer in Philadelphia and its satellite community of Easton.[9] Some of the most noted colonial Jewish families including the Phillipses, Simonses, Gratzes, Hartzes, and the family of Haym Salomon were of Ashkenazic stock.

These later Jewish settlers were part of a great population movement which, between the fourteenth and sixteenth centuries, saw Jews move from Western to Eastern Europe, and then revert to the West again. The westward flow which was to continue for three centuries, not only populated America with Jews of eastern stock but did the same for Western Europe. Eastern Europe served as the great population reservoir for the less prolific Jewish communities of the Western world.

Basically the motivation of the Ashkenazic immigration was the same as that of the Sephardic Jews. Their position was equally tenuous and they suffered trials no less tormenting. Between 1095, the year of the calling of the First Crusade, and 1348, when the Black Death descended on Europe, Jewish life was endurable, not because Christians gave them quarter, but rather because of the uncanny ability of Jews to create a human, even protective environment, under the most abysmal conditions. There may even have existed a modicum of fulfillment within their strong families and rich communal life not to be found in the outside world. But such resources could hardly compensate for the insecurity of their existence. They lived at the sufferance of their Christian neighbors.

Excluded from corporate feudal life, Jews were more subject to the vicissitudes of local wars which were the *sine qua non* of the feudal condition. In a society whose *raison d'être* was protection, there was no institution to protect Jews. As in Spain, Jews displayed a stubborn resistance to all attempts to convert them. A later age might respect such devotion, but in the age of religious zealotry it was a standing invitation to martyrdom. That, in fact, became the fate of hundreds of Jews in Europe. Against them was hurled every vile accusation that could be thought of. The Jew was a desecrator of the host, a ritual murderer, a seducer of Christian women. When the plague decimated Jews and Christians without distinction, Jews were accused by their hysterical Christian neighbors of poisoning the wells. If they were fortunate enough to survive Christian rage, they were then frequently forced to leave their homes to find shelter in the woods. And if allowed to return it was only to inhabit the dark congested ghettos, sealed off from the remainder of the comunity.

For Jews the crusades variously called in 1095, 1146, 1189, and 1208 proved to be a man-made disaster, for they, rather than more distant "infidels," became the object of the crusaders' zeal. The mob of declassed believers who rallied to the call of Pope Urban II in 1095 were barely able to distinguish between Jerusalem and the nearest sizable town. Why turn to distant lands to wrest the holy sepulchre, cried Peter the Venerable, "if the evil blaspheming Jews, far worse than the Saracens [live] not at a distance but in our midst...."[10] Accordingly, Jewish communities in the Rhineland, Speyer, Worms, Mainz, and Cologne were sacked and thousands of Jews came under the crusader's knife. French peasants were recruited for crusades by the promise that debts owed to Jewish moneylenders would be canceled, along with all mortal sins. The temptation to plunder scarce liquid assets in the hands of Jews proved impossible to withstand. Special taxes to pay for wars and the outfitting of crusaders were levied against the Jewish communities. Precipitous expulsion, such as Jews suffered in England in 1290 and Spain in 1492, became common in smaller communities.

Stigmatized, impoverished, and in all ways degraded, Jews were thrown back on their own resources. In their communities they developed resiliency and a rich family life which shielded them from the depredations of the outside world. But they paid a dear price for their isolation. Their genius lay in acting as catalysts and conduits between different classes, regions, and cultures and that role was restricted by the physical, cultural, and social isolation in which they were forced to live.

The fragmentation of papal power which occurred as a result of the Protestant Reformation in the sixteenth century offered the Jews a hope for better times. For the moment religious antagonism seemed to become an intra-Christian affair and the renewed interest in the Old Testament which Jews had never abandoned boded well for the "people of the book." But the hoped-for respite did not materialize. Martin Luther reverted to a murderous hatred of the Jews when his plans to convert them proved no more successful than those of his Catholic antagonists. At the same time, beset with a full-scale uprising, the Catholic world became even more anxious to maintain orthodoxy. It was the powerless Jewish community that was stamped by both groups as the source of their woes. Jews paid a bloody price in the religious wars which followed the Reformation.

Just as conditions in Western and Central Europe were forcing Jews out of their age-old settlements along the Rhine and lower Danube, there developed a strong pull drawing them to the East. Polish princes such as Boleslav and Casimir sought to make use of these pariahs. Aware of the important economic role Jews had played in the West, they undoubtedly hoped that the Jews would duplicate the feat in their own provinces.

These were still encrusted in static feudal relationships which kept them so overwhelmingly agricultural that there seemed little opportunity for developing an indigenous middle class. To the Polish nobility, locked in perpetual struggle with a sullen, hostile peasantry, often of different faith, the idea of importing a class which might serve as a buffer, while generating commercial activity at the same time, had an allure all its own. In 1264 Boleslav issued a "Charter of Privileges" which was extended in 1334 by Casimir the Great. The charter permitted the Jews to establish virtually an autonomous community within the kingdom of Poland. As word spread among the Jews of the promising developments in the East, the Jewish population began to shift to the Polish refuge. In 1501 it was estimated that only fifty Jews inhabited the area but by 1648 fifty percent of Europe's Jews, 500,000, had settled there.[11]

Jewish life in the Polish refuge may not always have lived up to the promise of Boleslav's charter, but it marked an improvement over what Jews had known in the West. In effect, Jews governed themselves through the local Kehillahs, an institution which exercised religious, economic, and judicial functions. In some cases, for example, the Kehillah imposed controls on rent and strictly regulated commercial transactions. By 1530 these Kehillahs organized themselves into a federated national assembly called the Council of Four Lands. Included in the Council were representatives of the Jewish communities of Greater Poland, Little Poland, Ruthenia, and Volhynia. A formal liaison with the Polish royal court was also established. Under such optimal conditions the possibility of building a "new Zion" in Poland was good. In the first half of the seventeenth century the Jewish community of Poland entered upon a rabbinic golden age. But two centuries later, under the influence of modern nationalism, the Poles began to complain that the Jewish community constituted "a state within a state."

Indeed, there was much truth to the complaint. Jews usually lived separately in small "shtetlach," a term derived from the German term for town with a Yiddish diminutive attached to it. There they were governed by their rabbis according to Talmudic law. The "shtetl" was more than merely a geographic location. For the first time since the exile a total Jewish environment had been created.[12] The "shtetl" gave Jews a strong sense of identity and a sense of shared community enterprise. Despite dire poverty and a siege-like relationship to the outside community, "shtetl" life was at the outset relatively free of symptoms of social pathology such as violent crime and disorder. It developed what can probably be considered the most intensely Jewish religious and social milieu in Jewish history.

If the "shtetl" was eminently successful as a transmitter of Jewish culture, it was unable to give the Jewish population the sense of physical security required for survival in the hostile Polish environment. The conspicuous position of Jews as middlemen, managers, and artisans was beset with dangers. Their roles as estate managers for absentee landlords, tax collectors, and wholesalers placed Jews in an exposed position in the continuing struggle between the Catholic feudal nobility and the peasantry which in the eastern provinces adhered to the Russian Orthodox faith. Jews tended to become a foil not only for the disaffected peasantry who saw in them a visible symbol of their exploitation, but also for the lesser nobility who envied their special position.

Bereft of any independent power, the "shtetl" was dependent for security on its liaison with the absentee nobility and more directly on the local strongman. Jews were also economically vulnerable because they were prohibited from owning land, the principal source of livelihood and status. Nor did their position as middlemen long remain unchallenged. A trickle of German merchants and artisans found their way to the eastern provinces to challenge the Jewish preponderance in commerce. Supported by the Catholic establishment of Germany, these merchants and artisans educated their Polish coreligionists in the Western tradition of placing economic prohibitions against Jewish commercial activity. The anti-Semitic practices so common in Western Europe found a fertile soil in a nation as rife with tension as the kingdom of Poland.

Gradually Jews noted a change in the favorable environment of Poland. As early as 1496 the newly founded Jagiello dynasty succumbed to anti-Jewish pressure and expelled the Jews from Lithuania. When the Jagiello dynasty died out in 1572, the Polish kingdom was on the verge of disintegration. The reign of Stephen Batory (1575–1586) saw the further extension of the nobility's power. Racked with internal and external troubles, what had formerly been a refuge for Jews became in many instances a bloody graveyard.

The decline of central authority on which Jews depended for protection was a signal for the peasantry, especially in the region between the Dniester and Dnieper rivers, to rise up against the hated Polish landlords. Poland's avaricious neighbors, Russia and Sweden, could not long resist the lure of land and booty which such a power vacuum represented. Between 1648 and 1649 and again in 1656 a cossack "hetman," Bogdan Chmielnicki, trading on peasant discontent, succeeded in welding together a coalition of Ukrainian cossacks, peasants, and Crimean Tartars. Together they ravaged the land, singling out as a special target the hapless Jews, thousands of whom were slaughtered in Kiev and other towns. Russia and Sweden invested the Polish kingdom and the devastation which followed broke the back of what remained of the Polish refuge for Jews.

What had once been enlightened rabbinic rule now became a conservative rabbinic establishment anxious above all to maintain security. The vitality of the Kehillah and "shtetl" life waned. It had once been notably free of class antagonism because under Talmudic law the attainment of wealth carried with it a special obligation to serve less fortunate brethren. These traditions gave way as the wealthy shifted the growing financial burden, caused partly by the levying of extortionist taxes against Jews, to those least able to pay.* The quality of leadership and learning, long distinctive among Jews, also deteriorated. Later the advent of conscription, which the wealthy also were able to shift onto

---

* The Council of Four Lands was dissolved in. 1764 because it proved to be an unsatisfactory tax agent for the Polish Sejin.

the poor by dint of their ability to pay for substitutes, became an additional cause for class bitterness.

Under such unhappy circumstances there were two alternatives for the Jews of Poland: (1) to embark on a spiritual migration through religious escapism and mysticism; (2) to migrate physically. The latter alternative was rarely available to Jews. The thousands of Jews who in 1648 and the years after came to believe devoutly that a Smyrnan adventurer, Sabbatai Zevi, was the long-awaited Messiah, was symptomatic of Jewish despair. By the same token, the rise of Hassidism, a pietistic movement which emphasized the efficacy of religious ecstasy and mysticism, was not only a reflection of this internal spiritual migration but a reaction against the ossified formalism of the rabbinic establishment which lacked genuine religious feeling. A small number of Jews, usually unattached and with readier access to the West, began the painful process of uprooting themselves. In the final decades of the nineteenth century that migration gained momentum and brought millions of eastern Jews to the United States.

In its earliest phases, however, only a handful were able to emigrate. Sometimes they were encouraged by an invitation such as that extended by Frederick William of Prussia in 1671 who invited sixty wealthy Jewish families to resettle in his kingdom. Undoubtedly he was prompted by the hope that these Jews would play the same role in Prussia that they had played in Poland. In 1648 the first Polish Jews made their appearance in Amsterdam where their Spanish coreligionists had already established themselves. Others reached the port of Hamburg and various towns in the interior of the German principalities. They soon discovered that the situation in the West was no improvement at all, especially for newcomers. Jews were ghettoized and sometimes forced, according to the edict of Pope Paul IV in 1555, to wear special, often demeaning, identification symbols. In the wake of the Thirty Years' War harsh measures were enacted against Jews including expulsion from Hamburg and Vienna.

The most daring and fortunate of these Jewish migrants sometimes succeeded in reaching England which then served as a way station to the colonies.[13] The earliest Jewish settlement in Georgia, for example, was composed of Ashkenazic Jews who were, in a sense, dumped in that colony in 1733 by Sephardic investors in the royal stock company chartered by George II in 1732.

The year 1654, when the bedraggled group of Jews landed in New Amsterdam, marks a critical juncture in Jewish history. It saw the final disintegration of one Jewish haven in Eastern Europe and the bare beginnings of another. It is not necessary to postulate that such a matching of good and bad fortune indicates the workings of a heavenly hand in Jewish history. Nevertheless such coincidences give the story of Jewish survival, which is the exilic history of the Jews, a uniquely dramatic quality.

The Jewish role in developing colonial America was less distinguished for the number of settlers than for the kind of settlers they were. Referring to their talent and daring in bringing together the several components of business, one historian has called them "courageous enterprisers."[14] It was a talent long associated with the Jews of Europe. They came to the New World ideally suited to play the role of nascent capitalists, for rather than having been steeped in an agricultural tradition they had been compelled by their circumstances to learn the "secrets" of the business entrepreneur.

The involvement of Jews in the commercial revolution, of which the discovery and development of the colonies was a part, can hardly be exaggerated. After the nations of Europe achieved a modicum of unity in the fifteenth and sixteenth centuries, they embarked upon a period of intense commercial activity in which territorial expansion and foreign trade played a prominent part. Appetites previously whetted by tales and goods brought back to Europe by crusaders and international merchants, sought to be satiated by the imagined wealth of the outside world. A series of voyages of exploration, sponsored first by Portugal and Spain, but soon followed by England, France, and Holland, established a link to the far-off places in the Far East, Africa, and the western hemisphere. Permanent settlement soon followed.

Excluded from the craft guilds and the ownership of land, Jews naturally gravitated to activities not yet preempted. In the feudal world they had fulfilled a limited number of commercial tasks, such as distribution of goods, money changing and lending, which were required by society but nevertheless despised. Unanchored in feudal society and therefore unbound by the accepted anti-commercial values, Jews were perforce better prepared to take advantage of the new commercial spirit. They were among the first groups to break through the pervasive localism of feudal life. The little international trading which persisted during those provincial years was sometimes conducted by a *Radanite*, a Jewish merchant who was familiar with the international trade routes and market conditions.[15] The chronicles left by these traders are among the richest sources of information we possess of life during the Middle Ages.[16]

What was a precarious source of livelihood in the feudal period became a formidable asset in the Age of Discovery. Jews were merchant-capitalists before it was fashionable to be so and their dispersion in the far corners of the world proved of practical advantage. The rich network of friends and relatives bound together, in the words of one historian, by a "community of language, race, blood [and] rules of conduct," helped establish the bedrock of trust and confidence on which commercial relations are ultimately based.[17] It helped lay the groundwork for a rudimentary financial and trade system composed entirely of Jews. The Jewish nexus in Europe became an important communications instrument linking the people of Europe together. "They are like the pegs and nails in a great bridge," observed one historian, "which, though they are little valued in themselves are absolutely necessary to keep the whole frame together...."[18]

Jews became involved in the full range of commercial activity which foreshadowed the development of capitalism. Teutonic knights sold their war booty, including Kievan slaves, to Jewish purveyors and middlemen who followed the army. Their connections with the Levant gave them easy access to slave markets. When Venetian traders began to tap the lucrative trade with the East it was sometimes in partnership with Jewish traders.

Exempted from the Church's strictures against usury, Jews developed the first rudimentary banking instruments, the concept of hiring money, letters of credit, and sale of securities. But once these practices were institutionalized, Jewish business pioneers were hard pressed to maintain them. In banking, for example, the Fuggers and the Medici, having government sanction behind them, soon outpaced Jewish bankers. Thereafter Jewish influence in banking, with the exception of certain periods during the seventeenth and eighteenth centuries, was negligible.[19] The possession of liquid assets by Jews was a constant temptation in an age when most capital was fixed in land. The cumbersome network of mutual obligations, which was the hallmark of the feudal world, would in time be discharged by payment of money. The practice, called scutage, made Jewish assets even more tempting. Jews were called upon to finance crusades and the construction of cathedrals, another favorite pastime of the medieval world. Jews then were among the first groups to make capital mobile. It was an essential prerequisite for the development of capitalism.

Since the Jews possessed a long tradition of involvement in commerce, it comes as no surprise to learn that Jews played a central role in the discovery and development of the New World. They helped finance the voyages of discovery, developed the navigational instruments which made them possible, and participated in the joint stock ventures under whose aegis settlement was undertaken.

A group of high-placed Marranos were among the first to sense the possibilities of Columbus's visionary scheme of sailing westward to get to the East. After Columbus failed to convince John II of Portugal of the feasibility of his scheme, he turned to Diego de Dega, the Marrano Bishop of Salamanca, who put him in touch with a group of Marranos in Spain, including Abraham Zacuto, the "map Jew." Between 1491 and 1493, Isaac Abravanel, Abraham Senior, Luis de Santangel, Gabriel Sanchez, and Juan Cabrero used their influence and purses to keep the scheme alive. It was to Luis de Santangel, whose family was subsequently liquidated by the Inquisition, that Columbus sent the first private letter detailing the discovery.

The second voyage was financed less voluntarily. Funds came from the sale of the confiscated property of exiled Jews and even Torah scroll covers were sold at auction to raise six million Maravedis for the voyage.[20] "Not jewels but Jews were the real financial basis for the first expedition of Columbus," observed the American historian Herbert B. Adams, anxious to put to rest the myth that Queen Isabella had pawned the royal jewels to finance the voyage.[21]

There has been considerable speculation that Columbus himself might have been a Marrano. The evidence presented to support such a theory is tenuous. Included is the contention that Columbus possessed a Jewish "visage" and Jewish personality traits. Others point to his disproportionate number of Jewish and Marrano friends and to archival evidence suggesting that he stemmed from a Marrano family originating in Galicia or Aragon which migrated to Genoa in the fourteenth century.[22]

If one can be skeptical about Columbus's Jewish ancestry, the role played by Marranos and Jews in the actual voyage seems indisputable. Portuguese and Spanish Jews possessed a long seafaring tradition and it was therefore natural that some should find their way to join Columbus's crew. As early as 1263, Jehuda of Valencia helped outfit a flotilla to conquer Murcia for King John I and in 1323 the Jews of Tortosa displayed a similar zeal in support of Portuguese naval activities.[23] It does not come as a surprise therefore that of the 120-man crew as many as six, most in key positions, can be identified as Marranos.[24]

The voyages of discovery of the fifteenth and sixteenth centuries would not have been possible without the development of a new technology of navigation and the systematic compilation of geographic data. These necessary discoveries were in some measure contributed by Jews. It was their proficiency in mathematics, a residue of their link to the more advanced Islamic culture, combined with their knowledge of world geography, gleaned from their travels, which placed them in a good position to make such a contribution.

Developments occurred in navigational instruments as well as maps. The astrolabe which was used by navigators to help measure distance from the equator was originally developed by the Greeks and subsequently improved by Arab navigators. In the eighth century a Jewish scientist, Mashala, the "phoenix of his age," improved the instrument and finally Joseph Vecinho Rodrigo, a brilliant mathematician of Marrano lineage employed at the court of King John of Portugal, brought the astrolabe to perfection. The quadrant, a device employed for measuring angles and altitudes using stars as reference points, has a similar history. In the fifteenth century it was improved by Abraham Ibn ben Ezra, Jacob ben Makhir, and Levi ben Gersom. Known thereafter as *Quadratus Judaicus* it was carried by all explorers who generally referred to it by the popular name "Jacob's staff."[25]

The almost exclusively Jewish art of map making was centered on the island of Majorca. The most renowned of the "map Jews" was Abraham Cresques of Palma. While attached to the royal household of Prince John of Aragon, Cresques composed and translated into Latin the most comprehensive compilation of nautical and geographical data then known to man, the *Catalan Atlas*. His son, Jehuda Cresques, carried on in the family tradition. At the age of sixty he became the leading figure at the nautical academy at Sagres which was established by Prince Henry the Navigator to gain nautical preeminence for Portugal.

On his voyages Columbus carried the *Almanac Perpetuum* which was composed by the Marrano Abraham Zacuto and had been translated from the Hebrew by Joseph Vecinho, his Marrano pupil. Vecinho went on to translate the works of Abraham Ibn Ezra but was opposed to Columbus's vision of finding a new world and used his influence as court physician in Lisbon to thwart his plan. On the other hand, Zacuto, Vecinho's teacher, was a strong supporter of Columbus and did all he could to help him from the vantage of his post as a professor of mathematics at the University of Salamanca. One story has it that Columbus once staved off a mutiny by using Zacuto's charts to predict an eclipse of the moon.[26]

Paradoxically, when the Inquisition came to Majorca in 1490 the scientific community was scattered; its delicate strands were never reassembled on Iberian soil. Naval supremacy passed on to the Dutch and the English and by mid-sixteenth century Europe's principal mapmaking center was Amsterdam where many Marrano Jews had settled.

It is not unreasonable to postulate that at least part of the reason for Spain's loss of naval preeminence was attributable to the Inquisition whose effect was to scatter this highly skilled group.

From whence came the Jewish aptitude for things of the sea? We have seen that map making and the compilation of atlases were probably related to the Jewish involvement in trade. Jews, moreover, were culturally closer to the Arab sources from which much data could be learned. Yet one cannot help suspecting that something more lies behind the Jewish interest in things geographical. It is possible that the very insecurity of Jews and Marranos on the Iberian peninsula coupled with their cosmopolitan interests led to a search for possible havens of resettlement and the routes for reaching them. The Jewish interest in geography may have been due to their well-honed instincts for survival.

Strange to say the commercial potential of their new possessions did not arouse the full interest of the Spanish and Portuguese monarchs. Their thinking about colonies reflected the times. It was centered on the mercantilist notion of filling the public coffers with treasure from the New World. This they believed was the true measure of a nation's power. Such thinking led to the implementation of a pattern of trade which saw gold shipped to the mother country only to flow out again to purchase the goods Holland and other nations could offer. Spain became a consumer rather than a producer of wealth. The massive importation of precious metals tended rather to degrade further the lesser nobility whose fixed income, derived from land, could not keep pace with the inflationary price revolution. The new possessions were also thought of as ripe fields for the real mission of Christian nations—the spreading of the faith. On a more practical level a colony served as a kind of a safety valve. It was a place where the unemployed nobility and other restless elements could satisfy their craving for adventure and status.

The muting of a commercial instinct left a vacuum in the colonies which was ultimately to be filled in part by the more commercially minded Protestants and Marranos. They played the role despised and shunned by the Iberian "lumpen nobility" in the colonies.[27] In the northern region of the western hemisphere where the Dutch, Swedes, and English held sway the reverse situation was true. Peter Stuyvesant, for example, harbored a strong resentment against Jews because he feared that they would offer strong competition to the indigenous merchants.

Jews pioneered in finding ways to make the colonies commercially viable. One such discovery gave to the European world the dubious blessing of tobacco. It was Luis de Torres who first noted how Caribbean natives inhaled tobacco smoke through their nostrils. Tobacco and snuff were introduced to Venice and Holland in the early decades of the seventeenth century and the trade was in the beginning almost wholly Jewish. More benevolent was the introduction of sugar planting which was, in part, developed by the Jewish planters of Recife and soon spread throughout the Caribbean, becoming the economic mainstay of the area. The introduction of coffee and tea cultivation later was also pioneered by Jews. Staples such as vanilla and indigo, the latter to become an important crop of Georgia's economy, frequently appear on the invoices of Jewish merchants who traded with Europe. When wine growing was introduced to Georgia the first vintners were Jews. Jews also pioneered in the production of Castile soap which they had manufactured in Europe since 1371 and which James Lucena brought to Rhode Island in 1761. The development of the spermaceti industry in Newport, Rhode Island, which permitted the replacement of the more expensive tallow candles, was introduced by Jacob Rodriguez Rivera.

Sometimes the initiative came from Jewish industries already well known in the old world. Thus in a reverse Europe-to-America pattern, Luis de Santangel, the noted Marrano patron of Columbus, introduced grains and horses to the New World. Sephardic Jews who emigrated from Amsterdam to Recife brought with them a special knowledge of the trade in precious stones, especially diamonds. It became an important element of trade with the mother country.[28]

Despite their pioneering role in establishing the colonial economies, Jews played a relatively minor role in the institutionalization of capitalism. Partly due to residual anti-Semitism, partly to their relatively late arrival, their participation in the early joint stock ventures was minor. They were hardly represented when the Amsterdam stock exchange was organized in 1631. The wealth of the 200 Marrano households in Amsterdam in 1610 is generally exaggerated. They had few participants in the bank of Amsterdam or in the business ventures in the eastern trade. Jewish resources were too limited to play their customary role of making capital mobile. Their condition improved considerably after the Dutch captured Brazil, but Sephardic Jews in Holland became merely a rich group. According to the tax assessment of 1674, their wealth was far inferior to that of their wealthy Christian neighbors. The Dutch East India Company, organized in 1602, had only a small representation of Jews. Of the company's capital assets which came to 6,500,000 Florins only one tenth of one percent, 4,800 Florins, was invested by Jews. The capital of Jewish investors in the Dutch West India

Company, organized in 1621, amounted at its founding to one half percent. It rose to four percent a half century later.[29]

Jewish wealth, such as it was, proved acceptable for investment when the joint stock ventures had passed their peak or had suffered some calamity, such as the recapture of the Dutch colonies in Brazil in 1654. Nevertheless, even a relatively small investment proved sufficient to wring good treatment for Jews in the colonies. This was the case in 1656 when the Jews of New Amsterdam again turned to the directors of the company for redress when Peter Stuyvesant restricted their economic activity. At that time seven of the company's 167 stockholders were Sephardic Jews, a sufficient number to compel better treatment from the reluctant governor. A year earlier the directors had reluctantly rejected Stuyvesant's plea to ban the Jews from the colony "because of the considerable loss sustained by this nation, with others, in the taking of Brazil" and also "because of the large amount of capital which they still have invested in the shares of this company."[30] As early as January, 1655, the Jews of Amsterdam petitioned the company to allow their brethren to "traffic and live," as do the Jews of French Martinique and British Barbados.[31] Such rights were essential if Jews were to play their customary role as commercial catalysts.

Paradoxically, while the Jews of Amsterdam cited in their petition the precedent of Jews living in the British possessions in the Caribbean, Jewish influence in promoting capitalist institutions in England was also minimal. They had little representation in the British joint stock companies and were restricted to twelve members on the London stock exchange. In contrast to Amsterdam there were no Jewish stockbrokers in England at the close of the eighteenth century. This was partly due to the fact that Jews had not been allowed to trickle back to England until after 1655 when negotiations between Menasseh Ben Israel and Oliver Cromwell paved the way for their return. Marranos living in England before that date were reluctant to profess their Judaism openly since even after the mid-seventeenth century the indigenous merchant class was apprehensive about Jewish business activity. In its earliest form the British Navigation Act of 1663—the enabling act for British mercantilism—was entitled an act "to prevent encroachments in trade by the *Jews, French* and other Foreigners."[32] In the early decades of the eighteenth century suspicion of Jews was somewhat eased. The joint stock company seeking to develop Georgia commissioned three prominent Jews, Anthony da Costa, Francis Salvador, and Alvaro Lopez Suasso to help raise investment capital.

Thus it happened that Jews, scorned stepchildren of Europe, were compelled in the fifteenth, sixteenth, and seventeenth centuries to seek a haven where they could exercise their talents and energies. They found it in America, the land destined to become Europe's favorite child, which needed these talents and energies to develop its untapped resources. In a sense America and the Jews made common cause in the New World and that happy reciprocity has marked their relationship ever since. How the Jews utilized the benevolence of the colonial environment to play the role history assigned to them is the subject of the following chapters.

CHAPTER II

The Genesis of
American Religious Tolerance

THE PRESENCE OF SOME 3,000 JEWS IN AMERICA IN 1780 HARDLY OFFERS
a large enough target for historical speculation.[1] The 2,800,000 Americans, primarily agriculturalists, were in a sense separated from the
Jews, who were concentrated in the few nascent urban centers of New
York, Philadelphia, Newport, and Charleston. Jews were, physically at
least, an inconspicuous minority.

Yet it was during the Colonial period that the basic outlines of the
American-Jewish relationship were established. The Colonial period,
after all, nearly equals in length of time the period which stretches
from the Revolution to the present. It offered ample time to deeply
root those things of national habit and style which often are the major
ingredients in shaping intergroup relations. That relationship was even
for its time remarkably free from religious bigotry. Undoubtedly that
was partly due to the fact that Jews formed such a small minority. If
the Jews of Colonial America provide a small opportunity for historical
speculation, they were by the same token an almost unworthy target
for the projection of the many religious antipathies which Colonial
settlers carried with them to the New World. There were other reasons
as well which related to the social landscape of Colonial America.
Jews were only one group among many religious minorities, many of
whom were more aberrant than Jews.

Nor did tolerance spring fully blown in 1654 when Jews first settled
here. It was wrested gradually from reluctant local authorities over
several generations and it was won through making common cause
with other minorities. But it did occur and become a crucial factor
in fashioning the conditions under which American Jewry developed.
Certainly without the growth of such a tolerance the unspoken *quid
pro quo* between America and its Jews would not have materialized.

European observers were sometimes amazed at the degree of acceptance
shown to Jews in Colonial America. "The Jews . . . ," observed a Ger-

[20]

man mercenary in 1777, "have their own commerce and trade and are not identifiable because of their beards and clothes as is the case with [the Jews who live among] us."[2] It was more than their indistinguishability which made Jews acceptable. Sephardic Jews did not carry the trappings of piety as far as their Eastern coreligionists. In the new environment a further relaxation of religious standards often occurred. The general laxity in religious observance became vexing enough for officers of Jewish congregations to follow the example of Christian churches who did not hesitate to employ coercive measures against their members. They refused to officiate at interfaith marriages, they tried to impose fines when infractions occurred and in extreme cases burial privileges were withheld and the threat of excommunication imposed.

The same mercenary was amazed at the frequency of intermarriage among Jews and Christians. One historian later placed the rate as high as ten per cent.[3] Sometimes such marriages represented the liaison of two budding aristocracies such as the Franks and the Delanceys. But they occurred among the common folk too and reflected the scarcity of acceptable Jewish mates, especially in rural areas where no Jewish community existed. In such circumstances Jewish men sometimes established informal liaisons with Indian women or Negro housekeepers. Sometimes such marriages were the result of the new opportunities for contact between Jews and other groups which were available because of the many interfaith business partnerships and consortiums.

Religious tolerance had not always been the rule in early Colonial society. The American Colonies were in fact a seething cauldron of religious conflict and only in the final decades of the eighteenth century was some kind of *modus vivendi* established between the various religious groups. The early settlers were frequently religious zealots rather than advocates of religious liberty. Many had found their way to the New World in quest of greater religious freedom for themselves, but paradoxically they were not inclined to extend to others the freedom they sought for themselves. One need only recall the case of Roger Williams who was forced to flee the Bay Colony in the winter of 1635 and Anne Hutchinson who was exiled two years later. The Puritans sometimes flogged Catholics and in one instance hanged four detested Quakers on the Boston Common. They had disregarded a 1658 law and had returned to the colony after they had been banned. These were not tolerant folk.

The very strategy of establishing the English colonies was partly related to the religious struggle between Catholicism and Protestantism still flaring in Europe. It was hoped that the Protestant colonies would outflank the Spanish Catholic colonies in the southern half of the hemisphere. The British victory in the French and Indian War in 1763 partly allayed the fear of the Catholic menace, but did not totally dissipate it.[4] When, for example, the British Colonial administration imposed the Proclamation of 1763, attaching the area west of the Allegheny Mountains to Catholic Quebec, the Protestants of New England staunchly opposed the policy because they did not want to see their hinterland in the hands of Catholics.

For the tiny Jewish community religious liberty was desirable not only in its own right but for its direct bearing on their ability to function in the economic arena. Accustomed to measuring their position in terms of the situation in Europe, they were relatively content to let things develop slowly and took care not to antagonize the Christian community. In London, for example, Jews forbade the discussion of religious subjects with gentiles "because to do otherwise is to disturb the liberty we enjoy and to make us disliked...."[5] The indictment of Dr. Joseph Lumbrozo in Maryland in February, 1658, for "denial of the doctrine of the trinity" was a sharp reminder of the prudence of such self-imposed restrictions.

The situation of New Amsterdam's Jews is a good illustration of how religious animosity could lead to economic restrictions. The twenty-four Jews who landed in the colony faced a series of restrictions which stemmed from the general disapprobation of religious dissidence and the specific anti-Semitism harbored by Governor Stuyvesant and the colony's Church officials. New Amsterdam chose not to follow the precedent of its more tolerant namesake in Holland.

The religious situation in the colony was one of turmoil. The Dutch Reformed Church was officially established under the Charter of Freedoms and Exemptions which officially prohibited other forms of worship. While kindred Calvinists, such as Congregationalists, were tolerated on Long Island, dissident Quakers, whom Stuyvesant detested, did not fare well. He ordered them banned from the colony in 1657. Flaunting the provisions of a new liberal charter promulgated in 1654 which guaranteed to all "the right to have and enjoy liberty of conscience," the Quakers responded with the Flushing Remonstrances in which they proclaimed unequivocally their right to welcome "all sons of Adam who would come in love among us."[6] Quakers rather than Jews courted martyrdom by settling in New Netherland. Nor did the Lutherans fare much better. In 1658 a Lutheran minister, John Ernest Goldwater, was unceremoniously shipped back to Holland for attempting to establish a Lutheran congregation. He was in contravention of a

1640 law which expressly forbade dissident sects to worship publicly.

The insistence on religious homogeneity was augmented in 1647 when the autocratic Peter Stuyvesant was appointed Governor of the colony. Stuyvesant was taken aback by the lack of attendance at church services, public drunkenness, weakness for Indian women, and other examples of moral lassitude. To tighten discipline, Stuyvesant prohibited the sale of intoxicants on the Sabbath and made church attendance compulsory. Soon the atmosphere became even more unfavorable as more regulations were introduced to enforce conformity with the tenets of the Dutch Reformed church. In the midst of this activity the remnants of the Jewish community of Recife sailed into the harbor. It was not the Governor's first experience with Jews. His resentment of them had been stirred when as Governor of Curaçao he had clashed with Jewish leaders. His antagonism had recently been reinforced by the activities of a group of itinerant Jewish merchants who did business in New Amsterdam shortly before the arrival of the St. Charles group.

His distaste for Jews was based partly on religious grounds as well as on a commonly held belief that Jews were prone to sharp business practices which victimized the community. In his correspondence the two reinforced each other. In a letter to the Amsterdam Chamber of the Dutch West India Company he complained not only of their "usury and deceitful trading" but also requested that "the deceitful race—such hateful enemies and blasphemers of the name of Christ—be not allowed to further infect and trouble this new colony...."[7] He was echoing a theme stated more clearly by Johan M. Megapolensis, New Amsterdam's principal church official, who wrote to his superiors "that these people [Jews] have no other aim than to get possession of Christian property and to ruin all other merchants by drawing all trade to themselves."[8] The directors of the West India Company shared these fears and while they could not grant Stuyvesant's request they informed him that they "foresee therefrom the same difficulties which [he] feare[d]."[9]

Stuyvesant's opposition to the Jews is best viewed within the context of the general apprehension regarding religious dissidence. "Giving them Liberty," he wrote to the directors, "we cannot refuse the Lutherans and the Papists."[10] If the Jews could not be ejected, ample means were available to confine their activities and perhaps make their position so uncomfortable that they would want to leave voluntarily. By withholding the right to become citizen-freeholders, for example, a right which Jews possessed in Amsterdam and Recife, access to the colony's commercial life could be effectively blocked. The primary activities of merchandising and practicing a craft could thereby be denied to Jews. By withholding from them the right to take part in "watch and ward" duty, by means of which the physical security of the town was maintained, Jews would not only be isolated but they would have to pay a special tax levy instead. Fortunately, these measures to limit Jewish economic activity did not prove very effective.

When Dutch New Amsterdam was forcibly converted to New York on September 7, 1664, only one decade had passed since the Jews of England had been able to profess their faith openly. At first the disestablishment of the Dutch Reformed church in the colony did not perceptibly improve the situation of the Jews. The articles of capitulation guaranteed liberty of conscience to the Dutch inhabitants, but after a decade of indecision the English authorities decided that the Jews were, after all, Portuguese, and therefore not entitled to the rights freely granted to other sects. For the next four decades the British handling of the question of Jewish rights oscillated between tolerance and restriction. Jews were prohibited from public worship, and a petition in 1685 requesting permission for a house of worship was rejected. But Jews, in effect, built their synagogue, albeit under private auspices, and nothing was done by the authorities to prevent this seeming circumvention of the law. The establishment of a Jewish congregation, in fact, came earlier than that of the Catholics and Baptists. By mid-eighteenth century it could boast 855 members.

But the growth of a measure of religious freedom for Jews proceeded less from their struggle to attain it than from the inability of the Episcopalian establishment to impose its will on all the diverse religious sects in the colony. Such sects chafed at regulations which required having marriages performed exclusively by Anglican ministers. They also bitterly resented having to support the ministry of the established church. When Governor Cranberry arrested a Presbyterian minister for preaching without a license in 1707, the court found him innocent, and the Assembly promptly passed a statute granting all Christian groups the right to preach publicly. Once dissidents possessed political rights it proved difficult to force compliance with religious statutes.

The Jews had profited from the forced liberalization of religious strictures but they discovered that they could swiftly lose privileges which they had held for decades. Since 1700, for example, Jews had exercised the franchise but in the close election of 1737 when the Jewish vote made the difference betwen winning and losing, their right to vote was contested and they were disqualified. Such arbitrariness after more than three generations must have been difficult even for the most politically indifferent to accept.

In the long run the relationship of Jews with Congregationalists had a special significance because Puritanism was destined to have a profound effect in shaping the national consciousness. Yet there was precious little contact between the two groups because few Jews resided in areas dominated by the Congregationalists. As late as 1729 there were only four Jewish families in Boston and a few more in the Congregational areas of Connecticut.

Undoubtedly the scarcity of Jews in Puritan-dominated areas could be attributed to the difficulty experienced by outsiders living in tightly organized theocratic communities. After the Bay Colony was officially chartered in 1629 the all-pervasive church became, as a matter of course, linked to town government. The line between secular and religious affairs was indistinguishable. Since each congregation was autonomous, each town was, in effect, a closed religious corporation allowing little room for religious divergence. In such a situation, breaking the conventions could mean bringing the wrath of religious as well as secular authority down on one's head. Puritans, moreover, had more reason than most to stress conformity because like most Protestant groups the danger of religious fragmentation was ever present once the search for revelation and salvation became a matter between each congregant and his God. Protestantism thus possessed a built-in centrifugal force which, if allowed full play, could threaten the continuity of the religious community. The Puritans guarded against this possibility by a zealousness for religious conformity which often outdid that imposed by the Inquisition.[11] If the inculcation of an overwhelming sense of moral righteousness did not suffice to suppress dissent then the threat of physical punishment would.

To the citizens of the Bay Colony the Jews were an enigma. They were treated with considerably more circumspection than the Quakers and Catholics. Jews did not disrupt Congregational religious services like the Quakers or display unforgivable religious pomp like the Papists. They asked only to be left in peace to worship privately. Puritans were sometimes uncommonly generous to Jews. In 1649 a Puritan court rejected a request by Solomon Franco, a poverty-stricken Jewish merchant, for a commission to supervise the shipment of goods to Major Edward Gibbons and his military garrison. But the court did grant him the generous sum of sixty shillings for ten weeks so that he might keep body and soul together.[12] By 1749 Jews residing in Boston suffered no particular disabilities.

Much of this fortunate situation is attributable to the Puritan love for things Hebrew. Like all fundamentalist groups, the Puritans held the Old Testament in high regard and because they were religious zealots they were not simply content with the English or Latin translation. It had to be in Hebrew—the language in which it was originally written. Men like Governor Bradford set themselves to learning Hebrew so that he "would see with his own eyes the ancient oracles of God in their native beauty."[13] Puritan Hebrew learning can be traced back to Emmanuel College at Cambridge where it was taught by converted Jews. It was brought to Massachusetts by Cambridge graduates. Once rooted here, it continued to be nurtured by Jews. Judah Monis, a Sephardic Jew from Holland, presented Harvard with his *New Hebrew Grammar* in 1720 and was awarded his Master of Arts degree for it, the first Jew to receive such a distinction. With Monis the Puritans also achieved their fondest wish, to convert the Jews.

The study of Hebrew became a distinctive feature of the Harvard curriculum. Included in the theses offered by the first class of Harvard graduates in 1642 was one entitled "Hebraea est linguarum Mater" (Hebrew is the mother tongue) and "Consonantes et vocules Hebraeorum sunt Coaetaneae" (Hebrew consonants and vowels are of equal age). Until 1817, many a scholar anxious to demonstrate the extent of his learning delivered his orations in Hebrew.[14] The *Bay Psalm Book,* a favorite seventeenth-century Puritan prayer book, was a direct translation of the *Hebrew Book of Psalms.* The Puritans went so far as to have special Hebrew type cut so that certain passages could be reproduced in the original Hebrew.

So enraptured were the Puritans with the Old Testament that they literally fashioned the structure of their community after the ancient Hebrew civilization. They became, in the words of one historian, "a cachet of the Hebrew old-testament spirit."[15] Their Christianity seemed truly to be a mere continuity of the ancient Judaic spirit. Christmas was considered a time of fasting rather than a season of joy and an over-exuberant celebration could be punished with imprisonment.[16] Celebration of the Sabbath was begun on the preceding evening as it was in the Jewish tradition. Children's names originated in the Old Testament as did much of local law and conventions. Sometimes the ancient Hebrew scriptures could be put to less than righteous use. Thus Cotton Mather cited as precedent for the Salem witchcraft trials the story of the hanging of the witches of Gaza in the Bible. Other times the identity with the ancient Hebrews was carried to extraordinary lengths. Puritans seemed more convinced that the Indians were the ten lost tribes of Israel than Jews and Catholics. They spent a great deal of time and effort not only in propounding the myth but in fruitless attempts to remind the Indians of their noble past.

The Puritan understanding of the ancient Hebrews was necessarily marred by their own preconceptions. Thus they caught and imitated only the stern moralistic fervor of the Hebrews and missed entirely the counterbalancing joyous component. Their conception of the ancient Hebrews, moreover, did not correspond to the facts of ancient Jewish life and certainly not to Jewish life in the seventeenth and eighteenth centuries. Jews, for example, were never an ascetic people as were the Puritans. They took seriously the admonition to "choose life." Small wonder then that when the Puritans came in contact with the real Jews they were puzzled. Surely these could not be the "children of the book." And if they were not, then the Puritans must be. New England became the "promised land" flowing with "milk and honey" and the Puritans were the real "children of the covenant."

Puritan love of things Hebrew did not necessarily carry over into love of the Hebrews who lived among them. It was confusing as the Puritans, thinking of themselves as the real Hebrews, sought to draw the professing Jews among them back into the fold from which they had supposedly strayed. The conversion of the Jews became so critically important in their theology that it was thought there would be no second coming of Christ until that occurred. The high priority given to the conversion of the Jews could lead to ridiculous extremes. Cotton Mather, for example, was wont to seek out Jews to discuss matters of faith and in 1704 cited a false biblical text in an effort to convert a Boston Jew. In 1714 he composed a history of the Jews as part of his *Biblia Americanuum,* which like William Penn's *Visitation to the Jews,* written in 1695, presents a congeries of misinformation concerning the Jews and the urgent need to convert them.

The Puritans then did much to form the basic context in which Colonial America viewed the Jews. In that context there was a peculiar ambivalence, for the Puritans combined at once the wish to use the ancient Hebrews as a model and yet seemed unable to accept contemporary Jews because of their stubborn refusal to accept the true faith. Consequently they looked upon Jews as offering an appropriate field for missionary work. The desire to convert the Jews was prevalent during much of the Colonial and early national period in American history.

In other communities the degree of religious toleration varied not only with the period but also from colony to colony. In general some form of religious restriction was the rule rather than the exception in all the Colonies. In Virginia, for example, Jews were simply excluded at the outset. The establishment of compulsory Anglican services in 1619 in that colony did not affect Jews. Yet it was in Virginia, over a century and a half later, that George Mason and James Madison successfully wrung the first statute guaranteeing religious liberty from a reluctant state legislature. It became the model for similar statutes in other states, but, ironically, the restriction faced by Jews settling in the colony in the early period, meant that there were few Jews to enjoy religious liberty later. There were only some six Jewish families settled in Richmond at the time of the Revolution.

Because of their concentration in Philadelphia, religious restrictionism in Pennsylvania had a more drastic effect on Jews. William Penn's "Holy Experiment" featured greater restrictions against Jews than Catholics, the alternate pariah group. But here, too, restrictionist statutes were more often honored in the breach than in the practice. While the Jews could not legally vote, hold political office, or participate fully in business and were also forbidden to hold public worship, in practice these restrictions were ignored. Philadelphia's first Jewish congregation, Mikveh Israel, was in existence by 1747 and Jewish business ventures thrived in that city. Penn shared with the Congregationalists a solicitous attitude toward Jews. Dreaming of their ultimate conversion, he viewed them with "tender compassion." But his primary interest was in establishing a haven for Quakers. In this endeavor he was only partly successful.

Pennsylvania became the most conglomerate of all the Colonies and the new groups, the Scotch-Irish Presbyterians especially, found little use for the Quaker establishment which appeared to them to be ignoring their security needs along the frontier, where they had settled. They felt that Quakers were over-solicitous about the welfare of the Indians with whom they were often locked in mortal combat. Eventually they wrested control of the colony from the Quakers. Like New York, New Jersey, Delaware, and Maryland, Pennsylvania offers a good illustration of how religious and ethnic diversity effectively prevented the imposition of an established church. For Jews of Colonial America that diversity had yet another significance. It prevented the focusing of religious animosity exclusively on them.

Maryland's Catholic origins made that colony an anomaly. The unpromising situation for the Jews remained fairly constant even while various Christian groups vied for control of the colony. Under the Catholics, Jewish unwillingness to profess belief in the Trinity disabled them in theory, and under the Congregationalists, who won the colony in 1654, and the Episcopalians, who won control in 1702, numerous political and economic strictures were added which disabled them in practice. Maryland's tolerant religious beginnings stand in sharp contrast to the stubbornness with which the state held on to its religious test for office. Thomas Kennedy, a Jeffersonian Democrat, tried vainly in 1811, in 1820, and in 1821 to convince the state legislature to permit Jews to be sworn into office on the Old rather than the New Testament. His efforts met with partial success in 1822 but not until 1826 did Maryland pass "An Act to Extend to the Sect of People Professing the Jewish Religion the Same Rights and Privileges That Are Enjoyed by Christians." It was the last state to do so.

Of all the Colonies, the tolerant atmosphere of South Carolina was most favorable for the development of the Jewish community. It was the first state in which Jews could exercise the franchise and hold political office. That happy condition was attributable largely to John Locke, the seventeenth-century thinker, who, more than any other person, stressed the advantages of religious toleration. His friend, the Earl of Shaftesbury, Lord Ashley, Chancellor of the Exchequer, had invited Locke to join him in writing the charter for the colony. It gave Locke the opportunity to include some of his favorite ideas on religious toleration in the "Fundamental Constitution of Carolina." For Carolina the advantages were soon discernible since it attracted talented dissidents such as Jews and Huguenots to that population-starved colony. Despite the existing spirit of toleration the Episcopalians did try to gain supremacy, but they hoped to persuade rather than coerce "Jews, heathen and dissenters from the purity of the Christian religion" to come into the fold. But the Episcopalians were not conspicuously successful. The first recorded Jew in the Colonies to hold political office was Francis Salvadore, a wealthy Sephardic Jew from England who represented the colony at the first and second provincial congress in the early 1770's.

Georgia, the last of the Colonies to be chartered, in June, 1732, was from its inception involved in the larger international religious conflict. One of the motives for its settlement was to serve as a counter influence to the Catholic Spanish settlement in nearby St. Augustine and the French Catholics in Mobile. The charter granted to James Oglethorpe read: "there shall be liberty of conscience allowed in the worship of God to all persons . . . except Papists."[17] Catholics, rather than Jews, were slated to be anathema in Georgia, but the circumstances surrounding the arrival of the first contingent of Jews in 1773 almost reversed the intentions stated in the charter. The trustees of the colony strenuously opposed what seemed to them the dumping of indebted Ashkenazi Jews by their wealthier Sephardic brethren.[18] Paradoxically no such complaints were heard when the sparse population of the colony was augmented by dredging up of likely convict settlers from the prisons of England and Scotland. Nor were they subject to the accusation that they were fleeing unpaid debts, as the Jews were, even though most of these settlers came from debtors' prisons.

The remaining colonies displayed varying attitudes toward Jews. Delaware, for example, followed the Swedish precedent of simply barring all Jewish settlement, a situation which did not change until the Dutch took over the colony in 1655. Then the new Jewish settlers in New Amsterdam became active in the lucrative fur trade in the South River vicinity. In Governor Berkeley's New Jersey on the other hand, the situation was far more favorable for Jews. That colony's charter, probably written by the enlightened William Penn, contained guarantees of liberty of conscience. Connecticut was for a time a kind of no-man's land in which the Congregationalists and the Dutch Calvinists of New Netherlands contended for influence. Neither had much use for religious dissenters. Few Jews settled in the area, which ultimately became the domain of the Congregationalists, whose church was not disestablished until 1818. A Jewish congregation was not legally chartered there until 1843. As late as 1776 North Carolina flew in the face of the times by inserting a clause in its constitution prohibiting Jews, Catholics, Quakers, and atheists from holding office. But a Catholic was elected governor in 1781 and a Jew won a seat in the state legislature in 1808. The election of a Jew, Jacob Henry, was challenged and while the restrictive clause was not enforced, it was not removed from North Carolina's constitution until 1868.

The circumstances surrounding its founding made Rhode Island, like South Carolina, an environment conducive to Jewish settlement. When Quakers and Jews learned of Roger Williams's opposition to the idea of a formally established church, they were naturally encouraged to settle in Rhode Island. Williams harbored a strong distaste for Quakers but, like most Puritans, stood in awe of Jews whom he viewed as living descendants of the Old Testament patriarchs. Like Cromwell, Williams supported the idea of allowing the Jews to return to England when he briefly visited there in 1655. Ultimately Rhode Island did develop a strong Congregationalist establishment, but it was not financially supported by the public treasury and permitted the open organization of a Jewish congregation in 1658.

Predictably the successful American Revolution went far to loosen the hold of the Episcopal church which was bound to the mother country. The logic of the revolutionary ideology, expressed in such documents as the Declaration of Independence, undercut the notion of religious uniformity. The struggle for freedom of conscience preceded the Revolution and formed part of its agitational background. The break-through in Virginia, of which Jefferson was so proud, served partly as the precedent for the compromise on the religious question which was achieved at the constitutional convention in 1787. Two constitutional provisions assured freedom of conscience: Article VI, clause 3, states that "no religious test shall be required as a qualification to any office or public trust under the United States" and the first amendment forbids Congress to establish a church or prohibit the free exercise of religion.

Nevertheless, even after the ratification of the Constitution it took several years for the idea of religious liberty to win acceptance on the local level. In 1775 most of the states had some form of an established church. Virginia, North Carolina, and Georgia severed their connection with the Anglican church after the revolution, but Maryland and South Carolina continued for a time to maintain the old ties. Nor did such severance of ties indicate the disestablishment of the church. New York and New Jersey continued for a time to maintain vestiges of an established church and connections with the Anglican church in England. Only Rhode Island, Pennsylvania, and Delaware had no established church whatsoever in 1775. Religious tests for office-holding continued to be common in most areas. Massachusetts and Maryland required acceptance of the Christian religion while Georgia, New Hampshire, New Jersey, and North Carolina maintained more specific Protestant tests, such as belief in "God the Father and Christ the son." Delaware, for example, sought "faith in God the father, and in Jesus Christ, His only son, and the Holy Ghost. . . ." Pennsylvania on the other hand was satisfied simply with the belief that "God was the rewarder of the Good and the punisher of the wicked."[19]

For Jews the thrust of these restrictive provisions was clear—the nation thought of itself as Christian. But the seeds for a more secular approach which had been planted in Virginia and the Constitution were also manifest. They could not fail to come to fruition. What Jews of the nineteenth century could not yet perceive was that secularization which opened the road to complete religious freedom also removed the bars to assimilation and would some day pose a serious threat to their own survival as a group.

The religious openness which came to characterize the American social environment was hardly attributable to a specific Jewish struggle, but, rather, to the conditions existing in the American Colonies and the effects of the Protestant Reformation. The nature and size of the Jewish community in the Colonies did not present insuperable obstacles to integration. That was the other side of the formula which guaranteed Jews religious freedom. They would be absorbed into the national community, a prospect which contained its own threat to Jewish survival.

There was in the Colonial pioneering situation a great need to play down religious antagonism. Religious struggles in Massachusetts, Pennsylvania, and New York displayed a dangerous tendency to divide the polity into "ins" and "outs." It added a bitter note to political discourse and in extreme cases threatened the very stability of community life. The imposition of religious uniformity could in many cases only be achieved by tearing the community apart. In any case few of the established churches possessed sufficient power to impose their will on the conglomeration of sects, Quakers, Baptists, Catholics, and pietist sects like Arcans, Mahumetans, Familists, Adamites, Raantrees, Levellers, Anabaptists—all representing fragments of the Protestant Reformation which sought shelter in Colonial America. Nor were such minor religious aberrations surrendered lightly since they were anchored in the heterogeneous ethnic stock of which the Colonial population was composed. In 1790 the white population of 3,172,440 could be subdivided into five major groups and dozens of smaller ones.[20]

For Jews such diversity served as a greater guarantor of security than formal verbal declarations. Dissident religious groups tended to act like a foil absorbing some of the hostility that might otherwise have been directed solely against them. The other-worldliness and eccentricity of the pietists tended to be far more of a nuisance than the Colonial Jews who were content to worship privately in their homes. The German Pietists and Quakers, for example, who refused to bear arms during the French and Indian War displayed an easy tolerance of frontier massacres perpetrated by Indians. It made them anathema to the Scotch-Irish Presbyterians who had settled along the frontier and had first-hand experience of the Indian mode of warfare. In Georgia, where Catholics were unwelcome for geopolitical as well as religious reasons, it was risky to hinder an already sparse population from expanding further. What mattered religion in the face of some man-made or natural disaster? A way had to be found to moderate the fierce religious conflict which in its own right posed a danger to the community. Ultimately a formula for religious peace developed which stressed a bland interchangeable religiosity rather than the highly particularistic pious religious groups which populated the world of the sixteenth and seventeenth centuries. There would be three primary religious groups, Protestants, Catholics, and Jews, and they would emphasize the tenets all held in common, rather than their theological differences.[21] For Jews the intriguing thing about this formula was that it placed Jews, a relatively minor group and traditionally conceived of by Christians with the utmost hostility, on an equal footing with two major Christian groups.

The existence of vast land space could make the suppression of religious dissidence difficult. That is the story behind the founding of Rhode Island which might serve as an illustration that what would have led to a new religious sect in Europe produced merely another colony in Colonial America.[22] But once the land was settled such a safety valve vanished. The Mormons had literally to leave American land space in order to achieve the right to worship as they pleased.

In the case of the Episcopalians, the distance from England and finally the close association with the loyalist cause during the Revolutionary period virtually ruled out all opportunities for the establishment of some form of religious hegemony under their aegis. On the other hand, the Congregationalists suffered from an internal weakness, the fact that the center of power was to be found in the individual congregation, an unlikely container for a national religion. Massachusetts itself proved to be too much for the Puritans to hold. The colony lost its charter in 1688 and the new charter of 1691 granted religious freedom to all, except Catholics and Trinitarians.

The absence of a powerful institutional nucleus meant that the nascent American national feeling was never linked to one specific religious community as it was in Spain. While generally Christian, the cultural diversity of the Colonies ruled out the development of a religio-national culture. The culture was too plastic and ever changing for one group to impose its stamp on it. For Jews that diversity and dynamism proved to be a blessing, for how far could they depart from the cultural norm when the norm itself changed perpetually?

Sometimes the very fervor of religious feeling in the colonies militated against the orthodox established groups. The "Great Awakening" (1733–1744) tended to widen the gap between those older established middle-class groups whose earlier religious passions had been replaced by a desire for decorum and respectability, and the lower classes who favored, perhaps required, a religious outlet for their untamed emotional fervor. The "Great Awakening" kept the religious pot boiling by encouraging religious fundamentalism which was at the heart of much religious dissent. Nonconformist groups grew in strength and frequently were able to challenge the established church at the parish level. The principal proponent of the "Great Awakening," Jonathan Edwards, stressed the importance of individual conversion and revelation. The institution of the church was relegated to the administrative realm. The "Great Awakening" breathed new life into fundamentalist groups like the Baptists and Methodists. They detested the deadly snobbery of the more established groups who in their opinion, did not have "real" religion. The feud would fuel intra-Christian conflict for several decades, leaving little inclination to get after those who did not accept Christ at all.

In some ways established churches were felt to be inimical to the commercial life of the Colonies. When, for example, the Episcopal church of Virginia sought a charter for William and Mary College in 1691, it gave as its reason its desire to save more souls. Soon an exasperated reply was received from the business-minded Lord of the Treasury in London, Edward Seymour: "Souls, damn your souls; make tobacco."[23] Again in 1750 the Episcopalian establishment of Virginia, locked in battle with the Presbyterians over control of the state, was advised by the Lords of Trade in London that "a free exercise of religion . . . is essential to the enriching and improving a trading nation. . . . We must therefore recommend it to your care that nothing be done which can in the least affect that great point."[24] When religious scruples interfered with the profits of the joint stock company, such as Stuyvesant's refusal to allow Jews to continue their trade with the Indians on the South River, the directors predictably opted for material benefits over those of the spirit.

The business-minded advice given by the Lords of Trade to the Presbyterians of Virginia was itself an indication of how the bourgeois spirit was helping to bank the religious fires which burned so brightly in seventeenth-century England. It was not achieved all at once. In 1753 an attempt to naturalize foreign-born Jews residing in England failed. Parliament's affirmative action on the Naturalization Act aroused such public furor that it had to be repealed.

But in the Colonies observers could note a moderation of religious passion with the approach of the Revolution. One could postulate that the passions heretofore devoted to the ethereal realm of religion had merely been transferred to the more earthly one of politics. By the mid-eighteenth century the struggle to establish a new nation had all but been won and the fervor and singleness of purpose, frequently imposed through a religious instrument, was no longer necessary. Later generations could no longer muster the same intense idealism as their forefathers, nor did it seem compelling that they do so. Seventeenth-century Puritans had little difficulty in publicly testifying to their conversion experience, but their grandchildren did. The attempts to convert the Indians, a favorite pastime of the forefathers, declined, as did church attendance.[25] The two decades following the Revolution were a low-water mark for religious adherence. The denominational colleges passed through a "cult of irreligion."[26] The new age would be characterized by a climate of rationalism. Washington, Jefferson, Franklin, and John

Adams restricted their religious sentiments to a low-flame back-burner. They thought of themselves as Deists, which meant that they approached the concept of God and institutionalized religion in cerebral, non-denominational rather than in emotional terms.

Not least important among the factors which contributed to a specific toleration of Jews was the religious outlook of Sephardic Jewry whose customs held sway in the colonies. These Jews possessed a relatively urbane outlook on life which included a greater tendency to accommodate to the secular environment than the later Ashkenazi immigrants of the nineteenth and twentieth centuries. Brought up in the ghettoes and shtetlach of Eastern and Central Europe, few of these latter Jews had any contact with gentile society. On the other hand, Sephardic Jews had learned over a period of centuries to compartmentalize their religious practices so that they did not interfere with their active participation in the temporal affairs of the community. Their practices were in some respects forerunners of Reform Judaism, for while they maintained a fierce loyalty to Judaism, they were not as particularistic as Ashkenazi Jews. Nor did their mores and manners set them so radically apart from the Christian community. They fit well into the Colonial social landscape.

The religious tolerance ultimately produced in Colonial America was, we have seen, an essential prerequisite for the full development of American Jewry. The Colonial approach to Jews seemed all the more exceptional when compared to the practice of the Old World. There history had produced an organic concept of nationhood, which, at best, encouraged the viewing of the Jewish community as a foreign body within the nation, and at worst as a pariah group. America had no such backlog of history to depend on for defining itself. It was an artificial contrivance based on rationalist principles. Rather than being based on the historical experience of one group, the national community could be broken down into a constellation of ethnic and religious and racial groups whose history and interests were often at sharp variance. In order to survive, a formula which allowed the various sub-communities to live in harmony with each other was derived. From the beginning Jews were included in this agreement, which is at the very heart of the American polity. It subsequently became difficult to single Jews out officially as a pariah group without threatening the delicate mechanism which bound this disparate nation together. The development of a pluralistic society in America, in effect, removed the special onus under which Jews had traditionally been compelled to live.

CHAPTER III

Jews in the Colonial Economy and in the Revolution

WE HAVE SEEN THAT THE RELIGIOUS ACCEPTANCE OF THE JEWS DURING the Colonial period evolved as part of a general prescription for the development of national unity. Composed of a highly variegated population with but a short period of history in common, Colonial society required such a formula. For the tiny Jewish communities of Colonial America the fact of their acceptance had special significance. Its members were conditioned by their previous history to play the special role of economic catalysts which they would now be allowed to fulfill with energy and skill.

The Colonial enonomy in which Jews found themselves was overwhelmingly agrarian. With the exception of minor production of staples like rice, tobacco, and indigo, farming was largely of a sustenance variety. It produced little surplus to support urban concentrations. So all-pervading was the agricultural cast of Colonial life that no area of the economy—merchandising, shipping, or crafts, was far removed from the soil. Like most colonial economies it possessed little depth.

For Jews this condition held both promise and problems. Historically excluded from agriculture, Jews could not alter their role overnight. The alternative was to concentrate their activities in the dependent under-developed commercial sector. The advantage inherent in this condition was that the distribution sector of the economy was undeveloped. They became resident-merchants, peddlers, Indian traders, shippers, purveyors, and artisans. Because Jews were relatively unaffected by the anti-business mental set of farming life and historically conditioned to innovate, they were ideally suited to develop the economy. There was a disadvantage in commercial concentration in that business enterprise tended to remain dependent on the well-being of agriculture. The life of a businessman in Colonial America held out the hope of his becoming wealthy but it was also tenuous and insecure. There was little guarantee that there would always be enough to eat, a guarantee that was the farmer's.

For those Jews who were skilled artisans the Colonial economy, chronically short of labor, offered new opportunities. The attempt to solve the labor scarcity by importing indentured servants and slaves served to increase the labor force, but it did little to increase the pool of skilled labor. The situation was aggravated by the fact that labor received a comparatively high wage and was being continually reduced in number by the ever-present lure of the land. There was thus little incentive to go through the lengthy process of apprenticeship to learn skills. The craft guild system was not easily transplanted to such an inhospitable soil. Instead, Colonial America gave birth to a jack-of-all-trades who could do many things adequately, but few things with the expertise that European craftsmen possessed. A degradation of artisanship in the Colonial setting was inevitable.[1]

Under such circumstances, the European precedent of excluding Jews from fulfilling such roles was a luxury the Colonial world could ill afford. In New Amsterdam, for example, the effort to exclude Jews from crafts did not endure. Jews became bakers, tailors, peruke makers, braziers and generally participated in the myriad crafts by which pre-industrial America produced goods and services. One of them, Meyer Meyers, was elected to the presidency of the Colonial silversmith society.

The Colonial economy operated within a mercantilist framework, but the depressing effect on economic activity that such an enforced dependency on the mother country might have had was not in evidence. From the outset the situation of lower classes seemed much improved in the New World. Their labor power was anxiously sought and generously rewarded, with the result that enormous new energies and talents were released. In the Colonies the poor dared hope that their lot might be improved by their own efforts. It was that spirit which accounted for the restless, seething activity which de Tocqueville later recognized as the "super abundant force" of the American people.[2] Certainly that force was most in evidence in the Jews of Colonial America, who given an unprecedented degree of freedom and security, energetically sought the means for improving their lot.

Such means were not always easy to find for what would become true in theory was not always discernible in practice. Colonial authorities were not at first willing to have Jews fully participate in the economy. There was a fear of economic competition which the stereotype of the shrewd, grasping Jewish merchant made all the more real. In New Amsterdam the effort to withhold trading licenses and bar Jews from certain activities was rejected by the directors of the West India

Company. Jews were granted the right to "travel and trade to and in New Netherland."[3] Even so, Governor Stuyvesant chose to defy the instructions of the directors and prohibited Jews from participating in the fur trade in the Fort Orange and South River regions.

He had not abandoned the hope that the directors might yet be convinced of the danger of allowing Jews to do business in the colony. On October 30, 1655, he addressed still another letter to the directors in Amsterdam in which he warned of the dire consequences of permitting Jews to participate in the fur trade. Meanwhile Jewish merchants who had already invested in the trade on the strength of the company's first order again petitioned the directors as well as the Council of New Netherland to honor the previous order. The Council of the colony predictably denied their request, but decided to permit the Jews to carry on a token trade until a definite decision should be issued by the directors. Not until June of 1656 was the company's reply received. It unequivocally acknowledged the right of the Jews to partake in the fur trade and to purchase real estate and cautioned Stuyvesant to execute orders "punctually and with more respect."[4] But the same letter contained a new affirmation of Stuyvesant's right to prohibit Jews from becoming artisan-mechanics and from opening retail shops.

Each step on the road to complete access to the economic arena had to be fought for separately. The legal underpinning for the restriction of Jews related to the unresolved question of burgher rights and endenization. Small burgher rights had to be obtained and a twenty-guilder tax to be paid in order to carry on retail trade in an open establishment. In addition an oath "to bear the burden, expenses, expedition and watches like other burghers and citizens" was required.[5] The directors of the West India Company did not consider that Jews who had come from another Dutch colony possessed such rights. The New Amsterdam Jews were thus compelled to pay a special tax in lieu of the "watch and ward" which only citizens could perform. Step by step Jews fought for the rights of burghers. In the case of the "watch and ward" tax Jacob Barsimson and Asser Levy argued that as simple laborers they were unable to pay the tax and therefore wished to fulfill their burgher obligations by standing guard. The council denied the petition and instead contemptuously gave the two men "consent ... to depart whenever and whither it pleases them."[6]

The Jews of New Amsterdam did not rest easily with this decision. They maintained a steady flow of petitions demanding the rights which came with citizenship and eventually they were permitted to stand "watch and ward." In April, 1657, Asser Levy, who had been a burgher in Amsterdam, petitioned the Council for burgher rights. Predictably his claim was denied, but nine days later a group of Jews, reminding the Council that the Jews of Amsterdam possessed this privilege, again earnestly petitioned for them.[7] They were gradually wrested from a reluctant Director General and Council. In 1685, after a petition by Saul Brown, Hazaan of Shearith Israel, the right to participate in whole-sale trade was finally extended to the Jews of the colony. Ultimately, too, the prohibitions against Jewish participation in retail trade, purchase of real property and burial plots and the myriad of minor limitations designed to curtail the activities of Jews, were relaxed. Jews became full participants in the economic life of the colony.

After the English established their hegemony in New York and Dela-ware the endenization problem continued to hamper Jewish commercial activity. The British Navigation Act of 1660 was designed to bring trade to the mother country. Although it was not seriously enforced until after 1763 its legal provisions limiting trading rights to native-born English-men or endenized citizens were well established. The status of denizen referred to a form of naturalization which entitled foreigners or non-residents to certain of the rights associated with citizenship, such as the running of a retail business. Under the Dutch, foreigners could be endenized through an act of the colonial assembly. When the English established themselves in 1664, colonial governors, and in some cases colonial legislators, granted such rights and a number of Jews were naturalized in this way.[8] In 1683 a general naturalization was extended to all resident aliens in the colonies, but after that date its grant was limited to Protestants, although Jews might still obtain naturalization certificates from the governor or the assembly. Thus between 1705 and 1769, 44 Jews were endenized in New York, but in other colonies the procedure was more difficult.

The question of naturalizing Jews sometimes caused conflict. In 1685, for example, Major William Dyer, a diligent crown official, clashed with Governor Coddington of Rhode Island over the right of Jews to partici-pate in the molasses and sugar trade. Dyer insisted that seven Jewish men and women were illegally involved in the trade because they were not citizens, and tried to seize their property. But his action was chal-lenged in the courts which returned the property to the Jews and charged Dyer with court costs.[9] In another case, Moses Lopez, a kingpin in the economy of Rhode Island, who had been granted a ten-year monopoly to manufacture potash, was denied naturalization. Lopez was compelled to travel to Lancaster, Connecticut in 1762 to obtain the privilege.

Finally in 1740 Parliament passed a naturalization law which made the granting of naturalization uniform throughout the colonial empire.

It would be granted to Jews, like other aliens, after seven years of residence and they would be permitted to omit the words "upon the true faith of a Christian" from the oath of abjuration. Between 1740 and 1744 twenty-four additional Jews were naturalized and eventually two hundred Jews sought to be naturalized under the provisions of the new law.

Nevertheless, the implementation of the law was not uniform and Jews continued to experience difficulties. Sometimes these were caused by the persistence of suspicion of Jews among local officials. "David the Jew," a peddler from New Amsterdam, wandered into Congregational territory in 1659 to ply his wares. He was arrested and charged by the Hartford General Court with "going into houses when the heads of ye families wr absent, and tradeing provisions from children." Another, Jacob Lucena, was fined £20, later reduced to £10, for lewdly propositioning women.[10] It would take more than naturalization laws to eliminate completely the ingrained fear and suspicion of Jews which persisted in the mind of the public. But in time even that would be reduced to manageable levels.

Such occasional manifestations of anti-Semitism on the grass-roots level did not noticeably affect Jewish business activity. It appeared as if the small size of the Jewish community was inversely proportional to the number of Jews involved in some form of trade and commerce. They became especially prominent in the distribution network as merchants, Indian traders, and peddlers. But most important was their involvement in ocean commerce, which was a crucial activity in the Colonial economy.

The economic channels within which the Colonial economy operated were to some extent determined by a loosely enforced mercantilist policy. Horace Walpole's policy of nonenforcement of mercantilism, sometimes called "salutary neglect," allowed for the development of an extra-legal commerce with nations other than England. Several variations of a trade pattern, sometimes thought to be triangular, which featured as its three anchors New England, the west coast of Africa and Caribbean islands like Jamaica, Barbados, and Surinam, were developed. The Caribbean islands possessed some of the oldest Jewish communities in the New World, and Colonial Jewish traders, some of whom had migrated from the islands, possessed a natural commercial connection which they used to good effect.

Of the several ports which became involved in ocean commerce, it was Newport which best capitalized on the triangular trade. It served as the principal port for much of New England's foreign commerce.

In Newport, too, a flourishing Jewish community established itself. The fortunes of that port were in some measure related to the business activity of its Jewish community. The high point of its prosperity in the three decades between 1740 and 1770 corresponded in time to the summit of Jewish prosperity and the decline of the port, to the disbanding of the Jewish community during the revolutionary war.[11]

The first group of fifteen Jewish families who arrived in Newport from Holland in the spring of 1658 were simple folk—soap boilers, brass workers, and small merchants. Beginning in 1759 the first group of settlers was supplemented by a group of established merchants stemming primarily from Curaçao and Barbados. Included among the new immigrants were the Lopez, Rivera, and Hart families, all destined to leave their mark as successful traders.[12] At the peak in 1760 there may have been as many as a thousand Jews residing in Newport and its environs. They owned seventeen candle-making factories related to a wholly Jewish-owned spermaceti trust, twenty-two distilleries, four sugar refineries for the making of rum to be used domestically and for the African trade, five rope-walk factories, a Castile soap-manufacturing combine, several furniture factories, a potash trust, and several smaller merchandizing establishments. The Jews of Newport also maintained a sizable representation in the shipping and whaling industries.[13]

Jewish preeminence in the commercial life of Newport was based on the entrepreneurial skills which were part of their cultural baggage and a special talent for pioneering in new industries such as the manufacture of potash and Castile soap. Here Jews brought their knowledge of "industrial secrets" to bear. The manufacture of soap, for example, was a craft monopolized by Jews since the fourteenth century; its "secrets" were brought to Newport by Moses Lopez. The development of the spermaceti industry was a byproduct of the Jewish involvement in the whaling industry. It was a Portuguese Jew, Aaron Lopez, who perceived the advantage of spermaceti over tallow candles and together with a group of Jewish merchants organized the first American trust in 1761.

Jewish merchants early realized the long-range practical advantages of maintaining a good reputation for honesty and reliability. Two of their number were among the twenty-seven signers of a petition enjoining the Common Council of New York to restrain those who used sharp practices like the sale of "not merchantable" flour.[14] A story regarding one of the founders of the spermaceti trust, Jacob Rodriguez Rivera, illustrates the reputation made by some Jews for honesty in business. After suffering serious business reverses, Rivera was forced to declare himself bankrupt. But he remained distressed regarding the fate of his many loyal creditors. In a few years Rivera recouped part of his fortune.

Thereupon his creditors were invited to a special banquet. Each guest found beneath his respective napkin a check for the amount owed plus interest accrued.[15]

While honesty and punctiliousness in business went far in explaining Jewish success, its commercial basis could be found more directly in the existence of the Jewish-Caribbean nexus. Religious and family ties with Jews in the West Indies often allowed Jews to exercise a disproportionate influence in ocean commerce. From their private family correspondence Jews were often able to secure the commercial intelligence which was needed to learn of market conditions. In the days before the establishment of a commercial press such intelligence could make the difference between profit and loss.[16] In its earliest stages the trade between the Colonies and the West Indies was a rather random affair carried on through "huckstering" voyages. On such trips the captain of the vessel would act as a commercial agent as well. He would decide where to sell his cargo, at what price, and what goods to bring back in his hold. Frequently he was part owner of the company and shared in its profits and losses. Under such conditions, family or religious connections could prove to be the prime ingredient in carrying on profitable business. The Jewish merchants of Newport frequently relied on such connections.[17]

How deeply were the Jewish merchants of Newport involved in the ocean commerce? An examination of the cargo manifests and business books of Aaron Lopez, who owned a fleet of perhaps as many as thirty ships, presents a virtually complete listing of the type of goods involved in the ocean commerce of the Colonies. Horses, furniture, wheat, oats, rye, barley, flax, apples, live geese, turkeys, oak staves, copper, logwood, water casks, all kinds of spermaceti oil, candles, soap, honey, butter, cheese, haddock, and mackerel were shipped to the West Indies, England, and the west coast of Africa.[18] From England they imported cotton, hoes, and guns which were then transshipped to New Amsterdam. From Africa they imported slaves and from the West Indies they received molasses from which they distilled rum.

A key aspect of the triangular trade involved the notorious middle passage, the transportation of slaves from the west coast of Africa to the West Indies and eventually directly to the Colonies. Newport was the major Colonial port for this traffic in people, so that it comes as no surprise that Colonial Rhode Island boasted a higher proportion of slaves than any other colony.[19] Jewish merchants were involved in this trade, but it is difficult to determine the extent to which their fortunes were dependent on it.[20] Numerous transactions concerning the trade in slaves are recorded in the business ledgers of Isaac da Costa and Aaron Lopez.

In April, 1762, Isaac Eliezer and Samuel Moses, two of Newport's leading Jewish merchants, charged the captain of one of their vessels to "be particular careful of your vessel and slaves." If the voyage was profitable the captain would be allowed "the privilege of bringing home three slaves and your mate, one."[21]

The author of *The Story of the Jews of Newport*, Morris Gutstein, maintains that there were relatively few Jews involved in the slave trade and cites the census of 1774 to show that only thirty servants were employed in Jewish homes, all of whom, Gutstein assumes, were white indentured servants. The few Jews who may have owned slaves in Newport were none too comfortable with them. Their wills, according to Gutstein, often contained clauses ordering that such slaves be freed upon the master's death.[22] Jewish involvement in the slave trade should not embarrass today, as one suspects it did Mr. Gutstein. The application of twentieth-century standards of morality to eighteenth-century behavior can lead to twisted results. It was then not freighted with the moral onus it carries today. The traffic in human beings by the Portuguese, Dutch, French, and English was an essential ingredient of the early capital formation necessary for the development of the capitalist system, and Jews who were frequently found at the very heart of commerce could not have failed to contribute a proportionate share to the trade directly and indirectly. In 1460 when Jews were masters of the nautical sciences in Portugal that nation was importing seven to eight hundred slaves yearly.[23]

At the same time there is some reason to feel that the Jews of Newport, if they did not avoid the profitable business of trafficking in slaves, might have hesitated about owning them. But this might have stemmed from the British-Caribbean precedent from which area many Newport Jews had come, rather than from moral scruples. In the British areas of the Caribbean Jews were forbidden to own slaves because of the fear that under Jewish tutelage slave insurrection, a perpetual fear in slaveholding communities, would be encouraged.[24]

In the Colonies Jews became aware relatively early of the need for a distribution system to bridge the gap between the commerce and industry located near the coastal ports and the developing markets in the interior. The Indian fur trade was the first mainstay of Jews of New Amsterdam, and from there it was but a short leap to satisfying the growing demand for amenities among the rural frontier population. The Jewish peddler who carried his pack of "notions" containing such things as needle and thread, buttons and hooks was not an uncommon sight in the frontier communities. The earliest link between the new small factories and warehouses of New England and the Western market was established by a Jewish firm which shipped a cargo of goods down the Ohio to Fort Chartres in the Illinois country in 1768.[25]

These traders and peddlers were undoubtedly helped by a reputation for scrupulous honesty in their dealings with customers. "While they are close dealers," one Colonial newspaper reported, "they were as a class rather more honest than the English traders and they became friendly with the Indians."[26] It is not unreasonable to postulate that the Indian fur trade which led to a perpetual search for new beaver grounds and peddling awakened an interest quite remote from the Jewish ken—an appeciation of the value of land. Jewish traders played a pathfinder role in Kentucky, Illinois, Indiana, Michigan, the interior of Canada, and later throughout the Mississippi valley.[27] More important was their acquiring a taste for the profitable business of land speculation which sometimes was the instrument used by the humble trader to make his fortune. Examples of this early Jewish version of the American "rags to riches" story are not plentiful, but they do exist.

More likely was the rise from peddler to resident merchant. Once established, the Jewish resident merchant might become the source of furnishing merchandise and short-term credit to the less fortunate peddlers who served as his agents for extending his market over as wide an area as possible. This was necessary since in terms of purchasing power and numbers a single town or even a county rarely generated enough business volume to support such a business venture.

When the French and Indian War broke out in 1754 some of these Jewish merchants were in a good position to reap a handsome profit as purveyors for the local military contingent. They possessed the business acumen and, more important, the connection with Eastern suppliers and transporters to undertake such a venture. It was even possible, providing capital was available, to try one's hand at local manufacturing and distribution. The final step of a typical successful business odyssey was to invest in land which, with few interruptions, rose steadily in value throughout the Colonial period. Joseph Simon's career serves as a good illustration of this model. He began as a humble Indian trader and then joined the consortium of Trent, Levy, and Frank, which served incidentally as a means of capital accumulation. After the outbreak of the French and Indian War he joined Alexander Lowry to purvey supplies for the Continental Army. At the same time his growing fortune was increasingly earmarked for investment in land. By the 1760's Simon had achieved a relatively elevated station as a merchant and man of property in the Colonies.

With some variations a similar pattern was followed by other successful Jews. Michael Gratz, whose daughter Rebecca Gratz served as the model for Rebecca in Sir Walter Scott's *Ivanhoe*, Hyman Levy, a merchant and Indian trader, and his son Michael also achieved rapid mobility as merchants, purveyors, and land speculators. In the case of the Gratz brothers a connection in London, which gave them the ability to exert influence on the English court, allowed them to compete with the Christian firm of Baynton, Wharton and Morgan in exploiting the untapped Illinois country market.[29]

More often Christian-Jewish partnerships were formed to exploit the business opportunities offered by the opening of the first West. The Franks family of Philadelphia was notably successful in its investment in land, having secured large grants on the Ohio between 1760 and 1769. Sometimes, as in the case of Ezekiel Solomon who pioneered in the Michigan territory, Jews were the first pioneers in a newly opened territory. Typically these were individual enterprisers but sometimes a Jewish commercial concentration might form. This was apparently the case in the town of Easton, Pennsylvania, a fur-trading center near the fork of the Delaware River, which in 1780 boasted five Jewish resident merchants and numerous peddlers. Surviving tax records show that Jewish traders of Easton did quite well for a time.[30]

The life of these Jewish merchants was not always smooth; nor was success assured. During the French and Indian War the trade with the West suffered grievously because of marauding Indians. Joseph Simon and David Franks lost all their supplies in this manner and for a time faced ruin. Another, Hyman Levy, was taken prisoner by Pontiac, chief of the Ottawa tribe. Others lost their lives as well as their stock of merchandise.[31] Even in times of peace an element of risk attended trade with the Indians. Their lack of understanding of the concept of private property made them highly unpredictable customers at best.

What was misfortune for some proved a boon for others. The war opened up a new opportunity for shipowners who applied for commissions to prey on French shipping. Jews played some role in this temporary, risky but sometimes profitable business of privateering. Sampson Simon owned four such privateers, the *Hardy*, *Sampson*, *Union*, and *Polly*, while Hyman Levy outfitted two, the *Dreadnought* and the *Orleans*. A privateer with the impressive name of *The Duke of Cumberland* was owned by Judah Hay.

Provisioning the armies could also prove to be a lucrative business, especially since the market was guaranteed by contract and the connections for obtaining such provisions already existed for the resident merchant. Purveying was a conventional Jewish business role in the Old World and it was therefore not surprising that it should become one in the Colonial world as well. Again the Franks family of Philadelphia, especially Moses Franks and his Christian partners, Messrs. Colebrook and Nesbitt, became prominent in this venture on the side of the English during the French and Indian War. On the French side, another Jew, Abraham Gradis, played the same role. By the time of the Revolutionary War, purveying and sutling had become occupations associated with Colonial Jewry.

The Treaty of Paris in 1763 brought with it a decline of Indian "troubles" and a surge of new settlers for the West. For the Jewish merchants who were among the first to see the possibilities in the Western market, this development affirmed the accuracy of their vision. The increase in population would not only increase the size of the market, it was bound to lead to a rise in land values. The Indian trade now was dominated by larger consortiums, but at the grass-roots level the individual peddler continued to ply his wares, fullfilling in the process an essential distribution function in the remote reaches of the Colonial economy.

The establishment of the institutions of a capitalist economy, banks, stock companies, and exchanges, also had their Jewish representation. Three Jews, Benjamin Seixas, Ephraim Hare, and Joseph Bueno played key roles in establishing the New York Board of Stockholders, the precursor of the Stock Exchange. Numerous others gained prominence as private bankers and discounters.

In other respects the economic activity of Jews was frequently fashioned by the region in which they happened to reside. The commercial activities of Jews in the staple-producing economy of the South were somewhat different from the activities of the Jews of New England or the Middle Colonies. In South Carolina the prosperous Jewish community consisted of planters as well as of merchants and traders. In Georgia, Isaac DaCosta became the principal grader of the indigo crop and eventually became the "Surveyor and Inspector General of Indigo."[32] How rapidly fortunes might be made in this region is illustrated by the career of Francis Salvador, one of the most prominent of South Carolina's Jews. When he arrived in the colony in 1773 he was virtually destitute, having lost much of his estate in the failure of the Dutch East India Company. Within a short period he owned a 7,000-acre plantation and many slaves. Unfortunately his good fortune proved to be short-lived. He lost his life at the age of twenty-nine when he was killed in a skirmish with the Cherokee Indians.

In Georgia normal trading and merchandising was supplemented by participation in vine and silk growing ventures which were pioneered and developed by Jews.[33] The business career of Mordecai Sheftall, founder of the most prominent Jewish family of Colonial Georgia, illustrates the many business activities which might be combined to establish the family fortune. Sheftall was variously a planter, a rancher, a sawmill operator, a shopkeeper, and a ship's captain. In 1777 he became the Deputy Commissary General of Purchases and Issues for the state militia and eventually for all Continental troops in South Carolina and Georgia. During the war he and his son were captured and spent several years confined in a prison ship and in the West Indies. Georgia was a colony where the loyalist cause had considerable following and undoubtedly one of the costs to men like Sheftall, who was outspokenly sympathetic to the Revolution, was a decline in their business interests.

While Sheftall's sacrifices may have been anomalous in Georgia, they were quite in keeping with those of American Jewry. Whereas the majority of Americans were indifferent to the outcome of the War of Independence, Jews demonstrated an uncharacteristic recklessness in casting their lot almost exclusively with the Whig side. Why this should have been so it not very difficult to discern. One could reason that Jews were concentrated in that sector of the economy where the impact of the Greenville and Townshend programs were most severe among the merchants. They, therefore, ostensibly felt a special animus toward the mother country. The signature of six Jews on one of the Non-Importation agreements which followed hard upon the Stamp Act of 1765 might be used as evidence of the animus.[34] But then not all Jews were merchants, and historians have long since dismissed the quaint notion that all Colonial merchants were anti-British. It may have been that Colonial Jewry, being largely of Portuguese and Central European origin, felt little cultural affinity and loyalty to the British. But then how does one explain the relative passivity of the French, Dutch, and Swedish groups in the Colonies who also had little cause to love the British. Much of the Revolutionary leadership was in fact of English stock. It is more satisfactory to explain Colonial Jewry's preference for independence on the basis of characteristically Jewish post-emancipation ideological preferences which when combined with their Colonial experience made republicanism preferable.

Jews felt that the republican form of government held a promise for further improvement of their lot. When Benjamin Nones who possessed impeccable credentials as a Revolutionary soldier, was nevertheless subjected to a scurrilous attack by a Federalist organ in 1800, he expressed his republican anti-monarchical principles this way: "On religious grounds I am a Republican. Kingly government was first conceded to the foolish complaints of the Jewish people as a punishment and a curse; . . . . and so it has been to every nation who have been as foolishly tempted to submit to it. Great Britain has a king, and her enemies need not wish her the sword, the pestilence and the famine."[35]

That sentiment was reinforced by the relatively tolerant atmosphere in Colonial America which Jews, more than other ethnic groups, had reason to appreciate. The Revolution possessed a liberal bias which promised to extend further the openness of the American society. "The very fact that he had so many rights and privileges made a Whig of him," explained one historian.[36] We have seen that even the few disabilties under which Jews were compelled to live tended to give way as the Revolution approached. They came to feel that they belonged here and that it was a propitious environment for them, because it was free of the European ways. They were early believers in the concept of the two hemispheres which served as the ideological buttress for the early policy of isolation and the Monroe Doctrine. America was different from Europe; it was the hope of the world and must not be contaminated by the corruptions of the Old World. For the Colonial Jew, aware of the condition of his coreligionists in Europe, such a postulate had a special meaning. He had become an integral part of a new and different kind of national community. He became an American nationalist because he felt he belonged.

It was this feeling of being part of a new, still uncorrupted, community which best explains the precipitous actions of the Jewish community of New York and Newport. Both chose to disband and relocate rather than live under British occupation. Gershom Seixas, spiritual head of New York's Shearith Israel, removed most of his congregation to Philadelphia and Stamford, Connecticut, upon the approach of the British army. In Newport, too, the Jewish community led by Aaron Lopez dispersed rather than suffer British occupation. The nucleus of the congregation resettled in Lancaster, Connecticut.

In the Old World, Jews had not customarily taken part in military operations. It is perhaps the surest evidence of their changed status that they participated wholeheartedly in the armed struggle against Britain. Two Jewish officers, Benjamin Nones and Colonel Isaac Franks, served on Washington's staff. Nones began his military career as an enlisted man serving under General Pulaski and then under General De Kalb and Lafayette. He is credited with playing a key role in relieving the siege of Savannah by leading French troops through the British lines. During the bitter winter of 1777–1778, when the Continental Army was encamped at Valley Forge, it was Philip Moses Russel, Surgeon's Mate of the Second Virginia Regiment, who helped care for the frozen, forlorn soldiers. In the Colonies on a temporary sojourn from England

and Canada was David Franks who took the opportunity to give expression to his well-known Whig sentiments by joining a Massachusetts regiment. He became a major on Benedict Arnold's staff and barely avoided the stigma of treason associated with his superior. At his insistence a special court of inquiry was convened after the war to clear him of the charge. A "Jews Company," so dubbed because 26 Jews served in its ranks, was one of South Carolina's contributions to the Revolutionary cause. Connecticut could boast of the Pinto family which sent four of its members to the Continental Army. Like Mordecai Sheftell, Colonel Isaac Franks was captured by the British but proved too resourceful to remain long in captivity. Jews continued to be prominent as purveyors and sutlers during the Revolution and some, like Isaac Hart, were active in the lucrative but risky business of privateering.

Because of the popularity of the much-exaggerated activities of Haym Salomon, the role of Jewish financiers in the Revolution has been somewhat misunderstood. There was, of course, an element of risk in discounting the commercial paper so generously distributed by Robert Morris, the treasurer of the patriotic cause. Haym Salomon apparently did so generously and unfortunately did not live to see how costly it would turn out in the end and how ungrateful the descendants of the patriots would be. Supposedly his estate contained thousands of dollars of worthless paper for which Congress refused to compensate his family even while it praised his service to the Revolutionary cause. But it is also true that Salomon never lent money to the government as such but rather acted as a broker selling $200,000 worth of government securities for which he earned a broker's fee. What he did do is to lend money to certain delegates of the Continental Congress, likes James Madison and Edmund Randolph, for which he rarely charged interest. The myth that Salomon singlehandedly helped finance the Revolution was probably generated by his son anxious for the dividends of reflected glory.[37] Moreover the financier role was shared by other prominent Jews including Manuel Josephson, Mordecai Sheftall, Moses Hays, Isaac Moses, David Franks and the various members of the Minis family. There are no recorded complaints of these creditors.

Although Colonial Jewry largely favored the patriotic side, it did not completely avoid the community rifts which characterize every civil war. There was in the Jewish community a goodly representation of loyalists as well.[38] In Newport, the Harts and the Pollocks and John Lucena remained loyal and suffered dearly for it. Two brothers, violators of the Non Imporation Agreement, were stripped of all their property and driven out of town. Another "was inhumanly fired upon and bayoneted, wounded in fifteen parts of his body, and beat with their muskets in a most shocking manner."[39] For a time Ezra Stiles, a well-known philosemite, gave credence to the rumor that loyalist Jews of Newport had actually organized an intelligence network to funnel secrets to London.[40] The social tensions created by the conflict could trigger the release of residual anti-Semitic sentiment which undoubtedly was the basis for the rumor.

In Philadelphia, David Franks, son of Jacob Franks, and one of that city's leading Jewish merchants, openly espoused the British cause. He served as a purveyor for the British army and took pride in his daughter's marriage to an English officer who was later knighted. Like the Jewish loyalists of Newport he was to pay dearly for having chosen the losing side.

But such cases were the exception rather than the rule. Sometimes Jews adapted themselves to the political coloration of the area in which they lived. Thus the Jews of Montreal remained fiercely loyal. The case of Mordecai Sheftall of Georgia who was denounced by James Wright, the loyalist governor of that state, was exceptional. Even in New York City, where Jewish sentiment in favor of independence was fairly strong, there was a sizable minority among the wealthier merchants who chose to remain in the city rather than follow the lead of Gershom Seixas. There must have been some Jews too who shared the indifference of many other citizens. Those who remained behind in New York did business and fraternized with the Hessian troops. Jewish women "are very fond of the Germans and obliging towards them," observed Conrad Döhla in his diary.[41] Indeed, after the congregation Shearith Israel left the city, the rump of the congregation was serviced by Alexander Zunz, a Hessian officer of Jewish extraction.[42] Fifteen of these Jews signed an "Address of Loyalty" to the victorious Admiral Richard Howe and his brother General William Howe. Paradoxically, the brothers were themselves suspected of having Whig loyalties in England.[43]

But most Jews were fortunate enough to have chosen the winning side and had some claim to reaping the fruits of victory after the hostilities were over. In the parade in honor of the newly ratified Constitution in Philadelphia in 1789 a careful observer might have noted among the table of refreshments at the end of the parade route one which contained only Kosher food. It was placed there by the proud Jews of Philadelphia. Some Jews pressed their claim for office and honor for their role in the Revolution. Thus a group of New York Jews reminded Governor Clinton that "none has manifested a more zealous attachment to the sacred cause of America in the late war with Great Britain."[44] Some wanted more tangible rewards. Mordecai Sheftall, Solomon Bush, and

David Franks joined their gentile comrades-in-arms in requesting tracts of land set aside for veterans.

Undoubtedly as the war drew to a close many Jews felt that they belonged to America as much as America belonged to them. One newspaper put the case for the Jews succinctly: "The Jews have had a considerable share in our late revolution. They have behaved well throughout. Let our government invite the Jews to our state and promise them a settlement in it. It will be a wise and politic stroke and give a place of rest at last to the tribe of Israel."[45] Such generous sentiments attest to the culmination of a process already manifest in the late Colonial period. Jews had found "a place of rest" in America.

CHAPTER IV

Jews in the Antebellum Economy

FROM AN ECONOMIC POINT OF VIEW THE YEARS FOLLOWING THE Revolution were dreary ones. The independent colonies were now outside the British imperial system which meant that the important "sugar trade" was denied to them. Trade patterns established during the Colonial period were to some extent anchored in trade with the mother country and its possessions. These markets were no longer available to the shipping industry and at the same time Britain dumped cheap manufactured goods in its former colonial market in a last-ditch effort to strangle the economies of the newly-independent states. Meanwhile the creation of a national economy eluded the Colonies. Frequently one Colony was pitted against another in trade and currency wars. The overall effect was severe economic dislocation.

The slack in ocean commerce led enterprising New England traders to the Far East for markets and goods. Interest in the China trade had been awakened when in 1784 the *Empress of China* returned from the Far East with a cargo which yielded 110 percent profit. The trade grew apace so that by the time of Washington's inauguration there were fourteen American vessels in Canton's harbor.[1] Benjamin Etting, a well-known Jewish merchant involved in the oriental trade, discovered an easy market for the tea and silk "richly embroidered" and of "variegated colors," and two thousand boxes of firecrackers which would certainly be used for the Fourth of July celebration on Independence Day.[2] But Etting was probably an exception since most Jewish traders who survived the economic decline of Newport were not able to tie up their limited capital in such uncertain long-range ventures. For them the reopening of certain Caribbean ports by France, Holland, and Denmark offered an opportunity to enter once again into that lucrative commerce. But things were not the same even after the British relented and in 1830 allowed American ships to trade in their old Caribbean haunts. In the interim years the slave trade had earned the disapprobation of the opinion leaders in England and the United States. In 1833 that key element in the triangular trade was outlawed by Britain. Previously, in

1808, the importation of slaves had by constitutional provision become illegal in the United States.

The outbreak of war between France and England also had considerable impact on Colonial shipping. There were the usual opportunities to act as prize-masters for belligerent privateers, and one Jewish trader, Moses Myers, is reported to have done so with such success that the French appointed him as their official agent in the port of Norfolk. But such dividends have to be balanced against the liabilities caused to the nation's economy by a war which was fought as much in the commercial arena as it was in the military. Napoleon's Berlin and Milan Decrees, the backbone of the Continental System, were designed to encourage a European dependence on the French economy. England retaliated with its Orders in Council and by developing a lucrative trade with Spain's colonial possessions in South America. America's ocean commerce was caught in between. Washington's advice to isolate the nation politically while maintaining friendly commercial relations, seemed impossible to follow as American commerce proved unable to avoid the blockade of either nation.

The situation came to a head during Jefferson's second administration. Faced with the prospect of being drawn into the struggle, Jefferson first limited American commerce (Embargo Act of 1807) and then cut off trade with Europe entirely (Non-Intercourse Act 1809). His successor, James Madison, reverted to a policy of bargaining for concessions for the belligerents in return for trade (Macon's Bill, Number 2, May, 1810). The policy of limiting trade represented a calculated risk. In return for peace a portion of America's commerce would be sacrificed. But the gamble did not pay off for while the nation's ocean commerce declined, it did not stave off the war which came in 1812.

The effect of Jefferson's and Madison's policies on the nation's business life was drastic. Between 1811 and 1814 the value of exports dropped from $61,000,000 to $7,000,000 while imports declined from a value of $53,000,000 to $13,000,000. During the same period the tonnage involved in ocean commerce dropped from 950,000 to 60,000. Business activity declined sharply. The rise in prices of imported goods, on which the economy was still dependent, led to a rise in wholesale and retail prices and also in the cost of production. Credit became increasingly scarce. In short, the commercial sector, in which the greater number of American Jews were involved, entered upon meager times, whereas agriculture, which was still relatively independent of the cash economy, barely felt the rise in prices and the business downturn.

Some Jews were able to hedge against bad times by reverting to their former source of livelihood, the fur trade, which had in the interim shifted its activities from the Hudson to the Ohio Valley. Many Jews had abandoned the trade after the deterioration of good relations with the Indians during the French and Indian War. During that war only the trading post at Detroit escaped the scourge of Pontiac's warriors. A Simon and Lowry pack train was attacked at Blood Run and everything was lost. At least five Jewish Indian traders were captured. Most important, the war cut the source of pelts which came from Indian trappers.

Now the lure of the fur trade seemed again to be irresistible. The consortium of Franks, Simon and Trent regained its former preeminence. Stronger companies began to dominate the field. Destined to become the largest of these was the company organized by John Jacob Astor. He received his introduction to the fur business under Hyman Levy, who, incidentally, found him wanting in business sense.

Eventually the influx of settlers into the Ohio Valley and the growing availability of cotton and wool, both of which were cheaper and more convenient to use for clothing, began to affect the fur trade adversely. By 1840 the wearing of beaver skins was no longer considered stylish for men. It would be some time before women developed a taste for them. The trappers, now located primarily along the Missouri, fared less and less well.

Jewish business ventures, some now in their second generation of family ownership, suffered from another handicap. The simple partnership, which often became the standard business organization among them, proved singularly inappropriate for amassing the additional capital needed for expansion. Instead such businesses financed expansion through profits and trapped themselves in a capital scarcity of their own creation. Often growth might be further hampered by the fact that family businesses could not easily attract outside managerial talent as they grew in size. Often even a son, who could claim the business as his patrimony, was lured by the promise of the West. Even relatively successful businesses experienced difficulty in sustaining themselves beyond one generation. Frequently they became ingrown and moribund and left their original promise unfulfilled.

A major difficulty for American business in the post-Revolutionary decades was raising capital. Money was scarce and lacked flexibility and uniformity. During the War of 1812 capital tended to desert the moribund ocean commerce for the small manufacturing enterprises which were beginning to sprout in New England. Many stratagems were used to solve the capital scarcity problem; among the most common was the lottery. So popular did these lotteries become that Philadelphia alone boasted two hundred outlets. Jews particularly seem to have been attracted to them and used them not only for amassing business capital but also for financing synagogue construction.³ Prizes as high as $20,000 kept the lotteries sufficiently attractive so that capital could be collected in the form of suitable percentage for the house.

It was perhaps the pervasive shortage of capital that made private and public banking so attractive for those fortunate enough to have capital available. In the Jewish community Harmon Hendricks, who earned his fortune in mining, serves as a good example. Hendricks invested some of his fortune and established a private bank as well. At the end of his career he sat on the Board of Directors of several business establishments, including the Bank of Hartford. Other well-to-do Jews invested in local banks and in government bonds. Jewish international bankers also came into the picture. R. & I. Phillips and Company and J. I. Cohen Jr. and Brothers were the American agents for the Rothschilds in Philadelphia and Baltimore.

Naturally, Jewish bankers were not exempt from the vagaries of the business cycles and other conditions, such as the attack by the President of the United States, Andrew Jackson, which made banking a risky business. The Cohen Brothers of Baltimore with their connections with the Rothschilds hardly qualified as one of Jackson's "wild cat" banks which dotted the West like prairie flowers. Yet during the panic of 1837, brought on partly by Jackson's Specie Circular, the Cohens barely survived a run on their bank.⁴ The Rothschilds, who became the agents of the United States for the French spoliation claims in 1830, were not so lucky with some of their other agencies. Their agency in New York, managed by the Joseph brothers, went into bankruptcy on March 17, 1837. It was that bankruptcy which brought another Jewish banker, August Belmont, to the American financial scene. He became Rothschild's new agent on the New York Stock Exchange.

Jewish feeling of belonging is reflected in the frequency with which they turned to the government for succor. Usually they solicited positions as consuls, Indian agents, custom inspectors and collectors, treasury agents, auditors, marshals, and agents in foreign ports. One consul, Nathan Levy, was kept at his St. Thomas post despite several complaints of being overzealous in the fulfillment of his duties. In the case of Madison's appointment of Mordecai Noah to a consular post in Tunis, his Jewishness caused unforeseen problems. Noah was recalled in April, 1815, with a cryptic comment by James Monroe stating that at the time of his appointment "it was not known that the Religion which you profess would form an obstacle to the exercise of your consular function." Isaac Harby, a noted Jewish playwright, presented a near-classic reply to the charge: "I would ask since it was not *then* known whether it has been *since* discovered that Religion disqualifies a man from the exercise of his political functions."[5]

Sometimes, as in the case of granting a commission to Uriah Phillips, government officials were far more ready to grant them than were naval officers to accept those to whom they had been granted. Nevertheless, the employment of Jews in the Federal civil service, such as it was, was probably somewhat greater than their proportion of the population.[6] Their administrative skills, business experience, and their participation in local politics made Jews natural candidates for such positions.

A period of nationalistic enthusiasm swept the nation after the Treaty of Paris was signed in 1815. It momentarily concealed the growth of sectional specialization which would turn the South into a staple-producing agricultural section based on a quasi-feudal plantation economy utilizing the labor of slaves, while converting the North into an industrial area dependent on free labor. The first signs of the growing economic bifurcation came in the political arena over the issue of the tariff. Eventually it would engulf all issues, including the disposition of the Bank and Western lands.

The tariff, which had first been introduced as part of Hamilton's financial program and renewed in 1816, was designed primarily to protect New England's "infant industry." After 1824, the South, through its principal spokesman, John C. Calhoun, opposed the tariff because it meant, in theory at least, higher prices for the manufactured goods on which it depended. It also invited retaliation against its principal export, cotton. Nor was the South alone in its opposition to the tariff of 1828. Many small businessmen, Jews among them, were adversely affected by its inordinately harsh protectionism. Joseph Gratz, a Jewish trader who was involved in the Oriental trade, imported certain goods from India for transshipment to the West Indies. After the passage of the "Tariff of Abominations," Gratz discovered to his dismay that even though the goods were not destined to be sold in the United States, he would nevertheless be required to pay the higher duty. Accordingly he requested that Richard Rush, the Secretary of the Treasury, permit the goods to be repacked in the customs house under the watchful eye of a customs agent, so that he could avoid paying the additional duty.[7]

Foreign and domestic problems might momentarily block the basic thrust of the American economy toward growth and development but they could not alter its basic direction. Part of that growth was based on a population which doubled in size every generation, a continuing stimulant to the economy. The increased population had to be housed, fed, and clothed. It encouraged the growth of a mass market which in

turn permitted a greater division of labor. By 1840 the value of manufactured goods was $483,278,000; by 1850 it had risen to $1,055,500,000
and by 1860 to $1,855,861,000.

The promise of continued growth of the American economy stemmed
also from the nature of the new society. Americans seemed less resistant
to the consumption of mass-produced goods, especially in clothing. Nor
were resistant guilds, remnants of the feudal period, to be found here.
The American was unusually inventive. By 1830, 544 new inventions
had been patented; by 1860 there were almost ten times as many. The
American farmer, unlike the European peasant who remained literally
anchored to the soil, was peripatetic and not averse to joining the
consuming society. A gradual shift of the population westward was
evident in the Colonial period. It accelerated in the national period.
At the same time the number of people living in cities grew: in 1840
there were seven times as many cities as there were in 1790. To be sure,
urbanization was not uniform, occurring with greater frequency in the
Northeast than the South. The growth of cities was partly a reflection
of the American farmers' greater ability to support such urban concentrations. For American Jewry urbanization had a special meaning;
the city, the natural habitat of the Jew, seemed destined to become the
wave of the future.

The reordering of the population, its shift to urban areas and to the
West, would not have been possible without a parallel revolution in
transportation which made these areas accessible. Between 1790 and
1870 a three-phased revolution beginning first with the building of
roads and turnpikes, followed by canal building, and finally a protracted period of railroad building occurred. When it was all over the
nation had been furnished with a transportation grid binding its far-flung
section together so that its industry had access to all the nation's raw
materials and markets. In the construction of the transportation network,
the economy was incidentally subject to a massive public works program,
which acted as a primer pushing the economy to ever higher levels
of productivity.

Such developments had profound significance for Jews who were
concentrated in the chaotic underdeveloped distribution sector. The
development of transportation to the interior and the discovery of new,
more efficient, forms of business organization meant that the vacuum
into which Jewish merchandisers had stepped could now be filled. Distribution would be rationalized but that would not occur for several
decades, giving masses of new German Jewish peddlers an opportunity
to get their start.

After Elias Howe developed the sewing machine in 1849, the ready-made clothing business became virtually a Jewish monopoly. By 1880 fifty percent of all Jewish firms were concentrated in some facet of the ready-made clothing industry or allied trades. The firm of Hart, Schaffner and Marx, and the firm of Kuppenheimer and Sonneborn controlled ninety percent of the wholesale and eighty percent of the retail clothing trade.[8] Jews were almost alone in seeing the possibilities for the second-hand clothing market. The shoe industry which had discovered the benefits of mass production in the 1830's, albeit without as yet being able to differentiate between the right and left shoe, was dominated by a Jewish firm, Florsheim. The firm of Freudenthaler and Oestreicher was the first to exploit the Great Lakes fishing grounds. Another German Jew, Isaac Friedlander, was by the mid-1850's known as the grain king of Chicago. Nelson Morris pioneered in the meat-packing industry and was the first to ship cattle on the hoof to Europe in 1867. Still later, he developed the idea of shipping frozen butchered beef in newly-developed refrigerator cars.

Jews early became involved in mining. Harmon Hendricks built the first copper-rolling mill in Belleville, New Jersey, in 1812 and subsequently became the principal supplier of copper to such illustrious coppersmiths as Paul Revere. Hendricks supplied copper tubing, stills, and kettles required for the distillation of rum. The tradition of having at least some Jewish representation in the mining industry was carried forward seven decades later by the Guggenheim family, the first of whom arrived in America in 1847 to begin their business careers as humble peddlers. The company they bought in 1889, the Philadelphia Smelting and Refining Company, was itself the creation of three German Jewish immigrants, Leonard and Adolph Lewisohn and David Marks Hyman. Also involved in mining, albeit in a different capacity, was Adolph Sutro, later to become the popular Mayor of San Francisco. Practically untrained as an engineer, Sutro gained the reputation of being something of a genius in mining engineering when he devised a way to tap the virtually inaccessible Comstock Lode.

The business career of Solomon Lyon, a Philadelphia merchant, illustrates the number of bases touched upon on the road to wealth. At the close of the Revolution, Lyon's estate was assessed at £6,500. For its time it was a sizable fortune which enabled him to weather the bad times following the Revolutionary war. He was in fact able to profit during that period from a brokerage boom which accompanied the speculation in Western lands. He invested his profits shrewdly in bank stocks and public securities. He became the first Jewish stock-holder in the Bank of North America. Aware of the imminence of a population growth in the new urban centers of the West, Lyons invested in two development concerns, the company which was to build the water system for Philadelphia and the Pennsylvania Population Company. By 1795 his fortune had grown to the extent that he was no longer known merely as a merchant but as a "gentleman" of means.

Few economic restrictions were aimed specifically at Jews in the antebellum period. Washington's reply to the congratulatory letter sent by the Jewish community of Newport on the occasion of his inauguration stated that the nation would give "to bigotry no sanction." That was usually the way it was.

Jews remained an inconspicuous group, barely known to the general public. When Jacob Jonas, the first Jewish settler in the new Western metropolis of Cincinnati, encountered a lady who had never seen a Jew, a not unusual scene transpired. Learning that he was Jewish, she requested that he allow himself to be examined so that she might see with her own eyes what a Jew actually looked like. She had read so much about Jews in the Scriptures, she explained apologetically. But after close scrutiny the disappointed observer confided to the embarrassed Jonas, "thee looks no different than anyone else."[9]

Nevertheless, there were differences which were especially apparent in the established Jewish communities of the East. One might note that they considered Saturday their Sabbath rather than Sunday. Sometimes this led to altercations with local officials who took the universality of Christianity for granted and prohibited Jews from carrying on business activities on Sunday. Local courts tended to be harsh with people who trespassed on the "Lord's Day." Jews and Seventh Day Adventists continually fell afoul of the Sunday Laws until well into the twentieth century. Even so, these Sunday Laws were less harsh than the later "Blue Laws" and were more an expression of Christian religious zeal than a conspiracy against Jews.

The regional specialization which developed in the economy in the years before the Civil War gave the South its own distinctive character. Jews developed a separate and distinctive accommodation to the plantation economy. They were rarely involved directly in the production of staples by the use of slave labor. Rather they filled a commercial service role for plantation owners. They were resident and commission merchants, brokers, auctioneers, cotton jobbers, and, of course, peddlers. They furnished the slave owners with second-hand clothing for their slaves. Among the more successful, cotton and tobacco exporting was a favorite business. According to Frederick Law Olmstead, the noted park designer who traveled extensively in the South, Jewish merchants were less reluctant than others to trade directly with the large free Negro population resident in many Southern cities.[10]

There was a Jewish representation in what was perhaps the ugliest facet of the plantation economy, the trade in slaves. Usually they were part-time slave traders and made up only a small proportion of those involved in the business. In Richmond, for example, only three of the twenty-three slave traders were Jewish, and in Charleston there were only four Jews out of forty-four traders.[11] That was the reason the Reform leader Rabbi Isaac Wise suspected Harriet Beecher Stowe's use of a Jewish slave-trading firm (Davis) in her widely-circulated *Uncle Tom's Cabin* was an example of anti-Semitism among the abolitionists. The Davis family was, after all, one of the three smaller Jewish firms which were involved in the trade in the city of Richmond. There were twenty non-Jewish firms she might have selected in that city.

Jews rarely became plantation owners, but like other Southerners they accepted the values and code imposed on the South by this small group. Their model of success was represented by the genteel plantation life which, in reality, was the lot of a small group of large plantation owners. It comes as no surprise therefore that the small group of Jews who made their fortunes in commercial pursuits sometimes went on to affect the style of the large plantation owners. Judah P. Benjamin, for example, made his fortune as a lawyer, merchant, broker, and speculator and then purchased his plantation, romantically named "Bellechasse." He then went on to earn a reputation as an expert in sugar cultivation and to own a stable of 740 slaves, of whom, incidentally, only eighty were field hands. The business career of Moses Raphael is similar. He made his fortune as a commercial lawyer and then became a gentleman farmer by purchasing a plantation near Columbus, Georgia, which he named "Esquiline Hill." He owned forty slaves and experimented with the cultivation and marketing of peaches and plums, crops which were to become a mainstay of Georgia's economy.[12]

Precise figures on how many Jews owned slaves are difficult to determine. According to the authority on Southern Jewry, Bertram Korn, the figures vary considerably with time and place. One can, however, surmise that the number of Jews owning large numbers of slaves was relatively small, but the possession of one or two house servants was fairly widespread. As many as a quarter of the South's Jews may have fallen into this category.[13] This figure roughly matches that of slaveholding for the South as a whole and was probably slightly above that of other Southern merchants. It is a clue to the relative prosperity of Magnolia Jewry because slave ownership was also an indication of wealth and social status.

But the occupation of Jews as peddlers, merchants, and small business-men actually conferred a relatively low status in the Southern social system. These were despised activities, if only because they did not fit into the heroic-chivalric self-image of the Southerner. There were a small number of Jews who escaped this classification, but most lived with it, perhaps content with the knowledge that as a group they were better off than their Northern brethren. Then too there was a concealed advantage in living in a society which reserved most of its fear and rancor for its blacks.

For their own part, Jews were anxious not to be set apart from other Southerners, owning slaves, if not for labor, then for status. They imbibed generously of its pervasive racist sentiment and participated in the ritualized violence formalized in its "code duello." For example, Mordecai Noah narrowly escaped several duels during his Charleston years. A Jew, Dr. Philip Minis, dueled and killed a member of the Georgia legislature, James A. Stark, in 1832, for the insult of having been called "a damned Israelite" who "ought to be pissed upon."[14] In another case, August Belmont dueled with Edward Heywood of Charleston and paid for it with a wound in the thigh which left him with a limp for the remainder of his life.

Nor were Jews exempt from what, we are informed, was a widespread practice in the plantation system, the sexual exploitation of dependent female slaves.[15] There are some recorded cases of illicit cohabitation between Jews and Negro slaves but this is undoubtedly only the tip of the iceberg.[16] Isolated Jewish peddlers are known to have sometimes chosen Negro or Indian women as common-law wives. Sometimes generous bequests to Negro housekeepers in wills hint at deeper involvements. In one case in 1797, Moses Nunes of Savannah, acknowledged his concubine and the children he had with her, by willing her several of his remaining slaves. Similarly, land and money were willed by Isaac H. Judah to his two mulatto sons.[17] The most renowned product of such a union is Francis Lewis Cardozo, Jr., who, after being educated in Glasgow, Edinburgh, and London for the ministry, went on to become the incorruptible state treasurer of South Carolina's Reconstruction government. Francis was sired by either Jacob N. Cardozo, a well-known Southern journalist or his brother Isaac, grandfather of the Supreme Court justice.[18]

Such mulatto progeny could not have fared too well in the Jewish community which shared fully in the prohibition against miscegenation. The Jewish congregation of Richmond required only that its members be free, but Congregation B'rith Elohim in Charleston went further. Rule XXII of its 1820 charter stipulated that proselytes would be accepted "provided he or she, or they, are not people of color.[19] This did not mean, however, that blacks were forbidden in the congregation. There is one known case of a free Negro who regularly attended services in Charleston without interference.

We can fairly assume that Jews did not differ substantially from their fellow Southerners in their animus toward "people of color." Magnolia Jews approved of, or at least did not think of opposing, the slave system. This is so despite evidence of generosity towards their slaves in wills. One departed Jew entrusted the protection of a free Negro to his step-daughter and son-in-law, requesting that they "take him under the protection, to treat him as well as they would do me and to give him such cloth [sic] as they will think useful to him and never forsake him being the best friend I ever had."[20] A more common cause for generosity was given by Isaiah Isaacs of Richmond, who "being of the opinion that all men are by nature equally free . . . ," called for the phased emancipation of all his slaves upon his death.[21]

The somewhat idyllic image of Jewish benevolence to slaves should be balanced by examples of harsh treatment of them. Like others, Jewish slaveholders adhered to the practice of lashing and branding their slaves when they were caught in some illicit activity like stealing. They advertised for "nee'r do well" runaway slaves by offering rewards in the local newspapers. Jews undoubtedly felt the same terror regarding the imminence of slave uprisings as other Southerners, and they assiduously enforced the slave codes designed to safeguard against the possibility. There were even cases like that of Joseph Cohen of Lynchburg, Virginia, who was tried in 1819 for the murder of one of his slaves.[22] Southern Jews, in short, were part of the system, subject to all its weaknesses and strengths.

Of all the phenomena in nineteenth-century American history, the westward movement had perhaps the most profound economic, social, and, ultimately, political impact. The intrusion of population into the hinterland, first in the area beyond the Alleghenies and subsequently to the Mississippi and beyond, transformed the primarily coastal economy of the Colonial period into one whose center of gravity was now in the interior.

The crucial role the West came to play as a market for the developing industrial capacity of the Northeast and the role of the Northeast as a market for the produce of the West, can hardly be exaggerated. The completion of the Union Pacific Railroad in 1869, linked with steel rails the area that was already connected commercially. Some historians go as far as postulating that the Civil War was brought on partly by the

South's defeat in the struggle with the North for control of the West. Frederick Jackson Turner, the historian of the westward movement, has gone as far as maintaining that the "existence of an area of free land, its continuous recession, and the advance of American settlement westward, explains American development." The shape of the American polity and the American character, according to Turner, were conditioned by the frontier, which he viewed, not so much as a geographic location, but as a process. Such geographic determinism has, of course, not gone unchallenged but few historians today deny the importance of the westward movement. By 1830, after all, one out of four Americans lived west of the Alleghenies. The rise of new cities in this area must have had a special import for Jews who had cast their lot with the city.

Jews early sensed the economic possibilities of the West. Jewish land speculators like the Gratzes, Franks, and Simonses were persistent promoters of the new region. But more important was the influx of a new breed of German-Jewish peddlers whose story deserves a special chapter. Much knowledge also emanated from Jewish involvement in the fur trade which offered a good opportunity to survey the land. Such traders were frequently the first permanent settlers in the new area. Three Jewish fur traders, John Pedro and Manuel and Silvado Rodriguez, settled in Lancaster county, Pennsylvania, in 1652. They were joined by traders like Nathan and Isaac Levy who dealt with the Mango and Shawnee Indians before the land was granted to William Penn. Another Jewish fur trader, John Hays, settled in the Illinois territory in the 1780's. He was variously a farmer, postmaster, sheriff of St. Claire county, collector of internal revenue, and an Indian agent.

The fur trade figures prominently in opening for settlement the five states encompassed by the Northwest Ordinances of 1787 and later Kentucky and the Mississippi and Missouri Valleys. Jacob Franks, for example, established a fur-trading post in what is today Green Bay, Wisconsin, as early as 1804, only a year after the Louisiana Purchase. In 1793, a group of Jewish fur traders, including Michael Gratz, became involved in a project to drain the "dismal swamp" in what is today West Virginia and northeastern Kentucky. Another Jew, Benjamin Monsanto, was an Indian trader in Alabama before 1803.

Abraham Mordecai, who is credited with founding Montgomery, Alabama, might serve as a prototype of these adventurous traders. He was a squaw man, an innovator in introducing the first cotton gin to Alabama; he fought in the Continental army and spent much of his life living among the Coosarda Indians. Single-handedly he developed the trade in furs, pinkroot, and other medicinal herbs which he transported to markets in Pensacola, Augusta, and Mobile. On one occasion he was instrumental in arranging the ransom of some white captives from the Creek Indians. Sometimes such traders were noticeably more Indian than European. In 1805, the Indian chief Towerculla had Mordecai's left ear removed for fraternizing too closely with one of the chief's wives. The absence of one ear seemed only to enhance Mordecai's growing reputation as an Indian scout.[23]

Jewish financiers also played some part in establishing the transportation network which made the West accessible. Benjamin Gratz, who played a prominent role in the Indian trade, later became a major investor, director, and finally president of the Lexington and Ohio Railroad, the first line west of the Alleghenies. He was joined by Joseph Simon's son-in-law, Solomon Etting, who became promoter and eventually director of the Baltimore and Ohio Railroad. After the Civil War the tradition of investing in railroads was carried further by Jewish bankers like Joseph Seligman and Jacob Schiff, who invested not only their own capital but drew additional investment capital from Jewish banking houses in Germany.[24]

The activities of Jews in the West created a special awareness of its potential for commercial exploitation. "There is no doubt," wrote S. Meylert to his nephew August, "that in a fw years, Illinois will be one of the first states in America and I counsel you ... to strike as many roots there as possible."[25] Traveling in the West, David Nathan informed his father of "the most stirring and lively city I ever visited," Pittsburgh, and assured him that he intended to "pay strict attention to everything that may be advantageous to you."[26] Such informal intelligence proved useful to Jewish businessmen.

In its special pull on Jews, the westward movement posed a threat to the more established communities of the East. In cities like Charleston, the attraction of the rich bottomlands of Alabama and Mississippi, could denude the minuscule Jewish community. The same held true for the Jewish community of Richmond. Meanwhile, on the other end of the line, cities like Milwaukee were growing by leaps and bounds and with them new Jewish communities. In 1850 Milwaukee had perhaps seventy Jewish families; two years later there were one hundred, and in 1856 there were two hundred. A similar growth pattern was discernible in other Western cities.

In concentrating on the agricultural aspect of the westward movement, the development of towns in the area has not always received the attention it deserves. Yet this movement may actually have surpassed in scope the movement of population to the cutting edge of the frontier. Cincinnati, for example, rose from a population of 40,000 in 1830 to 161,000 in 1860; St. Louis from 10,000 to 160,000, and Chicago from a village of 250 to 109,000 in the same period. In addition, hundreds of smaller towns sprouted in the West. It is mentioned here because, although precise evidence is difficult to come by, the process of urbanization of the newly acquired Western territories marked the continuation of a process in which American Jewry has always been deeply involved. They were urbanizers par excellence. "Many a prosperous inland town," observed a Jewish member of the California legislature in 1870, "owes its rise and present solidarity to the pluck and perseverance of the Hebrew merchant who gave life to the places in which they were located and hastened new enterprise by personal encouragement and generous financial aid."[27]

The Jewish link to such towns as Louisville, Detroit, Aaronsburg, Easton, Reading, York, Schaefferstown, Heidelberg, and Lancaster can be gleaned from the frequency with which they became town boosters, interested in promoting business in their respective communities.

Customarily, Jews preferred urban living but there were always some individuals who followed agricultural pursuits. Aside from the lack of tradition, farming posed certain problems for Jews who must live in communities in order to adhere to certain aspects of the Jewish religious code. Naturally, farming colonies were considered preferable. Thus we find during the panic of 1837, a group of newly-arrived German Jews, petitioning their brethren in New York City for funds to establish a farm colony. The argument they presented was that not only would it "add so much lustre to the Jewish character" but it would virtually guarantee that they would not be lost to Judaism.[28] But once established such agricultural enterprises had a relatively short life span. The Jewish farm colony established in Warwasing, New York, with the help of the Jewish congregation did not last five years. The absence of a proper agricultural tradition and the weighing-down of such enterprises with idealistic goals almost predestined them to failure. Nevertheless, Jews continued to demonstrate an interest in it partly as a possible alternative for destitute Jewish immigrants in the cities. Sometimes we shall see that they were part of proto-Zionist schemes to bring Jews to America. Such was the scheme of Mordecai Noah, Julius Stern, and William Robinson. In 1851, B'nai B'rith sponsored the Hebrew Agricultural Society to encourage would-be Jewish husbandmen but there were few members.

The best known of the agricultural strategies to redeem Jewry sprang from the fertile imagination of Mordecai Noah, the Tammany sachem. Since 1816, he had involved himself in a series of schemes to bring Jewish immigrants to the United States. Finally, in 1825, a visionary plan which had been simmering in Noah's fevered imagination for six years was made public. He proposed a refuge for Jews on a 17,000-acre plot on Grand Island, northwest of Buffalo. This "New Zion" would be dubbed Ararat, after the mountain peak on which that other Noah's ark had ostensibly come to rest after the Flood.

Impressive dedication ceremonies were held on September 15, 1825, in Buffalo's Episcopal Church of St. Paul. Dressed in ermine robes, Noah had himself anointed as "Governor and Judge of Israel." Convinced that the Indians were descendants of the ten lost tribes, he made certain that some chiefs were invited to the ceremony. They stood in full regalia next to a representation of the local ministry, dressed in somber dark clothing. Then Noah delivered his address; speaking in sonorous tones, he declared, "In his name do I revive and *reestablish* the government of the Jewish nation under the auspices and protection of the constitution and laws of the U.S. of A."[29]

Noah was ridiculed for his theatrical posturing and, predictably, little came of his manifesto calling on Jews to settle in Ararat. Not everyone was ready to extend such a generous invitation. The *Niles Weekly register* (October 1, 1825) was convinced that Ararat was merely another Jewish scheme to "get money, honestly if they can, *but get money*."[30] It accused Noah of trying to make a profit on the tribulations of other people. Indeed, the accusation had a certain sting since it was attached to a land promotion idea. But more important for us is the type of thinking it represented. Noah, we shall see, was not alone in viewing an agricultural Zion as a possible answer to the Jewish problem. Samuel Myers, a Jewish merchant from Richmond, hit upon a similar scheme, and Henry Castro, a Jewish immigrant who took to calling himself Comte de Castro, and brought thousands of Germans to Texas, many Jews among them, was also convinced of the practicality of resettlement. Agricultural resettlement was to become a major plank in the Zionist program toward the end of the century. That, we shall see, was strongly influenced by the Russian Tolstoyan-Narodnik tradition. The American proto-Zionist schemes, on the other hand, seem to have been motivated by a combination of personal idiosyncrasy, Jewish messianism, and American romanticism. Agricultural communes with religious overtones were, for a time, also popular among Shakers, Rappites, Zoarites, and numerous utopian secular groups. Nor was Noah unique in envisaging an American role in Jewish redemption. Isaac Leeser and other early American Jewish leaders frequently shared that vision.[31]

It was as city builders and dwellers, rather than farmers, that American Jewry was destined to leave its mark on American history. It was a destiny which came closer to fulfillment upon the arrival of a new wave of immigrants from the German principalities. An examination of their impact on American Jewish history follows.

CHAPTER V

The Success Odyssey
of German Jews in America

BEHIND THE ECONOMIC AND SOCIAL CHANGES WHICH MARKED THE
antebellum period in American history lay a startling increase in population. It was caused partly by natural factors, partly by an increase in the
influx of immigrants after 1820. Of the 23,000,000 people in the nation in
1850, approximately 2,210,000 were foreign-born, mostly German and
Irish. Many entered the labor force so that by mid-century the majority
of workers were foreign-born. Moreover, what had begun as a trickle
of 100,000 immigrants in the decade of the 1820's, broadened into a
veritable deluge in the following decades so that by the end of the
century some 4,000,000 immigrants had settled here.

Within the German influx there existed a relatively small group of
German Jews who also chose to uproot themselves, albeit for different
reasons. They were barely distinguishable from the German immigrants
and frequently continued to live within a German social and economic
ambience. Often they became the principal cultural agents of the new
communities. They led the theater groups, glee clubs, gymnastic and
literary societies which richly embroidered the cultural life of the
German immigrants. Even their newspapers were often published by
Jewish immigrants so that often it seemed as if German Jews were more
anxious to sustain German culture in America than their Christian
brethren.[1] Sometimes, as in the case of the German settlement at
Tulpehocken Creek in New York State, in 1723 it appeared as if a
cultural merger between the two groups had occurred. In that town a
community known as Neue Denkers (new thinkers) developed which
observed the seventh day as the Sabbath, circumcised their male
children, and refused to eat pork.[2]

The influx of Jews from Germany, we shall see, altered the character
and internal cohesiveness of American Jewry beyond recognition. But
its most perceptible impact was the changed demography of the community. After 1790 the some 3,000 Jews in America were yearly supplemented by several hundred new arrivals, so that by 1830 the Jewish

[68]

population had doubled. Between 1830 and 1840 the figure leaped to 16,000 and thereafter it rose at an even faster rate, reaching 20,000 by 1848 and 150,000 by 1860. There were a quarter of a million Jews in the United States by 1880. Even more revealing is the rapid growth in the number of Jewish congregations. The six sizable congregations which existed in 1825 increased to 37 by 1850, and to 77 by 1860. Although nineteen states were subject to a German Jewish influx, New York and Pennsylvania were favorite areas and it was there that most new congregations were established.[3]

Nevertheless the growth of the Jewish community, rapid as it was, did not keep pace with the even faster growth of the national population. In 1820 it stood at approximately 10,000,000 but five decades later it had quadrupled. Despite its rapid growth, the Jewish community of America actually grew proportionately smaller, a fact which was to have special significance for American Jewish development.

If the exodus of German Jews was an integral part of a general German emigration, their motives for seeking a new home differed markedly from their fellow German immigrants. Whereas the latter migrated as family units, Jewish immigrants were more likely to be single men whose desertion of the family hearth was prompted by a deterioration of the economic and social situation of German Jewry between 1815 and 1848.

Following the French Revolution, German Jewry willingly accepted the idea of emancipation. Indeed, its more established elements positively looked forward to becoming "German citizens of Jewish persuasion." They would tuck their religion away into some inconspicuous corner of their lives in order to participate fully in the newly developing secular culture. The defeat of Napoleon unexpectedly led to a partial withdrawal of emancipation status. The century that had begun with great hope for Jews had by its midpoint become one of gloom and despair. When not entirely revoked, the citizenship rights granted to them were curtailed and the ghetto, symbol of their inequality, was resurrected. The tolerant atmosphere engendered by the French Revolution was replaced by harsh official anti-Semitism. Pogroms in Würzburg, Bamberg, Frankfurt, Darmstadt, Karlsruhe, Bayreuth, Hamburg, and Danzig brought suffering and ruin to the Jewish population.

On August 2, 1819, students from the University of Würzburg, rallying to the ancient anti-Semitic crusaders' marching chant of *Hep Hep*, pillaged the local Jewish community as in days of old. The initials represented the Latin words *Hiersolyma Est Perdita*, "Jerusalem is lost or destroyed." Indeed, for Jews it often seemed that their Jerusalem in

Germany was destroyed. In the Bavarian Diet shouts of "the Jews must clear out and go to America" were heard and apparently heeded by an increasing number of Jews.[4] The renewal of legal and economic disabilities, coming as they did after several decades of relatively enlightened rule, proved especially hard to bear. Again licenses for marriages were limited, a particularly harsh form of population control. In some cases the Jew's toll, a special tax paid upon entering and leaving towns, was reimposed, severely curtailing business activities. Access to apprenticeship training was restricted, limiting the possibility of Jewish young men to earn an honorable livelihood through the practice of a craft. Jews were more severely affected than most by the economic dislocation which followed hard upon the advent of industrialization. There seemed to be little that a young Jew growing up in the German principalities in the first half of the nineteenth century could look forward to. "The Jewish emigration," observed one German Jewish newspaper, "appears to be less due to greed for gain than to consciousness of being unable in any other way to achieve independence or to found a family."[5]

Supplementing the conditions which were pushing Jews out of their homes were allurements which attracted them to America. Letters from America often presenting economic details involved in starting a new life in America were standard features in the German Jewish press. Sometimes such letters presented idealized accounts of the situation in America. "A German is gladly accepted as a workingman in America," one such letter writer observed, "[and] the German Jew is preferred to any other."[6] Others spoke of better relations between Christians and Jews in the new country and the ample rewards for those prepared to work hard. This Jewish version of the "America letter" did much to catalyze immigration. More important perhaps was the mere existence of a Jewish community whose members might serve as models and furnish shelter and employment during the difficult early period of resettlement.

In the case of the Jews, those who made the difficult decision to uproot themselves early, were precisely those in direst need. These immigrants stemmed largely from the rural areas of Bavaria where the earning of a livelihood had become nigh impossible. After 1848 (although not necessarily as a result of the failure of the revolutions of 1848) a new breed of more established Central European Jews began reluctantly to sense the hopelessness of their situation.[7]

These too were compelled to turn to their compatriots in America for succor. In March, 1848, Leopold Kompert, a prominent Austrian Jewish novelist, paraphrased Jeremiah in warning the Jews of the Empire that they must find new homes: "The harvest is past, the summer is ended and we are not saved."[8] He was convinced that America held out the best possibilities since "the Jews do possess the qualities and virtues so indispensable for reconstruction in that country; foresight, sobriety, economy, discipline and loyalty."[9] Subsequently, Kompert implemented his plan by organizing the "On To America" movement among Jews.

Leopold Zunz, a prominent founder of the Reform movement in Judaism, was no less anxious to establish links to American Jews which might serve as a bridge for Jewish migration. On June 1, 1822, the *Verein für Kultur und Wissenschaft des Judentums* (Association for Jewish Knowledge and Culture), the Reform group Zunz headed, requested Mordecai Noah to "transmit every particular information of the Jew in America."[10] Again in 1825 he inquired about "the means of promoting the emigration of European Jews to the United States [for] those who ... have nothing to look for but endless slavery and oppression."[11]

We have seen how favorably Noah responded to this need for havens. As early as July, 1820, he requested John Q. Adams, then Secretary of State, to make him Chargé d'Affaires in one of the capital cities of Europe, preferably Vienna or The Hague, so that he might encourage Jewish migration to the United States. He held out the hope that such an infusion of Jews would profit the American economy. Perhaps the Jewish community of Newport might even be restored. "This is the only country where Jews can be completely regenerated," he informed Adams, so that they ought to be informed of the "great political and commercial advantages which await them in the United States." But Noah's request contained an important caveat. He wanted the government request to be addressed to "the most intelligent and wealthy." The less fortunate would have to shift for themselves.[12]

The thinking of the *Commercial Advertiser* of New York displayed a similar hardheaded business attitude toward the migration of Jews: "The wealth and enterprise of the Jews," the paper observed on October 16, 1882, "would be a great auxiliary to the commercial and manufacturing, if not agricultural interests of the United States."[13] The image of wealthy Jews enriching the American economy by investing their capital in American industry was perhaps a selfish motivation, but that could not be said of another immigration scheme proposed by W. D. Robinson, who in 1819 suggested that Jews be brought to the agricultural settlements of the West. That, he thought, would not only "ameliorate the unfortunate state of this class of human beings ...," it would also be an asset to the development of the country. Robinson had somehow arrived at the conclusion that "Jewish towns and villages adorning the banks of the Mississippi and Missouri" would be of mutual benefit.[14]

Others were simply stirred by the plight of the Jews. Penina Moise, a Jewish poetess, undoubtedly echoed the sentiments of many American Jews when she wrote:

> If thou art one of that oppressed race,
> Whose pilgrimage from Palestine we trace,
> Brave the Atlantic, hope's broad anchor weigh,
> A western sun will geld your future day.
> . . . .
> Zeal is not blind in this our temp'rate soil
> She has no scourge to make the soul recoil.[15]

Jews were asked to contribute funds to relieve the "distressed situation of a great number of Israelites."[16]

The influx of Jewish immigrants from a different cultural milieu could not fail to affect the internal cohesion of the American Jewish community. To be sure a trickle of Ashkenazi Jews were among the first to establish themselves in the Colonies. Jews from Central Europe probably formed the majority by the third decade of the nineteenth century, though the Sephardic religious ritual prevailed well after that time. When the reform leader Isaac Wise arrived in New York in 1846, he observed with some chagrin that the "Portuguese congregation was the oldest, and the oldest Portuguese was a Polish Jew."[17]

Although the transition was gradual, a degree of friction based on different cultural and religious practices was unavoidable. The stubbornness with which each group clung to its national culture exacerbated the situation. The Sephardic group thought of themselves as an advanced element of an advanced culture. Proud, aristocratic, cosmopolitan, and somewhat indolent, they might have served as a natural leadership group for the rural small-town Bavarian Jews who were anxious to learn the ways of the New World. But a barrier of "money, land and origins" divided the two groups.[18] The Sephardic group preferred to remain "an exclusive coterie" inaccessible to outsiders.[19] Undoubtedly some German Jewish immigrants were able to transcend this barrier by dint of marriage or business partnership.[20] Nor did marriage necessarily indicate that the difference in status had been forgotten. Rosa Content, daughter of a distinguished Sephardic family, married James Seligman, scion of German rags-to-riches parvenus and purportedly continued to refer to her millionaire in-laws as "the peddlers."[21]

The estrangement between the two groups went beyond differences in spoken Hebrew and religious observance. The Sephardic Jews had already experienced their Golden Age in Iberia so that from one point of view, their life in America represented a decline, at least in a historical sense. Moreover, there was a certain effeteness among them which often accompanies generations of unearned status. They were no match for the provincial, rough-hewn German Jews who, without capital or family connections, would often, by sheer hunger for attainment, create a comfortable niche for themselves in the New World.

They apparently did so in goodly numbers and quickly assumed the trappings of their newly earned position. "The German Jews in America," observed Francis Lieber, a prominent leader in the German-American community, "gains in influence daily, being rich, intelligent and educated or at least seeking education. They read better books than the rest of the Germans, the booksellers tell me. . . ."[22] They were, moreover, able to advance themselves largely without the help of institutions like Shearith Israel's Hebrew Benevolent Society which had been established to aid indigent Jews.

Like the Sephardim, they had undergone a noticeable lessening of religious zeal since the French Revolution but they tended to remain traditionally-minded, albeit poorly-instructed Jews. They seemed as reluctant to surrender their German culture as the Sephardim were to give up the Spanish. There was more than a little irony here, for both groups had been rejected by the national cultures they sought to preserve.

It was in the traditional role of peddlers that German Jews made their living and their first impact on the economy. Peddling attracted them for a practical reason. It offered a rapid means of accumulating capital while at the same time requiring almost no capital to start with. Moreover, the Jewish merchandising nexus was already established and could serve as sponsors and models for later arrivals.

The town of Easton which enjoyed a revival as a center for Jewish settlement after 1830 might serve again to illustrate the attraction of peddling. In 1840, 46 percent of its Jewish male residents were peddlers. By 1845 the percentage had leaped to 70 and 1850 it had again declined to 55. The approach of the Civil War and the arrival of a higher class of German Jewish immigrant caused a further decline in the popularity of peddling. By 1860 only 39 percent of Easton's wage earners were so involved and by 1870 only 12 percent.[23]

The decline may also attest to the success of the earlier arrivals who had by 1850 succeeded in becoming resident merchants or had found some less strenuous way of earning their livelihood. From the outset few thought of peddling as a permanent occupation. It was to lead to bigger and better things. So they swarmed behind the cutting edge of the frontier, carrying their packs of notions and possessing only a rudimentary knowledge of English. In the 1840's hundreds invaded Iowa, Illinois, Indiana, and the Southwestern states, including California. They sold their wares in isolated hamlets, cow towns, and mining camps and in the process underwent a rapid Americanization.

As often as not, the peddler's vision of a small business at the end of the rainbow was an illusion. Peddling contained various stages which had to be negotiated before the ultimate aim of becoming a resident merchant might be achieved and even that much desired profession was no bed of roses. Isaac Wise described it succinctly:

1. the basket peddler—he is yet altogether dumb and homeless   2. the trunk carrier who stammers some little English and hopes for better times 3. the pack carrier, who carries from one hundred to one hundred and fifty pounds on his back and indulges the thought that he will become a business man some day.[24]

If fortune looked kindly upon him, the peddler could hope to become a "wagon-baron," a kind of peripatetic department store on wheels, or to peddle specialty items like jewelry and become a "jewelry count." Finally he might become a "store prince." As Wise saw it: "At first one is the slave of the basket or the pack, then the lackey of the horse in order to become finally the servant of the shop."[25] The last stage was not often achieved. "As often as not he bore his pack until his back broke under it," one observer states, "and thereafter his food came from the toil of others, his wife, his children, [and] kindly neighbors."[26]

The peddling career could be full of adversity. He rose early to walk from twelve to fifteen miles a day with a heavy pack, over all kinds of terrain and through all kinds of weather. Often he spent an entire week on the road, lonely, barely able to speak the language and frequently despised because of an undeserved reputation for dishonesty caused by the persistence of the Shylock image and the reputation for dishonesty of the Yankee peddler, for whom he was often mistaken.[27] Carrying the heavy pack required enormous physical strength. There were, in addition, fierce dogs and unfriendly farmers to contend with.

Naturally some of the immigrants who took up this calling lived to regret it. One peddler, whose diary has come down to us, cautioned others not to follow his footsteps: "O youth of Bavaria, if you long for freedom, if you dream of life here, beware for you shall rue the hour you embarked for a country and a life far different from what you dream of. This land and particularly this calling—offers harsh cold air, great masses of snow, and people who are credulous, filled with silly pride, cold toward foreigners, and toward all who do not speak their language properly."[28] Undoubtedly there were compensations too.

The peddler would return to his hearth on weekends to rest and re-
plenish his stock. He settled his accounts from the previous week and
received new short-term credit. When he could take advantage of them,
the frequent number of holy days on the Jewish religious calendar
served as a welcome respite. For the pious among them, the inability to
adhere to religious practices on the road was the source of much distress.
"Thousands of peddlers wander about America," the same observer
noted, "young, strong people waste their strength through heavy carrying and walking in the heat of summer .... and wholly forget in the
course of it their creator, they do not lay tfilim, they never pray on a
weekday nor on a holyday, truly they have ceased having religion with
the bundle on their back."[29]

Yet such dire warnings did not prevent a growing number of robust
young immigrants from carrying their packs to the remotest corner of
the nation. They became a welcome link to the established civilization,
where such amenities as buttons, lace, needles, and perhaps even a bolt
of gingham were common. A special need for them developed in the
mining camps where the persistent fear of claim jumping made the
miners reluctant to abandon their claims to purchase supplies in town.
Carrying loads that staggered the imagination, the peddler charged
high prices for the services he performed. Straw brooms cost $5 and
a bowie knife was almost worth its weight in gold. But his profits could
be as easily lost as gained. There were special risks in doing business
in mining camps for no sooner had a peddler succeeded in making the
transition to "store prince" when the boom-bust cycle would convert
a formerly bustling community into a ghost town.

Peddling in frontier areas could be dangerous in other respects too.
Louis Nathan, Henry Levy, and Isaac Goldstein were but a few of the
known victims of Indian scalping. Others lost their lives as part of the
toll of living in areas known for their lawlessness. The pack of notions
he carried attracted not only honest customers but those who had less
honest transactions in mind. Some peddlers were killed by highwaymen,
others died of illness, some simply disappeared, perhaps frozen to death
in some remote inhospitable area, others began their journey and were
simply never heard from again. Even among themselves the general
atmosphere of frontier lawlessness took its toll. There were many types
attracted to peddling, including rootless adventurers, and those who
had never been domesticated. Far less steeped in morality than the
average Jew, they brought to peddling a code of behavior based on
survival. Thus we find August Heflin, a Jewish gambler, holding off
with drawn pistol a group of fellow Jews who objected to having another
Jewish gambler, who had been killed in a gun duel, buried in their

burial ground. The peddler Levi Abram was tried for killing a friendly Indian, seemingly without cause.

The frontier code approved of killing Indians under other circumstances, however. A Jewish peddler, Sigmund Schlesinger, distinguished himself as an Indian fighter in the battle of Arikaree Creek and his heroism was celebrated in a short ballad:

> When the foe charged the breastworks
>   With madness of despair,
> And the bravest of souls were tested
>   The little Jew was there.[30]

More often, Indian and Jew had a good working relationship. The Jew often served as the Indian's bridge to the world of the settler, and the Indian served as a source of skins for the merchant. Their rapid mastery of the various Indian dialects sometimes made Jewish interpreters indispensable at Army posts.[31] It was Otto Mears, an Indian trader, who as an interpreter, helped negotiate the treaties which brought extensive tracts of Indian country to the Colorado Territory.

Jewish merchants and peddlers sometimes introduced innovations in dress which thereafter came to personify the area. The best example are Levi dungarees, universally popular today, but formerly associated with the mining and cow towns of the West. They were introduced there in the 1850's by Jewish merchants (Levi and Straus), who having exhausted the supply of normal seaming used copper-colored yarn and metal rivets to reinforce and hold together the sturdy denim material. The ten-gallon and derby hat, the latter the hallmark of many a merchant, were introduced and distributed by Jewish peddlers. By pioneering in the cross-breeding of the rangy cattle which roamed freely in the southern Texas public domain, and finding markets for butchered beef in the East, Jews contributed notably to developing the cattle kingdom. It became a major source of income for the West. Since Jews were primarily retailers, it was natural that they be concerned and involved in the West's primitive transportation system. Many a stagecoach line was developed by farsighted Jewish entrepreneurs who were aware of the need to get goods and people to the West.

But Jews seemed to show their greatest talent in merchandising. Here they introduced, or sometimes further developed, innovations used by others: wide-scale advertising, installment buying (especially for the purchase of furniture), set price policies, and the idea of money-back guarantees. The mail order catalog, because it brought the widest choice of goods to the most remote corner of the nation, became the bible of rural America. The idea of mail-order houses had its genesis in Germany.

It was brought here by Julius Rosenwald, a Jewish immigrant, who purchased a small watch company called Sears, Roebuck and converted it to the world's largest mail-order house.

One can gain a picture of how widespread were the travels of Jewish peddlers and merchants from various place-names in different regions of the country. Thus several passes through the Rockies are named after Jewish trappers and peddlers who discovered and first traversed them. Towns such as Rockovsky, Rittmayer, Kohn Brothers, Solomonville, Helene (after Helena Goldberg) are named after the Jewish merchant who played a key role in founding the town. The well-known town of Tombstone was so named by Ed Scheffelin, a Jewish merchant who opened the first general store there. The early pioneering role of Jews in the West is also reflected in the frequency with which Jews served as mayors, judges, state legislators, and governors in Western states. The notorious Dodge City, a cattle center and the setting for hundreds of cowboy stories, had three Jewish mayors, one of whom served five terms.

More often, however, the rewards for Jews came in the economic rather than in the political realm. No group seemed better to personify the American success story. Only for them the climb from rags to riches typically led from peddler to merchant to department store owner. We shall see that in some few cases they were then able to enter the world of banking. In their hands the distribution system, especially of dry goods, became systematized. In the larger towns of the interior the general store ultimately gave way to the specialized shop for such products as hardware, furniture, clothing, shoes, and jewelry. The next step was to combine these items under one roof to make the modern department store. In that development, too, Jews played an important role as the names of Straus, Lazarus, Altman, Bloomingdale, Filene, Gimbel, Wertheim, Bamberger, Hecht, Saks, and hundreds of less well-known names attest.

The success of these fortunate few families should not be allowed to conceal the fact that relatively few Jewish merchants who began as humble peddlers became millionaire department-store owners. An exaggerated impression of the German Jewish success story is, to some extent, attributable to Isaac Wise and, more recently to Stephen Birmingham. Birmingham, especially, did not find that the many unsung immigrants who remained peddlers or joined the labor force as tailors (especially from Posen) or paperhangers or cigar-makers or cutters in the garment trade, made good copy.[32] Nevertheless, compared with those millions of immigrants who entered the agricultural sector, Jews did relatively well, achieving middle-class rank, often in less than one generation.

We turn next to examine this relatively small group of successful Jewish businessmen. For it is from their ranks that America's first ethnic commercial elite of bankers arose in the post-Civil War period. Ultimately this elite sometimes complemented and more often rivaled the great Yankee banking houses.

Actually it is inaccurate to trace the development of Jewish banking in America exclusively to German Jewish immigrants. Jewish banking houses and investment firms like the Seligmans, Guggenheims, Heidelbachs, Straus-Goldmans, Kuhns, Loebs, Lehmans, Wertheims and Baches received a generous infusion of financial and human resources from Jewish bankers in Germany. Among them were the Speyers, who came from Frankfurt in 1837, August Belmont, who arrived that same year and became the American agent for the Rothschilds, Jacob H. Schiff, who arrived in 1868 and eventually headed Kuhn, Loeb and Company, Adolph Ladenburg, who also came in 1868, and Ernst Thalman who did not land here until 1880. The two groups traveled in the same social milieu and by a series of strategic marriages, friendships, and informal liaisons, gradually coalesced into what Stephen Birmingham has called a "Crowd" and which more properly might be classified as a commercial elite.[33]

For our purposes the original immigrants who underwent the peddler-to-department-store-owner-to-banker odyssey are of great interest because they represent an extraordinary example of social and economic mobility. It outpaces the rise of the American industrial moguls who, it has recently been shown, usually stemmed from families who had already achieved middle-class rank.[34] Moreover, even within the elite the degree of success was by no means uniform. In the top rank were Kuhn, Loeb, Seligman, Speyer, and Belmont. Immediately below them were Hillgarten & Co., Goldman, Sachs & Co., Lehman Brothers, Heidelbach, Ickelheimer & Co., and Ladenburg, Thalman & Co. On the lowest rung of the ladder were Asiel & Co., J. S. Bache & Co., Albert Loeb & Co. (to become L. F. Rothschild & Co., in 1910), Scholle Brothers, and Adolph Lewisohn & Sons. The Straus family, the Wertheims, and the Guggenheims did not become bankers and stockbrokers until the first decade of the twentieth century.[35]

It was Joseph Seligman who first employed Horatio Alger as a tutor for his children and it is no accident that his business career serves as a classic example of the American Jewish "rags to riches" story. Joseph arrived in New York in 1837 and within a decade he had created a small merchandising network which reached from Pennsylvania to New York to Alabama and California. Like so many others he began as a humble peddler. The Civil War found the Seligmans about to embark on a clothing manufacturing enterprise, a business which would be greatly stimulated by government orders for uniforms. The Seligmans soon discovered, to their dismay, that the government, unable to pay cash, settled its bills with negotiable credit notes. To be converted into liquid assets these notes had first to be sold on the open market. Willy-nilly the Seligmans found themselves in the bond selling business. Of the $250,000,000 of bonds sold abroad between February, 1862, and June, 1864, the Seligmans marketed over half, performing in the process a great service for the Union cause and incidentally earning a better profit than in the cotton-starved clothing business. One historian, William E. Dodd, attributed to Seligman a service to the Union cause "equal perhaps to the service of the general who stopped Lee at Gettysburg."[36] Although a Democrat, August Belmont performed a similar service and in addition convinced the Rothschilds not to invest in Confederate bonds. But the Rothschilds were not the only Jewish banking family in Europe and ultimately Judah P. Benjamin, using cotton as collateral, successfully placed a loan with the Erlangers, a French Jewish baking family.

The rise of a Jewish commercial elite seems all the more remarkable when it is realized that they alone among the numerous ethnic groups in America produced such a phenomenon. There were isolated Italian and German bankers but they did not form themselves into a distinct group. Moreover, if one takes into account the Sephardic commercial nexus in the Colonial period, one could make a case for maintaining that American Jewry has done so twice in the short history of this nation. How does one account for this development?

At the root of the phenomenon of the Jewish commercial elite a combination of circumstances and attributes specific to Jewry can be noted. Many German Jews possessed a great deal of ordinary business experience which sharpened their ability to discover the opportunities for business in this country. In many cases their merchandising skills were already evident in Europe. Then, too, a major share of the phenomenon was due to the relative openness of the American economy in the period immediately before and after the Civil War, when most of the German Jews made their debut in America. There was almost no anti-Jewish discrimination precisely at the juncture when, stimulated by the Civil War, the economy entered upon a period of rapid expansion.

I say "almost" no discrimination because there was one form of private discrimination which indirectly contributed to the development of a Jewish commercial elite. Jewish investment capital had nowhere to go except to their own banking houses since Yankee banking houses rejected Jewish representation to which the massive amount of Jewish dollars entitled them. There is no record of a Christian banking firm ever taking on a Jewish partner, although an isolated Jew might occasionally be found on the board of directors.[37] Even after they had established themselves, Jewish banking houses were often forced to deal with the left-over, riskier issues which Yankee bankers did not want to handle.

Then, too, the ethnic and religious bond which tied Jews together contributed notably to their success. Common background, shared cultural values, often a common experience in business were reinforced by friendships and marriages which gave the group a cohesiveness and established a bond of trust and confidence essential for doing business in the capital market. Since they had entered banking precipitously, it became possible for the members of the group to substitute private knowledge of reliability for the established reputation which few of them possessed at the outset.[38]

While such group cohesiveness proved to be an important factor in achieving success it would have been as nothing if capital had not been available. That came from the prosperous group of Jewish merchants who made their assets available to the new group of Jewish bankers. Jewish banking was merely the visible peak of the remarkable success odyssey of Jewish business in America. It was supplemented by the connection with Jewish banking houses abroad from which they received not only knowledge of the latest banking techniques, but also investment capital to funnel into the expanding American economy. Eventually these connections were formalized. Thus Kuhn, Loeb became linked to Disconto-Gesellschaft in Germany and to the Ernest Kassel Banking firm in Britain; Hallgarten & Company was allied with the Darmstadter Bank in Germany, and the Seligmans had by 1890 formed branches in London, Paris, and Frankfurt. Once established, the new American Jewish banking houses were able to play an important role in attracting necessary investment capital to the American economy. The early capital needs of railroad construction, mining, the cattle business, and real estate development were in some part filled by the Jewish banking nexus.

The success of the German Jewish immigrants, on whose shoulders Jewish banking stood, is reflected in the business indicators of the time, such as they were. Between 1860 and 1870 the number of Jewish-owned firms warranting a business rating rose from 374 to 1740. By 1890 the more accurate Dun rating estimated a further rise of 20 percent in Jewish-owned businesses. By that year too, Jewish firms were growing larger. In 1870 only 10 percent of such companies were capitalized over $100,000. By 1890 the figure had risen to 25 percent. Jewish business activity was especially prominent in "dry and fancy" goods such as women's ready-made wear and to a lesser extent "gent's furnishings," glass and paint, the upholstery and bedding business, the distribution of tobacco and other smoking articles, wines and liquors, meat, wholesaling and retailing, jewelry and watch repairing, precious stones and optical goods, leather tanning, and marble and granite distribution. Their success was especially visible in New York City, 60 of whose 1,103 millionaires were Jews.[39] All things considered it was a remarkable showing for a group comprised largely of recently-arrived immigrants.

CHAPTER VI

Jews in the Politics of Antebellum America

THE DECADES AFTER THE AMERICAN REVOLUTION DID NOT PRODUCE A noticeable increase in political visibility for the small Jewish community. Doubtlessly, that was as much due to the continued qualifications for the franchise and office holding, especially for newly-arrived immigrants, as it was to a conscious choice among Jews to establish themselves economically rather than to concern themselves with politics. The small size of the Jewish constituency and the scarcity of good leadership also contributed to the low political profile.

However, it cannot be said that Jews did not possess political convictions. That would be highly uncharacteristic. At the beginning of the nineteenth century the great dividing line in politics was the issue of the French Revolution. Like Jews the world over, American Jews tended to favor the changes wrought by that revolution, if only because it seemed to extend further the great principle of emancipation also embodied in the American Revolution. A preview of how things would be under the new regime established in France came in 1791 when the French government abolished all official religious discrimination.

The French Revolution became the major issue of American politics and so heated did the debate become that sometimes it seemed as if it were being fought in America rather than in France. Despite Washington's admonition regarding the divisiveness of political parties (he called them factions), two groups, the Federalists and the Democratic Republicans, had already made their debut. The Federalists, aside from anglophilism and their Whig revulsion at the bloody turn of events in France, tended to favor what appeared to be class legislation, as reflected in Hamilton's financial program. The Democrats favored the Revolution, opposed the financial program and harbored a deep fear that behind Federalist political rhetoric was the desire to reestablish a strong central authority, perhaps even a monarchy.

Jewish commitment to the dramatic events in France determined their political preferences. They saw in Jefferson, the Jefferson who helped achieve the separation of Church and State in Virginia, the embodiment of their own political ideals. He was, moreover, the type of leader who has traditionally exercised a powerful attraction for the Jewish voter in modern times—a patrician who transcends his class, background, and interest to uplift the less fortunate and has, in addition, a claim to intellectual preeminence.

How powerful these pulls must have been is reflected in Jewish transcendence of certain group interests to favor Jefferson. They were, after all, members of a highly urbanized commercial group. Yet Jefferson, a physiocrat, frequently expressed revulsion and fear of rootless urban living and preferred to envision the future in idyllic agricultural terms. Their interests might just as properly have been centered on Alexander Hamilton, the leader of the Federalist party, who, if he did not possess Jefferson's impeccable aristocratic roots, nevertheless favored the advancement of the very commercial sector with which Jews had cast their lot. Undoubtedly some Jews did, for that reason, favor the Federalist party. But they could not have been very comfortable in it since there was soon to be ample evidence that it had little tolerance for foreigners generally (Alien and Sedition Laws of 1798) and Jews in particular.

In contrast to the Federalist party, local branches of the Jeffersonian persuasion such as New York City's Tammany, were accessible to Jews. Jews like Mordecai Meyers, Noah Jackson, Mordecai Noah, and Emanuel Hart later assumed leadership roles in it. Mordecai Noah, the grandest Sachem of them all, edited several newspapers for the Democratic party, including the important *National Advocate*. So did other Jews like Naphtali Phillip and Isaac Harby. In turn, the Federalists had little to show but an ill-concealed anti-Semitism which led them to refer to the opposition as "Shylocks" and to label the Democratic organs a "Jew Press" and the principles of the party as anti-Christian. Thomas Kennedy, a Democrat who devoted much energy to winning the franchise for Maryland's Jews, was calumnied by his Federalist opponent, Benjamin Galloway, for heading the "Jew Ticket" in an election campaign in Washington county.[1] James Remington, a former loyalist turned Federalist, condemned the opposition for associating with Jews who, he was convinced, were carriers of the vice of democracy.

At the termination of the "Era of Good Feeling" in 1824, the entrance of the West into the political and economic arena led to a political realignment. Eventually the sectional turmoil produced a new type of leader, a man of the frontier West, in Andrew Jackson. There is little agreement among historians as to the precise sources of the Jacksonian upheaval but Jewish preference, to the extent that it was visible, favored the fiery general. They joined in the general popular rejoicing following his election victory in 1828, and in 1830, when word of a second revolution in France reached American shores, Jews again celebrated what they considered as a victory for the spirit of human progress. The pattern continued in the next decades buttressed by the influx of German Jews, who, although not directly involved in the liberal upheavals which culminated in the revolutions of 1848, were nevertheless in tune with the spirit which caused them.

That spirit was manifest in America, too. A liberalization of the franchise in most states preceded Jackson's election. A surge of humanitarian reform movements including workingmen's rights to organize, women's rights, penal reform, and abolitionism, was an intrinsic part of the general reform ferment which characterized Jacksonian democracy. It possessed an earthier aspect as well. Jackson's concept of rotation in office was based on the idea that the average man could fill any office in the land. But practically it operated on the principle that "to the victor belong the spoils." Although the effect of the "Spoils System" was to broaden the membership of the office-holding class, it by no means made a clean sweep of the old office-holding aristocracy. Nevertheless, such measures apparently found favor among Jews whose leadership, Reuben and Samuel Etting, Jacob Cohen, Solomon Jacobs, Samuel Mordecai, Joseph Jonas, and of course Emanuel Hart and Mordecai Noah, staunchly supported "King Andrew."

But when it came to supporting Jackson's hand-picked successor, Martin Van Buren, there was a parting of the ways. Mordecai Noah, the most outspoken and best known of the Jewish political leadership, never enjoyed the favor of the "Albany Regency," a reformist faction in the Democratic party headed by Van Buren, which virtually controlled New York State. In 1832 Van Buren was linked to Duff Green, a member of Jackson's "Kitchen Cabinet" who supported John C. Calhoun, rather than Van Buren, for the succession. Most Jews continued to support the Democratic candidate and discovered that such loyalty yielded political dividends especially in gaining administration intervention for the series of problems abroad which began to concern American Jewry after 1840.

With the approach of the Civil War, American politics underwent a change which resulted in a new set of political principles for the Democratic party. It became increasingly associated with the slave-holding South and therefore less useful for American Jewry which was concentrated largely above the Mason-Dixon Line. Jewish allegiance was given increasingly to the newly formed Republican party, which if not opposed to slavery *per se* was at least opposed to its extension into the West. Already the new party had attracted the old Whigs, Know

Nothings, Free-Soilers and especially the German immigrants who were flocking to the West, and attached special significance to the word "republican." Jews followed the lead of their German neighbors because they often viewed themselves as belonging to that group. In some cases they took the lead in organizing the new party. In Chicago, for example, four out of the five founders of the local Republican organization were German Jews. That pattern held true in other states as well.

At the same time many Jews remained loyal to the Democratic party because of a regional accommodation or for personal reasons. Jews in the South and upland South (the southern part of Illinois and Ohio) tended to remain loyal Democrats. So did men like August Belmont. Refusing to change his political coloration, Belmont was a staunch supporter of Buchanan and managed Stephen Douglas's unsuccessful campaign against Lincoln in the election of 1860. His biographer gives him much credit for holding the Democratic party together during its dog days between 1860 and 1872, when he resigned as chairman of the Democratic National Committee.[2]

The outspoken political loyalties professed by men like Noah and Belmont were not characteristic of American Jewry. As the approach of the Civil War heated the political temperature to an uncomfortable degree, Jews reacted defensively. They were reluctant to be identified with any specific group or political position. The community had not yet produced a leader who might galvanize the latent political energy in the community. Such leaders as there were, operated outside the context of a Jewish constituency. They were "well intentioned laymen" who happened to be Jewish. Often Jews denied that such things as a Jewish interest or voting bloc existed. On October 1, 1832, when the tariff dispute was at its height, a letter to the *Courier* in Charleston, cited a resolution in which members of the Jewish community "wholly disclaim any wish . . . to be represented as a peculiar community."[3] The *Northern Monthly* noted with some amazement in 1858 that "we hear of the Irish vote, the German vote, but who ever hears of a Jewish vote?"[4] That, according to the *American Israelite*, is "the way things should be." "In regard to public and political questions there is no union among us," the journal claimed, ". . . a man's public record, not his private individual faith, either fits him or unfits him for the public position for which he aspires."[5]

Undoubtedly Jewish sensitivity to being looked upon as a voting bloc was stimulated by the appearance of the nativist Know Nothing movement in the 1850's. Strangely enough that party, which directed its animus primarily against Catholics, boasted a handful of Jewish members in its ranks. The best known was Lewis C. Levin, an attorney from Philadelphia, who helped found the Native American Party and three times was elected to Congress on its ticket. It does not appear so strange, however, when we realize that Jewish hostility toward the Irish, who made up a sizable portion of the Catholic community, had begun to manifest itself as a result of conflict on the local level and the infamous Mortara kidnapping case of 1858, which saw many Catholic spokesmen justifying the forcible conversion of a Jewish child in Italy. Most important, they did not see eye to eye with the Irish on the issue of slavery. When political leaders like Mordecai Noah gave vent to anti-Irish sentiment, they were no doubt echoing what many Jews had come to feel.

By the 1830's it was clear to astute observers that the slavery issue would come to occupy the center of the political stage. Already it was exercising a strong impact in the economic sphere and had found eloquent spokesmen in the South, like John C. Calhoun and George Fitzhugh, to sing its praises. By the 1850's it was apparent that the worst was coming to pass. A combination of weak political leadership and ideological fanaticism on both sides was tearing apart the still delicate fabric of the nation. Jews, for various reasons, were unable to avoid getting caught in the maelstrom.

Proponents on either side of the slavery question functioned in a milieu highly charged with religious conviction. Both sought in the Old Testament religious justification for their positions. An antislavery tract which invoked scriptures was published in the Massachusetts colony as early as 1700. A year later a pro-slavery rejoinder relying on the Old and New Testaments, came to the opposite conclusion. It was after all the Old Testament which suggested that "Ham was smitten in his skin" and it was Noah who told Ham that his "seed will be ugly and dark skinned."[6] Abolitionists, much of whose organizational strength was linked to the Congregational clergy of New England, were no less avid in seeking scriptural justification for their position. They argued vehemently that slavery was an abomination in the sight of God, who considered all men the children of Adam and therefore intended no man to serve as an animated tool for another.

Predictably, it was not long before Jews, "the people of the book," were called upon for an authoritative view. Indeed Abolitionists must have been gratified with the work of Dr. Moses Mielziner, of the University of Giessen, whose work, Slavery Among the Ancient Hebrews, concluded that the bible was basically opposed to chattel servitude. Pro-slavery forces were able to counteract the effects of Mielziner's work by citing the authority of Morris Jacob Raphall, Rabbi of B'nai

Jeshurun in New York City, who in his *Bible View of the Slavery* found some biblical sanction for the slave system. But Raphall had actually been very careful to emphasize the differences between slavery as it existed in the South and as it existed among the ancient Hebrews.

Nevertheless, the wide circulation given to Raphall's tract in the South was viewed with chagrin by the group of Reform leaders who supported the abolition of slavery. Michael Heilprin, the brilliant editor of *Appleton's New American Encyclopaedia,* wondered whether the "stigma of Egyptian principles be fastened on the people of Israel by Israelitish lips themselves."[7] Dr. David Einhorn, the abolitionist-minded leader of the Temple Har Sinai in Baltimore, could not resist inquiring whether "a disease perchance cease to be an evil on account of its long duration."[8]

Actually the bible had little bearing on the slave question in America. There were, to be sure, several references to slavery in Exodus and Leviticus and in several Talmudic tractates, but their relevance was doubtful because they could be interpreted to lend support to either side. Slavery among the ancient Hebrews was of a precapitalist variety and had virtually no commerce connected with it. Unlike the situation in the plantation South, it did not shape the pastoral economy of ancient Israel which in any case found little use for masses of slaves. Rather than being considered an animated tool, as he was in the South, the slave in ancient Israel was merely a member of society in dependent status. He was entitled to the full protection of the laws of the community.

The situation in ancient Israel was, moreover, complicated by the careful distinction drawn between Hebrew bondsmen who became slaves because of penury or the inability to make restitution upon being caught stealing, and heathen slaves who were captured in war or, on rare occasions, purchased from slave traders. It was this last-mentioned group of slaves who bore some resemblance to the status of slaves in the South. But the possession of these slaves was not common in ancient Israel.

For the more common Hebrew bondsmen the bible cautioned "Ye shall not rule over one another with rigor" (Leviticus XXV, 46). He was permitted to go free in the Sabbatical or Jubilee year; he was entitled, indeed compelled, like all Jews, to rest on the Sabbath. If he suffered bodily harm at the hand of the master, he was automatically set free. Nor could he be mutilated. That the ancient Hebrews did not view slavery as a natural state is best attested by the severe punishment reserved for those who kidnapped a man in order to sell him into slavery or those who returned a runaway slave to his master. Witness the fate reserved for Joseph's brothers. In practice, however, the system varied with the kind of slave involved. When a heathen slave escaped he had to be returned upon capture and could be severely chastised. The distinction between Hebrew and heathen slaves gave the Scriptures a certain duality which made it possible to use them for ideological justification by either side.

Despite the ambiguity of the bible on the score of slavery a number of Rabbis and informed Jewish laymen saw in the Scriptures a clarion call to oppose the slavocracy. Prominent among them were the afore-mentioned Michael Heilprin and David Einhorn, both of whom were at one point in their lives forced to flee their homes, threatened by the fury of pro-slavery mobs. Other Rabbis involved in the abolitionist crusade were Bernard Felsenthal and Sabato Morais, often to the consternation of their Philadelphia congregants.

There were also a number of ordinary Jews in the forefront of the abolitionist crusade. Jacob Benjamin, Theodore Weiner, and August Bondi marched with John Brown in Kansas. Moritz Pinner published the abolitionist *Kansas Post* and three Chicago lawyers, Leopold Mayer, Michael Greenbaum, and Adolph Loeb, earned some prominence as abolitionists. In New York, Gustav Pollack, Isidore Bush, and Philip Joachimsen, the last-mentioned an Assistant District Attorney who suc-cessfully prosecuted slave traders, formed a nucleus of militant anti-slavery crusaders. Others like Moses Judah were active in the manumis-sion society which successfully convinced several Jewish families to free their slaves. The daughter of a Rabbi, the Polish-born Ernestine L. Rose, might serve as a prototype for the Jewish radical, nineteenth-century vintage. She became an ardent atheist in her youth, went on to pioneer in the women's rights movement during the Jacksonian period and abolitionism, the major reform movement of the time.[9] Marx E. Lazarus, the scion of a wealthy Jewish family, was one of the rare Southern abolitionists of Jewish faith.

But for the most part the rank and file of American Jewry chose to follow the more cautious path of neutrality. Abolitionists were vexed by the lack of Jewish commitment to their cause. At the meeting of the American and Foreign Anti-Slavery Society held in New York in 1853, abolitionists, concerned over the steady increase of pro-slavery senti-ment in certain religious denominations, found the position taken by American Jewry wanting: "The object of so much mean prejudice and unrighteous oppression as the Jews have been for ages," read the annual report of the society, "surely they, it would seem, more than any other denomination, ought to be enemies of *caste* and friends of *Universal Freedom*."[10]

But Jews, mindful of the fact that other religious groups, such as the Baptists in 1854 and the Methodists and Presbyterians in 1857, had already been rent in twain by the slavery question, continued to avoid taking a position. No Jewish leaders raised their voice against the Mexican War which abolitionists viewed, in the words of James Russell Lowell, as a war fought "so's to lug new slave states in." Involved in establishing themselves economically, Jews preferred to heed the Talmudic admonition that "the law of the land is the law. . . . [for Jews]," rather than the prophetic vision distilled by the abolitionist Rabbis.

The sentiment of the community in which Jews lived thus had considerable bearing on the position they took on the critical slavery issue. Jews who lived among Germans readily adopted their viewpoint. As a group the Germans were generally opposed to the extension of slavery, although not inclined to disrupt it where it existed. Their view, in turn, was partly affected by their clash with the Irish who were moving into the Democratic party and shared its anti-Negro sentiments. As working people, they keenly felt the potential of competition from freed Negroes for jobs. The newly-arrived Germans, while harboring little love for the black man, also saw in the continued spread of slave labor, a threat to free labor.

By the same token the conformity of Southern Jews with that section's outspoken pro-slavery position was nigh complete. Speaking admiringly of the slave system's elevating effects on Southern society, Benjamin Cohen, a well-known Savannah merchant and community leader, believed "that the institution of slavery [is] . . . the only human institution that would elevate the Negro from barbarism and develop the small amount of intellect with which he is endowed."[11] The view that slavery was a practical transmitter of civilization was often reiterated by slave owners. As early as 1824, Isaac Harby, the noted Jewish essayist and dramatist, expressed his disdain for the abolitionists. In general the Southern rabbinate reflected rather than contravened the views of their congregants. Some, like Rabbi George Jacobs of Richmond, were themselves slave owners. Edwin De Leon became an important propagandist for the Confederate cause in Europe. Judah P. Benjamin, "the brains of the Confederacy" who was denounced by Benjamin Wade on the floor of the Senate as "an Israelite with Egyptian principles," and David Yulee, formerly Levy, the Senator from Florida between 1845 and 1861, were both staunch upholders of the slave system. So were other Southern Jewish leaders like Gustavus Meyers, Henry Hyams, and Raphael Moses. The last-mentioned was a "fire eater," the most extreme form of secessionist, who helped lead Georgia out of the Union and then enlisted with his three sons in the Confederate Army.

Yet not all Southern Jews were adamant in the defense of slavery or anxious to remove themselves from the Union. Mention has been made of Marx E. Lazarus. During the South Carolina nullification convention of 1832, the four Jewish delegates split their votes evenly on the momentous question of whether that state should nullify the tariff of 1832. Twenty-nine years later, at the secession convention of Alabama, Philip Phillips, who represented Mobile, and Edwin Moise, a physician and lawyer and scion of the renowned Moise family, voted against secession. In the cosmopolitan center of New Orleans, Jews could be found who came to grips with the moral dilemma posed by the slave system. One such was Michael Hahn, a Douglas supporter, and a firm opponent of slavery and secession. In 1864 Lincoln appointed him to the governorship of the repossessed state of Louisiana. But in general, Magnolia Jews went along with the system and shared the unfavorable view of the Negro which was at the base of the slave system.

Nor was such a view confined to the South, or to Southern Jews. The racist view of Rabbi Isaac Wise, the leader of the American Reform movement, approximated that of the aforementioned Solomon Cohen. He viewed the Negro as "representing all that is debased and inferior in the hopeless barbarity and heathenism of six thousand years." As far as he was concerned, the parallel, often drawn by the more liberally inclined, between the bondage of the Jews in Egypt and the Negro in the South was nonexistent. According to Rabbi Wise, the ancient Hebrew always cherished his freedom while "the Negro was never free; and his bondage in Africa was simply duplicated in a milder form when he was imported here."[12] His views of the abolitionists, who he felt were "demons of hatred and destruction," went further than most middle-of-the-road Democrats. His antagonism toward them was partly prompted by his awareness that in the abolitionist stronghold of Massachusetts, these abolitionist reformers had often opposed extending the franchise to the foreign-born. He suspected, moreover, that rather than being missionaries doing the Lord's work, an image which they liked to project of themselves, these reformers were actually power-hungry, would-be leaders, who were anti-Semitic in their outlook.[13] Spiritual leaders such as Jacob Raphall, Judah Wechsler, and Bernard Illowy often found themselves agreeing with Wise, although they were less extreme in their partisanship. The abolitionist reform movement proved not nearly as attractive to Jews as later reform movements such as the Progressives or the New Deal reformers.[14]

Jews were especially drawn to Lincoln. Lewis Dembitz, granduncle of Louis Brandeis, was one of the three local leaders who placed Lincoln's name in nomination at the Republican convention in 1860.

Another Jew, Abraham Jonas, like Lincoln a former Whig, campaigned for him in 1858 and 1860 and was subsequently awarded the postmastership of Quincy, Illinois. Some have noted a personal factor involved in Lincoln's attractiveness to Jews. They recognized a kindred soul in his light, self-deprecating humor, the seeming permanent melancholy, his humanity, and his concern for people. Isaac Wise, no friend of Lincoln's, claimed the President had confided in him that he believed himself "of Hebrew Parentage."[15] That is probably farfetched, but it does serve to indicate how anxious some Jews were to claim a good man as their own. We shall see that their faith in Lincoln was not misplaced.

In the sense that it placed the existence of the United States in jeopardy, the Civil War loomed as a threat to the continued well-being of the Jewish community. Jews knew from experience that such social upheavals inevitably proved to be a disaster for them. It is therefore something of a paradox to note that for Jews in the North, where most Jews lived, the war actually proved to be something of a boon. They had avoided the open breach of the troubled decade of the fifties and now during the war an acceleration of German Jewry's headlong leap into affluence could be noted. Once hostilities broke out, Jews cast their lot with their respective sections, those in the North fought and died for the Union and those in the South for the Confederacy.

About 10,000 Jewish men, far above their proportion of the population, fought in both armies. The South had 23 Jewish staff officers including David De Leon, who served as Surgeon General, and A. C. Meyers, who served as Quartermaster General. Four Jews attained the rank of General in the Union Army. A movement to follow the precedent set by South Carolina during the War of Independence of organizing separate "Jew's companies" developed in the Jewish communities in Syracuse, Buffalo, and Chicago. But such attempts proved to be impractical and were soon abandoned.

For a brief period the question of a Jewish chaplaincy caused some consternation among Jews committed to the Union cause. The Confederacy had passed a chaplaincy law which neither prohibited nor encouraged the establishment of a separate Jewish chaplain's office. But in the North, where a similar procedure was followed, the enabling act stated that a chaplain "must be a regularly ordained minister of some Christian denomination." Always in search of political ammunition against the Lincoln administration, the Ohio Peace Democrat, Rep. Clement Vallandingham, prodded by Isaac Wise, spoke out in favor of a Jewish chaplaincy. But despite pressure to act, the House of

Representatives still refused to sanction it. On July 17, 1861, Rev. Arnold Fischel, a Dutch immigrant, acting at the behest of the Board of Delegates of American Israelites, met personally with Lincoln regarding his application for a commission as a chaplain. A few weeks later Simon Cameron, the Secretary of War, rejected the application. The matter was next brought directly to Lincoln's attention and it became the subject of at least one cabinet meeting. But the matter was not satisfactorily resolved until July, 1862, when Congress amended the discriminatory clause.[16]

Such grievances did not appear to dampen the zeal of local Jewish communities to serve the "cause." Feeling themselves wholeheartedly involved in the fate of their respective sections, Jews participated actively in the volunteer infrastructure which sprang up on both sides. Philadelphia's Jewish community, long accustomed to organizing its own self-help institutions, established a Ladies' Hebrew Relief Association. Two years later it developed into the Ladies' Hebrew Association for the Relief of Sick and Wounded Soldiers. It became associated with the United States Sanitary Commission, the agency which then combined the roles of the present-day Red Cross and the United Service Organization. In New York City several wards of the Jew's Hospital (today, Beth Israel) were set aside for war wounded. Jewish communities in other cities followed suit. Raising money for the war effort became an important activity in which many Jewish communities participated. Following the precedent set by the Jewish community of Washington, D.C., some Jewish communities assumed the financial cost of supporting the families of soldiers at the rate of $11 per month.[17] As the war drew to an end and word of the devastation of Southern cities reached the North, some Jewish congregations responded generously to the call for help from their less fortunate brethren in the Confederacy. In 1865, for example, the Jewish communities of Philadelphia and New York shipped two-and-a-half tons of Matzohs, the special unleavened bread required for the Passover holidays, to the Jewish congregations in Columbia and Charleston in South Carolina.

Both in the North and the South the cataclysmic effects of the war released general intergroup hatreds which might otherwise have remained latent. In 1862 Judah Benjamin, who had suffered much calumny because of his being Jewish, was censured by the Confederate Congress for failing to send war supplies to Roanoke and thus causing its loss to the Union Army. He did not reveal that if he had complied with Roanoke's request, Norfolk would have been left vulnerable. Jewish merchants in the Southland felt the sting of anti-Semitic slander as civilian goods became scarce. The town of Thomasville, Georgia, passed a resolution banishing all its Jewish residents, and another town found the Jews guilty of "evil and unpatriotic conduct." The *Richmond Examiner* filled its pages with anti-Semitic diatribes which began by complaining about Jewish war profiteering and ended by accusing them of being responsible for Confederate defeats on the field of battle.

On the Union side the situation was not far different and in one case revealed that anti-Semitic sentiment reached high up the chain of command. Grant's General Order Number 11, issued in December, 1862, was one of the rare instances in American Jewish history of official anti-Semitism sponsored by an arm of the government.

The background of the order includes the fact of cotton starvation in Northern textile mills and a critical shortage of certain kinds of medical goods and a surplus of raw cotton in the South. This created a situation in which big profits might be reaped if a commercial connection could be established which gave each side what it needed. The opportunity to do so arrived after the Battle of Shiloh which opened up the Mississippi River to commercial travel at least as far as Vicksburg. Soon a profitable business, with a volume estimated as high as $30,000,000, developed in the war zone. It attracted some Jewish traders, but primarily the business was in the hands of non-Jewish Army officers, treasury agents, and droves of small-time speculators. Aware of the temporary advantage the trade generated for both sides, neither the Union government nor the Confederacy prohibited the trade. It became so widespread, especially among army officers, that at one point Lincoln complained that "the army itself is diverted from fighting rebels to speculating in cotton."[18] Rumored to be playing a prominent role in the trade, especially in the obtaining of permits, was Jesse Grant, the General's father.

Late in 1862 a feeling that the trade was getting out of hand had permeated the officer ranks of the Army and government circles. In August, 1862, the shipment of gold bullion to the Confederacy was forbidden. On November 9 and 10, Grant issued orders to his commanders in Jackson, Tennessee, which hinted that he blamed Jews for the nefarious trade. The department was ordered purged of all traders "especially the Israelites because their travelling to and fro was such an intolerable nuisance."[19] On December 17, 1862, Grant again made known his distaste for Jews to C. P. Wolcott, Assistant Secretary of the Army, by complaining that Treasury regulations were being violated "mostly by Jews and other unprincipled traders."[20] Finally in December, a sweeping order for the evacuation of all Jews living in the Tennessee Department, General Order Number 11, was issued by Grant. No appeal to headquarters would be permitted and the evacuation would be carried out within twenty-four hours.

Since the Jews were unaccustomed to being thus singled out for discriminatory action, Grant's order aroused consternation and anger in the Jewish community. Those not sympathetic to the government seized upon the order as further evidence of Lincoln's bad faith and disregard of basic civil liberties. The press of the Peace Democrats accused the Republicans of mustering a greater concern for blacks than they did for Jews, who, whatever else they were, were after all white.

But in the meantime some steps were initiated among the Jews of Paducah, Kentucky, one of the towns affected by the sweeping order. The President of the Paducah Union League was a well-known Jewish merchant, Cesar Kaskel. Joined by several others, he spared no effort to inform the Jewish community and the Lincoln Administration of the full significance of the order. Kaskel saw Lincoln on January 3, 1863, armed with evidence of the purposeful discrimination of the order. Two months later, on March 3, 1863, the effort finally met with success. Lincoln ordered General Halleck, General in Chief of the Army, to revoke it immediately. But by that time the Jewish community was up in arms and the issue had become a political one. The revocation of the order came too late for the Jews of Holly Springs and Oxford, Mississippi, and Paducah, Kentucky. There the order for mass evacuation was actually carried out.

In trying to find some deeper significance for this unhappy incident there is some danger of making too much of it. On the one hand, it may simply have involved a personal distaste for Jews by Grant, William T. Sherman, and probably H. W. Halleck. It may have represented an effort to cut down Jewish competition by the non-Jewish traders and smugglers. On the other hand, one can hardly make light of an order involving an arm of the government, indirectly punishing Jewish communities without "due process" of law. It was the type of collective punishment reminiscent of Europe in the Middle Ages. Although Grant went to great pains to deny the anti-Semitic intent of the order when he ran for the presidency in 1868, there seems little doubt today that the order actually represented the capstone of a feeling of anti-Semitism which permeated Grant's officer corps.[21]

There is also the possibility that at least part of the incident might be attributed to a misunderstanding within the Lincoln administration, who, blithely unaware of its potential for interfering with the war effort, looked benignly on the trade, while soldiers who were often called upon to sacrifice their lives, viewed commerce with the enemy as unseemly. But why single out the Jews when non-Jewish traders were so much more conspicuous in this commerce? There is no easy answer to this question. It is likely, however, that those predisposed to believe it, saw in this commerce the image of the shrewd, cunning Jew who traded while others were dying. The war strengthened tendencies and revealed dispositions toward anti-Semitism, which under normal circumstances might never have come to the surface. This is one of the costs of war too rarely figured into the final accounting.

CHAPTER VII

The Early Reform Movement in American Judaism

POSSESSING THE SPIRIT OF SELF-RELIANCE SO HIGHLY PRIZED IN THE NEW World, Jews generally were well thought of in the decades before the Civil War. An editorial entitled "Jews as Citizens" which appeared in the *Washington Sentinel* on May 21, 1854, began with a paean of praise, "Not a Single Jew Requiring Relief" and went on to extol the absence of crime and vice among them.[1] "Characteristic Traits of Jews," the title of a rather facile editorial which appeared in the *Sunday Dispatch* of May 25, 1854, similarly admired their hard work, perseverance, and "spirit of pride" which kept them "above want and charity."[2]

In their turn, Jews were grateful to live in a community where their talents, especially in business, were allowed full reign. In dedicating the building of Congregation Mikve Israel in Savannah on July 21, 1820, Dr. Jacob De La Motte wondered aloud "on what spot in this inhospitable globe does an Israelite enjoy more blessings, more privileges, or is more elevated in the sphere of preferment and more conspicuously dignified in respectable stations?"[3] For most Jews such benevolence was a new experience and they demonstrated their appreciation by a heartfelt love of country. They were punctilious in their observance of patriotic holidays. The pantheon of leaders who guided the nation through its troubled early years became national symbols and were held dear by people like Rebecca Gratz. In February, 1805, she complained to a friend about the "languid patriotism" of Americans. One would never have believed, she writes, that "only a few years have passed since the birthday of Washington was hailed with enthusiasm by every American, now it passes unobserved."[4]

It is a truism that group cohesiveness is strengthened in the face of outside hostility and tends to ebb when outside pressure diminishes. While some Jews reveled in the generally benign social environment of America, few could fathom that such benevolence carried with it problems of survival no less urgent than those generated by a hostile community. Not only did the free atmosphere tend to loosen community bonds, it required adjustment of Jewish communal and religious practices. What had been suitable for a hostile environment would not necessarily be found satisfactory for the free, highly-secular atmosphere of the United States. For many this accommodation was personified by a new form of Judaism which was produced by the Reform movement. To find its roots we must momentarily return to the Germany of the late eighteenth and nineteenth centuries.

A good date to begin might be 1791, the year when the French National Assembly proclaimed religious liberty throughout the land. That officially started the movement for change within European Jewry, although a ferment for change had been manifest much earlier. Finally in November, 1819, after more than a decade of experimentation with new religious concepts and rituals, a group of about fifty prominent Jewish intellectuals, including Leopold Zunz, Abraham Geiger, and Heinrich Heine, met in Berlin to institutionalize the movement for restructuring Judaism. They formed the Verein für Kultur und Wissenschaft der Juden (Association for Jewish Culture and Knowledge).

The Verein gave organizational shape to a movement for change which had begun when Jews first tasted the heady atmosphere of the Enlightenment. The early effects of the so-called emancipation was to stimulate the conversion of many high-status Jews to Christianity. Many more lapsed into nonbelief, or at least nonaffiliation with Judaism. They considered themselves enlightened free thinkers. The movement for emancipation of Jewry triggered by the French Revolution successfully eroded much of the potential leadership strata of European Jewry. It seemed that what centuries of persecution could not achieve, a few decades of the Enlightenment might. To halt the erosion some way of accommodating the basic principles of Judaism to the philosophy of the Enlightenment had to be developed. To achieve this the hold of the rabbinic establishment, with its vested interest in preserving the tradition which gave it preeminence, had to be broken. Once that was done, the bright light of prophetic Judaism espousing universalist principles, which incidentally coincided with the rationalist philosophy of the time, could shine forth and the Jew could partake in the developing secular society.

Gradually the Reform movement made inroads among the Jews of Western Europe. In the East, the rabbinic establishment momentarily held fast. Predictably, pressure for change was advocated primarily by those Jews anxious to join ranks with the rising new middle class. When citizenship was proffered to the Jews of Amsterdam in 1795, for example, the leadership rejected the offer for fear that its flock would be tainted with secularism. But the thriving port city had many wealthy Jews anxious for such legal status and within a year they succeeded in having the decision reversed. Carried forward by upwardly mobile Jews and the spirit of the Enlightenment, the movement for innovation seemed to be irresistible.

A new scientific reading of the scriptures which developed in the universities revealed that the Bible was not, after all, given to mankind directly from the hand of God. It was composed by mortals, and not by one man like Moses, but by many at different times and places. The revelation that the Bible, which served as the very foundation of Judaism as well as Christianity, was not a divine document but a historical one, proved sufficient to shake the faith of the most devout.

For Jews it was not only these discoveries which tended to undermine their faith. Unlike other creeds, Judaism prescribed an entire way of life above and beyond its system of belief. It was an entire culture which stood in the way of accommodating to modernism. Many were loath to abandon it entirely. Clinging hopefully to it, they sought to modernize it. Judaism, they reasoned, had always been able to change itself. That, in fact, accounted for its remarkable survival through the ages. Jews of old had known instinctively, without reading Hegel, that change was the rule of life. Modifications had to be made so that Judaism might survive. Yet how could one make the necessary changes if one was compelled to adhere to the *Schulchan Aruch*, a classification of rules to be followed by all Jews compiled in the sixteenth century by Joseph Caro. The *Schulchan Aruch* (ready-set table) designed for life in a different time and place prescribed the activity of a devout Jew for virtually every moment of his day. Every century saw more additions by rabbinic responsa and new interpretations of the Talmud. Truly, they believed, the rabbis had embedded Judaism in legalism so that its enlightened humanistic spirit no longer shone forth.

For those who had achieved a middle-class position the question of image also rankled. Religious services were unseemly and far from reverent. The cacophony of sound as each worshiper separately raced through the prescribed prayers as fast as possible, rarely understanding what the Hebrew words meant, lacked grace and solemnity. The separation of women was old-fashioned and the practice of "shenodering," the auctioning of honorific duties and titles, offended bourgeois aesthetics. Having just achieved middle-class status, they felt that the way things looked was inordinately important.

Although they often gave that impression, the motives of the reformers were not only aesthetic. What they really desired was to proscribe the all-encompassing practice of traditional Judaism so that one might function in the secular world. Once that was achieved, Judaism would become simply a religion among other religions. The first emphasis was to establish decorum in the service and almost without knowing it they sought their model for proper respectability in the dominant Protestant faith. To give the services solemnity there would be mixed choirs and the playing of an organ, family pews, joint congregational reading of prayers, an uplifting sermon delivered by the rabbi, and use of the vernacular so that the worshipers might understand what they were reading. Sometimes, as in the case of the new temple Beth Elohim in Charleston, the new edifice even looked suspiciously like a church.

But soon the reformers found it was necessary to develop a new exegesis to clothe their theoretic nakedness. Those things in the Judaic faith which stood in the way of assumption of the full obligation of citizenship in the modern nation state would be removed. As the reformers saw it, a principal roadblock was the traditional view that the exile was punishment for sins, a temporary condition from which Jews would be redeemed upon the arrival of the Messiah. How could one assume the obligations and privileges of citizenship if one, in fact, owed allegiance to a Judaic national entity which might at any moment be reconstituted?

The reformers had to change what Jews traditionally considered a curse into a blessing and what was a temporary situation into a permanent one. This was achieved by postulating that it was, in fact, God's purpose to make the Jews into his priestly missionaries among the gentiles. Rather than being a punishment, the exile was in fact a blessing, a sign of God's continuing covenant with the Jewish people. The Jewish people were a permanent fixture among the nations. Rabbi Gustav Posnansky, the reformist activator of congregation Beth Elohim in Charleston, put it succinctly in his dedication of the newly built temple: "This country is our Palestine, this city our Jerusalem, this house of God our temple."[5] Such principles would place the Reform movement on a collision course with Zionism by the turn of the century. That ideology would demonstrate the advantage of being able to offer everything which Reform offered, modernism, access to secular culture and Jewish peoplehood, while at the same time harnessing the most powerful ideological force of the nineteenth century, nationalism.

To modernize Judaism so that it could function in a contemporary rationalistic setting it would also be necessary to abandon the hundreds of prohibitions and obligations which had been collected over many centuries. "We wish to know," said Rabbi Max Lilienthal, a leader in the American Reform movement, "what in our law is God's command

and what is the transient work of mortal man." Rabbi Felsenthal put it more bluntly when he spoke at the inauguration of a new Reform congregation, Anshe Maariv, in Chicago on April 17, 1858: "We must separate the eternal and indestructible kernel of Judaism from its tattered encasing."⁶

It should be noted that the Reformists had no desire to destroy Judaism. They wished merely to make it usable in the new setting. "We wish not to *abandon* the institutions of Moses," stated the petition of the Charleston reformers in 1824, "*but to understand and observe them,* ... we wish to worship God, not as *slaves*, but as enlightened descendants of that chosen race, whose blessings have been scattered throughout the land of Abraham, Isaac and Jacob."⁷ But the influence of the Protestant model was openly acknowledged by Isaac Harby, the leader of the Charleston reformists. "The pen of Luther was the great intellectual lever which shook papal hegemony to its foundations, why may not the virtuous example of a few Israelites, then, shake off the bigotry of ages from their countrymen?"⁸ Clearly the Reform movement was to do for Judaism what the Protestant Reformation had done for Christianity.

In both cases it was an entrenched establishment which held back progress. The desire to purge Judaism of rabbinic interpolations was viewed not only in terms of making Judaism viable. It would permit the laity to understand what Judaism was all about. Since one could not theorize with the masses, one had to begin with concrete change. So the reformists in Germany began first to revise the prayer service, matters like abandoning the head covering; the confirmation service and dietary laws came later. By the time the reformers were through, the Judaism they had created was a fairly good approximation of a Protestant sect.

The buffeting effects of the Reform movement were felt first in Germany and there were similar vibrations in other Western European nations. But it was in the United States, the secular state *par excellence*, where the Reform movement found its most favorable climate for growth. The seeds of the Reform movement were carried to American shores by a group of rabbis, who were part of the German Jewish migration of the mid-nineteenth century. It included Leo Merzbacher who arrived in 1841, Max Lilienthal who arrived in 1845, Isaac Meyer Wise who came in 1846, David Einhorn who arrived in 1855, and Samuel Adler who did not arrive until 1857. They helped shape an organizational framework for the indigenous movement for reform.

From the point of view of the social conditions of American Jewry, the prospects for the kind of innovation advocated by the Reform movement were good. We have seen that the congregational polity of American Judaism disallowed a resistant rabbinic establishment, backed by the power of the state, from functioning. Each congregation determined its own course unhampered by a rabbinic hierarchy. By the second quarter of the nineteenth century one could note a fragmentation of functions heretofore controlled by the congregation. Unarmed with the backing of government authority, the synagogue lost control of many of its social, educational, and philanthropic activities and became, what it never was in the Old World, merely a house of worship. The most American of motives, the spirit of free enterprise, entered the Jewish community life, as the teacher, the ritual slaughterer, the winemaker and ultimately even the circumciser (Mohel) went into business for themselves.

Philanthropic institutions also acted independently of the congregation. *Bikur Cholim* societies were organized to visit the sick. Separate *Gemilath Chasodim* (mutual loan societies) made their debut. As early as 1801, the Jewish community of Charleston organized the first Hebrew orphanage. After 1850 Jewish communities began to establish hospitals which observed dietary laws. Cincinnati did so in 1850, followed two years later by New York City and Chicago in 1868. Jewish orphanages were established in Philadelphia (1855), Cleveland (1868), and New York in 1879. By the end of the nineteenth century few philanthropic functions remained linked to the religious congregation.

Most telling for the religious congregation was its partial loss of the fraternal function. In the Old World the *Beth Hamidrosh* (synagogue) had served as the locus of the communities' social activities. But in the New World the relative openness of the social environment and the movement toward secularism proved difficult for the congregants to resist. Social clubs, fraternal societies like the Masons, singing clubs and literary societies grew up outside of the congregation.

The establishment of *B'nai B'rith* (Children of the Covenant) in 1843 deserves special attention. It was founded by a group of German Jewish merchants, who resided below Chatham Square on the East Side of New York. Although some of them were already members of the Masons and the Odd Fellows, they had come to the conclusion that a Jewish fraternal order was required "to ameliorate the deplorable condition of the Jews in this our newly adopted country."[9] Within a relatively short period of time B'nai B'rith had branches in most of the nation's Jewish communities and by the end of the century it expanded overseas, the first American Jewish organization to forge a bridge to European Jewry. Everywhere it was established it served the needs of those Jews who could not gain entrance to, or did not find their social needs met by, Christian fraternal orders.

The middle-class types who were most drawn to Reform were especially prevalent in the United States. We have already taken note of the remarkable success odyssey of German Jewry in America. Anxious to obtain the good things of this world, they found it natural to mute those facets of traditional Judaism which interfered with their headlong drive to achieve middle-class status. They were perhaps more ready than most to accept the Protestant-determined model of proper bourgeois behavior. A disregard for the sanctity of tradition, moreover, permeated American life and Jews, no less than other groups, were ready to drop old forms in favor of the new. The Reform movement was in tune with the preference for innovation rather than tradition. Reform, for American Jews, was not so much a matter of religion, about which they knew precious little in any case. It meant the Americanization of an alien faith to parallel their own acculturation. Most important, it held out the promise of being able to enter fully into the life of secular America.

For those willing to see, it was apparent that secular America barely bothered to conceal its Protestant trappings. After 1840 the Protestant ethos was transmitted directly by the public schools. Jewish children attending them had Protestant teachers as models, imbibed Protestant standards of decorum, sang Protestant hymns of Thanksgiving, and learned from Protestants at Christmastime where Jews had gone astray. The Reform movement operated in a Protestant ambience and its influence, direct and indirect, had an important bearing on the shape reform finally assumed in America. It is no accident that in the final decades of the nineteenth century, in its more extreme manifestation, Reform resembled nothing so much as a liberal Protestant sect.

Evangelical Protestantism attempted to project an influence on Judaism directly by proselytizing among Jews. The conversion of the Jews had the highest priority among the early Puritan settlers. Later, the rise of several groups to promote Christianity by bringing the word of God to non-Christians indicated that the missionary spirit was still alive. Strangely enough, these missionary groups were primarily interested in converting the Jews in Europe and fairly ignored the small American Jewish community. They had considerable success in Europe, especially among upper-class Jews anxious to rise in society. Between 1820 and 1844 it is estimated that 2,200 Jews were baptized in Germany.

During the 1820's the American Society for Meliorating the Condition of the Jews turned its attention to the Jews of America. The organization brought some of its successful converts to a special colony in Harrison, New York. They were used primarily as models and to gain entree into the Jewish community. Their efforts were supplemented by periodicals with euphemistic titles like *Israel's Advocate* which preached the message of conversion to the "true faith" to the Jewish community. But the enterprise was never markedly successful because it tended to awaken latent Jewish survival instincts. Jews like Abraham C. Collins published a periodical, *Israel Vindicated* in 1820, to counteract the baneful effects of the missionary publications. In 1823, S. H. Jackson published a more formal journal titled *The Jew*, which, like Collins's journal, aimed at alerting Jews to the threat of conversion. Some trace the origin of the Anglo-Jewish press to this publication.

Conversion never posed the threat to Jewish survival that intermarriage did. Paradoxically, Christian opinion leaders were as opposed to it as were Jews. Sir Walter Scott's *Ivanhoe* and Maria Edgeworth's *Harrington*, both popular works of the time, raised in different ways, the question of the propriety of Christian men marrying Jewish women and concluded that it was not desirable. Apparently Christians were not yet fully prepared to employ this surest means of bringing Jews into the fold. Nevertheless intermarriage has probably been the single greatest cause of attrition in the Jewish community.

A more important link to Protestantism emanated from the desire of the leaders of the Reform movement to legitimize their cause by gaining approbation from Protestant leaders. Isaac Wise went out of his way to cultivate the friendship of non-Jewish leaders like Horace Greeley, Millard Fillmore, and Daniel Webster. At times he was accused of being more concerned with gaining the approval of the local Protestant clergy than of his own flock. When he inaugurated his Reform congregation, Anshe Emeth in Albany, he waxed enthusiastic not only about the prospects of the Reform movement in America, but also the fact that so many of the "most cultured non-Jews" of Albany had been present at the ceremony. There was more than friendly ecumenism involved here. He felt that these leaders were able to appreciate that the Reform movement was "activated by regard for the needs of the spirit of the age."[10] To succeed, Reform had to become American and that in turn meant association with America's principal religious creed.

Indeed Reformers did solicit agreement from non-Jewish spokesmen. When the first pangs of reform emanated from Charleston's Jewry in 1825 it elicited comment from Samuel Gilman in that most prestigious of scholarly journals of the time, the *North American Review*. Gilman approved of the developments. "The spirit of the age," he thought, "like the voice of Jehovah will gently and inevitably convert the present synagogue, with its obsolete ceremonials . . . into a more rational sanctuary."[11] On January 6, 1826, the aged deist Thomas Jefferson replied to

Isaac Harby's communication regarding the movement that he thought
the proposed innovations "entirely reasonable."[12] Even the fragmentation which American Jewish Congregations were to undergo in the
1830's and 1840's bears some resemblance to the denominationalism
which plagued Protestantism.

Dispersion of German Jewish immigrants in the West tended to enhance the opportunities of the Reform movement in that area. Dispersion
made it difficult to establish Jewish communities to take responsibility
for their religious needs and it made the abandoning of Old World
religion more imminent. Sometimes makeshift *Chevras* (informal associations) were organized in isolated areas but these proved hardly ade-
quate to furnish a full Jewish life. Letters home from the flock of Jewish
peddlers sometimes bemoaned the absence of a Jewish community and
the difficulty of remaining observant Jews in the new environment.
"God in heaven. . . . thou alone knowest my grief," noted one peddler
in his diary, "when on the Sabbath eve, I must return to my lodgings
and on Saturday morning carry my pack on my back, profaning the holy
days, God's gift to his people. I can't live as a Jew."[13]

Not all peddlers were so observant. More than likely a loss of religious
zeal had already occurred in the small towns of Bavaria and Hesse from
whence these peddlers stemmed. Moreover, by preselection, those who
were most likely to think in terms of emigration were, by the same
token, least likely to be traditional-minded. Hebrew learning in these
small German towns was in a low state and in the small towns of the
American West, to which these peddlers had transplanted themselves,
it was even lower. Touring through the West, Isaac Wise noted that
there "Judaism was like the dead sea." In Milwaukee "there was but
little interest in Judaism [and] several fashionable Jews had been
baptized."[14] Wise, who stemmed from Bohemia, suspected that the low
estate of Judaism was related to the low level of sophistication possessed
by these rural Jews. He had discovered, while delivering his sermons in
Albany, that a sermon suitable for a European congregation was above
the head of his Albany congregants. In order to win their attention he
was compelled to act "as though [he] were teaching school, possibly an
upper class."[15] Probably such despair tells us more about Wise than it
does about the simple hard-working folk who found little relevance in
his sermons. In any case, the new Jewish congregations, to Wise's gratification, seemed intelligent enough to buy what he was selling. Most
joined the Reform movement and made the West the citadel of Reform
in America.

American Jewry was not alone in experiencing an erosion of religious
commitment. The decade after the Revolution witnessed a sharp decline

in church attendance. In some cases less than 10 percent of professing Christians attended church on a regular basis.[16] But after the liberating effects of the Revolution had worn off, the Christian churches experienced a revitalization. Not so for American Jewry, which continued to languish. Many came to believe that Reform would reinvigorate the Jewish religious spirit. Even Jews living fairly close to large Jewish communities experienced difficulties in attending services because of lack of good transportation, which, in any case, they were prohibited from using on the Sabbath. It was clear that to be a practicing Jew one was either compelled to live in a Jewish community or bend the rules of behavior so that one might travel to one.

The absence of a Jewish community was a major problem. It led to frequent out-marriages among the new arrivals, many of whom were young and single. "They came alone," observed Lewis Dembitz, "[and] found no one to pray with and no one to mate [with] . . . ."[17] Rules were bent to make a community viable. In 1828 when the Jewish community of New Orleans was established, so many congregants had intermarried that the traditional rule of the Jewish faith passing down through the female line was abandoned. The last article of the Charter of Incorporation read: "No Israelite child shall be excluded either from the schools or the temple or from the burial grounds, on account of the religion of the mother."[18] Sometimes the fear of assimiliation could be used as a ploy to wring funds from the more prosperous congregations of the East. In January, 1824, for example, the nascent Jewish community of Cincinnati, requested aid from the Jewish congregation in Charleston, using as its primary argument "that many Jews are lost in this country from not being in the neighborhood of a congregation, they often marry with Christians."[19]

Wise used the same argument to advocate Reform Judaism. He pointed out to Isaac Leeser, his traditionalist-minded opponent, that of the original Jewish settlers in America "there were not two hundred families left that belonged to a congregation while the great majority had disappeared among the masses."[20] Surely Reform Judaism for such was better than no Judaism at all. Wise pointed out that in the West and many isolated areas in the East Jews were attending local church services, substituting appropriate words in the liturgy where they thought they belonged. Many Jews had already become "tinged with Christian thought" according to Wise. There were "Episcopalian Jews in New York, Quaker Jews in Philadelphia, Huguenot Jews in Charleston and so on, everywhere according to the prevailing sect."[21]

Wise may have exaggerated in order to highlight the inappropriateness of traditional Judaism in the new environment. But there was little doubt that newer Jewish communities found it nigh impossible to secure for themselves the supportive institutions required by a strict adherence to Jewish law. These included a ritual slaughterer, a ritual bath for women, a circumciser, a rabbi, and functionaries to form a matrix such as that offered by the *shtetl*. They were forced to improvise or to ignore certain practices and frequently the changes that were made bore a greater similarity to Reform practices than to Orthodox. If one could not read in Hebrew then why not in English and if one did not have a *minyan* (the quorum of ten male adults necessary to hold an organized service) then why not do without or include women?

In many cases proper ritual practices, if they had ever been known at all, had been forgotten through disuse. There were few in the country who could remind the congregants of what was proper. Talmudic scholars, traditionally accorded the highest status among Jews, were rarely tempted to risk the wilds of America, where, rumor had it, the quality of Jewish life was abysmally low. In 1838 Isaac Nordheimer, a noted Hebraist, was brought to New York University in the hope that an infusion of European learning would raise the state of Hebrew scholarship, but little effect could be noted. Hebrew scholarship was probably more advanced among Protestants than among Jews. There were few Jews who boasted an enthusiasm for Hebrew akin to that of Ezra Stiles. Gershom Seixas, the spiritual leader of New York Jewry, possessed only a faulty knowledge of Hebrew.

In the absence of trained rabbis and teachers, the education of Jewish youngsters in the ways of their faith was distressingly meager. For a time Isaac Leeser agitated in the *Occident*, a journal he sponsored to spread the traditionalist point of view, for the organization of Hebrew Sunday schools. With the help of Rebecca Gratz one such school was finally established in Philadelphia. Paradoxically, the very concept of Sunday school and the text that the school used were additional reminders of the pervasive influence of Christian practices upon Judaism.

The absence of ordained rabbis led amateurs, some talented, but many ignorant of the Jewish faith, to conceal their ignorance by affecting titles such as Minister or Reverend, in order to fill the vacuum. But even when the spiritual leader had good credentials there was little he could do to gain compliance from the reluctant or the indifferent. Monetary fines or threats to deny religious burial might momentarily bring a rebellious congregant to heel. But in the long run such measures were ineffective against the strong centrifugal pull of the secular environment. The Jewish worshiper became aware that the security derived from the religious community was not really necessary in the new environment which did not threaten Jews or Judaism. He no longer had to belong and when that disappeared the *raison d'être* for maintaining Jewish communities also vanished. Jewish community life became voluntaristic.

Considering the bitter conflicts which occurred within the religious congregations, the recalcitrant worshiper might have found a greater peace outside the congregation. The issues involved were complex. At times it concerned the matter of *minhag*, the order of the ritual, in which *nussach*, the order of prayer, played an important part. What prayer should come first and which second was merely the visible peak of conflict between Ashkenazim and Sephardim and also between various national elements within the Ashkenazic group. Splitting along national-cultural lines was sometimes supplemented by generational splits in which "young Turks" played an active role.

A classic model might look something like this. The arena is an old Sephardic congregation following a Sephardic *minhag*, though a good many of the congregants were actually of Ashkenazic background. The argument might be sparked by a question as to which prayer ought to be read in a given service. The conflict takes on a bitter tone because the *minhag* question is itself a manifestation of deeper class and cultural differences. "Everyone had his own minhagim," Isaac Wise observed, "and everyone wanted to have those minhagim observed generally. Blows passed in a certain synagogue in New York on Kol Nidre evening (the prayer which ushers in the Day of Atonement, the holiest day in the Jewish religious calendar) because the one party insisted that at the close of the service the ADON OLAM be sung first and then the YIGDAL, while the other insisted on the opposite.... A fight at the congregational meeting, the escape of the PARNASS (leader of the congregation in prayer) through a window in order to avoid threatened danger, lengthy and unprofitable altercations in place of debates—such things were not rare."[22] Sometimes the final step would be the splitting-off of the dissenters to form a separate congregation.

Something more than cultural and generational discord may have been involved in these conflicts. For these high-strung people disputation over form was part of a tradition which served Jews as an outlet for pent-up emotions. "Cut off socially from free and complete intercourse with the greater communities in which they existed," one historian observes, "these immigrants rubbed against each other.... Whatever pent-up energy and desperation induced by social boredom was in them burst forth into heated arguments in congregational meetings."[23] Conflict served as an emotional catharsis.

Motivated by the desire for reform or some other reason, one part of the congregation would split off from another. It would begin by a dissident or a small group of dissidents forcibly raising the issue. Thus in May, 1825, Baruch E. Cohen, a younger member of Congregation Shearith Israel, refused to make the standard offering for charity after having received the honor of being called to read from the Torah. The gauntlet was down. What would the officers of the congregation do regarding this open defiance of tradition? In this case they decided not to confront Cohen's defiance head-on. "Mr. Cohen acted from a mistaken view of the law and not from any desire to insult the Congregation," the officers decided.[24]

But the dissidents were not to be denied so easily. A few months later, in October, a number of attendants refused to don prayer shawls, claiming that they could not discover a religious reason for wearing them. This time the officers of the congregation were more courageous and ruled that the prayer shawls must be worn, to be sure not for any religious reason, but because not to do so would lead "to the subversion of all venerable & established usages in this Congregation."[25] They did not mention that to permit such defiance would inevitably undermine their own authority, which was probably the intent of the dissidents.

When the conflict had crystallized and clear sides were discernible, the dissidents would informally form into a Reform association frequently called *Kultus Verein*. They remained within the original congregation until such time as enough funds could be raised to found a separate congregation. This was the pattern in forming Har Sinai in Baltimore, Emanu-El and B'nai Jeshurun in New York, Har Sinai in Chicago, and Isaac Wise's own Anshei Emeth in Albany.

Splitting and forming new congregations resulted in a proliferation of smaller congregations. In New York, for example, the group who refused to wear prayer shawls formed a nucleus of a new congregation within Shearith Israel called Chevra Chinuch Nearim. It became the founding nucleus of Congregation B'nai Jeshurun, the first well-established Ashkenazic congregation in the city. But once started, the process took on the appearance of mitotic cell division. Three years after B'nai Jeshurun was founded a new group of Polish, Dutch, and German dissenters left to form a new congregation, Anshei Chesed. In 1835 a new series of splits occurred which saw the establishment of three new congregations, Chabei Zedek (1835), Sharei Zedek (1839), and Sharei Hashomayim (1839). In 1842, dissenting nuclei from Anshe Chesed and Sharei Hashomayim organized Rodelph Sholem and a year later Beth Israel was formed by a dissenting faction of Polish Jews who had withdrawn from Sharei Zedek.

Meanwhile class and wealth factors came into play. In 1845 a group of wealthier German Jews who favored the Reform ritual, moved uptown to establish Temple Emanu-El. That same year yet another split from B'nai Jeshurun, which might better have called itself the mother of congregations, resulted in the establishment of Sharei Tefilah. When it was all over there were twenty-seven congregations in New York where there had been five.

For a study of a model pattern of reform we turn naturally to Congregation Beth Elohim, the Sephardic congregation of Charleston. In the 1820's it was still the largest and wealthiest congregation in the nation, although it was not to remain so for much longer. The issues which caused a group of younger members to petition the Adjunta of the Kaal Kodesh (the directorate of the congregation) for reform in December, 1824, were not triggered by cultural antagonism. There were few Ashkenazic Jews in the congregation. But the youthful dissidents were familiar with the Reformist movement in Germany and cited a lengthy passage from the Reform-minded *Frankfurter Journal* to buttress their case.

The dissidents, sons of established Sephardic families, were most interested in typical Reform issues, decorum in the services and making the services meaningful to the worshipers. They wanted to counteract the "apathy and neglect" which they felt stemmed from "certain defects which are apparent in the present system of worship." "A more rational system of worshipping God," they thought, "should be available."[26]

The concrete suggestions for reform had a familiar ring. The services should be shorter and it might even be better to hold them on Sunday, the unseemly bidding for honors should be discontinued, there should be unified responses from the congregation, there should be family pews rather than separation of men and women, the service should be held primarily in the vernacular and of course there was the need for a mixed choir and perhaps organ music to beautify the services.

Predictably, the vestry rejected the memorial of the petitioners and the resignation of the twelve young dissident leaders followed automatically on November 21, 1824. Led by Isaac Harby, they established "The Reformed Society of Israelites," which in two years increased its membership to 45. Undoubtedly the conflict in Charleston's Beth Elohim contained a strong generational aspect. It featured a group of talented, strong-willed younger congregants clashing with a particularly paternalistic leadership who four years earlier had taken it upon themselves to write a clause into their constitution prohibiting the establishment of another Jewish congregation within a five-mile radius of Charleston.

Despite their energetic start the dissenters soon discovered the difficulties involved in sustaining and institutionalizing what they had done. Harby removed himself to New York and died four years later. Charleston itself began to lose its leading role as a port after the tariff of 1828. A good part of its population, including Jews, moved to the rich "bottom lands" newly opened in Alabama and Mississippi. There was not enough enthusiasm for things Jewish nor enough Jews to support two congregations in Charleston. In 1833, barely eight years after it had been formed, "The Reform Society of Israelites" was dissolved and some of its members rejoined Beth Elohim.

But the battle was not over. What the reformists could not do by organizing their own congregation they now achieved within the older one. In 1836 the now numerically stronger reform faction invited Rabbi Gustav Posnanski, a reform leader from Hamburg, to the pulpit of Beth Elohim. When the old building burned to the ground in 1840, a new impressive edifice was built which triggered a new conflict within the congregation. When the trustees rejected the idea of an organ, Posnanski overruled them. This time the traditionalists left the congregation. Secession was a well-established habit in South Carolina for Jews too. But in the case of the Reform movement at Beth Elohim the dissident traditionalist Jews turned to the law courts rather than the field of battle for redress.

The Reform movement found its leader in an outspoken rabbi who had himself been trained in the Orthodox tradition, Isaac Wise. The members of congregation Beth El in Albany, whose leadership Wise assumed in 1846, did not take long to discover that their rabbi brooked no interference from the congregation, especially where reformist innovations were concerned. Within a year he led a dissident reformist faction out of the traditionalist-minded congregation to establish Anshe Emeth. But Albany was too small an arena for Wise and when an attractive offer materialized to head the new Reform-minded B'nai Jeshurun Congregation in the bustling new western city of Cincinnati, he accepted. A year later his colleague and collaborator, Max Lilienthal, was invited to take the pulpit at the neighboring B'nai Israel congregation. These fortuitous circumstances and the fact that Cincinnati seemed destined in the 1850's to become the "Queen City of the West," and also contained a sizable German Jewish community, helped it to become the center of the American Reform movement.

In the following years Wise spent much of his energy in building an institutional framework for the Reform movement so that American Jewry might be unified under its auspices. But his first effort to establish a rabbinical academy, the Cincinnati Zion College Association, for the purpose of producing spiritual leaders to fill the vacuum in religious leadership, was unsuccessful. A parallel attempt to establish such an institution by his traditionalist-minded rival, Isaac Leeser, also proved futile. But in 1867, the year when Leeser's Maimonides College succumbed, Wise's fondest hopes were realized. The Hebrew Theological College opened its doors in Cincinnati and the first candidates for the rabbinate trickled into Cincinnati in 1875.

Aware that the question of *minhag* was everywhere splitting Jewish communities apart, Wise next attempted to impose some order. In 1875 he published a new uniform prayer book called appropriately enough, *Minhag America* (The American Way). It became the basis of a uniform service among Reform congregations until 1894 when the *Union Prayer Book* was published. In addition, two journals, the *American Israelite*, written in English, and the *Die Deborah*, for the still sizable number of German-speaking congregants, were published by the movement. What language should prevail was itself a source of some conflict within the Reform movement. Rabbi David Einhorn did not easily surrender his preference for German, whose research and science, he felt, served as "the hearth of the Jewish Reform idea."[27]

An attempt to provide American Jewry with a unified Synod to decide knotty problems of religious law proved to be premature. Non-Reform rabbis preferred to forward such cases to English and Continental *Beth Dins* (rabbinical courts). Despite such setbacks Wise worked tirelessly to establish a Reform framework for American Judaism. In 1875 he successfully unified all Reform congregations under one umbrella organization, the Union of American Hebrew Congregations. Four years later it was sufficiently strong to absorb the Board of Delegates of American Israelites, the major national organization of American Jewry established at the time of the Mortara kidnapping case in 1859.

Much effort was devoted to crystallizing a new Reformist philosophy. The results sometimes went beyond what the original reformers in Germany had intended. Kaufman Kohler, one of the founders of the movement in America, threw down the gauntlet to the traditionalists by articulating a radical Reform position at the Pittsburgh convention in 1885. One of the convention's resolutions read: "We hold that all Mosaic and rabbinical laws as regulate diet, priestly purity, and dress originated in ages and under the influence of ideas entirely foreign to our present mental and spiritual state... their observance in our day is apt rather to obstruct rather than to further modern spiritual elevation."[28] Such statements tended to polarize American Jewry by forcing a choice between the Reform position or some gradation of the traditional view. Not until the turn of the century would a suitable in-between position develop.

Four years later, in 1889, Wise successfully placed the finishing touch on the Reform organization by creating the Central Conference of

American Rabbis. All Reform congregations were unified under its auspices. In July, 1895, at its convention in Rochester, the theoretical framework of the movement was completed. The Reformists rejected the legitimacy of all post-Biblical and patristic literature, including Talmud, Responsa, and Commentaries. These, it was felt, have value as religious literature, but do not possess the force of immutable law.

Just at the point when the American Reform movement had completed its organizational and theoretical structure, developments in Europe conspired to alter totally the composition of American Jewry. The new arrivals from Eastern Europe, although frequently alienated from Orthodoxy, would find the Reform position difficult to accept. Moreover, certain weaknesses in the movement had already become apparent. It proved only partially successful in preventing the exodus of upper-class Jews from the fold. Whereas the first generation often found the Reform innovations helpful, it proved difficult to solve the major problem of any religious community—how to transfer the new faith to the next generation. In committing itself to modern-rationalist forms and content it had abandoned the myths and symbols and above all, the extra rational "magic," which is at the root of much religious sentiment. If one desired rationality it was after all more readily available in the secular world of science. In rationalizing Judaism the reformists, in their early enthusiasm, had thrown out the baby with the bath water. They cast out much that made Judaism distinctive. In many cases the acceptance of Reform became merely a *rite de passage* for transferring one's loyalty to one of the less Christologized Protestant sects, such as Unitarianism. The sons and grandsons of the affluent German Jewish immigrants often preferred such alternatives to the somewhat colorless imitation of Protestantism that Reformism seemed to be.

CHAPTER VIII

The Immigration Experience of Eastern Jewry

WE COME NEXT TO THE DEVELOPMENT WHICH MORE THAN ANY OTHER was to determine the character of twentieth-century American Jewry —the arrival of Jews from Eastern Europe. Strictly speaking, these were not "new" immigrants at all. Jews from Eastern and Central Europe may have composed the majority of the Jewish community as early as 1730. Of the 45,575 immigrants listed as Russian by immigration authorities between 1850 and 1881 it is estimated that 30,000 were Jewish. Yet the year 1881 which signaled the beginning of a massive inundation of Eastern Jews serves as a useful demarcation because the trickle of immigration before that year did not noticeably alter the demography and character of American Jewry. After that year nothing was the same.

We shall see that their motives for coming were not remarkably different from those which had brought German Jewry to these shores two generations earlier. The primary pressure for migration was economic. It was related to the erosion of the peasant-based economy on which the burgeoning Jewish population of Eastern Europe depended for its well-being. As in the case of the German Jewish migration these pressures were aggravated by official government anti-Semitism. Lastly, we shall see that the problems faced by the new immigrants differed in degree, rather than in kind, from those faced by their predecessors.

Eastern Jews bore only a superficial resemblance to the other ethnic groups which composed the "new immigration." True, their outer appearance allowed for the poetic classification of "wretched refuse," but in the level of artisanship and their keen ambition to rise in status they were reminiscent of the "old immigration." They were not displaced peasants, as were the Russian and Italian immigrants. The Jewish immigration was composed of a displaced middle and artisan class. They boasted a slightly higher literacy in their native tongues, Russian, Polish, and German. Those who emanated from Russia were overwhelmingly from towns and small villages whereas Russian immigrants were largely from rural areas.

They differed markedly from other immigrants in other respects. Fully 70 percent of the Jewish immigrants had been involved in some facet of industry or commerce compared to 13 percent of the other immigrants from the East. They possessed a virtual monopoly of the business life of the Pale and formed a significant portion of its mechanics and artisans. Of the Jewish male immigrants from Russia, 67.1 percent were skilled workers. They were distributed in thirty-five different trades, the most popular of which was tailoring, a fact which goes far to explain the attractiveness of the garment industry as a place of employment.[1]

While Jews were rarely involved in basic industries such as mining, fully one-third of the Pale's factories were owned by Jews. Predictably, their representation in the merchant class was overwhelming. Customarily Jewish businesses were not far removed from the agricultural activity which served as the base for the Russian economy. They were grain merchants, fur, cattle, and lumber dealers, owners of inns and store-keepers and peddlers.[2] With some allowances for regional variation, the profiles of Jewish immigrants stemming from Austria-Hungary and Rumania were roughly the same.[3] To be sure, as one moved westward the number of Jews found in the professions rose. In Galicia, for example, the proportion of Jews involved in the professions was ten times as high as their Christian counterparts. There, too, Jews frequently found employment as stewards and administrators of estates for the landed nobility.

Why one-third of the Jews in the East chose to uproot themselves when, at least in a statistical sense, they occupied an enviable position is not really as puzzling as it appears. The answer is to be found in the dynamic economics of the area rather than in static statistical surveys which tend to conceal the precariousness of the economic position occupied by Eastern Jewry.

In the last quarter of the nineteenth century the economy in all three areas from which Jews stemmed was in the process of rapid transition. Severe dislocation, particularly in the agricultural sector, was part of this change and it affected not only the economies of the nations in the East but American economy as well. The overproduction of grain was caused partly by the mechanization of agriculture and the intro-duction of new grain-growing areas in the United States and Argentina. That in turn caused a decline in the international market price on which Russia, a prime grain producer, was heavily dependent. Trouble in agriculture naturally adversely affected the middleman, who, in the unflattering words of one American populist, "farmed the farmers." A disproportionate number of these middlemen, we have seen, were Jewish. Farmers everywhere were in trouble, but in Russia the situation was aggravated by the emancipation of the serfs in 1862. That left the peasant so burdened with collective debt that his potential as a consumer was affected for generations to come. He could not buy what the Jewish merchandiser had to sell.

Eastern Jews possessed the energy, talent, and resources to carve out for themselves a secure position in the developing economy. But government-sponsored anti-Semitism which sought to capitalize on the fact of their preeminence as middlemen convinced the peasantry that Jews were their real enemy. The government successfully interposed Jews to deflect the growing peasant resentment that might otherwise have been turned against the regime. Meanwhile, in the wings there hovered a budding indigenous class of merchants and middle men, waiting for businesses to be abandoned by Jews. To help them, the government offered loans and other allurements and in turn native middlemen instigated boycotts of Jewish merchants. At the same time, the growth of large-scale farming enterprises and farm cooperatives made inroads in areas which traditionally were heavily infused with Jewish middlemen. Jews, in short, were gradually being displaced and forced into keen competition among themselves for the shrinking market which remained available to them.

Forced back upon themselves, crowded into towns with a shrinking source of livelihood, the position of the Jews deteriorated. By 1880 certain sections of Eastern Europe produced one Jewish peddler for every ten peasant customers. To make the picture gloomier the Jewish population was growing by leaps and bounds. The approximately 1,000,000 Jews living in Eastern Europe in 1800 had quadrupled by 1890.[4]

For the first time "black labor," work so brutalizing that it was considered unfit for Jews, made its debut. By 1890, 2 percent of the Pale's Jewish labor force was employed as agricultural laborers, cabmen, diggers, stonebreakers, ragpickers, teamsters, porters, and water carriers. The port of Odessa alone boasted 8,000 to 9,000 Jewish day laborers and 1,700 longshoremen. This last-mentioned occupation had traditionally been viewed as unsuitable for Jews because of their supposedly poor musculature and low physical stamina. "On the banks of the Dnieper," noted one observer, "are seen the Jewish porters who unload wood from the ships, some of them between 60 and 65 years of age, pass days of from 12 to 14 hours in water to their waists unloading boats." In Galicia before 1880, as many as 5,000 Jews are estimated to have died yearly from diseases brought on by malnutrition and sometimes by outright starvation. In the villages a new type of Jew made his debut.

He was popularly known as a *luftmenech,* literally a person who had no visible means of support and lived on air. In their feverish semi-starved state, such men would spend their lives dreaming unrealizable dreams building castles in the air. The *schnorrer,* a professional beggar, and the *gassmench,* an unskilled worker who was available for any work regardless of its hazard or legality, became commonplace.

The decline of the economy on which it was based dealt the heretofore socially self-sufficient *shtetl* life a mortal blow from which it never recovered. The sense of communal responsibility for the less fortunate, a hallmark of *shtetl* life, gave way to an embittered class antagonism.[5] Its remarkable social cohesiveness became fragmented. The rabbinic leadership no longer mustered the confidence of former times and became unresponsive. Scholarship, a prime focus of Jewish community life, deteriorated and philanthropic giving declined. The heavy tax burden and the onerous requirements of the conscription system, which was imposed in Russia in 1827 and in Poland in 1845, fell disproportionately on the poor. After 1847, when the Russian government insisted on exercising its prerogative of selecting those to be conscripted, a lifelong military service, which meant that the recruit had to abandon his Judaism, became an important reason for Jews to seek a new haven.

Changes in the intellectual culture of the community also became apparent. Religious piety often gave way to secularism and political radicalism. No longer protected by their community and subject to increasing economic hardships, Jews sought in socialism, anarchism, and Zionism the answer to their problems.[6] These were the ideologies they brought to the New World. Congestion and poverty in the towns brought in their wake family disruption, juvenile delinquency, crime and vice. In a word, the quality of Jewish life in Eastern Europe disintegrated and with it the moorings to which the Jews in the East had clung.

Most Russian Jews resided in the so-called Pale of Settlement, an area composed of Congress Poland, Lithuania, Byelorussia, and the Ukraine. Traditionally an area of heavy Jewish concentration, the Pale was confirmed as the official area of Jewish settlement at the time of the partition of Poland in 1772 and 1795. At that time Russian authorities restricted all aliens to where they were then settled. Thereafter the treatment of Jews fluctuated with each new regime. Some thought to repress Jewish culture and economic activity while others encouraged assimilation.

But after the assassination of Alexander II in 1881, government hostility assumed an ominous character hinting strongly at physical violence. It became apparent that Russian policy (and Rumanian) was directed at ridding the country of Jews by almost any means. A group of highly ethnocentric Russophiles gained control of the levers of power and determined to root out of Russian society all alien elements, Old Believers, Baptists, Molokans, Tolstoyans, and the numerous other religious sects, including the detested Jews, who were considered to be harbingers of Westernism and liberalism. Led by the Procurator of the Russian Holy Synod, Constantin Pobedonostev, a series of bloody pogroms were unleashed in 1881 in Elisavetgrad, Kiev, Odessa, Berdichev, Pereyaslav, and Warsaw.

Pogroms were not a new experience for Russian Jewry. Many recalled vividly the Odessa pogrom of 1871 and the countless smaller pogroms which occurred from time to time. But while they had sensed the government's indifference to their fate before, they had never experienced a situation in which the government encouraged pogroms as a matter of official policy. The authorities did their utmost to arouse peasant anti-Semitism against the Jews. It subsidized the publication of 2,837 anti-Semitic books and pamphlets. Nicholas II, who succeeded Alexander III in 1894, privately paid almost twelve and a half million rubles to sustain the production of anti-Semitic tracts. These dubious expenditures produced the classic anti-Semitic forgery of the twentieth century, *The Protocols of the Elders of Zion*. It was concocted by Sergii Nilus, a publicist and secret police official.

A year later a "cold pogrom" based on economic discrimination was initiated. Its object was to speed the Jewish emigration from Russia. Technically, the May Laws, which were at the heart of the pogrom, sought to restore life in the Pale to the way it had been before Alexander II had meddled with it. But in reality the object was to accelerate the pace of Jewish economic decline. Movement of Jews within the Pale was circumscribed. Resettling outside their towns was forbidden nor could one do business in the larger towns. Jews could no longer purchase real property or negotiate mortgages. Sunday Laws were strictly enforced, curtailing the time during which pious Jews might carry on their business. The May Laws were a staggering blow to the Jewish business economy because virtually all of the regulations had the effect of isolating the Jewish merchant from the peasantry which served as his primary market. One could, of course, get around the regulations by bribery which in fact became a way of life. But that too entailed a price because it tended to demean the giver as well as the receiver.

In 1886 a supplementary series of government ukases aimed a devastating blow at those Jews who still aspired to gain entrance to the developing indigenous middle class. A strict *numerus clausus* limited their access to university education. Within the Pale, 10 percent of the university openings would be reserved for Jews but outside—in cities like St. Petersburg and Moscow, only 3 to 5 percent could gain entrance. Access to professional careers in medicine and law were thus placed further outside the reach of most Jews.

In 1891 the privileged Jews who were fortunate enough to live outside the Pale in large cities, and had thereby been able to avoid many of the tribulations faced by their brethren, were subject to precipitous wholesale expulsion. Employing the rationale of illegal residence, the authorities had 10,000 Jews residing in the Zaryadye quarter of Moscow evicted. Other cities followed suit.

The Jewish plight enlisted the sympathy of outsiders. A Bavarian-born Jew who had earned a fortune as a railroad builder, Baron de Hirsch, approached the Russian government with an offer to contribute $10,000,000 for the purpose of reeducating Russian Jewry so that they could become more self-sustaining. It was rejected, but a second plan to resettle 3,000,000 Jews as farmers in Argentina and other areas was found suitable by the Russian authorities. The desire, after all, was not to Russify Jews, nor to alter their class character, but to be rid of them.

In milder form the story was not far different in Rumania and Austria-Hungary, the two other areas which furnished emigrants to America. Despite moments of respite, the trend in all three areas clearly pointed to a decline in Jewish fortunes. With the Kishinev massacre, a bloody three-day pogrom, which was followed by other outbreaks in 1903, the realization of threat to life and limb as well as of economic decline became unavoidable. Russia's defeat in the Russo-Japanese War was conveniently blamed on the hapless Jews. The gory massacres in Zhitomir, Odessa, Bialystok, and Siedlec followed as a matter of course. So did the rise of the Jewish emigration curve.

The image of America as a haven for Jews did not rise suddenly full-blown in the last decades of the nineteenth century, nor was it the only haven thought of. As early as 1846 Jewish leaders in Vilna addressed a letter to Sir Moses Montefiore which sounded a desperate cry for help. "Do not leave us in this land which hates and despises us. . . . Why are you silent brothers in Germany, France and England?"[7] In 1869 German Jewish leaders met in Leipzig to decide on a plan of action to cope with the masses of Russian Jews who, stalked by famine, had left the northwestern provinces of the Russian empire and moved west. But by 1880 America was clearly the preferred destination for emigrants. "Give us a chance in your great and glorious land of liberty," reads one plea for help received that year. "Come, brothers of Israel in America, come to our help . . . let us touch the sacred soil of Washington."[8] "Amer-

ica," according to a Russian newcomer, Mary Antin, "was in everybody's mouth."[9]

Stories of the accelerated industrial development of the American
economy had reached even the remote interior of Eastern Europe.
Indeed, there was much substance to rumors of the fabulous prosperity
to be found in the New World. Between 1870 and 1890 the American
economy experienced a 28 percent growth in the number of industries
and a net increase in the value of production of 167.5 percent. The
small-town Jews of Eastern Europe could not fathom the significance of
such figures. But they did know by means of the Hebrew and Yiddish
press which published glowing reports of life in the New World, that
America was a "goldeneh medina," a glorious society. The drama of
America's discovery and early development was well-known to Eastern
Jews. In 1817 Hayim Chaikel Hurwitz published a Yiddish-Hebrew
translation of a German work, *Die Entdeckung von Amerika* (The
Discovery of America) which gained wide popularity among the Jewish
reading public.

As in the case of the immigration of German Jews, those Eastern Jews
who had settled in America earlier served as catalysts for later immigration. It may well be that an uncle or cousin in America was a greater
attraction than all the abstract reasons usually given for causing mass
immigration movements. Such a relative could furnish room and board
until the immigrant could get on his feet and repeat the process for
someone else. The practical logistics involved in resettlement were apt
to generate awesome apprehension among people reared in small villages. The existence of a willing, or sometimes not so willing, relative
could make all the difference in the world for the potential immigrant.

To be sure not all Eastern emigrants viewed America as their destination. A group of perhaps 30,000 to 40,000 members of the Lovers
of Zion movement chose to resettle in Palestine. For a time arguments
over which was preferable were featured in the Hebrew press.[10] Eventually a small group of *Biluim,* an acronym formed from the Hebrew
phrase "House of Israel Let Us Go," settled in Palestine. Compared to
the millions of Jewish immigrants who came to the United States the
resettlement in Palestine formed a relatively insignificant counterflow.

America attracted its own Jewish pioneers from the East in the Am
Olam movement (eternal people). It shared many characteristics with
the Zionist pioneers, including a strong belief that human renewal
through contact with the soil was possible and that a new form of
community based on either the cooperative principle or socialism was
desirable. Both the Bilu and the member of Am Olam were influenced
by the prevailing Russian populist romanticization of agriculture. For

Jews, traditionally prevented from becoming farmers, the idea of working the land had an allure all its own, regardless of whether the transformation took place in Palestine or America. Abraham Cahan, a member of Am Olam, was as enthusiastic about becoming a farmer in America as any Zionist pioneer was about farming the ancient soil of Palestine. "I paced my room in a fever," he writes, after the idea was broached to him. "America! To go to America! To reestablish the Garden of Eden in that distant land. My spirit soared. All my other plans dissolved. I was for America."[11]

So apparently were millions of other Eastern Jews. Between 1881 and 1910, 1,562,800 Jewish immigrants arrived from the East; 1,119,059 from Russia, 281,150 from Austria-Hungary, and 67,059 from Rumania. In the next four years the total reached 2,000,000. Before 1924, the year which marks the official end of the mass immigration, another quarter million Jews arrived.[12] The Jews from Russia composed 71.6 percent of the total inflow and their arrival falls into two major periods. The first between 1881 and 1892 and the second between 1892 and 1896. The Austro-Hungarian empire contributed 18.6 percent of the total and its peak year was 1903. Rumania contributed the smallest share, 4.3 percent who arrived mostly between 1901 and 1904, the years of the passage of the Hawkers' and Artisans' Law.[13] (Both laws had the effect of severely curtailing Jewish economic activity in that country.)

Of the millions of immigrants who entered the United States between 1881 and 1924, Jews composed only a small fraction but compared to the people among whom they had lived in East Europe, a far greater proportion of Jews chose to uproot themselves. Only 12 percent of the population of Galicia was Jewish, for example, but they made up 60 percent of its emigrants. But the principal impact of the immigration was not in the country they had left, but in America among the Jews who received them. The influx of several millions of additional Jews totally altered the demographic and cultural profile of American Jewry. Of the 4,200,000 Jews who lived in the United States in 1928, 3,000,000 were of East European origin. American Jewry had been re-Europeanized. Also, for the first time in their history they became a rather conspicuous minority. While the general population increased 112 percent between 1881 and 1920, the Jewish population increased by 1,300 percent—eleven times as fast.

Like the German Jewish migration, they came in waves. Although there were many significant exceptions, one can generally assume that the first to uproot themselves were those with the least to give up, those with the least *Yichus*. (A term used by Jews denoting status derived from lineage and wealth.) These arrived between 1870 and 1900 and were followed in the next decades by Jews who had resided in larger cities, Odessa, Warsaw, Lodz, Cracow, and Vilna, which had offered them at least temporary security from the harshness of the depredations.[14] The later immigrants were economically more secure, often possessing important marketable skills, or, better yet, a measure of wealth which offered a certain immunity from the harsh condition of Jewish life in the East. Israel Zangwill, the novelist, who became director of the Jewish Colonization Society, thought them "the most civilized element in the whole immigration."[15]

In contrast to other immigrant groups, Jews migrated with their families. One out of every four Jewish immigrants was a child below the age of fourteen. Moreover, once he arrived he was less likely than other immigrants to decide to return. Such a decision was made by thirty of every hundred immigrants who arrived here, but among Jews only eight out of every hundred chose to go back. Usually these were very pious Jews who preferred to avoid the intense pressure for secularization in the New World. Of the three groups, Rumanian Jews were least likely to return to Rumania.[16] In its affirmative mood, the Jewish migration differed sharply from that of other immigrant groups.

For these provincial people who rarely passed beyond the radius of a few kilometers of their villages, the decision to travel beyond the ocean to start a new life must have been a momentous one. They came first to the town of Brody in eastern Galicia which had over the years become a processing center for Jewish immigrants. From there they were transported to Berlin or Breslau or directly to Hamburg where for $34 one could purchase a steamship ticket to the New World.

Amidst scenes of bewildering confusion they were again processed, this time by German officials who displayed little sympathy for them. "Baggage [was] thrown together in one corner of the yard heedless of contents," one observer later wrote, "those white clad Germans shouting commands, always accompanied with 'Quick! Quick!' "[17] The officious manner of the German officials tended to convert the immigrants into helpless children. It left an abiding bad feeling toward them which was reinforced when the immigrants encountered German Jewish officials, of similar ilk, at the other end of the journey.

The voyage, which took anywhere from thirteen to twenty days depending on the time of year, added to their discomfort and anxiety. For most it was an experience never to be forgotten. The primitive sanitary conditions in steerage, the crowding, the touch of seasickness must have made more than one immigrant rue the day he decided to uproot himself. What sustained many through the difficult crossing was the thought of the new life which awaited them in America. "In our minds," Cahan tells us, "we were coming to a country of wonders and mystery. I had imagined that all Americans were tall and slender and that all men wore yellow trousers and high hats."[18]

The processing immigrants had to undergo at Castle Garden at the tip of the Battery, and after 1891 at Ellis Island, was sufficiently grueling to dispel the idyllic image many had harbored about their new home. Ellis Island was soon dubbed *Trernindzl* (Isle of Tears) and protests about the processing flew hot and heavy. Immigration officials tended to be political appointees, often of the lowest caliber. At peak periods they were sometimes compelled to process as many as 4,000 immigrants a day, a load so staggering that it ruled out sympathy for the human being behind the tag each immigrant wore.

As part of his processing he was interviewed by officials from United Hebrew Charities and the Hebrew Emigrant Aid Society. Frequently the contempt these Jewish officials displayed for the "wild Russians" exceeded that of government officials. Emma Goldman, destined to become a leading anarchist, found the scene at Castle Garden appalling: "The atmosphere [was] charged with antagonism and harshness," she wrote in her biography *Living My Life,* "nowhere could one see a sympathetic face; there was no provision for comfort of the new arrivals. . . . The first day on American soil proved a violent shock."[19] Abraham Cahan whose expectations of the New World sustained him throughout the difficult crossing was also sadly disappointed when he arrived at Castle Garden: "My heart grew even heavier when they began to register us," he writes in his memoirs, "I felt we were being treated like recruits at a Russian summons for military service."[20]

There were nevertheless some exceptional officials who sympathized with the immigrants' plight. Among them was one, Philip Cowen, a German Jew in the employ of the Immigration Service, who gained a reputation for effectiveness in interceding with Federal officials for better treatment of Jewish immigrants. In 1905 he was given the opportunity to bring order to the chaotic immigration situation at its source, when Theodore Roosevelt appointed him to a special commission to investigate Russia's extrusion policy. Alexander Harkavy was another official who fell into this category. Editor of a Yiddish newspaper and of a Yiddish-English dictionary, Harkavy served as a HIAS agent on Ellis Island between 1904 and 1909. His attempt to humanize the processing procedure brought him to the attention of William Williams, then Commissioner of Immigration. Williams eased Harkavy's way in working some improvements, especially in the heartless deportation hearings for those immigrants who, for physical and other reasons, would never be able to support themselves in the new country. Often the target of bitter complaints by the Jewish organizations who were saddled with their support, these unfortunates were frequently weeded out and sent back to Europe. Harkavy arranged a screening procedure whereby obviously unfit immigrants would be weeded out at the port of embarkation, before rather than after they had made the difficult crossing. He also organized an immigrant employment bureau for those who reached America to prevent their falling into the hands of unscrupulous labor contractors who preyed upon the work-starved immigrants at dockside.

But when it came to finding a solution to the more deep-seated problems, like the dire poverty of many of the immigrants, men like Cowen and Harkavy could do little. The average Jewish immigrant arrived with less money and more dependents than the non-Jew. The need to find an immediate source of income was so compelling that he was forced to take almost any job which came along. He had not the financial resources nor the stamina to continue the journey into the interior. He settled in the port city often within a few miles radius of where his boat had docked. In effect, the transplantation, at least in its initial stage, often resulted in a worsening of his economic plight.

His problems in the New World were compounded by the difficulty of adjusting to a new life. Not only was the language unfamiliar, but the value system and the accelerated pace of life was loathsome, especially if he was an Orthodox Jew. Russia had not treated him kindly, but when he compared the new life to life in his little *shtetl*, the latter seemed infinitely preferable. The shock of transplantation and the sheer ugliness of the new environment lent to Old World life a golden glow. "I was seized with a longing for Slutzk," writes the poet Ephraim Listzky after spending his first lonely Sabbath in Boston. "In my mind's eye I saw it day and night, its streets, its houses, its people, its meadows, gardens and orchards—and it appeared to me like a heavenly city in an eternal world."[21] The writer, Anzia Yezierska, was saddened when, as a child, she viewed her new home from the vantage of an East-Side tenement window. "Where was there a place for me to play? I looked out into the alley below and saw palefaced children scrambling in the gutter. 'Where is America?' cried my heart."[22]

But if the scene which greeted the Jewish immigrant was grim, he also found things in it which raised his spirits. The heady atmosphere of freedom was everywhere. "I used to marvel how freely I could walk about," one newcomer wrote. "No policeman or gendarme stops me and brusquely demands to see my passport.... Jews speak whatever language they please in public, they wear whatever clothes they wish...."[23] There was something in the atmosphere, perhaps the feeling that hard work would be rewarded by advancement. There was the possibility of hope.

Jewish organizations played a special role in facilitating the movement of the Eastern immigrants. In 1882, representatives from the Board of Deputies of British Jews, the Alliance Israelite Universelle and a group of German organizations, soon to unify themselves by forming the Hilfsverein der Deutschen Juden (German-Jewish Help Association), met in Berlin to map a strategy for the mass population movement they knew was about to take place. Private philanthropic agencies also became concerned. One of the first in the field was the Baron de Hirsch Fund which, as has been pointed out, interceded with the Tsarist regime and proposed its own long-range solution to the Jewish problem. A subsidiary agency of the fund, the Jewish Colonization Society (ICA) established offices in virtually every major town of the Pale to facilitate resettlement. In Britain the Mansion House Committee was established for the specific purpose of helping those Eastern immigrants who chose Britain as a stopping-off place on their way to the United States. It was, however, the Jews of Germany who bore the brunt of the burden. By 1901 under the aegis of the newly-organized Hilfsverein, elaborate machinery was created to speed the immigrants on their way.

Paradoxically, organizations representing American Jewry were at first disinclined to involve themselves. But supplementary voluntary organizations, the hallmark of Jewish life, had since 1870 been active in easing the lot of the immigrants. The Hebrew Emigrant Aid Society and the Board of Delegates of the American Israelites were early in the field. They were aided in September, 1881, by a grant of $114,000 from the Baron de Hirsch Fund which helped weld several voluntary groups into the Russian Emigrant Relief Committee. For a time it filled the vacuum which the Union of American Hebrew Congregations seemed hesitant to fill. A program to process the immigrants at the docks, a function eventually assumed by United Hebrew Charities, was initiated. In February, 1882, Eastern Jews themselves entered the picture with the Hebrew Emigrant Auxiliary Society, headed by the beloved Michael Heilprin. At the same time a Hebrew Sheltering Society was organized to house and find employment for the new arrivals. Slowly a network of organizations assumed responsibility for settling the new immigrants.

Shortly before the expulsion of the Jews from major Russian cities in January, 1891, Russian Jews already settled in America established the Jewish Alliance of America for the purpose of extending aid to Jews remaining in Russia. Eleven months later the Baron de Hirsch Fund again stepped in to bring order to the chaotic overlapping of the volun-

tary immigrant organizations in the United States. All groups concerned
with the welfare of immigrants were convened and an umbrella organization, the American Committee for Ameliorating the Condition of
Russian Exiles, was established. A special fund of $400,000 was set up
to finance the relief effort. Thus, by the second decade of the mass
immigration, American Jewry, with a generous infusion of financial help
from abroad, had established an elaborate network of organizations to
smooth the transplantation of the Eastern immigrants. By 1897 an
omnibus agency, the Hebrew Sheltering and Immigrant Aid Society
(HIAS), which combined under one roof facilities for temporary housing, interpreters, legal aids, an employment agency, and even training
for new skills, was in existence. The finishing touch was achieved in
1900 when the Jewish Colonization Association (ICA), was joined to
HIAS to form HIAS-ICA. It has remained the principal Jewish agency
concerned with immigration.

We have seen that German Jewish organizations were reluctant to
assume responsibility for the new immigrants. The Union of American
Hebrew Congregations, early withdrew from the effort stating that it
"no longer assumes any charge of the subject of material aid for the
emigrants arriving in the United States."[24] They had grown suspicious
that the British, French, and German organizations were dumping the
Eastern immigrants on American Jewry without bothering to determine
whether they could support themselves. The immigrants themselves
were increasingly viewed as a permanent drain on hard-pressed charity
organizations. It may have simply been blind resentment which prevented American philanthropists from seeing that the nation's liberal
immigration laws, rather than Jewish organizations abroad, were at the
heart of the problem. There was little that could be done to stop a
determined immigrant from coming to America.

The resentment of the German Jewish community over the Eastern
immigration went beyond the high cost of maintaining it. Much of the
financial cost had in any case been footed by the Baron de Hirsch Fund.
It was traceable to class and cultural factors. Having but recently attained middle-class status, many of the German Jews were still too
insecure to accept with equanimity the rude reminder of their own
roots posed by the poverty and the distinctive Old-World character of
the Eastern Jews. By 1890 barely a trace remained of the old peddler
origins of these former immigrants. Many had moved to the comfortable
brownstone houses on the West Side of Manhattan. According to a
study based on the census of 1890, 40 percent of them had at least one
servant and 10 percent had three or more. The class gap between the
"uptown" and "downtown" Jews, 8 percent of whom were so dependent

that they were compelled to become domestic servants, usually to "uptown" wealthier Jewish families, was wide and deep. The Eastern immigrant often experienced his first taste of hostility from the original settlers on the day of his arrival, when he came in contact with German Jewish officials. That they would ultimately react was predictable. In the fall of 1896 a group of Eastern Jews protested against the overbearing behavior of the agents of the United Hebrew Charities organization on the docks. More importantly, Eastern Jews, we have seen, rapidly began to develop their own self-help agencies to ameliorate the condition of the new arrivals. "It is up to us Russian Jews to help our poor countrymen," one founder of the Hebrew Sheltering Society declared, "to keep them from being insulted by our proud brethren to whom a Russian Jew is a schnorrer [beggar], a tramp, a good-for-nothing."

Neither side could see the other for what it really was. The Eastern Jews, oversensitive and possessing an injured pride, saw only arrogance on the part of their mentors. The original settlers, most of German-Jewish background, were more concerned with operational efficiency than recognizing the humanity of the new arrivals, who seemed to them to be something less than sensitive human beings. The misunderstanding was overlaid by a clash of national temperaments, the conflict of Teuton and Slav played out in a Jewish context. One outlet was to develop abbreviated verbal slanders for each other. The German Jews became "Yeckers," or something worse, when anger was high and Eastern Jews became "Kikes" (after the many "kis" in their names), or "mad Russians" or "Hinter Berliners" for the Galician Jews. "It wasn't only the difference in our daily language and manner of speaking that got in the way," Cahan explained. "It was deeper differences in inherited concepts and customs that separated us. With the best of intentions in the world and with gentle hearts they, unknowingly insulted us."[25]

The problem of financing exacerbated the situation, especially after the depression of 1893 dried up some sources of philanthropy. Inland Jewish communities to which many Eastern Jews had been transshipped now began to consider the financial outlay required to support dependent Eastern Jews as a kind of unjust tax levied without their consent. In 1886 the Conference of Managers of the Associated Hebrew Charities passed a resolution condemning the transportation of paupers into the country. "All such as are unable to maintain themselves," the resolution read, "should be forthwith returned whence they came."[26] True to their word, the organization's agents recommended that 1,082 of the immigrants be returned in 1887, 1,396 in 1888, 1,118 in 1889, and 1,204 in 1890. But even such action was insufficient to stop the complaints, especially regarding the arrival of widows and children or deserted wives, all of whom, it was felt, were destined to remain dependent on charity.

Undoubtedly a certain proportion of the new immigrants were forced to depend on charity, especially in the initial period of adjustment. But there is some reason to think that, considering the number of immigrants involved, the German Jewish agencies' complaints may have been exaggerated and overlaid with hyperbole. The overwhelming majority of new arrivals wanted to work and were usually able to find employment in the expanding economy. It is estimated that only 5 percent of the newcomers turned to the agencies for help and the percentage declined after 1900. Of the 128,984 Jewish immigrants who arrived in 1905 only 10,015 depended on the relief agencies for help.[27] In 1906 United Hebrew Charities was able to note that the new arrivals appeared to be sturdier and that the number of applicants for assistance had declined. Apparently by that year the Eastern Jews who had arrived earlier were established enough to absorb much of the cost of maintaining the new arrivals, often their friends and family members.

Nor should we allow ourselves to fall into the error of assuming that the German-Jewish community in America allowed its distaste for Eastern Jews to interfere with the obligation it felt to help its religious brethren. True, they often did not display much grace in fulfilling their obligations, but in most cases they did what had to be done. Thus, when the Secretary of the Treasury sought to exclude Russian Jews under the 1891 law restricting immigration of those "likely to become public charges," American Jewish organizations protested vigorously against the Secretary's impending action. The regulation was never implemented against penniless Eastern refugees since Jewish charity agencies assumed responsibility in such cases. There were also people like Emma Lazarus, Henrietta Szold, Michael Heilprin, Kohler Morais, Jacob Schiff, Moritz Ellinger, and Benjamin Peixotto, who sympathized with the difficulties faced by the immigrants and who were able to ignore the cultural differences under which the human potential of Eastern Jewry was hidden.

The negative general reaction to the "new immigration" manifested itself fully in the 1890's and was not enacted into law until the 1920's. In the period of the 1870's and 1880's one could find surprisingly tolerant reactions to the pending inflow of Jews. In September, 1869, the *New York Herald*, having heard that San Francisco had organized a society to bring more Jews to that city, expressed its approval: "The Israelites prosper in this great and free country. . . . Let our rich Israelites bring their oppressed brethren to this new land of promise. Here at least they will be free men, and milk and honey will not be found wholly wanting."[28] A dozen years later the *Herald* was ready to acknowledge that some of the Jewish immigrants did indeed look "vicious." But it had not totally given up its belief that there was a vast potential in this human material: "Statistics have shown many times in the history of the world that the laws Moses left to his people have had the virtue of making the race peaceful and abstemious. Such virtues are admirable foundations upon which to raise the superstructure of ideal citizenship. They are virtues that might well be cultivated by the most American of Americans."[29] But in 1881 when the paean of praise was composed, few American newspapers were ready to share these sentiments. Ten years later they positively rejected them.

Nor could such singular examples of philosemitism assuage the growing apprehension of "uptown" Jews regarding the inundation. Having observed at first-hand the intense piety of the new arrivals and noted that sometimes it was converted overnight to an equally intense political radicalism, they despaired of the possibility of Americanizing the Easterners. They feared that the high visibility of the new arrivals would generate anti-Semitism and affect their own relatively secure middle-class position. That fear was manifesting itself especially in the larger cities of the Eastern seaboard, where a "critical mass" of Eastern Jews had developed sufficiently to generate its own distinctive culture. Resentment grew as the older community felt control slipping away from it. In 1880, for example, New York City had 85,000 Jews primarily of German derivation. Two decades later it had almost a half million Jews, only 20 percent of whom were of German origin. By 1914 the figure had declined further, to 10 percent.[30] Uptown Jews watched apprehensively as their city and community were metamorphosed from something they knew and loved to something that was strange and unattractive to them.

It was a reaction which resembled nothing so much as that of the nativist elements who also came to believe that the country was being taken away from its rightful owners. That was a prime motive behind their restrictionist sentiments. Yet for "uptown" Jews it was not so easy to divide the world they knew into "ours" and "theirs" because the Eastern immigrants were, in a sense, "theirs" too. Ultimately they set aside their conflicts and reservations and acknowledged the link to these strange newcomers. They made a clear choice to oppose the growing sentiment for immigration restriction.

CHAPTER IX

The Lower East Side: Shtetl *in Macrocosm*

FROM ONE POINT OF VIEW THE JEWISH COMMUNITY WHICH DEVELOPED on the Lower East Side was a collective expression of all those Old World *shtetlach* from whence the newcomers stemmed. But like many composite communities, its sum was greater than its parts. It was more than a mere physical environment in which Jews from Eastern Europe lived together. The Jewish ghetto was a "state of mind" and a strategy for survival.[1] At the root of its development there was the idea of easing the pain of accommodation, and that could best be done by the creation of a temporary transitional culture.

Ghetto culture wove the social and cultural threads of the old way of life into a new pattern. The *landsmanschaften*, the *shtiblach*, the *shuls*, the cafeterias, the benefit performances at the Yiddish theater, and the labor unions retained something recognizable of the old East European culture. But there was in them something distinctively new as well. It was an amalgam of religious and secular Jewish modalities to form a kind of *shtetl* in macrocosm. The life span of that distinctive culture was roughly one generation. Then it succumbed to the centripetal pulls of the new environment. As the immigrant became Americanized he no longer lived delicately suspended between two cultures. Ghetto culture left in its wake an afterglow which still weakly nourishes some elements in contemporary Jewry today. It is that culture which this chapter seeks to examine.

If the ghetto was a state of mind, it was more apparent to those observers who wrote about it *a posteriori*. For those who lived within its nucleus, a twenty-square block area south of Houston Street and East of the Bowery, it possessed a concrete, sometimes odoriferous reality. In the 1830's and 1840's the Lower East Side had been an ethnic enclave for German and Polish immigrants who settled in what is today New York's Chinatown. When the Eastern Jews arrived they pushed east into Division, Allen, Christie, and Henry Streets and north, to Stanton, Ludlow, Clinton, Attorney, Rivington, Pitt, and Houston Streets. These

Anglo-Saxon street names became the reference points in the block culture developed by the children of the ghetto. After 1865 the ghetto began to expand northward to encompass the older German Jewish settlement north of Houston Street along the numbered streets between Avenue A and B to Fourteenth Street.

The impoverished circumstances of the new arrivals made striking out into the interior, in the manner of their German Jewish predecessors, impossible. But that is hardly sufficient to explain the development of a distinctive new American-Jewish ghetto culture. Something also drew the new immigrants to these areas of primary concentration in New York, Boston, Philadelphia and Chicago. The small towns of the Midwest offered no bustling Jewish communities where one could comfortably worship in the manner to which one was accustomed and where one could speak the old language which came easily to the tongue. They did not offer a half-way house to the new culture. More important, the ghetto offered the possibility of employment by Jews. By 1890, 77.8 percent of the apparel industry was located below Fourteenth Street. It was that industry which was destined to play a key role for the new arrivals.

But if the social and economic adjustment was easier in the ghetto, its physical estate, especially its housing stock, was not sufficient to absorb the masive influx of immigrants. Sometimes idealized as thriving or bustling or even as possessing a "consumptive flush," the true hallmark of the ghetto was its congestion.[2] In 1904, 64,000 people were squeezed in about 5,897 tenements. The census of 1890 indicated that in the area below the Harlem River the population density was among the highest in the world, 143.2 people per acre. In some subsections of the Lower East Side it reached the astronomical rate of 986.4 people per acre. Only Bombay boasted a higher density in 1895.[3] When the population of the Lower East Side reached its peak of 542,061 in 1910 it was literally bursting at the seams.

Actually the extreme manifestations of congestion lasted only a short period of time. After 1901 new building codes which outlawed the dumbbell tenement began gradually to ease the situation. Rapid economic mobility which permitted the immigrants to move to Harlem or Yorkville and across the Harlem River to East Bronx or the East River to Williamsburg, Brownsville, and Borough Park allowed for a precarious balance between newly arriving immigrants and available flats. The completion of the Brooklyn Bridge in 1883 and the first interborough subway line in 1904 made these areas accessible. Everywhere the immigrants settled they established satellite ghettos which in vibrancy and teeming humanity emulated the distinctive character of the parent ghetto on the Lower East Side.

The influx of Jews also altered the character of the city. Not only the congestion but the babble of Yiddish complete with characteristic hand gestures, the distinctive dress of pious Jews, the thrust of commercialism, the hordes of unattended children on the streets, the appearance of Yiddish newspapers on the stands (with script reading from right to left) added something new and strange. Small wonder that when Henry James returned from Europe in 1907 after a long stay abroad, he was taken aback at the "extent of the Hebrew Conquest" of New York.[4] Like those German Jews who formed the core of the preexisting Jewish community, it gave him a feeling of having been dispossessed.

Had Henry James been interested he would have been able to note the effects of the new immigration on the economic life of the city. The apparel industry was the primary recipient of the commercial and craft skills possessed by the immigrants. Over 60 percent of the ghetto's working population was employed in some facet of this industry, whereas only 5.9 percent found employment in the construction industry, cigar making, or in some other trade. Fully 23.5 percent of the immigrant breadwinners found their way into some facet of business, whether as humble peddlers or "store princes." "De Ate," the largely Jewish 8th Assembly District, boasted 144 groceries, 131 butcher shops, 62 candy stores, 36 bakeries, and as many as 2,440 peddlers and pushcart vendors.[5] Some 1.4 percent of the work force was employed in servicing the religious needs of the community. They were *melamdim* (talmudic scholars), Hebrew teachers, cantors, rabbis, sextons, and ritual slaughterers. There was a growing representation in the professions as well.

Piety and poverty remained two of the most conspicuous characteristics of the new settlers. The piety of the ghetto dwellers had little of that mock sanctity and concern for decorum so noticeable among their "uptown brethren." Religion was simply part of their lives; it was taken for granted even among those who no longer believed.

Taken less for granted was the condition of poverty in which many of the immigrants found themselves. Jewish immigrants possessed a keen ambition to rise above their impoverished circumstances, and many ultimately did so. But in the early years of their new life most immigrants were poor, many of them desperately so. Strangely enough, in many cases their dire poverty stemmed not so much from a lower income but rather from the many things that had claim to part of that income. The Jewish wage earner was responsible for more dependents and assumed numerous additional financial responsibilities. In Orthodox homes it was not customary to allow the women of the house to supplement

the family income by working. Frequently a portion of the family income was earmarked to repay passage money or to save enough to
offer the same largesse to yet another relative anxious to emigrate. Sometimes savings from meager wages would be accumulated so that a little
business could be capitalized or to send a promising son to school.
Moreover, lack of familiarity with the cost of life in the New World
meant the immigrant overestimated how far his income could be
stretched. A wage of $5 per week seemed an incredibly high sum when
translated into rubles. Sometimes a boarder was taken in to lighten
the burden.

There is some reason to believe that the choice of becoming a small
businessman was less a reflection of the much vaunted Jewish love of business than it was a poor second choice for those who possessed no craft
skills which would give them a livelihood. Immigrants who possessed
skills were held in high esteem among their compatriots and were relatively well compensated. Conversely, to become a peddler held no great
honor. After 1880, when the sign—"no peddlers or beggars allowed"—
began to appear on the doors of private homes, the humblest cobbler
considered himself more fortunate. But for the "Eydems oif Kest," the
numerous scholar-grooms slated to be supported by their fathers-in-law
in the *shtetl*, who subsequently abandoned their dependent position to
seek their fortune in the New World, there was little choice. Peddling
still offered some opportunity to rise, especially if one became a "cus-
tomer peddler" with steady accounts. Then one could hope to become
a "store prince" in the manner of his German Jewish predecessor.

The reality of life in the New World hardly corresponded to the
idealized notion which many immigrants held when they mustered
their courage and energy to take the biggest step of their lives. True,
many opportunities awaited the newcomer, but life was also difficult.
Most people labored hard and long in the Old World but they had been
able to proceed at the more human pace of a preindustrial world. Here
working in a sweatshop meant payment by the piece which required
an inordinately fast tempo in order to earn a livelihood.

Frequently a loss of status accompanied hard work. A new immigrant
who held the highly esteemed calling of scholar or intellectual in the
Old World soon discovered that there was little "psychic income" to
be derived from such distinction in the new. The lowly wagon driver of
the old *shtetl* earned more and therefore achieved a status higher than
the scholar. Under such circumstances, memories of the real life in
the Pale were forgotten. It suddenly appeared to be a good life in
comparison. Articulate intellectuals gave vent to their resentment by
playing with the Hebrew words *Ama Reka*, which sounded like America,

but translated into Hollow People. Many immigrants sympathized with the bitter jest of a character in a popular Yiddish novel published in Warsaw in 1894: "Who ever asked him, Columbus, to discover America?"[6]

If it is true, as one author suggests, that the Jewish immigrant possessed no "sense of ease at living on this earth," then that was so because their life in the New World gave them precious little to be "at ease" about.[7] Yet Eastern Jews, especially the pious, brought with them their own notions of how one ought to live on this earth. Their sense of the good life derived from non-secular sources and contained elements of grace unavailable to the impious or the gentile of similar station in life. After the frenetic pace of the workday week, an observance of the Sabbath in which all physical exertion was prohibited, could be a welcome change. On that day even the humblest Jew considered himself a king. It offered an opportunity to reacquaint oneself with one's family and to enjoy the company of like-minded Jews in the synagogue. The Jewish religious calendar was marked with numerous religious holidays, each with its own set of symbols and ritual. That could add meaning to life, especially in a world of secularism which offered little to set the days and years off from each other. Orthodoxy offered a built-in social, intellectual, and, in many cases, an economic context.

Yet the number of Jews who chose to enter fully into the secular world, rather than to remain in the self-contained religious one, grew larger each year. The transplanting process caused an awesome wrench in the lives of the religious, and accelerated the craving for modernism already apparent in the Old World. Heretofore dormant ambitions were released in the New World where one could hope to rise. Under such circumstances, the need to pray three times a day, to wear certain types of clothes and cut one's hair in a certain way, the need to obey the stringent regulations of *Kashruth* (dietary observance) and the numerous additional regulations proved difficult to observe.

The problems of transmitting these customs to the next generation seemed virtually insurmountable in the New World. A pious Jew could follow the difficult path of Orthodoxy, but how could he compel the younger generation, subject to the full impact of secular values, to follow his example? The question of religious adherence was, in fact, frequently to be found at the heart of the generational conflict which characterized life among the pious. Unfortified by a commitment to religion and barely able to sense the advantages it held out for some, the young shed the old values at the earliest opportunity.

Everywhere in the ghetto one could encounter forces which worked to tear down the old religious spirit. Although religious Jews viewed the activities of evangelic missionaries with trepidation, they were in reality the least effective conduits out of the Jewish milieu. The instruments chosen for this work were usually converted Jews, many of whom had been attracted to Protestant missions by the need for money. They were treated with contempt even by the impious: "The converted Jews who preach," observed one reporter, "are followed by jeering mobs...struck and reviled...and spat upon."[8] Indeed, if the rabbis grieved on the one side because of the lack of religious observance among Jews, the missionaries grieved on the other for lack of success in converting them. "In all matters pertaining to their religious life...," one missionary complained, "they stand, the east-side Jews, where the new day that dawned at Calvary left them standing, stubbornly refusing to see the light."[9]

Reform Judaism might well have shared the missionaries' complaint. In 1903, for example, Dr. David Blaustein, director of the Educational Alliance, characterized the Alliance's religious program as being singularly free of "superstition" and "bigotry." (These were terms Reformists usually reserved for the Orthodox ritual.) But he was compelled to admit that in freeing the program from these two abhorrent characteristics he had also freed himself of any potential immigrant worshipers at the Alliance. The people considered it "no religion at all," he complained. "Our school is free, but the people will not send their boys to it. They prefer to pay $5 a month to send them to the rabbinical school."[10] There were 279 such schools, or *shtiblach*, on the Lower East Side in 1903 but they too could boast of little success with their charges. If the reformists were too modern, too un-Jewish, the Orthodox were too Old Worldly and too devout. The new generation would select a path in between the two extremes. That path would lead to the establishment of yet another branch of Judaism.

It is doubtful that the immigrants made a conscious choice about the role religion would continue to play in their lives. It was determined by a kind of calculus of pleasure and pain in which the intensity of the original devoutness played a major role. It could not, however, have escaped their notice that as one climbed the economic ladder fewer Orthodox Jews were to be encountered. Economic mobility and piety appeared to be almost mutually exclusive. Ambition to rise was perhaps the most important countervailing force drawing Jews away from Orthodoxy.

That drive also had a powerful impact on the stability of ghetto life. While there was a continuous influx of newcomers, there was also an exodus of those grown affluent enough to move to "better neighborhoods." There was, of course, a hard core of permanent settlers on the

Lower East Side, but much of the population was also in flux. Unlike other ethnics brought in by the New Immigration, Jewish sense of community did not include a territorial imperative. Jews learned to think of the ghetto as a temporary stopping place. Contemporary idealization of ghetto life tends to conceal the fact that the most pervasive ghetto dream may well have related to finding a strategy to leave the ghetto. The immigrants became the most avid believers of the American dream of success, and no price seemed too high to achieve it. That many converted their dreams into reality is reflected in the fact that after 1905 virtually all new immigrant workers found employment with "bosses" who were themselves former immigrants. They lived in tenements owned by Russian Jewish landlords. Often the employer and the landlord still retained the telltale signs of their own recent arrival. They served as constant reminders that success was within easy reach of all who dared try.

Of all the strategies to achieve success, formal education and professional training proved, next to a business career, the most attractive. The quest for education represented something more than hunger for success. The formally educated man has always been held in high esteem among Jews, perhaps uncritically so. Through education there was the possibility of earning psychic as well as economic gratification. Medicine, about which there is a special aura in the Jewish community, was a favorite choice of profession and law followed a close second. To become a doctor or lawyer often took the better part of a decade. Yet many were able to achieve it. In the decade after 1897 the number of Jewish doctors in the ghetto doubled and the number of lawyers increased almost as fast. The number of dentists and pharmacists increased even faster. By 1910 the ghetto boasted a relatively rich network of doctors and hospitals and even an independent medical society which published its own journal.

All forms of education and training were generally sought after. Of the 77 institutions of higher learning surveyed in 1908, 8.5 percent of student enrollment was Jewish. At the time they formed less than 2 percent of the population. A statistical breakdown of the Jewish student population shows 18 percent studying pharmacy and 13 percent preparing for law careers. Careers in teaching and dentistry were also popular. Naturally colleges in the New York metropolitan area were among the first to experience heavy Jewish enrollment. By 1888 each graduating class of City College contained 25 percent Jewish students, and of the 280 graduates of the New York Normal College, 50 were Jewish.[11] By the turn of the century, City College had earned the unflattering title of "Jewish College of America." But what the school lacked in ivy and in prestige, it made up in the vibrancy of its intellectual atmosphere. It was filled with keen Jewish students whose enthusiasm for intellectual pursuits was the source of much comment.[12]

The motivation for academic achievement was instilled by the parents. According to Mary Antin, Jewish parents brought their children to their first day of school "as if it were an act of consecration."[13] That concern was sustained throughout the child's school career. The public school teachers, who were usually of humble Irish origin, must have been a little overwhelmed to discover that Jewish immigrant parents considered them models for emulation by simple virtue of the fact that they were teachers. Teaching had always been considered a high-status profession among Jews. Jewish students maintained good class decorum and a high attendance record. Jacob Riis, who frequently viewed the Jewish condition in the ghetto with a jaundiced eye, waxed enthusiastic about the "ease and rapidity with which they [Jewish children] learn." It was equaled "only by their good behavior and close attention while in school. There is no whispering and no rioting at these desks ... as in the Italian ragged school."[14] A similar observation was made by a reporter for the *Evening Post*: "The rapidity with which these children acquire knowledge is a constant source of surprise.... Those who come in contact with them are continually amazed at the evidence of precocity they display."[15]

The public library was deluged by the new arrivals. "Lines of children reaching down two flights may not infrequently be seen at the Chatham Square branch...," one observer noted, "the Jewish child has more eagerness for mental food, it is an intellectual mania.... No people read so large a proportion of solid reading."[16] Indeed, in the circulation of books in the fields of history and science the libraries of the ghetto ranked first in the city.

After toiling a full day, immigrants frequently attended public and a growing number of specialized private evening schools. Free lectures, such as those sponsored by Cooper Union People's Institute, were packed to capacity by the culture-hungry East Siders. There was, of course, no special secret to account for their ready ability to assimilate formal learning except that they were highly motivated, sometimes unrealistically so. Suicides, normally an infrequent occurrence among immigrant Jews, were not unknown among disappointed aspirants for education.[17] The mania for self-improvement through education pervaded all strata of the Jewish population. If one scratched the lowliest worker or peddler one was likely to find a frustrated scholar. The hunger for education was a distinguishing characteristic of the Jews of Eastern Europe and is related directly to their rapid mobility.

Immigrant officials frequently remarked about the low physical state of the Eastern immigrants. Indeed, between 1887 and 1890, some 5,000 Jewish immigrants were sent back because in the judgment of these officials they were "unfit for work." It was believed that generations of physical disuse and poor diet had taken their toll by giving the Jewish immigrant a stunted appearance. But in the ghetto he proved to be a relatively hearty specimen. The mortality rate of 17.4 per thousand in the virtually all-Jewish Tenth Ward, was the lowest in the city according to the *Tenement House Committee Report of 1894.* In comparison, the Fourteenth Ward, populated largely by Italian immigrants, had a mortality rate of 35.2 per thousand. It seems clear that the oft-noted poor physical state of the Eastern immigrant may have been a reflection of the severe economic hardships and malnutrition experienced in the Old World. Perhaps some of it, too, was in the eyes of the beholder who generally found little to admire in immigrants.

Even the far from ideal environment of the ghetto was sufficient to create a remarkable difference in appearance between the immigrant generation and their American-born offspring. "The children," Cahan observed, "grew tall and strong and were better built than their parents. It was not uncommon to see a sixteen-year-old boy towering over his father."[18] Various theories have been advanced to account for the comparatively good health enjoyed by the Jewish immigrants. The ghetto boasted a fairly effective medical care network composed of private doctors, hospitals with special low-cost out-patient clinics and also pharmacists acting in the capacity of paramedical personnel. Jacob Riis attributed Jewish physical durability on the Lower East Side to the sobriety and temperateness of the Jewish immigrants. Except for an occasional religious ceremony, Jews rarely drank to excess. They preferred seltzer (an artificial carbonated drink) to alcoholic beverages. Nor were the sanitary facilities in the tenements they inhabited superior to those of other groups. Jewish men were addicted to the "schwitz" (turkish bath) and religious women were required to attend the ritual bath at least once a month. Together with certain religious dietary regulations this might have given some slight advantage in comparative health to Jewish immigrants. More likely is the fact that the negative judgments regarding the health of Jewish immigrants were culture-bound, based on superficial factors such as musculature, complexion, height, and general appearance.

If Jewish immigrants were less likely to succumb to tuberculosis and more likely to survive in infancy, they also had distinctive, if less serious, maladies. The reverse side of their sobriety and achievement orientation was a prevalence of maladies associated with severe nervous stress.

They were more subject to hypertension, neurasthenia, ulcers, facial tics, and other psychosomatic disorders. Venereal diseases, virtually unknown among Jews in Europe, also made their appearance among Jews in the new environment. Neurosis attendant on the stress of adjustment to the new way of life produced family disruption, juvenile delinquency, criminality, and mental breakdowns.

Particularly baneful was the inability of the immigrant generation to closely supervise their offspring as had been the custom in the *shtetl*. Here the children went to secular schools and used the congested street as their playground. Gang fights and exposures to street vice were the most obvious surface dangers inherent in the situation. It was a cause of great distress for traditionally-minded parents who watched helplessly as their children developed an ethos more suitable for survival on the streets. The new ethos often entailed breaking the cycle of religious adherence so that a pious father could no longer be certain that he would raise a pious son as he was commanded to do by Jewish law. It was this problem which often caused unhappiness, especially in Orthodox families.[19]

Life for the first generation of adolescents living with parents who could not see the need for a period of limited responsibility before the assumption of adult obligations, could be difficult. Child labor was common on the Lower East Side since the need for additional income was pressing. The small, crowded apartments offered few opportunities for the young to entertain their friends. Instead, much of the social life of ghetto youth was transferred to the teeming streets where they banded together in pursuit of their own interests. The values generated by this "street corner society" were sharply at odds with traditional Jewish values. The young, in effect, lived in two worlds. They were participants in the culture of the block but they also were compelled to attend some small *cheder* (one room school) to receive what passed for religious education.

Other strains on the traditionally close-knit Jewish family produced the highest divorce rate of the city.[20] Couples who may have led satisfactory lives in the static environment of the *shtetl* were likely to experience marital problems in the new environment where each partner adjusted at a different rate. Many women were quick to grasp the greater degree of independence permitted them in the New World, often to the dismay of their already hard-pressed husbands, whose status may have been previously undermined by the new order of things. Often a couple, reunited after a period of separation, found that their relationship had become insupportable. In the interim, the husband had assumed the trappings and values of an American. He discovered that the Old World garb and manners of his wife no longer suited his fancy. Husbands who preceded their wives to the New World sometimes simply forgot that they were married and took new wives.

In spite of the disturbing new influences, tranquility and order predominated in the ghetto and was a source of pride to the immigrants. Dean Howells noted with some amazement that despite degrading physical conditions, Jewish neighborhoods were orderly: "I saw none of the drunkenness or the truculence of an Irish or low American neighborhood among them [Jews]. There were no policemen in sight and the quiet behavior that struck me so much seemed not to have been enforced."[21] The immigrants placed an inordinate faith in law and the police whom they called at the slightest provocation. According to the census of 1890, Jews and Germans contributed less than their proportion of recorded crime, while those of Irish, Italian, and English extraction produced more. This does not mean that Jewish immigrants were always tranquil. In extreme situations such as the provocation which occurred during the bakers' strike of 1895 and during the struggle to organize the garment industry, Jews on both sides resorted to open violence.

The picture of a relatively crime-free Jewish community is idyllic in another sense. It applied primarily to crimes of physical violence. In 1898 Jews boasted the lowest crime rate in the nation for crimes like assault. But Jewish representation in commercial crime such as embezzlement, forgery, failure to pay wages, fraudulent insurance claims, and especially failure to heed the Sunday Laws was considerably higher. That the Irish police enforced these ordinances with zeal is attested by the high rate of indictments of Jews for violating corporate ordinances, 17.7 percent as compared to the national average of 12.3 percent.[22] Mary Antin describes the plight of her merchant father whose beach-front business was ruined by the enforcement of the Sunday Laws in Boston: "We had driven a feeble stake into the sand. The jealous Atlantic in company with the Sunday Laws had torn it down. . . ."[23]

The charge by several Progressive reformers that Jews were dominant in vice rings is more difficult to explain. When Police Commissioner Theodore Bingham, writing in the *North American Review* of September, 1908, assigned to New York Jewry the responsibility for generating 50 percent of the city's crimes, the emotional reaction was such that the outcry for the Commissioner's scalp was long and loud. Sensitive to the charge that vice existed among them, Jews naturally attributed such charges to the Commissioner's anti-Semitism. To be sure, Jews had learned from hard experience that certain government officials were not able to view the Jewish immigration objectively. George Kibbe Turner, a progressive reformer, was convinced that Jewish participation in the white slave trade was ruining the moral fiber of America, especially in its cities. Echoes of that charge found their way into the *Immigration Report of 1911.* "There are large numbers of Jews scattered throughout the United States who seduce and keep girls," the report read. It drew a picture of Jewish men of mysterious prowess in lovemaking who lured innocent girls into prostitution.[24]

Such charges revealed more about the Progressive patrician reformers who made them than about the actual vice situation in the cities. Many of these reformers had little love to spare for the Tammany-voting immigrants who crowded into city slums and seemed unwilling to assimilate to American life. The Jewish immigrant in particular assumed extraordinary dimensions; he was shrewd, mysterious, subversive, and lecherous. Hence the charge of vice against the Jews. For Jews such charges merely represented a sophisticated version of the same old anti-Semitism spewed forth under the guise of reformist rhetoric. For men like Turner, they reasoned, there was a need to view urban vice as a foreign import rather than a native product. The "New Immigrant" served as a foil. The net effect of these charges and the emotional reaction of the immigrants to them was to prevent an objective picture of vice in the ghetto from being drawn. Instead there ensued a battle of words and statistics which muddied the waters further.

Perhaps the reason why Jews reacted the way they did to Bingham's charges was that, underneath it all, there was a small element of truth in them and they were concerned about it. Discussions of delinquency and vice in the Jewish community were common fare in the Yiddish press and social service journals. The Lexow and Mayet investigation of 1894 and the Frank Moss study, three years later, found Jews, no less than other groups, implicated in organized vice. For those able to see, moreover, there was visible evidence of prostitution and protection rackets in the Jewish districts, as there was in every poor district in the city. Much of it came from outside the districts but some was bred at home. Most Jewish youngsters were undoubtedly as familiar with the names of Jewish gangsters like "Kid Twist" (Max Zweibach), "Yuski Nigger, King of the horse poisoners" (Joseph Toblinsky), "Dopey Benny" (Benjamin Fein), "Kid Dropper" (Nathan Kaplan), and "Gyp the Blood" (Harry Horowitz) as they were with the names of Jewish prizefighters who assumed Irish aliases in order to get into the ring.

Insecure and more accustomed to thinking about Jewish talent rather than vice, Jews reacted negatively to the charges. A few weeks after Turner's accusations were published in *McClure's,* Jewish authorities denied the allegation of a connection between the Jewish community and prostitution. A battle of statistics raged for months after the publication of Bingham's charges. One study of convictions in New York's Court of General Sessions indicated that Jews produced 50 percent less crime than other groups.[25] It did much to restore injured racial pride. But that was soon countered by the findings of the unfriendly Immigration Commission. These showed that Russian (i.e., Jewish) women surpassed all others in convictions for soliciting. Jewish pride received another mortal blow in July, 1912, when the revelations of the Rosenthal murder case were made public. Before he was felled by an assassin's bullet, Herman Rosenthal revealed the existence of a vice ring operating with police protection. With the exception of the police lieutenant involved and one hired gangster, all of the major figures involved were Jewish. After that episode one could deny the existence of vice in the Jewish community only by deliberately closing one's eyes to it.

Yet it was also true that vice and crime were confined to a relatively small proportion of the ghetto dwellers. Had the reformers bothered to observe it, they might have noted that typically the ghetto dweller was achievement-oriented, perhaps too much so. His primary goal was to "make it," to succeed, and for some the drive was so strong that the traditional sense of morality went by the board. Jews drawn to vice and crime were rarely burglars or "holdupniks." They eschewed crimes of violence. It may well be, as one author has suggested, that the crime of the ghetto represented merely the seamier side of the intense desire to rise.[26] They differed from their peers in business or in night school only in the unacceptable means they chose to employ. But after a generation there would be few to inquire by what means, fair or foul, they had risen.

Predictably, no one was more disturbed by the revelations of vice in the ghetto than the original Jewish settlers. When they viewed it together with the political radicalism of some of the immigrants, or their religious piety and their other idiosyncrasies, it seemed as if nothing less than a catastrophe had befallen them. "If there should grow up in our midst a class of people ... who ... adhere to customs and practices abnormal and objectionable to our fellow citizens," read the proceedings of the 19th annual convention of the Union of American Hebrew Congregations, "all of us will suffer ..., the question is largely one of self-preservation."[27] The more established original Jewish settlers sought to remold the new arrivals to save the community from the anti-Semitism which the "abnormal and objectionable" practices of the new arrivals were certain to arouse.

CHAPTER X

The Old and the New Immigrant: Conflict and Philanthropy

IT IS A TRUISM THAT AT THE ROOT OF MIDDLE-CLASS BEHAVIOR IS A STRONG desire to conform lest one lose respectability. New arrivals to the middle class appear to bear more than their share of concern for appearances. They want, above all else, to be acceptable and are often willing to go to extreme lengths to achieve respectability. They accept almost any cue received from the middle-class style-setters and opinion leaders. Imagine then the pressure on Jews who want to enter the middle class! They would be compelled to undergo a religio-cultural as well as normal class alterations. We have seen that the mainspring of the Reform movement was an attempt to assume respectability by adopting the trappings of acceptable modes of worship. Such people worried about decorum. Predictably, they were very much concerned with the arrival of their religious brethren from Eastern Europe, who in manners and dress were anything but middle class. Would these newcomers interfere with their headlong drive to achieve middle-class respectability?

The portents were not good. The coming of the Jews from Eastern Europe coincided in time with a rapid growth in nativist sentiment. It began in earnest during the period of the Gilded Age (1870–1880) and continued almost unabated into the first decade of the twentieth century. Its opprobrium was directed against all groups associated with the "new immigration." Sometimes nativism assumed a ludicrous form. Michigan, for example, found razors in the hands of the foreign-born to be a threat and prohibited them from becoming licensed barbers.

Naturally what disturbed Jews most was the strong anti-Semitic component of the new nativism which capitalized heavily on the Shylock image and stories of Jewish business chicanery. Some insurance companies discontinued selling fire insurance to Jewish businessmen. What most aroused the concern of the Jewish *arrivistes* was their gradual exclusion from the exclusive summer resorts, private schools, college fraternities, and desirable neighborhoods where the wealthy lived and fraternized.

[142]

The most celebrated case of exclusion occurred in the summer of 1877 when the Grand Union Hotel in Saratoga Springs refused to admit Joseph Seligman whose name meant wealth and class in the Jewish community. The event became a *cause célèbre* among Jews and sparked a boycott of the A. T. Stewart Company, a wholesale firm whose president, Judge Hilton, was associated with the Grand Union Hotel. The firm was forced into bankruptcy, but it was clear that economic coercion could not reverse the tide of exclusion, especially in the smaller hostelries which followed a restrictive policy. To the dismay of the "uptowners" it appeared as if nothing could be done to prevent their being barred from the acceptable middle class. In 1893, the Union League Club, which Jews helped establish in New York, closed its doors to them.

Moreover, such snubs were nothing compared to the physical assault experienced by Jews in the deep South during the 1880's. There, debt-ridden farmers stormed into towns to sack the stores of Jewish merchants. In 1893 nightriders burned dozens of farmhouses belonging to Jewish landlords in southern Mississippi as part of a drive to push Jewish merchants out of the area.[1] In 1913 the Southern brand of anti-Semitism culminated in the conviction for murder of a Jewish manager of a pencil factory in Atlanta, Leo Frank. When the governor of Georgia came into possession of evidence which clearly pointed to Frank's innocence, he commuted the sentence to life imprisonment. The mob thereupon removed Frank from his cell and lynched him.[2] Further north in New Jersey three days of rioting followed when Jewish workers were hired for the glass factory in Millville.[3]

While the "uptowners" blamed the immigrants for the unfortunate turn of events, the new arrivals, who did not visit fancy resorts or send their sons to exclusive schools, were not inclined to accept gracefully the guilt assigned to them. Compared to a pogrom, a residential covenant which prohibited Jews, or a policy of not accepting Jews at certain high-class resorts, were mild inconveniences. What were the rich Jews getting excited about and why did they want to hobnob with rich gentiles anyway? The resentment of the "uptowners" against them must have seemed greater than the resentment of the Christian community with which they had little contact in any case.

The *New York Times*, owned by rich "uptowners," was wont to complain about the stench of the ghetto. "Cleanliness is an unknown quantity to these people," complained one editorial. The editors were certain that these Jews could not be "lifted to a higher plain because they do not want to be."[4] The anti-Semitism faced by the "downtowners" was of an earthier variety. It consisted of Jew-baiting, which usually occurred during the high holy days, or sometimes of a direct physical confrontation, such as the attack on the funeral cortege of Rabbi Jacob Josef in 1902. The "downtowners'" reaction was different, more down to earth; perhaps because in the ghetto they formed a compact physical majority. Moreover, they probably did not expect better behavior from the Christian world. For the moment it was their uptown brethren who suffered most. The newcomers would become involved only when anti-Semitism affected them directly.

By 1890 several strands were discernible in the broadened anti-Semitic reaction. There was the original nativist sentiment rooted primarily in the discontent of the agricultural population. This was supplemented by the anti-Jewish antagonism of the displaced patrician class, of whom Henry Adams is a good example. Then there was the anti-Semitic feeling, of a different variety, harbored by the urban Irish who were in closest contact with the Jews. At the turn of the century, for example, Church officials forbade Irish maids to work in Jewish homes.[5] Still another strand furnished the intellectual rationale which made anti-Semitism respectable. Triggered by the Dreyfus Affair in France, certain European intellectuals developed the notion of a specific Semitic spirit abroad in the Western world. Jews were pictured to be pleasure-loving, indolent, and overly intellectual in sharp contrast to the spirit of Christianity which was ascetic, hard-working, and above all heroic. The work of Ernest Renan, Count Arthur de Gobineau, and Houston Chamberlain went far to make anti-Semitism respectable for all classes. They set the stage for forcibly separating the Jews from the Western culture of which they so much wanted to be part. But that would occur only four decades later.

Jewish leaders like Theodor Herzl and many established American Jews sought the cause of anti-Semitism in the Jewish people itself. That was one of the reasons they wanted to change the Jewish religio-culture. But in the American case there is good reason to believe that neither the conspicuous success of the German Jews nor the aberrant customs and appearance of the newly-arrived Jews from Eastern Europe were the source of anti-Jewish animosity. The embattled farmers of the West and South who projected their hostility on Jews during the 1890's had little direct experience with Jews. What the farmer wanted was a simple, all-encompassing, personalized explanation for the loss of his farm and for the loss of status in relation to other groups in American society, both of which occurred with distressing frequency. A Jewish conspiracy offered a simple explanation of the action of market forces which he barely understood. It gave him a personal, yet remote, object against which to vent his frustration.

Jews were not alone in feeling the farmers' wrath, nor were farmers the only group which used Jews as an outlet for their resentments. Throughout the 1870's and 1880's the railroads and middlemen, on whom farmers had become increasingly dependent, were blamed for their woes. Eventually they hit upon the banking system and government fiscal policy as an all-encompassing explanation for their troubles. There was just enough truth in each of these allegations to make them appear reasonable. Currency had contracted at the juncture when an increase in production and population required an increase in the amount of money in circulation. The farmer, who had borrowed heavily when the currency was relatively inflated, was caught in a deflationary cycle. He borrowed a cheap dollar and now discovered that he was compelled to pay back with a dear one. Farmers accepted the belief that a conspiracy existed to cheat them of their hard-earned bread by manipulating the currency. Currency inflation for the purpose of restoring to them what was believed to be rightfully theirs, became a principal plank of the Populist program.

Once they discovered the idea that a conspiracy existed to deprive them of their rewards through the manipulation of currency in circulation, it was but a short jump to fantasize about the "money changers in the temple." It was the Jews living in the hated cities from whence this conspiracy emanated, who were responsible for their woes. Were there not international Jewish bankers like the Rothschilds, Lazard Frères, Kuhns, Loebs, and Seligmans conspiring to take over the world? The idea of an international Jewish conspiracy, already common coin in Europe, now became a popular image in the United States.

The popularization of the image was aided by the writings of patrician intellectuals like Henry Adams. He placed a Jewish character, Hartbeest Schneider Koupon (coupon clipper), "decended from all the Kings of Israel. . . . prouder than Solomon in his glory," at the center of a novel he wrote anonymously in 1888. Soon the conspiring Jewish money prince became a stock character in dime novels. In his novel *Caesar's Column*, the Populist leader Ignatius Donnelly pictured a degraded society ruled by Jews, who, because of centuries of unjust persecution by Christians, were placed by God at the helm of society. But even that reason for the rule of what Donnelly called the "noble race" did not make it palatable to readers. In *Coin's Financial Conspiracy*, published in 1894, a map showed England as the center of the gold conspiracy, but in place of England the name "Rothschild" was printed in bold letters. The farmers' money difficulties were traced to the menacing character of "Baron Rothe'" in one popular novel by William Harvey and a popular magazine suggested that Baron de Hirsch influence his coreligionists to "loosen the coils about the money bags of the Wall Street bankers."[6] The image of a parasitical race who had accumulated wealth by illegal and immoral means made rapid inroads into the public imaginings.

Until recently it was assumed that the vehicle for proliferating such an illusion was Populist spokesmen who found that the conspiratorial view of the farmers' decline could easily be validated by underpinning it with the preexisting Shylock image of the Jews. Populist anti-Semitism was assumed to exist in virulent form by such historians as Richard Hofstadter, Oscar Handlin, Irwin Unger and, to some extent, John Higham. But that assumption has been challenged by another group of historians, including Norman Pollack, C. Van Woodward, Walter Nugent, and Frederic C. Jaher, who find little evidence to indicate that the Populists were more anti-Semitic than other groups in American society.

Nor was the conspiratorial image of a corrupting Jewry confined to America. It gained even wider currency in other areas of the world. When Moses Montefiore and Edmund Rothschild appeared at the Brussels Monetary Conference in 1894, it was taken as a certain sign that a conspiracy was in the making. Similarly when the Zionists held their first international conference in Basle in 1897, word spread that a plot to conquer the world was being hatched. An "invisible empire" populated by Jewish bankers was imagined to be at work behind the scenes. How else might one explain the fact that Austria-Hungary, Japan, and Russia had in the 1890's deserted bimetalism in favor of the gold standard, and all within a few years of each other? In America the equivalent was Bryan's sprinkling of his diatribes against the gold standard with Christian images. He was simply adding fuel to the conspiracy theory. When farmers, or their spokesmen, talked of crucifixion upon "a cross of gold," Jews predictably became wary.

Lest the picture become overdrawn, however, one should add that unfavorable stereotypes of Jews were frequently ambivalent as was the attitude towards Jews in reality. Nor was the unfavorable image universally shared. Ignatius Donnelly, for example, projected a rather heroic image of Jews. He employed a Social Darwinian rationale to explain their superiority. Centuries of persecution had honed their survival ability so sharp, that Jews had actually become more fit to survive.[7] Moreover, to balance the anti-Semitic sentiments of men like Henry Adams, Thomas Wolfe, and Edward Canning, there were community leaders like Henry Ward Beecher, Charles Henry Parkhurst, Josiah Royce, Nathaniel S. Shaler, Robert Ingersoll, George William Curtis, Oliver Wendell Holmes, and Mark Twain who were philosemitic. They often expressed appreciation for the leavening influence Jews had on

American culture. Some prominent authors like Lincoln Steffens, Hutchins Hapgood, and Dean Howells were drawn to the East Side, attracted by its electric cultural atmosphere. Lincoln Steffens became as infatuated with the Lower East Side as an Eastern boy with the "Wild West." "I went to the synagogue on all the great Jewish holydays," he relates in his *Autobiography*. "Yom Kippur I spent the whole twenty-four hours fasting and going from one synagogue to another. The music moved me most."[8]

Whatever the case may be concerning the rise of anti-Jewish feeling in the final decades of the nineteenth century, one thing seemed certain: feeling both against and for them had come to the fore. They had become a more conspicuous group and it was this fact which made certain members of the original American Jewish community more than ever anxious to present the proper appearance. The new immigrants would have to be made over.

We have seen that it was the established Jewish community which felt most threatened by the seeming loss of goodwill. But rather than attribute it to their own conspicuous rise, they preferred to believe that it was caused by the arrival of the new breed of Jews from Eastern Europe. They assumed that Americans would not differentiate between them and the new arrivals and that they were thus all being tarred with the same brush.[9] If one did the "right" thing, however, if one maintained the proper middle-class values and decorum, anti-Semitism would vanish or at least be mitigated. The way the new arrivals lived was wrong because it tended, they thought, to bring down the wrath of the larger community. "We belong to the minority, and the minority is always judged by its lowest representative," an uptown spokesman declaimed, "our great duty therefore is to raise our race...."[10] It had, according to the same spokesman, become "a question of self defense." Israel Zangwill's play *The Melting Pot* became immensely popular among the "uptowners." It proposed a solution. The sooner the new immigrants would give up their cultural characteristics and melt into the undifferentiated mass, the sooner anti-Semitism would disappear.

The uptown proselytizers soon discovered that molding this Eastern clay would be no easy task. Despite their poverty, the Jews from Eastern Europe were proud and hardly viewed the German Jews as a suitable model. They sensed that the position of the "uptown" Jews lacked a certain pride. Many chose to live in the ghetto because they hesitated to give up their culture, or at least wanted to abandon certain parts of it at their own rate. Having had more experience with the basic irrationality of anti-Semitism, they refused to accept the notion that certain actions or certain accommodations would solve the problem or satisfy their antagonists.

The problem was made complex by the wide cultural and class gap between "uptowners" and "downtowners." As recipients of "uptown" charity, East European Jews naturally resented the givers who even when they were not haughty seemed to look down on them. A German Jewish lawyer speaking before a cultural society composed of East European Jews thought he would begin his address by complimenting the audience. "Who would believe," he told them, "that this is a gathering of Russian Jews. Everyone looks handsome."[11] The speaker was pleasantly surprised. More often the decorum-loving German Jews were treated to blow-by-blow accounts in the press regarding Kosher meat wars or some other internecine dispute which the immigrants fought with great vigor and zest. It was all so embarrassing.

The politics of the new arrivals was found especially unsuitable by the more established settlers. They feared that the clannishness of the immigrants would be reflected in the formation of a political voting bloc. They had spent years assuring their gentile friends that no such cohesion existed among Jewish voters. The Zionism which some of the newcomers proudly displayed particularly rankled German Jews of the Reform persuasion. "Judaism must drop its orientalism and become truly American in spirit and form," the Reform leader Kaufman Kohler declaimed. "We cannot afford any longer to pray for a return to Jerusalem. It is a blasphemy and lie upon the lips of every American Jew."[12] More aggravating, perhaps, was the growing evidence of political radicalism among the new arrivals. It seemed to the "uptowners" that when the immigrants were not Zionists they deviated in the direction of anarchism or socialism. Apprehension about the loyalty of the Eastern immigrants was never far from the surface.

Immigrants dependent on charity caused hot resentment among older settlers, especially in the interior. "Were it not for the poor Russians," wrote the *Detroit News* on September 13, 1896, "...there would be hardly any need for Hebrew charitable organizations in the city...it is very rare that a German Israelite seeks relief from anybody...."[13] Such complaints were echoed in Syracuse, Milwaukee, Albany, Hartford, and other middle-sized American cities where Eastern immigrants had been settled. At times these Jewish communities went beyond mere complaining. In July, 1882, the Jewish authorities of Providence threatened to return two Russian immigrants for every one sent to them, insisting that they had all they could handle. Russian immigrants were variously accused of being lazy, shiftless, a curse, and underminers of the peace and tranquility of these Jewish communities.

Under such circumstances there was little social mingling between the two groups. The cultural and social clubs of the "uptowners" were "off limits" for the new arrivals who would have felt uncomfortable in them in any case. B'nai B'rith, which less than two generations earlier had been founded by German immigrants who lived in similar impoverished circumstances on the Lower East Side, now denied a charter to Polish Jews living in the same area because they thought them unfit to be members of that august organization.

Formal day-to-day contact in which the "uptowner" usually served in some official capacity, tended to exacerbate the bad feelings. Julia Richman, for example, who was well known in the ghetto for her lectures at the Educational Alliance and for the high position she held as an Assistant Superintendent of Schools, compromised her reputation for concern about the children of immigrants by her insistence on the rigid enforcement of the statutes against pushcart peddling by which many immigrants eked out a living. Laws were laws, she maintained, and should be obeyed no matter what the consequence. That lack of understanding on her part led Joseph Barondess, a popular labor leader, to petition the Board of Education to transfer "this self constituted censor of our morality and . . . patron saint of the slum dwellers" to another district.[14]

Amidst such group tensions there were some among the original Jewish community who were able to sense that beyond the strange appearance and behavior of the Jewish immigrants there lay a great human potential. Rabbi Leo Franklin of Temple Beth El in Detroit, where feelings seemed to have been particularly bitter, reminded his congregants that, as Jews, their first obligation was to help the unfortunate. "Oppression has temporarily taken the manhood out of the Russian Jews," he observed, "yet he is our brother . . . how dare we expect the world to look with unprejudiced eyes upon us so long as Jew stands against Jew."[15]

It was partly the desire to "Americanize" the immigrants, partly a residual feeling for *K'lal Yisrael*, the community of Israel, an example of which was given by Rabbi Franklin, which caused an outpouring of charitable aid from the established Jewish community. Organized charity became a principal bridge between the "uptown" and "downtown" wings of the Jewish community. In the minds of the philanthropists there was no conflict between the dual motivation which prompted their giving. To help these immigrants to become good Americans as quickly as possible would, they reasoned, be the greatest service they could perform for their religious brethren. The idea that the immigrants also possessed a cultural heritage worth preserving rarely entered their minds. The object was to make the Jewish immigrants over in their own image.

The program of the Educational Alliance was one of the major "uptown"-sponsored social and educational instruments designed to achieve this end. Its charter provided that the agency offer programs "of an Americanizing, educational, social and humanizing character...."[16] Predictably, the Americanizing aspect of the program became a bone of contention between the proud Yiddish-speaking ghetto intellectuals and the trustees of the institutions. Americanization in practice meant that English, German, and even Russian were employed in the various citizen education courses but Yiddish, the actual language of the ghetto, was not. It was considered to be an inferior form of German. By 1905 the situation had changed considerably. It was clear that the "uptown" Americanizers, rather than the ghetto dwellers, had been reeducated. Yiddish lectures on subjects as varied as American history, Bible history and Jewish philosophy, delivered by popular ghetto intellectuals, were presented side-by-side with programs in English and German. The program of the Educational Alliance eventually featured a complete offering of vocational training courses as well as free medical examinations, cheap wholesome lunches, and summer camps for ghetto children. As Eastern Jews began to play an important role in managing and funding the institution its far-flung program won great popularity in the ghetto. The Educational Alliance's somewhat aloof, outsider image began to give way to a warmer one by the turn of the century. The surest sign that resistance was melting came when ghetto dwellers began to fondly refer to it as "the Edgies." When ghetto dwellers used diminutives it customarily indicated love and familiarity.

The Education Alliance was but one of several institutions created to service the ghetto's social and vocational needs. The Hebrew Technical Institute, sponsored by the Baron de Hirsch Fund, taught useful trades to ghetto youth. A matching institute for girls taught domestic arts. (Its charter stipulated that 10 percent of the student body must be composed of Christian girls.) Another agency which taught vocational skills was the Hebrew Free Trade School Association which was sponsored by United Hebrew Charities. In addition, a number of agencies were established to help ease the difficult transition to which immigrants were subject.

The increased services for the newcomers were reflected in ever-rising budgets of the philanthropic institutions. As early as 1880 an additional $46,000 was required to supplement the budget of the United Hebrew Charities. After that year the budget rose by leaps and bounds until, in 1895, in the heart of the depression, it reached the then astronomical sum of $116,000.[17] This did not take into account the efforts of individuals to better conditions in the ghetto. Thus Isaac Seligman used his own knowledge of the construction industry and his own funds to build a model tenement on Cherry Street in 1885. The city's first kindergarten was founded on the Lower East Side by Felix Adler and proved to be a boon for the beleaguered families of the ghetto.

Of all the social agencies in the ghetto undoubtedly the settlement houses, which made their debut in the 1880's, proved to be most beneficial. Not exclusively an outgrowth of established Jewish philanthropy, the settlement house proved to be especially useful in offering productive activities for the ghetto's unsupervised youth. They were prey not only to silent street wars between rival gangs but also to ghetto vice which was visible everywhere. The most important of these houses, the Educational Alliance, actually moved beyond mere social work. It became an intellectual and cultural center for the ghetto. Other settlement houses furnished similar activities, each possessing its own personality.

In 1886, the Neighborhood Guild, known after 1891 as the University Settlement House, was established at 147 Forsythe Street, in the heart of the ghetto. In 1903 it was moved to the corner of Eldridge and Rivington Streets, where it soon became a familiar sight to ghetto dwellers. It was directed by Dr. Stanton Coit, a leader of the Ethical Culture Society, which, ghetto rumor had it, served as a kind of halfway house for upper-class Jews who wanted to be rid of the burden of their Judaism. In 1893 it was joined by the Nurses' Settlement founded by Lillian Wald and Mary Brewster. It was soon dubbed the Henry Street Settlement after the street on which it was located. It was joined in a few years by the Madison Street Settlement House and other smaller enterprises.

Aside from helping to solve the myriad social and economic problems which beset the slum dwellers, the social workers offered a model with which ghetto youth would ordinarily not have come in contact. Often stemming from patrician Jewish and Protestant backgrounds, these social workers were imbued with the concept of service to the less fortunate. In many ways they represented the finest human resources America had to offer. Their influence on ghetto youth was an unforeseen dividend, as was the challenge they posed to the corrupt practitioners of local machine politics. An experience in settlement-house work often proved sufficient to convince these social workers that the ameliorative work in which they were engaged was futile if it was not accompanied by structural changes in the society which could be achieved only through political action. It was no mere accident that former settlement-house and social workers like Herbert Lehman, Henry Morgenthau Jr.,

Belle and Henry Moskowitz, Gerald Swope, Joseph Proskauer, Eleanor Roosevelt, Frances Perkins, and Harry Hopkins became known as political activists in favor of humanitarian change. Their influence was felt first by the local ward heelers of the political machine. In some cases they made their weight felt on the state and national level.

Belle Moskowitz, "the woman behind Al Smith," and Harry Hopkins, who played a similar role vis-à-vis Franklin Roosevelt, carried their enthusiasm for social reform to the highest levels of political power. The former was responsible for much of the pioneering program of social legislation passed during Smith's tenure as governor of New York and the latter played a key role as dispenser of Federal relief as administrator of the Federal Emergency Relief program. On the precinct level the settlement house made obsolete the services by means of which the local political machine gained the goodwill of the immigrant voters. The settlement house extended the same services and aid without demanding political loyalty in exchange. To some extent, they became an alternative to the Irish-dominated political club which was anathema to many Jews because it reeked of corruption.

The most important self-help institution in the Jewish community emanated neither from "uptown" Jewry nor Protestant patricianism. The *landsmannschaften*, a widespread network of mutual aid societies which formed the core of the ghetto's social organization, was an indigenous creation. They took their names and, in the initial stages of their development, their membership, from the East European towns from whence the immigrants originated. Often they began as smaller *vereins* or *chevras* which were linked to the numerous religious congregations on the Lower East Side. One of the earliest officially registered *landsmannschaft* was the Bialystok Mutual Aid Society which was chartered in 1864. By 1877 there were 22 major societies in existence and dozens of smaller *vereins*. At the height of their popularity in 1910 it is estimated that a half million immigrants belonged to them. Some of them merged with national fraternal orders such as the "Workmen's Circle" which came to the fore after 1900. Others jealously maintained their organizational integrity, often assuming insurance and medical-care functions.

The *landsmannschaften* seemed to spring up spontaneously to fill a need of East European immigrants for closer social relationships. Naturally such relationships were formed most readily with the *landsleit* (compatriots) from the old country. Jews apparently were the only immigrant group who generated a social infrastructure above and beyond its power-oriented labor movement, to concern itself with social service functions. The societies offered burial functions including plots and funeral benefits, insurance and credit facilities, health services and social and recreational functions. Frequently it also served as an informal employment agency. A newly minted "boss" turned naturally to the *landsmannschaft* to find a likely *landsmann* to work in his shop.

Strong ethnic and religious ties also spurred the establishment of special hospitals, orphanages, nursing and old age homes which offered Yiddish-speaking doctors and adherence to dietary laws. Beth Israel Hospital was established in 1890 and was followed by the Jewish Maternity Hospital and Lebanon Hospital in the Bronx. In the decades after 1900 virtually all neighborhoods of the city where Jews lived had their own Jewish hospital. In addition, new synagogues, yeshivas, political organizations of various complexions, labor union locals, philanthropic organizations had sprung up. There was even to be an attempt by the Jewish community at ethnic self-government. It is no exaggeration to state that by 1910 the East European Jews in America possessed the most elaborate organizational structure of any ethnic group in the nation.

One response to the social problems which came in the wake of ghetto congestion was the attempt to disperse and then to deflect the immigrants to the interior of the country. A subsidiary drive, but one that was directly related to this strategy, was the attempt to create a class of Jewish farmers.

The idea of dispersion was probably as much related to the feeling that the nexus of related characteristics created by the existence of a critical mass of Jews in the ghetto was a roadblock to Americanization, as it was to the feeling that ghetto crime and vice were related to the congestion of the ghetto. Dispersal of the East European immigrants into the interior, where they would be unable to depend on a Yiddish-speaking community would force them to learn more rapidly the language and ways of their adopted country. "Uptown" philanthropists viewed the ghetto as a foreign enclave which tended to perpetuate a foreign life-style. Americanization was possible only where American models were visible. They were rarely to be found in the ghetto.

Similarly, the idea of making Jews into farmers related partly to a dissatisfaction with the Jewish character. Like other philanthropic schemes the desire was not only to Americanize the subjects but to rid them of their class character which was thought to be unbalanced. Jews produced too many merchants and virtually no farmers. Philanthropists were not alone in holding to the idea that contact with the soil would produce a spiritually more wholesome people. Steeped in the Tolstoyan-narodnik tradition which idealized the simple rural life, many Russian-Jewish immigrants were prepared to join forces with the philanthropists, albeit for different reasons. Both groups were oblivious to the fact that the nirvana they sought was no longer available in agriculture. Farming was being rapidly transformed so that it actually required many of the talents of the businessman to thrive. The sturdy independent yeoman who was to serve as the model for remolding Jews had been forced to retreat to the backwaters of history.

Nevertheless, dispersion and agricultural conversion were implemented. In 1882, 2,617 immigrants were sent to 166 different localities in the interior. We have already mentioned that the result led frequently to the hostility of the established community who considered the newcomers to be a burden. Despite the difficulties plans to disperse Jews into the interior continued to be made. Also it was felt that if the influx of East European Jews could be kept moderate, conflict between Russian and German Jews in middle-sized cities could be muted. Thus in 1890 a new organization, the Jewish Alliance of America, was created with the special task of aiding the dispersion.

By 1900 an alarming report of the consequences of congestion issued by the United Hebrew Charities resulted in a more serious consideration of the dispersal idea. B'nai B'rith, now a major national organization, became convinced of the need for dispersion. The Baron de Hirsch Fund, whose activities had encouraged immigration, now directed its energies to the ghetto problem. It brought the Jewish Colonization Society (ICA), which for a decade and a half had been involved in resettling East European Jews, to the United States where it adopted the name Jewish Agricultural and Industrial Aid Society. (The word Industrial was dropped in 1922.) Primarily interested in bringing Jews to farming, the Society undertook to help finance 161 agricultural settlements in the United States. Dispersion would be a byproduct of these ventures.

The dispersion movement gained additional momentum in 1901 when a coordinating agency, the Industrial Removal Office, was established. Using the local branches of B'nai B'rith and other Jewish organizations as a base of operations, the agents of the new organizations would search out employment opportunities and otherwise endeavor to ease the infiltration of immigrant Jews into communities of the interior. But despite the considerable energies and funds expended the dispersion effort hardly dented the pattern of Jewish settlement which continued to favor the cities on the Eastern seaboard, especially New York. By 1901, 59,729 Jews had been resettled in 1,474 communities in every state in the Union.

In many cases the unhappiness of the resettled immigrants matched that of their hosts. "Brethren, no matter how bad conditions are in

Russia," one resettled soul wrote, "they are worse in Detroit."[18] Some
began to wonder if dispersion was a workable or just solution. The
director of the ITO (Jewish Territorial Organization), Israel Zangwill,
who was formerly a strong advocate of dispersion, changed his mind
when he realized how the immigrants must feel. "Let your millionaires
move to other cities," he imagined the immigrant saying, "I possess only
my Jewish atmosphere."[19]

But for the "uptown" advocates of dispersion, there was something
inherently attractive in tucking away an unseemly group in some remote
corner of the country. Ever bolder dispersion schemes were implemented. When, in 1906, Frank Pierce Sargent, the Commissioner General
for Immigration, suggested a scheme to deflect the immigrant stream
away from the Eastern seaboard to ports along the Gulf of Mexico,
Jacob Schiff was impressed enough to contribute $500,000 to put the
Galveston plan to work. By 1914, perhaps 10,000 additional immigrants
had been dispersed into the interior in this manner.

But rather than giving the breath of life to the dispersion idea, the
Galveston scheme seemed more like its death rattle. As early as 1907
the Industrial Removal Office admitted the futility of removing people
who did not want to be removed. "If mere enthusiasm were the proper
rule for the success of our work," the report read, "it would certainly
proceed apace. But when the real facts are faced it becomes at once
apparent that no wholesale solution of our problem is possible."[20] Ultimately perhaps 100,000 East European immigrants left the crowded
ghettos of the East, mostly under their own steam. Rather than proving
attractive to indigent immigrants, relocation in the interior appealed to
small businessmen who saw in cities like Cincinnati, Cleveland, St.
Louis, Detroit, and Los Angeles an opportunity to enter into small
business. Perhaps as many as 35 percent of those who ultimately chose
to uproot themselves again were composed of these businessmen. Rather
than grandiose hopes about renewal through farming or labor, it was
the traditional petit-bourgeois motivation, so widespread among Jews,
which convinced a small portion to strike out anew.

In its broad outlines the story behind Jewish farming bears a parallel
to the dispersion effort. It was encouraged by philanthropists for ulterior
motives, proved difficult to implement in practice, and in the end had
to be abandoned as impractical. The sixteen ventures in establishing
agricultural settlements after 1881 were all doomed to fail.

Although it is commonly associated with Russian Jewry, the dream
of converting themselves to tillers of the soil has respectable American
Jewish antecedents as well. There were proto-Zionist ventures in creating
farming settlements by American Jews in 1819, 1826, and 1837. By the

time the East European Jews were ready to try their hand at agriculture these unsuccessful ventures were only dim memories.

Jewish farmers were not the only agriculturalists who failed after 1881, but there were specific reasons why their chances for success were limited. Most of the collective ventures were hastily planned under great stress. Little attention was paid to such factors as proximity to markets, quality of soil, and the spiritual and physical fitness of the participants. The settlements were usually underfinanced, poorly led and administered, and subject to internal social stress. For instance, one of the first settlements established in 1883 and located between Little Rock and Memphis, was apparently purchased sight unseen. It turned out to be located in the midst of a forest with no access to a market. Furthermore, there was prevalence of malaria and yellow fever in the area. The settlement lasted but six months before the 150 settlers fled for their lives.

Sometimes the vagaries of weather took their toll. The Am Olam settlement on Sicily Island off the coast of Louisiana was ruined by flood. The settlements in South Dakota, Cremieux, Bethlehem, and Yehuda, were subject to hail storms, followed by drought and prairie fires. The settlement in Colorado was also wiped out by a prairie fire. The "lost" colony of Bersheba which sustained itself on the rolling plains of Kansas for four years between 1882 and 1886, was finally ruined by a combination of disasters, including a man-made one which created acute social tensions among the settlers. Among the factors causing the final demise of the New Odessa colony in Oregon was the scarcity of women.

As much as Jews might believe in the spiritually renewing properties of farming life, few possessed the mental set required to follow it. For the majority of East European Jews, farming was associated with the depressed life of the serf-peasant of rural Russia. Farming smacked of downward mobility. They had little familiarity with the relatively high-status American farmer who combined the qualities of tiller of the soil with the good sense of the businessman. It was therefore not surprising that even the highly motivated Am Olam group found the realities of farming difficult to adjust to. Many were intellectuals who found tilling the soil monotonous, back-breaking labor. They had idealized agriculture and now they found little that was ennobling about it. These Jewish intellectuals possessed none of the peasant passivity and fatalism which made such a life easier to bear. Some soon left the commune and turned to peddling. "We came to lead a quiet, honest and independent life as Jews and as free citizens," complained a disillusioned member of an Am Olam settlement, "instead we have to live in filth and tumult and eke out a living in petty, beggar-like trades. . . ."[21]

Only those settlements in southern New Jersey, Alliance, Carmel, Woodbine, and Rosenhayn, which were located near the large urban markets of Philadelphia and New York and modified their collectivist organization in favor of individual enterprise and cooperative organization, seemed to possess any staying power.[22] Such flexibility and good fortune were rare. It would take more than dispersion and the farming life to restructure Jewish character. Jewish destiny in America seemed irrevocably linked to the urban scene.

The actual contribution such farm colonies made to relieving ghetto congestion was infinitesimal. By 1900 there were perhaps 1,000 Jewish farm families and by 1908, perhaps 2,409. In 1909, the peak year, it is estimated that there were 3,040 Jewish farm families in the nation, a total of 15,000 people.[23] Even such meager results entailed considerable organizational effort. The Jewish Agricultural Society established a rural sanitation commission and planned many of the agricultural enterprises with the people involved. It also published a newsletter, *The Jewish Farmer*, which contained not only helpful marketing and crop hints but also news regarding Jewish agriculturalists in different parts of the nation.

In the last decades of the nineteenth century the established Jewish community reacted to the influx of their East European brethren with something less than a friendly welcome. Triggered by anxiety over an increased anti-Semitic sentiment among the general population, they sought, by a series of poorly planned haphazard programs, to remold their coreligionists as rapidly as possible. Theye were convinced that "Americanization" would be in the interest of the immigrants too and rarely sensed the cultural arrogance involved in their posture. What was needed to achieve the goal of remaking the immigrants was a massive social engineering effort and for this they lacked the knowledge, the finances, and the coercive power. The programs they did sponsor—settlement houses, vocational training, dispersion to the interior, and agricultural resettlement—were random and haphazardly planned. They had little effect in changing the life patterns of the Jewish immigrants. They continued to develop their own peculiar version of ghetto culture which was neither completely European nor American, but somewhere in-between. With time, however, the American component would gain the upper hand, but it would never win a complete victory. The ghetto proved to be a rich source of new organizational forms among which the *landsmannschaften* were significant. But of all the organizational adaptations to America the Jewish labor movement was to have the most far-reaching impact.

CHAPTER XI

The Making of the Jewish Labor Movement

MOST EAST EUROPEAN JEWS BECAME WORKERS AND IT IS IN THE CONDITION of their working lives that the historian finds a key to the development of American Jewry in the twentieth century. The Jewish labor movement, the principal institution developed by East European Jewry in America, was forged on an anvil uniquely Jewish and American. Its development is evidence, even for the most skeptical, that the Eastern Jewish-American amalgam was a stable one.

Considering the petit-bourgeois character of the East European Jewish immigrant and his tenuous relationship to the factory system, his development of a working-class consciousness seems anomalous. There was little that predisposed these independent artisans and petty merchants to such consciousness. Then how did it develop? It stemmed in part from the conditions to which the Jewish immigrant was subject in the new environment and partly from the activities of a small group of radical intellectuals who made him aware that he was a member of the working class. Paradoxically, this group itself stemmed from middle-class backgrounds and possessed middle-class aspirations. But they became so imbued with the anarcho-socialist critique of capitalism that they successfully transmitted their reasoning to large sections of the immigrant population. Their rationale was accepted because, temporarily at least, it seemed to correspond to the immigrants' condition and interest. The route by which the Jewish worker came to the American labor movement thus differed markedly from other groups. He was organized from the top down and carried an ideological cargo rarely found among American workers.

Another factor which distinguished the Jewish labor movement from the general American one was the fact that its struggle to organize and improve the lot of the workingman occurred almost entirely within a Jewish economic ambience. It would be that remarkable group of successful Jewish entrepreneurs who would be challenged by Jewish workers led by a no less remarkable group of Jewish labor organizers. It would lend a special bitter-sweet flavor to their conflict.

Most important, however, in giving the Jewish labor movement its unique character was the raw human material of which it was composed. Sixty-four percent of the Jewish immigrants who arrived between 1900 and 1925 were skilled craftsmen, rather than simple factory "hands" (compared to 8.5 percent for the comparable non-Jewish immigrant group). In Europe these craftsmen customarily combined entrepreneurial and craft skills. They were independent tailors, cobblers, itinerant metalsmiths, butchers, bakers, and makers of religious articles. Once settled in their new homes many soon discovered that such a fortunate combination of being both worker and entrepreneur was not possible in the more industrially-advanced world of America. Fully one-third of these craftsmen were displaced and forced to seek other means of making a livelihood. Many found such employment in the garment industry which was readily accessible through an ethnic bridge as well as geographic proximity. By 1900, 85 percent of the production of men's clothes and 95 percent of women's apparel was being produced by Jewish manufacturers.

Historians of Jewish labor have speculated that it was the Jew's poor physical condition combined with bad working situation which caused his unhappiness.[1] More likely, the socialist rhetoric, which came so easily to his lips, was caused partly by his precipitous displacement and subsequent loss of status. In the "Old World" the idea of a trade was held in high regard. "A trade is a kingdom," descries a Jewish proverb. It was also a far cry from being merely a "hand" in a shop, a position which he was frequently compelled to take in the new country. Despite his unhappiness and unfamiliarity with the factory system, the Jewish immigrant earned a reputation as a good worker. The 17th annual report of the United Hebrew Charities issued in 1891 spoke of the employers' general satisfaction with these new workers. As immigrants with even higher skills arrived, management satisfaction grew apace.[2]

To be sure, the feeling of Jewish workers for their jobs did not usually match the satisfaction of the "bosses." "There was no one who liked his work," observed one worker, "all hated it and all sought a way of being free of it. All looked upon the boss as upon their enemy...."[3] But rather than sparking a feeling of solidarity with his fellows and suggesting the idea of unionization, the solutions sought by the Jewish worker often were more in the direction of rising above his class rather than with it. He was an upwardly mobile worker who tended to view his sojourn in the shops as temporary. He might momentarily sympathize with the socialist intellectuals who spared no effort to inform him that he was the source of all value, but in his heart of hearts he continued to view success in petit-bourgeois terms; he wanted a shop of his own. He was receptive to the Jewish radical's creed but not to his goal.

The immigrants' strong motivation to achieve made the Jewish labor movement largely a one-generation phenomenon. The Jewish worker was neither the son of a worker nor would he produce a son who was a worker. Middle-class aspirations required that he earn more. A son's education could mean a longer period of dependency in which potential income for the family was not available. As a rule marriage for a Jewish woman meant an end to her career as a worker. As the day of marriage approached, she trundled her machine to the middle of the shop floor, a symbol that her shop days were over.

The arrival of masses of new immigrants served as a prod to achievement. While it is undoubtedly true that immigration tended to depress wages it also had the effect of improving the mobility of more seasoned workers. The new inexperienced arrivals served as an under-class which gave the older immigrant opportunities for supervision and perhaps a motivation to use this available cheap labor in his own business. The latter alternative, the temptation to join the ranks of the numerous contractors, was always present. It required hard work and the scraping together of a little capital out of his own meager wages. The effects of such ambition could be drastic: "Over and over again," observed Jacob Riis, "I have met with instances of these Polish or Russian Jews deliberately starving themselves to the point of physical exhaustion while working night and day at a tremendous pressure to save a little money. An avenging nemesis pursues this headlong hunt for wealth and there is no worse paid class anywhere."[4] When Max Pine, Secretary of the United Hebrew Trades, enthusiastically broached the idea of an eight-hour day to an audience of Jewish workers, he noticed to his chagrin that they remained largely unmoved. After the talk one worker approached him to explain: "These ignorant asses just don't understand that if we succeed in working shorter hours, then we can work for two bosses; eight hours for one, eight hours for the other, and double our pay. . . ."[5] Such was the attitude of many a Jewish worker. In season he toiled fourteen hours a day, six days a week. Accustomed to piecework, the idea of maximum hours and minimum wages eluded him. It was this gluttony for work, according to Morris Hillquit, which made the Jewish worker so submissive and listless and therefore difficult to organize.[6]

But in the objective situation of the Jewish worker, good reasons for becoming organized were also present. There was a social vacuum left by the process of transplantation; conditions of work in the garment industry were uniquely miserable; and, most important, there existed a group of self-conscious radical intellectuals whose world view assigned to working people an especially high place and a special role as societal change agents.

The need for community, for the fraternity of men of similar station and circumstance, is an important element in any human organization. It was especially important for the new Jewish worker because his isolation stemmed not only from his work but from his being uprooted and settled in a strange social milieu. For Jewish workers the union hall became the secular equivalent of the Beth Hamidrosh, the house of prayer and learning in the *shtetl,* where he could fraternize with his fellow townsmen. The Jewish labor unions came to serve, not only as social moorings in an alien world, but also as a new container for the old messianism which Jews traditionally possess in good measure. The assumption that progress toward a new and better order of things was possible, became an article of faith for many Jewish workers. It almost seemed as if they were acting out on the temporal scene the search for justice and righteousness implicit in the Judaic faith many had just abandoned. When strikes occurred, the issues were rarely simply a question of "bread and butter" as it was for the American Federation of Labor. Jewish unions planned to educate, to uplift the worker and to make him into an actor in the drama of history. With such ideological zeal and sense of mission every strike, no matter how small, tended to turn into a struggle for "a new day."

The intense ideological climate brought out the best in the leadership and the rank and file, but it proved to have disadvantages as well. It was difficult to keep the budding locals on an even keel. They tended to burn themselves out after each strike and had to be reorganized from scratch. Intense emotion could not sustain itself over a period of time.

If the union hall offered a kinship formerly associated with the House of Prayer, the radical intellectuals who assumed a key position in organizing the Jewish labor movement, played a role analogous to the rabbi. For many socialism became the new orthodoxy: "I am a Socialist," writes a new convert to the "Bintel Brief" section of the *Forward,* "my boss is a fine man. I know he's a capitalist, but I cannot hate him. Am I doing the wrong thing?"[7] One still needed to know the rules of the newly adopted faith and follow them undeviatingly just as one did the *Halacha* (the myriad regulations of Orthodox Judaism) in former times.

The low propensity for collective action among Jews was also balanced by the urgent need to improve conditions in the garment industry, where one-third of the immigrants had found employment. A spurt of growth occurred in the industry during the 1890's which saw the value of production in women's ready-made clothing rise 133 percent. With a few exceptions profit margins in the industry were low, even though some ordinary production costs such as plant and machine maintenance could be avoided as a result of the industry's unique organization. As the industry was organized in the 1880's, small contractors and workers were compelled to assume much of the costs, rent, machinery depreciation, overhead and management salaries, which under normal conditions belonged to the entrepreneur.

An uneven flow of work caused by the vagaries of the market compelled workers to toil at incredible rates of speed during the "season" only to find themselves idle once the season was over. During a depression such as the one which began in 1893, there might be no "season" at all and there was no unemployment insurance on which the worker might fall back. At such times union leaders momentarily set aside their revolutionary objectives and reminded their "capitalist" bosses of the traditional role of Jewish charity. During that depression the United Hebrew Trades distributed a circular requesting all to lay aside their bitter feelings of hatred and help the hard-pressed Jewish workers: "TO ALL HELP! TO EVERYBODY WITH A HUMAN HEART, BUSINESSMEN! CONTRACTORS! CAPITALISTS . . . . If your heart is not made of stone be human. Help your workers. . . ."[8]

Considering the working conditions in the industry it might seem as if unemployment was almost preferable to working in the "sweat shops." The industry used a kind of "putting out" system prevalent in the era before the factory system. The entrepreneur organized and financed the factors of production, but the actual manufacture of the garment was given over to outside contractors who competed fiercely for the available contracts. Operating in apartments or lofts, the contractors in their turn parceled out work on the basis of tasks. A task for a worker might consist of the completion of twenty coats which took fourteen hours to achieve. If the utmost speed were employed and nothing interfered, the worker might complete five such tasks in a six-day week. According to some observers, the tempo of work in the sweatshops was so grueling that the effective life span of an operator was twenty years. By their mid-forties most workers were too worn out to muster the necessary speed.[9]

The sweating system was made possible in part by the continued influx of immigrants in desperate need of immediate income. The inordinate ambition of the Jewish worker also played a role in maintaining the system. As the number of contractors proliferated, the margin of profit decreased. In order to obtain a contract an even lower bid was required. The entrepreneurs naturally encouraged the cutthroat competition between contractors. When the Brotherhood of Tailors struck in 1895 to end the sweating system, the major producers refused to negotiate. Their argument was that "the piece work system is best, for under it, the best man makes the best wages."[10] It was merely a Jewish version of the Social-Darwinist argument so popular at the time. When one realizes that until 1907 most workers had to provide their own "katerinka" (sewing machine), even paying a 50¢ freightage charge for transporting it from place to place, and were charged for thread, electricity, broken needles, worn leather belts and fined for damaging garments, the workers' plight becomes clear.

The marginal contractor was not much better off. Upwards of 60,000 children of these contractors were either employed as finishers or forced to mind children, so that the wife could help. Most sweatshops operated outside housing laws which limited the number of persons and uses to which apartments could be put. Child labor was also technically illegal. But it proved virtually impossible to enforce the laws, if indeed there was a desire by the authorities to enforce them. It would have required an army of inspectors to control the hundreds of small shops scattered all over the city. In 1913, for example, when the sweatshop had already passed its peak, there were 16,552 "factories" associated with some facet of the garment industry in which a variegated work force of 311,245 was employed. The average sweatshop employed only five workers while the larger shops, which developed during the war, employed about twenty workers.

The fragmentation and geographic dispersion of the industry proved advantageous to employers in other ways. It was a major roadblock in unionizing the labor force. When added to the myriad craft divisions which were frequently overlaid with ethnic divisions, organizers faced almost insurmountable difficulties. The cutters, originally Irish or German-Jews, considered themselves an elite group and looked down at the newcomers. Jewish tailors from Posen, who served as original operators, considered themselves superior to the Russians, many of whom were "Columbus" tailors, having learned the trade only after arriving in America.

Yet the garment industry became the arena in which the Jewish labor movement was tested. To make workers aware of the injustices visited on them was no easy task for in spite of its hardships the industry offered certain advantages to the immigrant Jewish worker. The proximity of the industry to his place of residence meant little time lost in travel. Moreover, amidst the killing pace of work a certain "homey" atmosphere prevailed in the smaller shops. Many workers were related by family ties and stemmed from the same town, and thus knew each other intimately. Spontaneous singing of the old songs or reading the latest novella from the Yiddish newspaper by a member of the contractor's

family made the work day pass quickly. Compared to the austere atmosphere of the modern factory, the shop was small enough so that the
sense of shared enterprise and satisfaction in producing a completed
garment had not yet been completely destroyed by the minute division
of labor characteristic of modern production. Special provisions could be
made for Orthodox Jews who were required to pray three times a day
and did not work on the numerous religious holy days. Employers like
the cloakmaker Reuben Sadowsky gained a good reputation for their
generosity in such matters.

Then, too, contemporary observers have tended to lose perspective
on the question of working conditions. From an absolute standard, conditions in the sweatshops were bad. But the East European Jewish
immigrant's idea of good conditions was not fashioned by an absolute
but by what he had been conditioned to in the Old World. He often
took such conditions in his stride. It took a flagrant injustice and some
persuasive talking to convince him that conditions were bad and that
the answer was unionization.

The garment industry was not the only source of employment available to Jewish immigrants. Fifty-five percent of the cigarmakers and
half the tanners were Jewish. There were 900 Jewish house painters
and carpenters and a great many blacksmiths and construction workers.
A good many Jews avoided becoming workers by entering small business. There were 140 groceries, 36 bakeries, and innumerable butcher
shops, bakeries, delicatessens, candy stores, and clothing stores in the
ghetto. The conditions of life for these petty merchants were not necessarily superior to those of the workers. In order to earn a living they
had to keep their shops open long hours. Often the merchant lived with
his family in cramped quarters behind the store. In a word, the "business," such as it was, owned him as much as he owned it. Nor did the
workers necessarily envy or feel inferior to these merchants. If the
socialist ideology taught him nothing else, it fortified his self-esteem.
He had a trade and made an honest living by the sweat of his brow,
which was more than one could say for the petty merchant.

If the sweatshop worker's situation was not a particularly fortunate
one, he might by some stretch of the imagination have gotten some
vicarious pleasure out of the knowledge that it was his sweat, his productivity, which enabled immigrant entrepreneurs to undercut and finally
eliminate the "Giants of Broadway," the German Jewish manufacturers
who founded the industry. It was the first major economic foothold
gained by East European Jews, a conspicuous symbol of their success.
East European hegemony in the garment industry was fairly complete
by 1890. After that year German Jews continued to dominate only cer-

tain retail outlets and the custom-tailoring element of the industry which catered to a well-to-do clientele.

In that decade, too, mechanical innovations, many of them conceived by German Jews, brought about the "inside factory" which was ultimately to sound the death knell of the sweatshop. In its classic outlines, the sweatshop thus had a relatively short life span. By 1903, 20 percent of the coats manufactured were produced in these new factories which utilized new technology and a minute division of labor. The making of a coat, for example, was broken down into twenty separate operations. Each required one operator who worked at nothing but his specialty. The result was typical of the introduction of mass production techniques in other industries. There was an increase of production both in quality and in speed and a drop in per unit costs. But rather than improving the lot of the garment workers the reverse occurred. By transferring skills from workers to the machine, the wage scale of the majority of workers actually declined, while those of an elite minority, cutters, managers, pattern makers, rose. Moreover, the piece-work system, at the heart of the sweatshop, was still operative. To be sure, working conditions, lighting, ventilation, proper sanitary facilities improved markedly, but the basic grievance of the garment worker, the uneven flow of work, long hours, and low wages, remained.

An incidental effect of the new system of production, of which all parties were only dimly aware, was that by gathering more workers under one roof they had created the solution for one of the major problems which stood in the way of organization, the dispersion of the work force in many small shops. Now there would be a ready audience for the group of self-conscious Jewish radical intellectuals who were determined to organize and lead the Jewish workers.

The social consciousness it brought to bear on every problem made the Jewish labor movement unique on the American labor scene. Much of that spirit was infused into it by a remarkable group of radical intellectuals who viewed the creation of the Jewish labor movement as part of a larger plan to improve, or at least change, the world. Radicalism and radical types had, since the Enlightenment, become well known to the Jewish community. When the heady atmosphere of emancipation and enlightenment, after the French Revolution, became mixed with the prophetic vision of justice and righteousness embodied in Judaism, the desire for social justice became almost irresistible.

There had been some Jewish contribution to the Jacksonian reform movement and several Jewish Reform rabbis supported the abolitionist crusade, but for the most part Jews maintained a low political profile in the reform movements of the nineteenth century.[11] The "golden age" of American Jewish radicalism awaited the arrival of the Russian Jewish immigrants. These immigrants possessed a strong sense of idealism, so much so that Israel Zangwill feared that it might interfere with their adjustment in the new community which was known for its practicality.[12]

The mélange of anarchism, socialism, and Russian populism which won the allegiance of East European Jews represented to them the path to modernism, to a world in which Jews would be fully accepted. In short, radicalism, especially socialism, played for East European Jews the same role that the Reform movement played for Jews from Western Europe. They believed that the "Jewish question" would only be solved when the universalistic message of justice and equality was accepted by all. Ironically, the imbibing of a radical secular ideology was accompanied by opposition to Judaism in which the very principles of the humanistic ideology they now espoused were embedded.

When the Russian government successfully deflected peasant revolutionary ferment by turning it against the Jews, thus bringing about a series of bloody pogroms, many Jewish radicals despaired of backward Russia ever accepting the spirit of universalism and modernism. They came to the United States to begin life anew. Some came as part of the Am Olam movement, an agriculturally-oriented collectivist group strongly influenced by Russian populism. More often they arrived as unaffiliated secularized Jews who had imbibed a measure of socialist doctrine as part of the intellectual ferment of the *shtetl* or in the Jewish labor movement of Eastern Europe. In 1900 an organization representing East European Jewish workers, the Bund, established a branch in America. That was a precursor to the rejection of merger with the Russian socialist movement in 1903. In one sense it was an East European socialist seed which was transplanted here. It would have to undergo considerable alteration in order to thrive in the soil of the new environment.

Once settled in the new community the radical intellectuals frequently proved to be natural opinion leaders. They quickly gained a following among East European immigrants who traditionally, and somewhat uncritically, held intellectuals in high esteem. The pervasive secularism of the American society in a sense prepared the immigrants for accepting the message of the intellectuals. The immigrant worker was alienated, was exploited, was, in a word, ready to believe that there was something redeemable in his situation. It would help him to reinvent and celebrate himself. Socialism and unionism offered hope of better things to come and a bridge to the modern world which most Jews were anxious to enter.

The role of "educating" the Jewish worker fell to the radical intellectuals and it was they who ushered their potential rank and file into the newly created locals. They were different from other labor organizers, however. They viewed the unions, not so much as indispensable in their own right, but rather as instruments in the "class struggle." By controlling organized labor they thought they would be able to refashion society, which in the long run would also be the surest way to improve the workingman's condition.[13] Such ideological thinking placed Jewish radical intellectuals at polar opposites to the rapidly developing American Federation of Labor, which under Samuel Gompers's leadership, aspired to "bread and butter" objectives.

Lest the impression is created that Jewish immigrants were manipulated by a group of clever intellectuals, one should add that the rank and file was made of the same stuff as the leadership. Both had experienced the dependent powerlessness of Jews in Eastern Europe. It predisposed them for revolutionary fantasizing. Possessing no power and no experience in how to exercise it responsibly, Jews allowed their ideologizing to run far afield. In the words of one observer Jews produced an "ideologue of luft" (air).[14] Its telltale signs were to be seen everywhere in the ghetto, a love of theorizing, highly developed pseudo-analytic faculties, a love of debate with almost no attention paid to the practical steps necessary for implementation of their goals. Never having experienced power, Jews concealed their innocence behind radical rhetoric. But in most cases their radicalism was an intellectual exercise rather than an exercise in revolution. They were the children of the Pale's petit-bourgeoisie who sought in the dream of revolution to break the fetters of the confining Judaism.

While radicals devoted a great deal of thought to the role of labor in the society of the future, precious few had actual experience in communicating with the group they professed to admire. As intellectuals they preferred to speak to each other in Russian instead of Yiddish, the actual language of the East Side proletariat. Not until August 19, 1882, when Abraham Cahan presented a simple explanation of the theory of socialism in Yiddish to an East Side audience were many of his compatriots finally convinced that in order to educate and lead the "masses" it was necessary to speak their language. Cahan was exceptional, not only because he possessed a good working knowledge of Yiddish, but also because he was wise enough to realize that the immigrant labor force could be organized if one were ready to abandon dogmatism and ideology to discover what practical techniques worked.

Such flexibility was not common among the radical intellectuals. Jewish anarchists, for example, initially opposed the thrust toward trade unionism because it smacked too much of amelioration and not enough of revolution. They were convinced it would blunt the edges of the class struggle. While Jewish intellectuals were more drawn to the structured world view of socialism, they supplied anarchism with some of its most creative theoreticians. Anarchism, particularly the humanistic rather than the bomb-throwing variety, had sufficient drawing power among Jewish workers to cause one of the myriad splits that would plague the Jewish labor movement. The more operational-minded intellectuals, such as Cahan, eventually lost interest in the undifferentiated utopianism of anarchism. But even after the Haymarket Affair of 1886 cast it into disrepute, anarchism continued to exercise some drawing power among Jewish intellectuals and workers. That power was partly due to the character of Johann Most and partly to the fact that anarchism shed much of its revolutionary utopianism at the turn of the century to become somewhat more practical.

Most radicals harbored a strong sentiment for the Russian underground revolutionary scene. They brought with them the habit of opposing the government, rarely noting the more democratic atmosphere in which they were permitted to operate in America. When they discovered eventually that America was not Russia and that they could agitate to their hearts' content without fear of arrest and Siberian exile they missed the drama of revolutionary conspiracy. "What kind of socialism could it be without conspiracy? What good was the fruit if it wasn't forbidden?" asked Cahan.[15]

In the unrevolutionary atmosphere of the New World, the Jewish radical intellectual felt strangely unfulfilled. Neither revolution nor intellectualism was held in high repute in America. Cut off from the general stream, radical intellectuals capitalized on those aspects of socialist doctrine which the immigrant workers found attractive, those which celebrated their historical importance as a class and promised improvement of their condition.

Jewish radical intellectuals succeeded in placing their stamp on the Jewish labor movement. There were, of course, various Jewish unions that had sprung up without the help of organizers. These would now be drawn into the United Hebrew Trades and furnished with a binding ideology. The unionization movement began with the realization by a few of the less hidebound intellectuals in the mid-1880's that a drop in business opportunity and the influx of immigrant laborers were rapidly proletarianizing the Lower East Side. Men of the ilk of Abraham Cahan, Bernard Weinstein, Morris Hillkowitz (later Hillquit), and a coterie of activists were ready to mute their revolutionary objectives and direct their energies to ameliorating the conditions in the sweatshops.

It gradually occurred to Abraham Cahan that despite their radical talk Jewish workers were not revolutionary at all but rather anxious to become American and participate fully in American life. They had already experienced the trauma and emotional exhaustion of the immigration and transplantation process. That experience served as the immigrant's personal revolution. Now he was ready to retrench and establish himself. The saturation point beyond which human beings could not remain perpetually in a state of upheaval had been reached. Immigrants, Cahan discovered, wanted to restore equilibrium to their lives. This would have to be taken into account in organizing the Jewish locals.

Existing locals before the radical intellectuals turned their attention to them had not fared well. Jews had played a role in the tailors' strike of 1850 and in the successful cap-makers' strike of 1874–1875. The last-mentioned action resulted in the formation of the cap-makers' local but it lasted less than a year. Locals in the garment trades had been organized with some regularity since mid-century but they had difficulty sustaining themselves for any length of time. In 1877, for example, a union of men's-coats tailors was established. It lasted two years. That same year the cigar-makers' union which had a heavy representation of Jewish workers went on strike against Kenney Brothers. However, even this union with such practical types of Jewish labor leaders as Leo Strasser, Ludwig Yablonovsky, and Samuel Gompers, experienced difficulty in sustaining itself. In 1883 a strike over the question of importing cheap labor virtually broke the union and organization had to begin all over again.

Between 1884 and 1886 a "great upheaval" occurred on the Jewish labor scene. On August 14, 1886, 1,500 cloakmakers left their workbenches. "They were not used to slave conditions," observed Abraham Rosenberg of the high status operators who led the walkout, "and frequently pulled others along with them."[16] That strike was followed in the spring of 1886 by a strike of 4,500 cloakmakers who promptly organized themselves into the Cloakmakers Benevolent Association.

But as a rule these strikes were only partly successful. Jewish workers were courageous and self-sacrificing during a strike but displayed little talent for the pedestrian task of building an organization and maintaining discipline. The strikes of the 1870's and 1880's were a kind of seasonal sport which resulted in almost no permanent organization or accumulation of experience.

When, in 1888, Branch 8 and 17 of the Socialist Labor Party, the citadel of the radical intellectual organizers, surveyed the field of Jewish labor, they found only two Jewish locals to be alive, the typesetters and the choristers. Not only were Jewish workers indifferent to organization, the influx of new immigrant workers offered the employers a ready source of strikebreakers. In order to succeed these immigrants would have to be continually educated anew. Moreover, constant friction and disunity were caused by the innumerable craft and ethnic subdivisions within the garment industry. Then, too, the radical intellectual leadership itself posed certain problems. They tended to be too theoretical and short on practical experience and as intellectuals they were continually riven by splits regarding nuances of socialist theory which the workers barely understood.

The problem of remaining organized was not unique to Jewish unions. It plagued the larger federations as well. The Haymarket Affair of 1886 dealt a death blow to the Knights of Labor, a loosely organized national federation of locals and all those friendly to labor. Organized by Samuel Gompers in 1881 along more durable craft lines, the American Federation of Labor showed promise of more strength and durability. But in its early decades it could not attract the budding Jewish locals because of its restrictionist position on the crucial immigration issue. Moreover, Gompers's brand of "bread-and-butter" unionism was anathema to the radical intellectuals, who, paradoxically, accused Gompers of lacking true working-class consciousness. In their turn, the Gompers group was appalled at the arrogance of the Jewish radical intellectual organizers who toyed irresponsibly with the lives of working people in the name of some esoteric doctrine which they thought would improve the world. The two groups held each other in contempt.

The drive to bring Jewish workers into the Jewish labor movement was begun in earnest in 1885. In that year Abraham Cahan and Bernard Weinstein established a Russian Jewish Worker's Association to which hopefully Jewish locals would attach themselves. But despite the organization of an Anti-Sweating League and a Yiddish newspaper, the *Yiddishe Folkszeitung* (Jewish People's Newspaper) the Association remained an umbrella organization without membership. The 1880's was not a good time for ventures in labor organization. Nevertheless, in 1886 another attempt was made to establish a central federation for Jewish locals, this time significantly dropping the word "Russian" from its title. This attempt was also a failure. The panic created by the Haymarket Affair and the subsequent trial of the anarchists brought the issue of anarchism to the fore. The socialist-oriented radicals argued incessantly over anarchist infiltration into the movement. The withdrawal of the anarchist faction from the Jewish Worker's Association in 1887 and the affiliation of the rump group with the Socialist Labor Party provided the necessary cohesion for the eventual formation of the United Hebrew Trades.

For a time the UHT remained a "federation without federates." Then a spontaneous walkout among the knee-pants makers, gave the UHT leadership an opportunity to demonstrate its mettle. After a week the strike culminated in a victory for the strikers and incidentally brought the UHT a reputation for winning. Independent locals were drawn to the UHT for affiliation. First came the leaders of a Jewish actors union, its delegates wearing formal dress and insisting on being addressed in German. They were followed by the shirtwaist makers, a favorite trade of Jewish radical intellectuals who needed temporary work. By 1890 the UHT had forty affiliated locals. Included were garment workers, actors, musicians, tombstone engravers, bank clerks, writers, bakers, seltzer bottlers, painters, bookbinders, printers, chorus girls, rag pickers, newsboys, and even bootblacks. A Jewish labor movement had finally come into existence.

Almost before it had the opportunity to establish itself, however, the UHT hit upon the shoals of disunity. Predictably, the difficulty was not in the rank and file but among the radical leaders. The question was a basic one. Were the Jewish unions to be an instrument of the Socialist Labor Party under whose auspices they were federated or were the radical intellectuals, who had become leaders of the UHT, to serve the rank and file? Daniel De Leon, a Sephardic Jew originally from Curaçao who headed the Socialist Labor Party, argued staunchly for the first position. The unions were envisioned as the power base for the revolution which was surely coming. The party needed the unions so that the major federations, the ailing Knights of Labor and the American Federation of Labor, could be brought under socialist control. But when De Leon ordered some UHT locals to detach themselves from the A. F. of L. and join District Assembly #49 of the Knights of Labor which he hoped to bring under control of the Socialist Labor Party, he found that few heeded his call. He discovered that he was a leader without followers. The UHT leadership had become autonomous.

The conflict was a protracted one. In 1895 the SLP established an alternate federation, the "Socialist Labor and Trade Alliance," to wean away locals from the more powerful A. F. of L. It was hoped to use the German and Jewish locals as levers. But rather than bringing organized labor under the flag of the SLP, the party split and nearly wrecked the budding UHT. In 1889, most of the Jewish leadership of the UHT, Cahan, Hillquit, London, Winchevsky, Miller, and Hurwich, gave their allegiance to the more moderate Debs faction of the Socialist Party. During the period of chaos, many of the UHT locals, so painfully organized, withered on the vine. But in a few months, the leadership group, now wiser and more practical, recouped its losses and went on to build on firmer foundations.

Eventually the Jewish labor movement came to be based on a triad of related organizations: the UHT, the *Forward*, which served as its organ, and the Workmen's Circle, a giant fraternal order whose medical and insurance benefits attracted many unaffiliated Jews to labor's banner. Originally established in 1892 for "mutual assistance to members in time of need and trouble," and to "promote the organization of cooperative business enterprises" the Order was plagued by legal problems and did not at first fare well.[17] The efforts of B. Feigenbaum, a journalist who became the Circle's general secretary in 1901, put the order on its feet. Thereafter the membership of the organization rose rapidly. In 1901 it had only 872 members but by 1905, when it was finally granted a charter by the New York State Insurance Department, its membership had risen to 6,776. A decade later it boasted nearly 50,000 members.[18] By the turn of the century, after nearly three decades of trial and error, a Jewish labor movement had come into existence. Its unlikely rank and file was matched only by an even more unlikely leadership. What had occurred between the two was more in the way of a mutual transaction rather than a missionary conversion of one by the other. The workers nominally accepted long-range socialist goals in turn for which the radical leadership gave first priority to ameliorating the conditions under which the worker was compelled to toil. The socialist society about which its leaders dreamed would have to wait. Furnished with the first consciously Jewish power base in America, the Jewish labor movement now set about to solve the more practical problems.

In 1903 the International Ladies Garment Workers Union with its 10,000 members, only one-third of whom were women, was the largest unit associated with the UHT. It was, however, in many ways, a giant with feet of clay. Its membership was spread over several cities and composed of various ethnic groups, creating problems of communication. When a sharp economic downturn occurred in 1903, the ILGWU was hit hard and proved too weak to offer its membership much protection. But despite its obvious limitations workers apparently felt that a union, even a weak union, was better than none at all. New unions were continually being formed. In 1901 a new cap-makers' union made its debut and a year later the fur workers were organized.

The path to organization was not always a smooth one, especially in the men's branch of the garment industry. The United Garment Workers, an umbrella organization for the several locals in the men's clothing industry, was plagued by internal strife which finally came to a head in 1914 and the rival Amalgamated Clothing Workers was established by Joseph Schlossberg and Sidney Hillman. Furthermore, the establishment of the United Hebrew Trades did not mean that the attempts to divide the Jewish labor movement had magically ceased. The remnants of the De Leon group, joined by the IWW, continued to raid the Jewish unions and sometimes set up dual unions for the purpose of weaning away the workers from the original locals. More troublesome for the organization of Jewish goals was the resistance of established craft unions, especially those in the construction industry, to the establishment of Jewish locals.

Despite the many problems, after the turn of the century the Jewish labor movement grew in numbers and power. A test of strength with the employers, who were loath to make improvements in working conditions, thus became imminent. The period between 1907 and 1909 saw increased tensions within the garment industry. When the shirtwaist makers, the most militant unionists in the industry, voted to leave their workbenches in 1909, the bubble burst. That strike ushered in a five-year period of labor unrest which is usually called the "Great Revolt." When peace was restored, neither the garment industry nor the Jewish community was the same. A new and powerful force had made its debut among the Israelites of America.

The shirtwaist industry which furnished the spark for the "Great Revolt" employed some 30,000 workers who were predominantly of Jewish extraction, but included also a sizable representation of Italians. There was seething discontent among the workers and the existence of the union had not noticeably improved working conditions. Many workers became convinced that only by striking could conditions be improved.

On November 22, 1909, the union convened another in a series of meetings at Cooper Union. Its purpose was to decide on a course of action. As the meeting wore on with the customary long speeches, the audience seemed restless. Suddenly the normal course of the meeting was drastically altered. A young operator, Clara Lemlich, rose and addressed her fellow workers: "I am tired of listening to speakers who talk in general terms," she announced, catching the mood of the audience. "What we are here for is to decide whether we shall or shall not strike. I offer a resolution that a general strike be declared now."[19] Pandemonium broke loose in the packed hall as the workers enthusiastically voted for the resolution.

Although the shirtwaist makers had only 2,000 members in their local, a fraction of the work force, the enthusiasm for the strike was contagious. Twenty thousand workers, mostly women, left their workbenches. Eleven weeks later the strike was over. The union had won a clear-cut victory: a fifty-two-hour work week, four paid legal holidays, and recognition of the union. Local 25 emerged from the strike with a five-fold increase in membership. The union leaders learned that the best way to recruit members was to win strikes. The reverse lesson would not be long in coming.

In July, 1910, the 60,000 members of the New York Cloakmakers Union, followed by the smaller Chicago local, went on strike. This time things were different. After the initial enthusiasm, a deadlock occurred. Neither side seemed able to compromise. For two months bitter recriminations, followed finally by violence, wracked the industry and when peace was finally established it proved to be an uneasy one. There was sporadic violence, including the use of armed thugs by both sides. The changing of the power distribution in the industry, which had to precede the improvement of working conditions, was no easy task.

The bitterness of the Jewish labor-management conflict, where both sides shared a common faith and culture, seems anomalous. It was almost as if such commonalities served to heighten antagonism. At times labor strife in the Jewish community assumed the character of a civil war. As in all wars between brothers it possessed more than the normal intensity of emotion and passion. The employers had scratched their way to the top the hard way, through hard work and self-denial. Once in positions of power they tended, like all self-made men, to assume that everyone worth his salt would adopt the same life strategy. Like all *arrivistes*, they were often inflexible and far less bound by humanitarian considerations than their German-Jewish predecessors. In the early stages their businesses had been marginal affairs, barely maintaining themselves on a narrow profit. The new "boss" frequently worked side by side with his workers. They were worker-entrepreneurs, forced to exploit their own families in order to earn a livelihood. Naturally such types found it difficult to understand, much less sympathize with, labor's plight. They were more likely to wonder why everybody did not work hard to become a "boss," as they had done. They were wont to remind recalcitrant workers that no one had helped them reach the top.

Nor was much more flexibility forthcoming from the ideologically hidebound labor leaders who looked upon employers as "capitalist exploiters" and to workers as the source of all value. As for the worker, no Horatio Alger stratagems could explain away his poverty or his fatigue at the end of an incredibly long working day. The union was becoming a hope for escaping from the cruel situation in which he found himself. For that reason he gave it his support.

Eventually, both sides in the cloakmakers' strike, aware that the deadlock was causing grievous harm, turned secretly to the neutral "uptown" leadership to find a way out of the dilemma. The "uptowners," who were appalled at the bitterness of the strike, wanted it settled quickly.[20] There was a Jewish tradition for mediation by the rabbinate but in the new environment the rabbis no longer possessed the leverage to make their will felt. That was to some extent now held by the group of wealthy "uptown" philanthropists who took an active interest in the Jewish community. Moreover, while the strike was a bitter one, the bonds which tied Jews together, a common faith and a high value set on justice, were shared by both sides. Louis Marshall and Jacob Schiff, the leaders of the "uptown" coterie who were held in high esteem by both sides, now urged that negotiations be started.

Under their sponsorship, Dr. Henry Moskowitz approached Lincoln Filene who had had some previous role in settling a labor dispute in Boston. Moskowitz's initiative was spurred by his inside knowledge of the dire situation of the strikers. In his turn Filene again approached his attorney, Louis Brandeis, who had earned something of a reputation for precision and wisdom in representing Boston cloak manufacturers in a prior strike.

In the ensuing negotiations the major difficulty proved to be the question of the union shop, which the employers refused to accept. But during the second phase of the negotiations both sides became more amenable. Public opinion again sympathized with the strikers as it had during the previous shirtwaist makers' strike. At that time society women like Mrs. Belmont and Miss Anne Morgan (sister of J. P. Morgan), among others, created sympathetic headlines in their effort to publicize the plight of the "heroic girls" fighting to improve the conditions of the workers. Now many clergymen, some under the influence of the Christian Socialist movement, used the cloakmakers' strike as an opportunity to sermonize against the rapacious manufacturers. Public sympathy for the strikers, combined with Brandeis's prowess as a mediator, finally laid the basis for breaking the two-month deadlock. Brandeis recommended the "preferential union shop" which gave the union substantially what it wanted while allowing the employers to save face.

The "Protocol of Peace" which brought momentary stability to the industry was a landmark in the history of labor-management relations. By abolishing the contracting system, it sounded the death knell for the sweatshop whose days were in any case numbered because of technological advances in the industry. Other provisions of the Protocol reduced the working week to an average of fifty hours, introduced permanent arbitration machinery, a Grievance Board to handle complaints on a day-to-day basis and a Sanitary Control Body to monitor standards of cleanliness in the shops. To those who had for years struggled for a recognition of the rights of labor it seemed as if a new day was dawning in the garment industry.

As things developed, however, the problems of the industry proved to be far from over. The machinery established by the Protocol to insure peace was dependent on the goodwill of both sides. After years of bitter conflict marked by mutual suspicion labor peace could not be created overnight. Industry-wide peace came to depend rather on the delicate balance of power between labor and management. That balance was partly destroyed by the depression of 1913 which reduced union strength and created pressure on the employers to reduce costs. The unilateral abrogation of the Protocol by a group of manufacturers in May, 1915, followed as a matter of course. In April, 1916, 25,000 clothing workers again found themselves on the street and remained away from their workbenches for fourteen weeks. The benefits derived from the first strike had to be fought for all over again.

It became apparent that amelioration of conditions through the actions of labor unions alone would not be sufficient to bring needed changes to the garment industry. The fact was brought home by the tragic Triangle Waist Company fire on March 25, 1911. The fire which broke out in a supposedly fireproof building located on the northwest corner of Washington and Greene Street claimed the lives of 146 women operators. The tragedy made it clear that government regulation to enforce compliance with safety and sanitary regulations was needed. Indeed, within the next decade Federal and municipal inspection of the new "inside" factories became widespread.

In 1910 the United Hebrew Trades had 100,000 members affiliated with 89 unions. By 1917 the membership figure had risen to 250,000. Despite an internal conflict between Yiddishists and universalistic-minded socialists, the Workmen's Circle had by 1918 succeeded in raising its membershinp to 60,000. The rising circulation figures of the Forward, now a daily approaching the highest readership in the community, served as yet another reminder that Jewish labor had made its mark. With their own labor federation, their own fraternal order, their own newspaper, a rapidly rising membership in the Socialist Party (118,000 in 1912), it seemed as if the group of radical intellectuals who had initiated the movement three decades earlier had succeeded beyond their wildest imagination.

For a group whose presence in the union halls was largely a one-generation phenomenon, the Jewish impact on the American labor movement is a remarkable one. The radical intellectuals who acted as catalysts for the organization of Jewish unions began by viewing the Jewish worker as an instrument to effect social change. But with experience they learned to inject into their idealism a modicum of practical hardheadedness which brought immediate improvements to the worker. They still believed that socialism would ultimately bring the better world but in the meantime a shorter workday and better wages should not be rejected. Socialist doctrine was relegated to the background and served to generate the high idealism which impelled Jewish unions in the direction of seeking social justice. But rather than seeking to sharpen "class struggle" they pioneered virtually every technique for maintaining labor-management peace found in the field of labor relations today.

The unions themselves became laboratories for testing social welfare programs. Jewish unions pioneered many of the major labor welfare programs implemented by the New Deal. Included were the forty-hour, five-day week, paid vacations, unemployment and health insurance, pensions, medical care, educational and recreational facilities, low-rent housing cooperatives, and credit unions.

Jewish unions welcomed the concept of labor-management cooperation to improve productivity and went as far as instructing some members in scientific management so they could further improve efficiency. They were among the first unions to employ trained professional labor organizers. The union hired its own economic analysts so that employers were often startled when union agents came to the negotiating table with a more comprehensive knowledge of the business and better theories of what ailed the industry than the management team.

At the same time the background of union officials in the socialist movement gave them a special concern about participating in the political process. The formation of the Political Action Committee of the Congress of Industrial Organizations in the thirties was an embodiment of the same principle writ large. The Jewish labor movement, especially its largest component, the ILGWU, was instrumental in 1938 in organizing the American Labor Party, for the purpose of maximizing the political strength of the labor vote and to give Jewish socialists an opportunity to vote for Roosevelt without compromising the socialist principles by voting for a capitalist party.

In short, when socialist principles were combined with practical experience, these radical intellectuals developed a core of leaders remarkable for their imagination, incorruptibility, and keen sense of service and social justice. They were instrumental in developing the first real power base for East European Jews in America. It was in that sense, in learning how to use power rather than building castles in the air, that the Jewish labor movement was an important Americanizing agent.

CHAPTER XII

A New Religious Synthesis: Conservatism

VASTLY OUTNUMBERING THE JEWISH COMMUNITY EXISTING IN AMERICA before them, the East European Jews and their descendants were in time destined to occupy the center of the American Jewish stage. They would bring to it a distinctive Jewishness which differed markedly from that with which America had become familiar. That difference could be found primarily in the way the newcomers came to terms with the fact of their Jewishness. Whether pious or simply ethnic, East European Jews suffered little from the cultural ambivalence of those Jews from Central Europe who had undergone several generations of Americanization. Fiercely Jewish, they were for the moment good material to kindle a new Jewish cultural spirit in America. So conspicuous a demarcation did their mass arrival produce in American Jewish history that the historian soon realizes he is dealing with a new American Jewry which, while superimposed on the old, is only tangentially connected with it.

As part of their cultural baggage, the new immigrants carried with them a strong sense of religious and ethnic self-consciousness, a sense of peoplehood. Stemming from that consciousness there developed among them two related phenomena: a new branch of religious Judaism called Conservatism and a complementary secular ideology known as Zionism. It is the examination of these two developments and the general reordering of American Jewish life accompanying their introduction which is the subject of this and the following chapters.

For the German Jews who settled here in the nineteenth century, the response to the prevailing Protestantism of the new environment was to adapt their outer religious forms to the Protestant model. That was the essence of the Reform movement. While the pervasive secularism of the new environment was bound to make adherence to a rigid religious orthodoxy problematical, new immigrants were repelled by the Reform accommodation of American Jewry. Its tint of Christian forms was to them a form of betrayal which made it less acceptable than having no religion at all. Moreover, in the historical milieu from which they stemmed even such an extreme accommodation held out no reward because they could never have hoped to become Russian or Polish citizens "of Jewish persuasion." In Eastern Europe the unrelenting quest among Jews for modernism took the form of commitment to new secular ideologies like socialism and Zionism. Both marked a break with the Orthodox tradition, but not necessarily with the ethnic, or folk, tradition which also prevailed in the Jewish community. That, we shall see, proved to be a great boon for the Zionist movement.

Socialism, on the other hand, offered, in theory at least, a path to the larger society and sometimes led to a brand of self-negating Judaism. An exchange of religious orthodoxy for a revolutionary one was the path followed by a growing number of Jews from Eastern Europe. Unlike the Reform movement of the West, such an exchange required a rejection of all religion. One of the most popular works among Jewish radical intellectuals was Johann Most's *Die Gottespest* (The God Plague) which became popular in 1888, after its translation into Yiddish. East European Jews made up a disproportionate part of the membership of the various branches of the socialist movement, albeit more were attracted to the moderate Menshevik than to the Bolshevik position. Only ofter the bloody pogroms of the nineties was there a growing realization among Jewish socialists that the automatic solution to the Jewish problem which they foresaw in a socialist order, was chimerical. It was then that the Jews formed a separate Socialist Labor Alliance, called the "Bund," to work for the realization of a socialist society in which Jews, as a group, would also find a place.

The radical intellectuals who came to America were products of a resistant social order. Since they had accepted socialism, there was little that could serve as a brake from their headlong flight from religious Judaism in a similar way to what the Reform movement had done for the Jews of Central Europe. Eventually they too were compelled for practical reasons to revert to those elements in Judaism—language and ethnic traditions—which permitted them to maintain a connection with the Jewish masses they sought to influence.

A confusing transitional situation prevailed among the Jewish immigrants from Eastern Europe. They read a socialist newspaper which viewed religion as the "opiate of the people," joined a socialist-oriented labor union, frequently voted the socialist ticket, but at the same time they still observed dietary laws at home and attended synagogue. They were in an in-between stage, no longer able to rely completely on the old faith for succor, but not yet willing to cut themselves loose from it. They booed actors who dared smoke on the stage during the popular

Friday night performances of Yiddish plays, even though they were themselves in the theater rather than in the synagogue. They still held to the general tradition of Judaism, if not to the specific regulations of the religious creed.

Nevertheless, since the religion had lost its base in *shtetl* life and was no longer threatened by a hostile host culture, some erosion of the spirit which bound Jews together was a foregone conclusion. "Suddenly the walls of the ghetto were removed," observed the philosopher Morris Raphael Cohen, "and we found that the Jews had not been the only conservators of wisdom and civilization."[1] Having noted the richness of the secular culture, many Jews desired to taste its fruits. That required a shifting from orthodoxy to the ethnic component of Judaism. The high degree of ritual elaboration characteristic of Orthodoxy was abandoned as were its myriad rules of observation. With characteristic humor, Jews were able to laugh at what was happening to them under the impact of secularism. The Have Emma (lovers of the faith) congregation in Chicago was jestingly labeled the Halba Emma congregation (half faith) because many of its peddler members were compelled by distance to ride to the services in horse and wagon. By 1913 almost half of the stores and pushcarts on the Lower East Side were open for business on the Sabbath.

For some Jewish radicals it was more than a case of drifting away from the old faith. They insisted on demonstrating a deliberate hostility to it. During the 1890's Jewish anarchists sponsored a "Day of Atonement Ball" which featured "music, dancing and a buffet" rather than fasting. But by 1900 even the anarchists were able to sense the strong attachment the immigrants still felt for their religious traditions and put an end to their anti-religious activities. The Orthodox branch of Judaism hardly offered a suitable target.

Of the 533 Jewish congregations in existence in 1890, 316 adhered to the Orthodox service. But many of these congregations were small, poor, and transitory. The Reform movement would have served as a more suitable target since in terms of financial resources, buildings, organization, and number of worshipers, it dominated the American Jewish religious scene. Whereas the Orthodox branch was concentrated largely in the ghettos of the Eastern cities among the new immigrants, the Reform movement was becoming national in scope by founding congregations in the West and South.[2] Since it was anchored in the Jewish middle class, it was perhaps the class status associated with it which prevented the new arrivals from considering the Reform movement as a possible alternative. Despite its glow of health, the dominance of the Reform movement was destined to be short-lived. Not only had it confined itself to what was becoming a minority of American Jewry; the generation of German Jews, who had furnished the impetus for the Reform movement, was passing from the scene and no new generation was being groomed to take its place. In many cases the movement had served as little more than a gateway out of Judaism. It called for little commitment to Judaism, and after seeing the Reform of the parents the new generation found the leap to unchristological Protestant sects, such as the Unitarians or the bland humanitarianism of Ethical Culture, relatively easy to make.

Thus at the turn of the century there existed an Orthodox branch, seemingly unable to cope with the secular environment, a Reform branch unable to regenerate itself and unacceptable to the new immigrants, which composed the majority of American Jewry, and a movement for secularization in all sections of American Jewry which featured ideologies, often with a distinct anti-religious bent. The Jewish religious scene contained a vacuum which a new religious modality that would neither cramp the desire for secularization nor trample on cherished traditional religious symbols, could readily fill. The Conservative movement seemed ideally suited to do that.

It sought to serve as a kind of halfway house between the ghetto-oriented Orthodox branch and the assimilationist Reform movement. Conservatism offered no new religious dogma but held out instead the prospect of religious continuity with a modification of the exacting requirements of Halacha, those numerous regulations which encompassed the life of the Orthodox Jew. It sought acculturation within a new Jewish context which could happily harmonize tradition and change.[3] The historic religious tradition of Judaism would be preserved, but the actual credal regulations would be determined by what one of its founders called "the conscience of Catholic Israel." By this was meant the religious practices currently in vogue in the "living body" of Israel.[4] Regulations would be determined by collective conscience rather than being imposed by a priesthood. Traditional principles, the centrality of the Torah, the observance of the Sabbath, the keeping of dietary laws, the laying of Tefillin, and a "collective commitment to the people and the land of Israel," would be maintained, but necessary innovations of specific regulations would also be assured by basing them on the normative practices adhered to by committed Jews.

In practice many innovations of the Conservative movement were borrowed from the Reform branch, especially those concerning decorum in the service. The status and role of women, for example, which served as a major point of conflict with the Orthodox branch, were upgraded in keeping with the tenets of modernism. There would be mixed seating and women would be permitted to play a role, ultimately a major role, in the congregation. Even so, Conservatives would not go so far as to permit women to become rabbis or read from the Torah during services. Like the Reform movement, certain concessions were made to middle-class aesthetics. There would be joint responsive reading and singing but the rabbi, rather than the cantor, would conduct the service. Order and decorum would be maintained by ushers and commercialism would be kept out of the service. The congregation would support itself by annual membership dues. Unfortunately the funds produced by this method have not always proven sufficient to keep the congregation solvent; hence psychological means of encouraging the wealthier congregants to display their wealth are sometimes resorted to, as are bazaars and other fund-raising devices. But "shenodering"—the pledging of money in exchange for honorific duties—and the high holy day "appeal" are generally frowned upon.

Otherwise, the Conservative ritual tends to be closer to the Orthodox than to Reform Judaism. Heads are kept covered and accompaniment to singing by an organ is not customary. The rabbi is held in high esteem and, in a nominal sense, is considered the spiritual leader of the congregation. (Actual power and control of the purse strings is in the hands of the Board of Trustees of the congregation.) An indirect relationship between the Orthodox branch and the Conservative has also developed, because many Conservative rabbis were at one time products of Orthodox overproduction. The rabbi of a Conservative congregation is expected to serve as a model of religious observance, a kind of custodian of the faith.

The hallmark of Conservatism is its emphasis on historical Judaism and continuity with the past. A warning about too radical a deviation from historical Judaism was included in Solomon Schechter's address at the inauguration of the Jewish Theological Seminary in 1902: "Judaism is absolutely incompatible with the abandonment of Torah. . . . We must either remain faithful to history, or go the way of all flesh and join the great majority."[5] When the flagship organization of the Conservative movement, the United Synagogue of America, was established in 1913, its constitution similarly advocated "loyalty to Torah and its historical exposition," by which was meant those rabbinic interpolations of the scriptures which went under the heading of Talmud.

Among the Conservatives, sermons usually concerned themselves with general problems rather than with biblical exegesis, which makes up the substance of Orthodox sermonizing. Predictably too, religious piety is of lesser intensity among Conservative Jews. Today only 50 percent of Conservative congregations conduct daily services, but religious holy days and, to a lesser extent, Sabbath services are well attended. In order to attract worshipers, Conservative congregations have resorted to advertisement in the press, telephone squads, guest lecturers, and refreshments, all of which are a far cry from the piety and devotion which bring Orthodox Jews to their synagogues.

Rather than a planned strategy to fill the gap between two unviable alternatives, the development of Conservatism occurred naturally. Its earliest exposition can be traced to Breslau, Germany, where Rabbi Zachariah Frankel and a group of disciples took leave of the highly rationalistic position advocated by Reformers in favor of "positive historical Judaism." Others like Isaac Leeser in the United States, who advocated "traditional Judaism," came to the same position independently. Within the Reform branch too, there were some congregations which veered close to the Conservative position and eschewed the more radical Reform measures. The fact that in all branches of American Judaism, real power was found on the congregational level, rather than in the central organization, made such variations possible.

Leadership for Conservatism was never in short supply. In its early stages Sabato Morais, an Italian rabbi who succeeded Leeser as spiritual leader of Philadelphia's Mikveh Israel, and Alexander Kohut, formerly a leader of Hungary's Conservative movement, played prominent roles. To this list should be added the name of Morris Jastrow, a Polish-born rabbi who had already shown evidence of a rebellious temperament when he lent his support to the Polish struggle against Tsar Alexander II in 1861, for which he spent some time behind bars. Jastrow was among the first of the American rabbinate to make common cause with the budding Zionist movement, an association which would later differentiate Conservatism from the Orthodox and the Reform branches. Another was Benjamin Szold who became spiritual leader of Congregation Oheb Shalom in Baltimore and who authored the first Conservative modification of the Orthodox prayer book.

The formal organization of the Conservative movement was triggered by a seemingly unimportant event, a banquet given by the Reformist Union of American Hebrew Congregations to celebrate its eighth council meeting and incidentally to honor the first graduating class of the Hebrew Union College in 1883. The invited guests, some of whom adhered to dietary laws, were shocked to find listed on the menu, "little neck clams," a non-kosher food. The banquet broke up in confusion and became a *cause célèbre* in more traditional-minded religious circles, where it was soon dubbed the "*trefa* banquet."

The incident served to crystallize the sharp differences which had developed between Reformists and more traditional-minded Jews. The

Orthodox and Conservative journals condemned the planners of the banquet, while Reformist-minded journals such as the *American Hebrew*, rose to their defense. Religion, they argued "centers not in the kitchen and stomach."[6] But in Reform Judaism there seemed to be precious little heart as well. It seemed as if the breaking of dietary rules at an ordination ceremony was planned by Isaac Wise's business backers in Cincinnati. Considering the attacks upon the banquet as a pretext to subvert the Hebrew Union College, they rallied round the flag. Grand Lodge Number 4 of the Free Sons of Israel, a major backer of the institution, provocatively organized similar banquets in other cities which included the serving of oysters. Isaac Wise, himself an observer of dietary laws, was prevailed upon to speak out on the subject: "There is a law which stands higher than all dietary laws," he observed, "...that is 'Be no fanatic,' which translated [means] 'Be intelligent, and allow your reason to govern your passions, propensities and superstitions.' "

Such advice was well suited for Reformist-minded Jews who had in fact replaced religious passion with reason, but it showed woeful ignorance of the mind and heart of traditional Jews, who were so committed to their religion that they insisted on duplication of hospital and other institutional facilities when regular facilities did not adhere to dietary laws. To them, the Reformist declaration which read "Mosaic and Rabbinic law as regulate diet, priestly purity and dress, originated in ages and under influence of ideas altogether foreign to our present mental and spiritual state," was anathema.

Orthodox Jews were not ready to make such concessions to "the views and habits of modern civilization." In Detroit a clash occurred over the question of dancing and card playing in the synagogue. The Orthodox community branded the synagogue which allowed such goings on as a "modern Sodom" and established its own congregation. The original Jewish settlers were convinced that it was precisely such accommodations which led to Americanization. "Our religion is distinctively American," commented the *Detroit Journal*, a local Reformist organ, "totally differing from the homeless Orthodoxy of the world which cringes before kings and princes."[7] Yet it was readily apparent to the newcomers that if the older settlers did not cringe before kings and princes, they placed an excessive value on the good opinion of a lesser breed, their Christian neighbors. They were apprehensive lest the strange and open manner in which immigrants bore their Judaism might adversely affect their standing in the community.

Two years after the *"trefa* banquet" the Reform convention at Pittsburgh formalized the difference between the traditionalists and themselves in a series of resolutions. Particularly noteworthy was the anti-Zionist resolution introduced by Kaufman Kohler which disapproved of any attempt for the establishment of a Jewish state. "Such attempts show a misunderstanding of Israel's mission," the resolution read, "[the] object of Judaism is not political nor national, but spiritual." It delineated a crucial difference between the old and the new settlers. It was the political and national aspects of Judaism, especially the idea of Zionism, which would become increasingly important to those Jews who desired to maintain their links to Judaism while at the same time coming to terms with the secular spirit.

Led by Sabato Morais, the Conservatives began in 1886 the slow process of establishing an alternative to Reform and Orthodoxy. First came the Jewish Theological Seminary which would train a new clergy to counteract "the baneful influences which have perverted the Cincinnati Institution" and would keep alive "the true Judaic spirit." The new rabbis would be trained "in a spirit of devotion and fidelity to the Jewish law."[8] With much hope the Seminary program was begun in rooms made available by New York's oldest congregation, Shearith Israel.

But the hope proved to be forlorn. Cut off from financial aid of the wealthy "uptown" Jews and held in contempt by the stand-pat Orthodox Jews, the new branch of Judaism did not fare well. Of the eleven congregations which affiliated with the Conservative branch, six were won over to the Reform movement by 1900. The Seminary, on which so much hope had been placed, attracted only 21 students and three teachers between 1886 and 1901. Only 17 were ordained during that period and even these few experienced some difficulty in finding suitable pulpits. When Morais died in 1897 the Seminary verged on bankruptcy.

An attempt by his successor to bring the Conservatives and Orthodox closer together by establishing a formal link in 1898 did not prove successful. The early recruits of the Seminary were usually young men of Orthodox background attracted to the Conservative movement for practical, if not always for reasons of principle. The new congregations which were destined to be established in the smaller middle-class cities and in the areas of second settlement outside the ghettos where a growing number of Jews were relocating, were associated with the Conservative branch. Despite the lack of formal ties an informal reciprocal relationship in which the Orthodox branch furnished young rabbinic candidates for pulpits in Conservative areas developed.

It was this reality which Cyrus Adler, an Arkansas pupil of Morais and Professor of Semitics at The Johns Hopkins University, made known to Jacob Schiff in the hope that the purse strings of uptown philanthropy would be loosened to place the Seminary on its financial feet. It is partly due to Schiff's anxieties regarding the Americanization potential of the new immigrants that his acceptance of the plan to refurbish the Seminary can be attributed. Here, it was thought, was a possible bridge which Orthodox Jews might cross to the American mainstream. The new Conservative movement might succeed where the Reformists could not. Together with Daniel and Simon Guggenheim, Leonard Lewisohn, Mayer Sulzberger, and Louis Marshall, Jacob Schiff raised a half million dollars to get the plan underway. Themselves associated with the Reform movement, these "uptown" philanthropists were nevertheless able to come to the aid of a competing branch of Judaism. Altogether it was a remarkable display of patrician intelligence.

In order to be fully successful the Seminary required a charismatic leader. The search for such a person, conducted by Louis Marshall, head of the Seminary's new Board of Trustees, and Cyrus Adler, its chief administrator, soon centered on Solomon Schechter who seemed to be the perfect embodiment of the Conservative idea. Lured from his post at Cambridge, where he was Professor of Rabbinics, by the prospect of pioneering a new branch of Judaism in America, which he was convinced was destined to become the most vital Jewish community in the diaspora, Schechter arrived to head the Seminary in 1902.

A remarkable personality, Schechter was born into a strictly Orthodox Rumanian family in 1850. Intellectual precocity gave him entree to the University of Vienna from which he was recruited as a tutor for the son of Claude Montefiore, the renowned leader of British Jewry. His reputation was enhanced by the discovery of the lost Apocryphal book of Ecclesiastes known as *The Wisdom of Ben Sira* in the Genizah (store room) of a Cairo synagogue. The discovery was testimony to Schechter's unmatched knowledge of scriptures. He was able to trace the find from a small crumbling scrap of parchment which came into his hands by coincidence. Later publication of *Studies in Judaism*, an eloquent exposition of his views on Judaism, established him as a foremost exponent of that unique mixture of the traditional and the innovative which was at the heart of Conservatism.

In contrast to Orthodox scholars, Schechter placed great confidence in modern scholarship and believed that it could serve to invigorate Judaism. But at the same time he continued to be intrigued by Jewish mysticism and the unexplainable in the scriptures. He harbored an abiding distaste for the German higher criticism of the bible because he believed it to be over-rational and so too was the Reform approach to Judaism which had imbibed many of its lessons. Most important, Schechter was a dedicated Zionist when it was hardly acceptable for a spiritual leader to be so. Moreover, his Zionism reached beyond a merely political credo. It found its roots in his religio-cultural point of view which believed passionately in the redemption of Israel and the ultimate triumph of the universal idea of Judaism.[9] It transcended the nineteenth-century variety of nationalism which spurred the Zionist movement forward, finding its strength instead in the mystical idea of Jewish peoplehood which bound Jews, especially the Jews of Eastern Europe, together.

Schechter attracted a distinguished coterie of scholars, Louis Ginzberg, historian-biographer as well as Talmudist, Alexander Marx, an authority on medieval history and literature, Israel Friedlander, a bible expert, Joseph Asher, an authority on homiletics, and Israel Davidson, a biblical scholar and essayist, who gave the Seminary a new lease on life. Even before Schechter had come to the Seminary, there were portents of a quickened interest in its activities. A group of graduates had banded together to form the Rabbinical Assembly of America, a Conservative counterpart to the Central Conference of Reform Rabbis. In 1913 the capstone of the Conservative organizational structure was set into place when Schechter gathered together sixteen Conservative congregations to establish the United Synagogue of American Hebrew Congregations. The establishment of that organization also marked the completion of the religious triangulation of American Judaism. Each branch was now furnished with its own central organization, infrastructure, and conviction that it represented the wave of the future for American Israel.

Two years later, in 1915, Schechter passed from the scene and his place was taken by Cyrus Adler; he served as the Seminary's president until 1940. Adler was succeeded by Rabbi Louis Finkelstein, a noted Talmudic scholar, whose tenure lasted until 1972, when Gerson Cohen, a scholar of considerable repute, took over the helm.

The vigor of Jewish religious life in America was reflected in the growth in the number of congregations. By 1900 there existed 1,769 congregations in the nation, an increase of 239 percent over 1890. Of these 1,112 were located in the North Atlantic states where the majority of Jews continued to reside. The North-Central region boasted 344 congregations, most of them in and around the city of Chicago. The South-Central region had 133 congregations while the Far West had only seventy. The distribution of congregations reflected the pattern of Jewish settlement. Within that distribution, small, often unaffiliated Orthodox congregations predominated in the core city areas, while Conservative and Reform congregations shared influence in the remaining areas. By 1916 the Conservative branch dominated in areas of second and third settlement, even though in terms of wealth, especially property, the Reform branch continued to hold an edge.[10] In 1918 the minority status of the Reform branch was confirmed by the *Jewish Communal Register of New York City*. Today Conservatism clearly predominates even in former centers of Orthodox strength in New York City. Its organizational vitality and potential for further growth are unmatched.[11]

The growth in the number of congregations and other indications of health notwithstanding, serious trouble spots were also developing on the American Jewish religious scene. Omitted from the statistics showing increased religious affiliation was the growing number of second-generation Jews who rejected all contact with religious congregations. By 1930 fewer than one-third of American Jewish families were members of any religious congregation. The increase in the number of congregations after 1900 actually occurred while the proportion of Jews choosing to commit themselves to institutional religious affiliation was on the decline. Furthermore, such increase in congregation membership as did occur represented more an adherence to acceptable middle-class behavior patterns than to an increase in genuine religious enthusiasm or piety. The increase in the number of religious buildings appears to be inversely proportionate to the quality of religious feeling contained therein. None of the three branches of Judaism has had notable success in halting the headlong flight of young Jews to a total secular life.

While Conservative Judaism would prove to be the most successful synthesis, it was not immune from the bane of Jewish organizational life, fragmentation and division. To be sure, the Reconstructionist idea was, from one point of view, a further elaboration of Conservative tenets, rather than a conflicting branch.

Founded by Mordecai Kaplan, one of the Jewish Theological Seminary's early graduates and a former teacher of homiletics at that institution, Reconstructionism focused primarily on the cultural aspects of Jewish civilization. Convinced that there was too much theocratic deadwood and not enough emphasis on the Jewish spirit, Kaplan sought to deemphasize further the purely religious element in Judaism in favor of its cultural component. He thought of Judaism as an all-encompassing civilization in whose framework the central religious element shared influence with historical, cultural, and ethnic factors. If Judaism were to survive and grow, all the elements of Jewish civilization must be recognized and held sacred.

At the same time Kaplan would streamline the credal system which served as the main buttress of religious Judaism. The concept of the covenant which was at the core of the Judaic faith and which stressed the special position of Jews in relation to God, was viewed by Kaplan as being more appropriate for an insecure nomadic tribe wandering isolated in the desert than for the modern urbanized Jew. He felt strongly that Judaism must be able to give meaning to the mysteries and complexities of the universe in contemporary rational terms, or risk decline. At the same time he recognized that the Reformists had erred in becoming ultra-rationalistic. They had thrown out the baby with the bath water. Religion had at its base certain extra-rational human needs including the need for myths, magic, and mystery. To ignore them produced the kind of sterile religion which he sensed the Reformist branch had become. Like the Conservatives he stressed the importance of historical continuity in Jewish tradition and culture. Included in such continuity was not only the centrality of the Torah but also its heroes, distinctive holidays, and its symbols. These Kaplan called *sancta*, and it would be these rather than *Halacha* which would be at the core of Reconstructionist practice. Whereas Reformists were strongly influenced by the new criticism, Kaplan seems to have fallen under the sway of the new anthropology. The awe-inspiring Jehovah Godhead would be internalized and in its place the idea of Jewish civilization and peoplehood would be substituted.

In 1922 Kaplan put his theory into practice by founding the Society for the Advancement of Judaism. The prospect for Reconstructionism was good since it seemed, at least in theory, to be ideally suited for the new immigrants who were groping their way to middle-class status. The growing class of professionals and secularized intellectuals, highly rationalistc in their approach to life, yet anxious to maintain something of the Jewish tradition, ought to have been drawn to the Reconstructionists. Indeed many were, but Reconstructionism never succeeded in attracting many congregations and its influence remained largely in the realm of ideas. It became a kind of theoretic midpoint between the Conservative and Reform movements attracting only ten congregations during the thirties. Paradoxically, it was Kaplan, rather than the more extreme Reform rabbinate, who drew the ire of the Orthodox. In 1945 they mounted an unsuccessful effort to excommunicate him, but the effort only revealed again how difficult it was to achieve such an action in the absence of hierarchical authority.

If the Reform movement and Jewish anarchists underestimated the hold of traditional religion on the Jews of Eastern Europe, the Orthodox branch, in which that tradition was contained in its purest form, was not very successful in capitalizing on it. Plagued by poorly-trained rabbis, ignorant of the problems posed by life in a secularized environment, Orthodox leadership was slow to grasp the fact that Old-World religious authoritarianism could not be transferred wholesale to the New World. In the new environment, with its congregational polity and its voluntaristic character, the automatic leadership of the rabbinate was not accepted without question. Orthodox success in establishing a thriving flagship congregation in 1852, the Beth Hamidrosh Hagodol, and numerous smaller congregations, momentarily concealed from the leadership that the coercive power it formerly possessed in Europe was not effective among the Jews of America. Furthermore, they seemed only dimly aware of the steady attrition taking place in their ranks.

The attempt to build a permanent Orthodox institutional framework began in earnest in 1887 with the establishment of the Etz Chaim Talmudic Academy. A year later Joshua Rothstein, a wealthy cap manufacturer, joined with several other affluent Jews and Orthodox leaders to import a "chief rabbi." Selected for the position was Jacob Josef, a well-known talmudic scholar from Vilna. From the outset the importation of a "chief rabbi" created a furor. The Orthodox congregations who did not partake in the selection refused to recognize his leadership while at the same time, "uptown" Reformists remained indifferent. In addition, Josef's supporters planned to finance the venture by taxing kosher food products, a tax which they had no power to levy. They were still thinking in the Old-World manner. Rabbi Josef turned out to be a genuine Old-World scholar, possessing few of those leadership attributes which were necessary for success. Little progress was made in extending his leadership before he died in 1902.

The failure of Rabbi Jacob Josef in New York and that of another imported leader, Jacob Wilowski, who was brought to Chicago for a similar purpose in 1903, might have served a useful purpose for the Orthodox community had they given some thought to the reasons behind the failure. The nostalgia for the authoritarian religious structure, which had in fact already failed in Europe, was merely part of a larger pattern marked by a neglect to train an indigenous leadership which might better come to grips with the situation in America. Slow to adapt and seemingly unable to master the organizational skills required for nationwide organization, the Orthodox branch seemed destined to decline in the New World. Its deep-seated problems were concealed by an artificial glow of health created by the continued influx of Orthodox immigrants from Europe.

To be sure, the Isaac Elchanan Theological Seminary's merger with the Etz Chaim Talmudic Academy in 1915 boded well for Orthodoxy. Under the leadership of Bernard Revel the combined institution became the nucleus of Yeshiva University, ultimately to become the largest Jewish religious institution of higher learning in the United States. Revel proved to be a fortunate choice since by training and circumstance he was hardly in the ordinary mold of Orthodox leadership. His experience in the oil business in Oklahoma gave him a familiarity with the American scene and a practical business-minded approach to building an organization. Moreover, he was relatively free of the fundamentalism which might interfere with combining Orthodoxy and higher learning. He saw no conflict in teaching modern science to Orthodox youngsters.[12] In 1928 an Arts and Science division was added to Yeshiva College. Later, under the leadership of Samuel Belkin, the Albert Einstein Medical Center and other graduate components in social work, education and mathematics became part of Yeshiva University.

When considered jointly with the expansion of the religious day schools (yeshivot), the Orthodox branch seemed to outpace the other branches in the crucial area of education. Even so in 1908 only 20 percent of the ghetto's children were receiving some kind of religious training, hardly sufficient for the needs of the Orthodox community. By the second decade of the twentieth century a new impetus for organization emanated from Europe where the Orthodox élan was still fairly intact. A new rigidly Orthodox organization, the Agudath Israel, was established in 1912 in Katowice, Poland. Its stated goal was to solve "all problems which arise in the life of Israel in the spirit of Torah and Jewish tradition."[13] The movement soon sprouted branches in the United States, but rather than fostering unity it seemed only to lead to further fragmentation in the Orthodox branch. The much-desired central direction would prove to be an elusive goal.

It was an impossible task to get Orthodox congregations, some led by poorly trained lay people and others merely transitory groupings of people drawn together by the need for a quorum, to accept the idea that guidance from a central authority was necessary. The Orthodox scene was populated by small independent congregations and numerous religious schools, a good proportion of which were marginal and actually required little in the way of organizational superstructure. Piety and commitment were matters between man and God; they were personal rather than organizational. Ultimately, however, two groups were established to bring some organization into the confusing Orthodox scene, the Rabbinical Council of America and the Union of Orthodox Rabbis of the United States and Canada. We shall see presently that the chaotic condition in the kosher food business was given a modicum of order only with the help of an outside agency and state law.

The tradition of religious consciousness brought to the New World by the East European immigrants was not lightly abandoned. Yet the impact of secularism did perforce lead to a form of accommodation based on a practical synthesis between the need for continuity and the need for change. That synthesis was at the heart of American Conservatism. But rather than magically unifying American Jewry under its banner, the Conservative movement became a viable mediating third branch of American Judaism. The Reform and Orthodox branches continued to claim the loyalty of those Jews whose special needs they met.

Zionism, the secular reflection of Jewish peoplehood, played a mediating role not unlike that of the Conservative movement on the religious front. The two polarizing forces were Jewish religious particularism and assimilation which in Eastern Europe often assumed the guise of universalism.

CHAPTER XIII

The Genesis of American Zionism

IN CONTRAST TO THE PROGRESSIVE WEAKENING OF THE RELIGIOUS ELEMENT
of American Judaism at the turn of the century, secular Zionist sentiment began to show signs of growth. The rise of one of and the decline
of the other were no coincidence. Since they were anxious above all to
"Americanize" the East European immigrants, the chagrin of the
"uptown" Reformers must have been considerable when they discovered
that the erosion of Orthodoxy did not solve their problem. Beneath it
could often be found a strong Jewish folk tradition, and a separatist
ideology which posed a serious challenge to Americanizers.

To those willing to perceive it, the existence of a distinct Jewish folk
culture was already apparent in Eastern Europe. It was rooted primarily
in the religious tradition and particularized by centuries of enforced
isolation from the host nation. The *shtetl* and the ghetto served as a
cultural incubator in which Jews developed their own language, literature, music, distinctive values, and folk tradition. In their domination
of the Pale they might even be considered to have possessed their own
territorial space. Under such conditions assimilation meant more than
simply the abandonment of one's religion, it meant the surrender of an
entire cultural heritage. It was a difficult path to tread, especially if
one became aware that the host culture was hostile toward such converts. In Eastern Europe assimilation, which often occurred under the
rubric of universalistic radicalism, frequently meant in practice assigning oneself to a cultural limbo. How much more comfortable it was to
adapt to the unrelenting impact of secularization within a Jewish cultural context! If one could not be a modern Russian "of Mosaic
persuasion," then one might as well remain a Jew, albeit of the secular
ethnic variety.

The Zionist idea of a separate Jewish national-cultural entity with
its own territory grew naturally out of these circumstances. It was
fueled in the second half of the nineteenth century by the appearance
of a new strident form of anti-Semitism whose primary argument was
not that Jews were clannish and refused to assimilate, but that they

[194]

were all too ready to assimilate and work their evil designs on the host nation. The bloody pogroms which began in earnest in 1870 went far in awakening a countervailing nationalism among the Jews.

Among the earliest to examine the possibility of a Jewish national cultural regeneration was an assimilated Odessa physician, Leon Pinsker. In his book, entitled *Auto Emancipation,* he boldly suggested that the assimilationist solution to the Jewish question was unworkable and that the still dormant ingredients for creating a Jewish nation could be developed if some suitable territory were found. Pinsker was not the first, nor would he be the last, to discover the possibility of developing a separate Jewish national culture, but the year 1882, when his book was published, was a fortuitous moment for that age-old dream to take root among the Jewish masses.

It started slowly with the organization of Lovers of Zion clubs and various Zionist colonization societies throughout the Pale. The earliest dreams of regeneration did not necessarily focus on Palestine, the ancient homeland of the Jews. Pinsker himself was uncertain whether this strategically important area was the best locale to establish a Jewish national homeland. Moreover, in practice, the need to find a haven for the Jews of Eastern Europe antedated the crystallization of the Zionist idea. Most immigrants from the East chose America as their Zion. But from the outset there was a small counterflow of perhaps 25,000 who cast their lot with Palestine, then part of the province of Syria in the Ottoman Empire. These pioneers joined the small Jewish community which had existed in the area since time immemorial, founding fifteen agricultural settlements, one of which they called *Rishon Lezion* (First in Zion).

The idea of reestablishing a Jewish homeland did not gain the support of the East European Jews all at once. Orthodox Jews who awaited the Messiah's restoration of Zion found in the presumption of the secular Zionists anathema. The revolutionary-minded socialists, who had in 1897 established the General Jewish Workers' Alliance (Bund), sought the solution of the Jewish question in the universal rule of socialism. They reasoned that the roots of anti-Semitism were to be found in the capitalist system which, when abolished, would liberate all peoples from their fetters, including the Jews. They viewed the Zionist ideology as a reactionary bourgeois nationalist throwback. A just universal order was the wave of the future, not the tribalism advocated by the Zionists. A writer for *Shulamit,* the journal of the "Lovers of Zion" movement, described the nature of the opposition to the Zionists succinctly: "The very religious consider us heretics who wish to bring on the redemption before it is time. The liberals look upon us as fanatics, who obscure the light of civilization with this new-fangled idea. The 'Know Nothings' are against us from sheer inertia."[1]

The nascent Zionist movement appeared to thrive on such opposition. Its leaders were convinced that the synthesis it offered would in the long run prove irresistible to the Jewish masses. Indeed, it soon began to find acceptance in the West where a practical brand of that ideology, spurred on by the apparent failure of Jewish emancipation, made its debut. The trial and degradation of a French army officer, Alfred Drey-fus, in the early months of 1895 was witnessed by a Hungarian-born journalist, Theodor Herzl. Although an assimilated Jew, Herzl was never-theless profoundly moved by the infamous affair. He became aware of the difficult position Jews occupied everywhere in Europe. He was motivated to publish a practical proposal for the founding of a modern Jewish state which he called *Der Judenstadt* (The Jewish State).

No ordinary journalist, Herzl possessed charismatic qualities of leadership which stood the Zionist movement in good stead. The move-ment suffered from internal dissension which Herzl's strong leadership would partly eliminate. Moreover, the Zionist idea would under Herzl's direction begin to gain support from Jews in the West while at the same time reviving the languishing "Lovers of Zion" movement in the East. Herzl's stature was such that he could undertake to negotiate directly with the crowned heads of Europe, especially the Turkish Sultan, to bring the idea of a Jewish state into reality. The new energy and skilled leadership infused into the movement went far to arrest the erosion of the early settlement. Many of the "Biluim," the name given to the early pioneers in Palestine, had been compelled by circumstance to abandon the pioneer settlements; they survived largely on the financial largesse of Edmond de Rothschild. In 1897 leaders of the two streams of Zionism, the folkish ethnic Zionism of the East and the political philanthropic Zionism of the West, were brought together in Basle, Switzerland, to meet in the first Zionist Congress.

Like all movements in the Jewish world, Zionism was not exempt from division. Less than a decade after the Basle Congress the question of where the Jewish homeland should be established split the move-ment asunder. Israel Zangwill and other leaders took a simple position—resettlement and nation-building should take priority over having the Jewish nation established in a specific geographic locale. The terri-torialists, the name given to this faction, were little concerned about the traditional Jewish historical settlement in Palestine. Any suitable territory would do for the venture in nation-building and when the British offered the territory of Uganda, they favored accepting it. But the more mystic, historically-conscious Jews of the East insisted that Jewish hope must have its roots in Israel's ancient homeland. Without historical continuity there was nothing, because it was not a mere haven which was desired but a regeneration of the Jewish people. Rooted in deep differences in how they approached their Jewishness, the two opposing positions proved to be irreconcilable. Under the leadership of Israel Zangwill, who headed the Jewish Colonization Society (ITO), the territorialists competed with the Zionist pioneering effort in Palestine for decades to come.

Virtually from its inception American Jewry, and certain American Protestant groups as well, were strongly drawn to the Zionist idea. When Moses Malki of Safed and Hayim Isaac Karigal, who visited the American Jewish community in 1759 and 1773 respectively for the purpose of raising funds for the indigent Jews in Palestine, they found the small American Jewish community generous. As early as 1832 a special fund-raising organization for the Jews of Palestine was permanently established among the Jews of America. One of the best known of the early experiments of American proto-Zionism was sponsored by Mordecai Noah in 1825. Ararat was not Noah's only venture in Zionism. In 1843 he penned his "Discourse on the Restoration of the Jews," which called for the purchase of land in Palestine in preparation for the redemption of Israel.

For their own reasons Protestants often shared with Jews a nostalgia for the restoration of Zion. Sometimes it took the form of sympathy toward the idea of Jewish redemption. That was probably what John Q. Adams meant when he wrote to Mordecai Noah after hearing of his proto-Zionist scheme: "I really wish again in Judea an independent nation."[2] The Zionist impulse which many Protestant sects harbored was religiously motivated, rooted as it was in the Old Testament. Often the many fundamentalist sects which dotted the American religious landscape considered themselves to be the "children of Israel" en route to the promised land. The peculiar Puritan relationship to the Jews (and to the Indians) was partly based on this self-image. It was even more evident among the Mormons whose history virtually reenacts that of ancient Israel. The restoration of Zion in the great salt valley of Utah was foretold by their prophets Joseph Smith and Brigham Young who, incidentally, bear an uncanny resemblance to Moses and Joshua in the Old Testament. The remarkable Mormon migration across the "Great American Desert" is in many ways a recapitulation of Israel's exodus from Egypt to wander in the desert of Sinai for forty years until they could enter the Promised Land. Once they were settled in their Promised Land of Utah, the Mormon Zionist rhetoric became even more pronounced. The Colorado River was renamed the Bashan, after the river mentioned in the bible. The Utah landscape, in fact, produced a complete atlas of biblical place-names. Like the Puritans, Mormons came close to considering themselves descendants of the ancient Hebrews, so much so that at one point in their history they contemplated the introduction of circumcision.[3]

Most of the dissident Protestant sects who chose to resettle in the New World contained within themselves a strong biblical Zionist strain which came out in their culture and in the way they viewed themselves in America. Sometimes it was in fact Christian proto-Zionism which served to awaken Zionist longings among the Jews. The publication of George Eliot's Zionist novel *Daniel Deronda* in 1876 and Laurence Oliphant's *Land of Gilead* in 1881 went far to create a consciousness of Zion among Jews. One such was Emma Lazarus who in 1882 wrote her own Zionist tract, *Epistle to the Hebrews*, which served to awaken Zionist stirrings among American Jews.

Among the most fascinating examples of Christian proto-Zionism was that of Warder Cresson. Scion of an established Quaker family, Cresson showed early evidence of being something of a religious enthusiast. Before his startling conversion to Judaism, he was variously a Shaker, Mormon, Millerite, and Campbellite. It was his growing interest in Judaism which led him to become the unofficial American Consul in Jerusalem. There he became convinced of the need to reestablish a Jewish homeland in Palestine "where the Jewish nation may live by industry, congregate and prosper." His eccentric religious proclivities and his activities in Jerusalem caused concern at home and the post he occupied was abolished. Charges of religious lunacy were brought against him by his son but after a celebrated trial in 1848 they were dismissed. Cresson's conversion to Judaism had led him to change his name to Michael Boaz Israel. After the trial he returned to Palestine to "witness the ingathering of Jews by divine means." To help the ingathering in the temporal realm he composed a circular letter demanding the "restoration and consolidation of all Israel to their own land. . . ."[4] But like Orthodox Jews, Cresson waited in vain for the hoped-for miraculous ingathering, and suspicion of his motives grew. Chief Rabbi Abraham Gaggin suspected that Cresson aimed to proselytize among the Jews. The fundamentalist character of other Protestant activities in the Holy Land had created hostility among the largely Sephardic Jewish community of Palestine which had been subject to such efforts for centuries.

Cresson's attraction to Judaism was singular, but his idea of settling in the Holy Land was duplicated by several other American Fundamentalists. In 1850 a group of such religious enthusiasts led by Clorinda Minor, wife of a wealthy Philadelphia merchant, settled on a tract of land near present-day Tel Aviv. Calling their agricultural colony Mount Hope, they planned to lead a simple ascetic life of work patterned on that of the ancient Hebrews and await the second coming of Christ. Before that could occur, Arab hostility and the absence of such practical things as a market for their produce brought the experiment to an end in 1857. It was followed in 1866 by a second proto-Zionist Christian colonization venture composed of 150 religious pilgrims from the State of Maine led by their spiritual leader, Rev. Adam. It too failed in short order.

A remarkable example of Christian zeal for Jewish national redemption was that of William E. Blackstone, a minister of the Gospel from Chicago. Blackstone visited the Holy Land in 1888 and came away with the idea of resettling Jews there. On March 5, 1891, he sent a memorial to President Benjamin Harrison urging that he "consider the condition of the Israelites and their claims to Palestine as their ancient home" and that he use his good offices to effectuate that goal.[5] The Memorial was signed by 413 prominent Americans including Speaker of the House "Czar" Reed, Cyrus McCormick, Cardinal Gibbons, J. P. Morgan, J. D. Rockefeller, Cyrus W. Field, William E. Dodge, and Philip Armour.

The reaction of American Jews and Christians exemplified by the Blackstone Memorial are best viewed against the backdrop of Russian depredations against Jews. Concern for the Jews of Russia had become manifest and had spilled over into the Christian community. The diplomatic dispatches of General Lewis Wallace, author of the popular novel *Ben-Hur*, who served as the American Minister to Turkey, displayed a typical compassion for the wretched Jewish refugees who were forced to flee from the Russian pogroms and were flocking to the United States. He suggested to the State Department several times that Palestine rather than the United States was the most suitable haven for Jews. For different reasons, the Harrison administration looked with favor on such schemes. When Secretary of State James Blaine arranged a meeting between Blackstone and Harrison, the Minister learned of the Administration's keen concern about the flood of penniless Jewish immigrants which the Russian pogroms were bringing to this country.

It was not the Administration which opposed Blackstone's scheme. The authorities were receptive to any scheme that promised to deflect the immigrant flow and had already diplomatically interceded with the Russian government for that purpose. Opposition came from an unexpected quarter—the Reformist and Orthodox branches of the Jewish religious community. Although eight rabbis and seven prominent Jewish lay leaders had signed the Memorial, the Reformist leader Rabbi Emil Hirsch, acting as spokesman for a group of Reform rabbis, stated unequivocally that Jews did not wish to be restored to Palestine.[6] At the same time a group of Orthodox Jews, prompted by an article in the *Yiddish Courier*, became convinced that the Blackstone scheme was a concealed attempt to convert the Jews to Christianity. Unfamiliar with the Jewish community and the stirrings of modern nationalism by which they were motivated, the philosemitic Blackstone had no way of anticipating the hornet's nest of opposition his proposal would stir up among the powerful anti-Zionist elements.

American Zionism was a slow-starting affair. In the 1880's and 1890's it attracted only a small number of Jews. After the defeat of Turkey in the Russo-Turkish war in 1877 there was some hope among the small group of American Zionists that America or Britain would receive a protectorate in the area. But such a scheme was visionary, if only for the reason that an American-sponsored Jewish restoration in Palestine faced the prospect of stern opposition from the more established sections of American Jewry. Zionism seemed destined to become a "downtown affair."

It was among the newly-arrived immigrants that the first "Lovers of Zion" chapter was organized in 1884. Like the initial phase of the organization of the Jewish labor movement, American Zionism experienced great difficulty in simply keeping itself alive. The economic difficulties experienced by immigrants between 1883 and 1886 and again between 1893 and 1897 put a damper on all organizational activity. Barely a trace of the original "Lovers of Zion" chapters could be found in 1896. Such energy and leadership as was available among the immigrants gave first priority to the organization of their social institutions and the labor movement. "Uptown" leaders, such as Rabbi Richard Gottheil, who were attracted to Zionism, were hampered by the fact they could muster little enthusiasm for dealing with the East European Jews who formed the rank and file of the movement. But even among Eastern Jews Zionism won little popular acceptance because it raised a disturbing issue among the hard-pressed immigrants. It ran counter to the wish to reroot oneself here in America. In addition, virtually all organized elements in the community, including the socialist labor movement and the "uptown" reformers, were distrustful of the solution proposed by Zionism.

In its formative period, therefore, Zionism remained a local, not overly popular idea among American Jews. The name of Herzl was largely unknown and those few who had heard the name were suspicious.

The *American Hebrew* thought he might be an imposter or worse, a false Messiah.[7] When the call for the first Zionist Congress sounded in 1897, it went virtually unheard in America. Several unofficial observers, Rabbi Richard Gottheil, Adam Rosenberg, Rosa Sonnenschein, and Leon Zolotkoff were present at the momentous gathering but the enthusiasm for Zionism of the only official delegate, Dr. Schepsel Schaffer of the Orthodox synagogue of Baltimore, waned soon after the Congress.

But the Congress itself seemed to act like a tonic on the small American Zionist movement. A Chicago group hit upon a method of attracting membership by capitalizing on the love of secret rituals and insurance plans which captivated the average American. Changing its name from "Chicago Zionist, Organization Number One" to "Knights of Zion," the new group employed an organizational scheme based on gates which were the equivalent of lodges in older fraternal orders. At the same time a breakthrough occurred among the older German-Jewish community. In 1897 the *Zentralverein Amerikanischen Zionisten* (Central Organization of American Zionists) was founded. The momentum was taken up by the budding Conservative movement which specifically favored the Zionist idea and whose leader, Solomon Schechter, gave it additional prestige. A small group of Orthodox Jews organized themselves into Zionist clubs. There was an increased tempo of Zionist organizational activity in Philadelphia, Chicago, and other Jewish metropolitan centers. When Gottheil returned from Basle he organized the first nationwide Zionist organization, the Federation of American Zionists. He was president of the organization from 1898 to 1904 while Stephen Wise, a young Hungarian-born rabbi from Oregon who was already gaining recognition as a magnificent orator, became its secretary.

While the Federation was hardly the national organization its title suggested it was, over 100 local Zionist groups, mostly located in the large cities of the East, had affiliated with it by 1898. And with the growth of the organization leadership talent became attracted to it as well. By 1900 the Federation boasted about 8,000 members and five years later that figure had more than tripled.

But American Zionism was not out of the woods. Only a handful were actually active in the movement. The federated organizational principle employed by American Zionism created problems by allowing the decision to be made on the local level. The implementation of a national strategy and national objectives was difficult. The bane of Jewish organizational life, fragmentation and petty rivalries, presented themselves the moment the organization seemed viable enough to play host to them. There was much dissatisfaction with the leadership of Richard Gottheil, especially among the East European Jews. In 1898 the "Lovers of Zion" chapters, which had initiated the movement, took leave of the Federation. Gottheil's support of H. H. Sarasohn's journal, the *Tageblatt*, created further acrimony. Moreover, all was not well in the Federation's relationship with the world Zionist headquarters located in Vienna. The Federation was loath to remit the proceeds from the sale of *shekels*, the certificates purchased by members to entitle them to vote for delegates to the Zionist Congress, when there was such dire financial need at home. Having $11,000 in its treasury, the Federation transmitted only $4,000 to the victims of the Kishineff pogrom. Herzl's charge of mismanagement was not long in coming. In 1901 yet another quarrel between the Federation and *Alliance Israelite Universelle* broke out. The strife took its toll. Between 1902 and 1903, sixty-three local Zionist societies, comprising over a third of the membership, withdrew from the Federation of American Zionists (FAZ). Included in the group who resigned were many of the Hebrew-philes and traditionally-minded Jews who had comprised the backbone of the early movement.

To balance this loss the movement attracted a gifted administrator and organizer, Louis Lipsky. Born in Rochester and a trained attorney, Lipsky possessed the kind of energy and talent which the Zionist movement required for its growth. Lipsky founded and edited the *Maccabean*, which became the official organ of the FAZ, while at the same time occupying the position of managing editor of the *American Hebrew*, the leading Anglo-Jewish journal. By 1912 he was head of the Executive Committee of the FAZ and a leading personality within the American Zionist movement.

A second personality who came to the fore of the Zionist movement, albeit through a more devious route, was Jacob De Haas. De Haas was Herzl's personal emissary to the American Zionist movement; he became secretary of the FAZ in 1902, and later the editor of the *Boston Advocate*, one of the better Anglo-Jewish journals. But personality factors and the unfortunate circumstances of having, in a sense, been foisted on American Zionism, curtailed his usefulness. He remained a "gray eminence" in American Zionism. Perhaps the greatest service he performed was in bringing Louis Brandeis to the movement. We shall see that it was that, more than anything else, which made Zionism respectable for middle-class Jews.

In contrast to De Haas, who was English-born, Emma Lazarus stemmed from the very heart of the older established Jewry of America. Born in 1849 of Sephardic ancestry, Emma Lazarus came late to full consciousness as a Jew and a Zionist and then had only a brief opportunity to project her spirit on the American Zionist scene. She died in

1887 at the age of thirty-eight. But in that short period she played a role in bridging the gap between the mystical, often Christian-inspired Zionism, of antebellum American Jewry, and the practical political Zionism of the twentieth century. Her advocacy of Zionism was sparked by the outrage she felt at the Russian and Rumanian pogroms during the final decades of the nineteenth century. A belated recognition that not all Orthodox immigrants could satisfactorily adjust to a society which was "utterly at variance with their time-honored customs and most sacred beliefs," contributed further to her conversion. She became convinced that especially for these Jews, Palestine would offer a transition less destructive of their culture.[8]

The trials of the Zionist movement, already in evidence in the 1890's, continued unabated in the first decade of the century. In 1901, led by Rabbi Philip Klein, the religious Zionists took their leave of the FAZ. Their hope to form an American branch of the international religious Zionist movement, Mizrachi, whose center was in Vilna, Lithuania, was not immediately successful, but neither was the split easily healed. The group sent their own delegate, Dr. Joseph Bluestone, to the World Zionist Congress which met again in Basle in 1903. At the same time another faction of Zionism representing a socialist labor view, Poale Zion, made its debut. Its first branch founded in March, 1903, desired to counteract the attraction of the socialist-oriented Jewish labor movement, but, predictably, it was at loggerheads with the religious Zionists as well. Poale Zion hoped to merge the socialist and Zionist idea. "The national struggle and the class struggle far from being mutually exclusive are branches of the same trunk," read one Poale Zion resolution. Extreme left-wing Zionists came to idealize the work of Ber Borochov, who ostensibly offered a workable synthesis between the two opposite schools of thought. The new branch became an autonomous body in 1909 and affiliated with the World Federation of Socialist Zionists, which had been established two years previously as an autonomous body within the World Zionist Organization.

The myriad cultural, religious, and political divisions to which Jewry was heir were being faithfully reflected in American Zionism. In the middle were the general Zionists and their organizations, the Order of the Sons of Zion, Young Judea, and Hadassah, the Women's Zionist Organization of America. (By 1912 the last-mentioned organization served as an umbrella for the Daughters of Zion and other women's groups who did not always see eye to eye.) On the left were the various groups associated with Labor Zionism whose variations consisted of all the gradations between the moderate Social Democrat position to the orthodox Marxist one. On the right were the religious Zionists to be joined later by the Revisionist Zionists who looked for leadership to Vladimir Jabotinsky.

For each group Zionism had come to mean something different. The religious wing envisaged a Jewish sovereignty from which the study of the Torah could go forth to regenerate the religious spirit of diaspora Judaism. For the labor Zionists it offered the hope of creating a Jewish secular classless society based on the socialist model which could serve as a model for the world. For those in the center, Zionism meant simply the creation of a modern industrial state, a *Musterstaat*, which might serve as a model for a humanistic middle-class social order. Finally, for the thousands of unaffiliated Jews Zionism was the most complete and positive expression of twentieth-century Jewish secular culture; it meant simply a revival of Jewish community.

Wracked by internal conflict, it appeared in 1910 as if the American Zionist movement was destined to languish. In 1913 the National Zionist Convention held in Cincinnati was sparsely attended, and at the following convention in Rochester there were only 15,000 *shekel* buyers, an increase of merely 3,000 since 1912. Hostility from the Reform movement, harping on the danger of "dual loyalties," and the Jewish labor movement, and its universalistic solution to the "Jewish question," curtailed the flocking of the immigrants to the Zionist banner. While the Zionist Labor idea might mute the hostility between Socialism and Zionism, the adamant opposition of "uptowners" was not so easily resolved, despite the fact that a handful of Reform rabbis had in fact cast their lot with the Zionist movement.

We have seen that the older Jewish establishment was anxious above all to rid East European Jewish immigrants of their distinctive alien culture so that they might become Americans as quickly as possible. Predictably, a nationalistic creed such as Zionism was considered an impediment to that process. For them "eternal Judaism" was not tied to a certain piece of land, it was not conditioned by space, it played its role throughout the world in the spiritual arena.[9] Zionism tended to bring out the latent insecurities of the original Jewish settlers. "To my mind," said Rabbi David Philipson, among the most outspoken anti-Zionists in the Reform rabbinate, "political Zionism and true Americanism have always seemed mutually exclusive. No man can be a member of two nationalities, Jewish and American. . . . There is no middle way."[10] In a similar way Jacob Schiff argued bitterly in a letter to Bernard Richards that "thanks to the preaching and machinations of Jewish Nationalists we are gradually being forced into a class by ourselves . . . whose interests are different than those of the . . . American people."[11]

In order to thrive American Zionism had urgently to find a response to the loyalty question. For a brief moment a visit from Herzl was contemplated. It was hoped that his charisma and respectability would soften the "uptown" opposition, but the idea had to be abandoned when it was realized, in the words of one Zionist spokesman, that not even "the Messiah could succeed in budging the German Jews from their new Zion."[12]

But Philipson and his Midwestern claque of Reform rabbis were in some ways more extreme in their opposition to Zionism than the constituency they represented. Many original settlers did not in fact oppose colonization in Palestine and the economic development of that area. Some retained enough of their loyalty to Judaism to favor such projects on general principles. Others may have seen Palestine as an alternative haven for the swarms of Jewish immigrants who were flooding the country and ruining their image of respectability. It was primarily political Zionism, the idea that a sovereign Jewish Commonwealth must be established, that was anathema. It led to the appeal of some Reformists to "scrap Zionism and build Palestine."

In 1914 and 1915 certain developments served to strengthen the American Zionist movement. The first was the recruitment of Louis Brandeis and the second was the discovery of a partial solution for the long-standing organizational difficulties within the FAZ. In 1915 that umbrella organization was restructured so that individual members could join it directly rather than having to join one of the several constituent organizations. Individual membership in the Federation, now renamed the Zionist Organization of America, could now balance the strength of the individual chapters which together were not coordinated enough to give direction to the organization.

It was in the recruitment of Brandeis that the Zionists finally found the way to clothe their cause with respectability, especially as it related to the charge of "dual loyalty." Brandeis came to Judaism late in life. Born in St. Louis in 1856, his formative years were spent in the patrician atmosphere of Boston where he received his formal education. He was in his mid-fifties when he began to think about Zionism. There is little agreement among scholars on what precipitated his "conversion." It may have been the belated influence of his uncle, Lewis Dembitz, a lawyer and staunch Zionist whose middle name he bore.[13] He found his way to the movement a few years after his uncle's death in 1907. The model of his uncle's life may have helped resolve a late identity crisis in Brandeis's life. Undoubtedly, the role he played as chairman of the arbitration board which produced the "Protocol of Peace" for the garment industry in 1910 also influenced him. He noted in his acceptance address of the Chairmanship of the Provisional Executive Committee of the ZOA that his experience at the negotiating table made him feel "the Jewish people had something which should be saved for the world." He thought he detected a deep concern for "social justice" and "love of democracy," concerns incidentally which occupied most of his adult professional life.

Other motivations have also been suggested. One theory maintains that it was the search for an outlet for his Progressive ideals based on smallness, efficiency, and the muting of the self-interest aspects of business enterprises that brought him to the Zionist movement.[14] Another historian upholds an earthier view by picturing Brandeis as a "marginal man" who came to the Zionist movement seeking compensation after Wilson veered away from his Progressive program and rejected Brandeis for a cabinet post in 1913. It was a Brandeis in search of a Jewish constituency, especially its business element, who came to the Zionist movement.[15]

Whatever the case, his late entry into Jewish organizational life made him self-conscious about the leading role he was called upon to play in the American Zionist movement. "I feel my disqualifications for this task," he admitted upon his election as head of Provisional Committee in August, 1914. "Throughout long years which represent my own life I have been to a great extent separated from Jews. I am very ignorant of things Jewish. . . ."[16] As a newcomer he perhaps overidealized the "deep noble feeling" and "sense of brotherhood" which he saw as the "fruit of three thousand years of civilization."[17] But as his attacks against privilege estranged him from some sections of his Brahmin Boston circle, he was able to draw sustenance from his newly discovered Jewish consciousness.

It was actually through his own initiative that Brandeis was drawn into the American Zionist movement. He penned a brief note to Bernard Richards, secretary of the FAZ, expressing interest in the coming tenth anniversary celebration. Sensing his interest, Richards prevailed upon him to chair a Boston meeting to honor Nachum Sokolow, a Zionist leader who was visiting the United States. After the original contact had been made, the influence of De Haas and Aaron Aaronsohn became paramount.

Brandeis brought to Zionism a first-rate mind, capable of digesting prodigious amounts of information and sending it forth again in a systematized, meaningful way. He possessed uncommon mental discipline and sense of organization which would stand the chaotic Zionist organization in good stead. Most important, however, was the fact of his commitment to the Zionist movement. It helped shatter the idea that "uptown" respectability and Zionism were mutually exclusive. Moreover, Brandeis was able to attract many of his talented circle to the movement. Men like Judge Julian Mack, Felix Frankfurter, Nathan Straus, Mary Fels, Benjamin Victor, and Louis Kirstein added stature to American Zionism. They made it American.

Brandeis continually returned to the charge of "dual loyalty" to mitigate its baneful effects. "Let no American imagine that Zionism is inconsistent with patriotism," he acclaimed; "multiple loyalties are objectionable only if they are inconsistent. A man is a better citizen of the United States for being loyal to his family and to his profession or trade...."[18] At times he was even more specific: "There is no inconsistency between loyalty to America and loyalty to Jewry.... The Jewish spirit, the product of our religion ... is essentially American." According to Brandeis "loyalty to America demands rather that each Jew become a Zionist."[19]

Many American Jews began to follow his lead. When he joined the movement membership had already climbed to 150,000. Five years later it had risen to almost 173,000. Money began to flow into the coffers of the Zionist organization. During the war America was chosen to serve as the headquarters of the international Zionist movement. But the testing of the mettle of American Zionism, the measuring of its newfound strength, awaited the end of hostilities when the crucial peace negotiations would offer a rare opportunity to put its program into effect.

CHAPTER XIV

The Elaboration of
Jewish Organizational Life, 1900-1920

DURING THE FIRST TWO DECADES OF THE TWENTIETH CENTURY THE elaboration of Jewish organizational life took place. Behind the proliferation of new and different types of organization was the startling growth in size and complexity of the American Jewish community. Some of the new organizations merely reflected the "uptown"-"downtown" division and duplicated the philanthropic, religious, and social functions of existing organizations. Others stemmed from the need to do something about the deteriorating conditions of Jewish communities in Eastern Europe. The models here were the national defense organizations which already existed in Britain, France, and Germany. The period also saw a unique experiment in ethnic self-government based on the model still extant in the Jewish communities of Eastern Europe. When the development was completed the organizational framework of American Jewry had been altered beyond recognition. It possessed the most elaborate organizational structure of any hyphenate group in America, and incidentally the most contentious one.

Feeling threatened and repelled by the newcomers, the "native" Jews's unwillingness to integrate, at least until certain "Americanizing" prerequisites had been met, was predictable. The unofficial membership policy of the New Harmony club, then the very pinnacle of genteel German-Jewish society, was "more polish and less POLISH."[1] The social gap between the two groups was exacerbated by the different manner in which each group proclaimed its Judaism. The result was a desire on the part of the new arrivals to establish their own fraternal orders, hospitals, orphanages, and a unique new type of social organization, the *landsmannschaft*.

The "downtown" organizational developments were made possible by the new sources of funds which became available as a growing number of immigrants successfully established themselves. These "new rich" were more than ever subject to the imperative of *Tzedakah* and naturally much of their giving flowed to the newly established institutions.[2] Frequently the establishment of a new hospital or old age home was precipitated by conflict over dietary and other forms of religious observance in an existing institution. Differences in class and station also tended to make the new arrivals uncomfortable in the oaklined carpeted offices where uptown charity was dispensed. The rigid formal protocol of the German-Jewish philanthropic institutions lacked the easy familiarity to which Jews from Eastern Europe were accustomed. Then, too, "downtowners" were put off by what seemed to them to be an arrogant attitude on the part of the "uptown" dispensers. The result was a proliferation of new organizations and institutions of charity. By 1918 the *Jewish Communal Register* reported the existence of 3,637 organizations in New York City alone. That meant one organization for every 410 Jews.

Undoubtedly it was partly the sheer number of Jewish organizations which served as the impetus for bringing some order into Jewish community life. Ever since the Board of Delegates of American Israelites had been absorbed by the Union of American Hebrew Congregations in 1894, no central nationwide secular organization existed within American Jewry. In the meantime the composition of the community had been radically altered by the influx of immigrants from Eastern Europe. This had led to a modicum of local coordination. As early as 1869 a half dozen Jewish charitable groups in Philadelphia had organized themselves into a Society of United Hebrew Charities. Coordination on the philanthropy level was encouraged by large givers, such as Jacob Schiff, who conditioned their donations on the elimination of wasteful duplication. Self-help and charitable organizations, cognizant of the unified model presented by the national Conference of Charities and Corrections, which was established in the Christian community in 1873, were better able to avoid the divisive spirit characteristic of other areas of Jewish organization life. One by-product of this fortunate situation was the rapid progress professionalization, especially in social work, was able to make. A career in social work proved especially attractive to Jews, and it was in part from their base in this profession, rather than from the political club, that many a Jewish reformer found his way into politics.

By the mid-1890's, Jewish communities in Cincinnati and Boston had followed Philadelphia's lead and systematized their philanthropic organizations. In 1896 the newly organized Federation of Jewish Charities of Boston eliminated the need for separate appeals by conducting a federated fund-raising campaign.[3] It was a practice soon to be followed by other Jewish communities. By 1900 the influx of new immigrants underlined the urgency for streamlining charity fund-raising and distribution methods. It spurred a new wave of reforms in the existing system. In order to improve the planning on the national level, the National Conference of Jewish Charities was established in 1900. The same was done by local federations established in Baltimore in 1907, Brooklyn in 1909, San Francisco in 1910, and Los Angeles and Pittsburgh in 1912. But the coordination and rationalization process frequently proved difficult to impose. The Boroughs of Bronx and Manhattan, which contained a considerable proportion of America's Jewry, were not federated until 1917, and Brooklyn did not join in making one large metropolitan federation until years later. It was the forty-sixth community to do so.

Once established, the local federations set community priorities in regard to need and centralized the collection of funds. In New York City, for example, 116 agencies concerned with charity were incorporated by the Federation. Included were hospitals, old age homes, child care centers, YM and YWHAs, family service agencies, settlement houses, and some educational institutes. The rise of the federations did not, of course, magically solve all the old problems. Conflict, especially over priorities, continued to occur. But there now existed a professional context in which these conflicts could be ironed out and prevented from becoming political issues. Sometimes, as in the case of Chicago and Boston, the federations themselves fell victim to the "uptown-downtown" polarization.[4] But these were exceptions. In the majority of cases philanthropy and fund-raising, the latter perhaps the most important activity in the Jewish community, became shining examples of efficiency.

Not unexpectedly, as the collective wealth of American Jewry grew, the pressure to contribute to the relief for hard-pressed Jewish communities overseas did too. Not that such giving was unprecedented. It had in fact been presaged in the pre-Civil War period when emissaries from Palestine and other communities learned firsthand of the generosity of the virtually unknown Jewish community of America. Individual examples aimed at promoting the welfare of Jews overseas were embodied in Mordecai Noah's somewhat visionary scheme to "save" the Jews of Tunis. Such generosity was prompted by nostalgia and memory of the links which still bound the isolated Jews of the New World to their compatriots in other parts of the world. There was, for an example, an outpouring of goodwill and money during the infamous Damascus Blood Libel Case in 1840. When the Russian pogroms began in earnest thirty years later, American Jews were again called upon for help. Their greatest contribution came in absorbing the immigrants produced by the depredations, a task which they sometimes proved reluctant to undertake. Yet throughout the troubled period additional funds were found for overseas relief. One fourth of the monies collected for the rehabilitation of the victims of the Kishineff pogrom emanated from American sources. When the Zionist movement came to the fore at the turn of the century with its separate need for financial assistance, it too came to rely heavily on American Jewish largesse. The Jewish National Fund, established in 1901 to purchase land in Palestine, raised over 25 percent of its capital among American Jews.

As in the case of domestic charity programs, it took the crisis of World War I to create an awareness of the need to place overseas relief on a similar rational footing. Several new relief agencies had arisen to aid the communities of Eastern Europe devastated by the war. By October, 1914, the "Central Committee for the Relief of Jewish War Sufferers" was in existence. It was primarily a "downtown" affair because it was the new immigrants who through their personal contacts with the victims gained a firsthand knowledge of the extent of the devastation. Soon the "uptowners" through the newly organized American Jewish Committee joined in the effort. Later a third group, the "People's Relief Committee," representing the Jewish labor movement, joined in. In November, 1914, the three groups, the *landsmannschaften*, the American Jewish Committee, and the People's Relief Committee combined to form the "Joint Distribution Committee of the American Friends of Jewish War Sufferers." Later the name was shortened to the American Jewish Joint Distribution Committee (JDC).

The JDC became the major American Jewish overseas relief agency. Felix Warburg, its first chairman, was the scion of America's leading Jewish banking family. Carefully avoiding the shoals of Jewish community politics, the JDC thought of itself as an administrative organization which collected funds through existing organizations and distributed them through the established channels of the overseas relief network. If fund-raising is any indication, this neutral posture, added to a reputation for effectiveness, proved eminently suitable for loosening the purse strings of American Jews. In 1915 the agency raised $1,550,000 for relief and by 1918, $16,500,000.[5] The agency's success continued under the administration of Paul Baerwald, who became chairman in 1932. It expanded in scope under the chairmanship of Edward Warburg, the son of the first chairman, who took over the reins of leadership in 1941. It was during the following years, the years of the holocaust, that the mettle of the agency was tested.

America's neutrality permitted the JDC to distribute its largesse to both sides until April, 1917. Its efforts were naturally concentrated in

Eastern Europe where the war proved devastating to the Jewish communities of the Pale and Galicia. It helped build schools and workshops to employ the destitute Jewish population, but most of these facilities were dissolved by a suspicious new Soviet regime after November, 1917. For relief in German-occupied territory the JDC channeled its funds through the American consul in Warsaw, who in turn transferred them to a German Jewish agency, the *Jüdische Hilfskomite für Polen und Litauen* (Jewish Aid Committee for Poland and Lithuania), which operated behind the German lines. So effective was the JDC that Herbert Hoover, who directed the massive postwar government relief effort, singled it out for special praise. According to Hoover, it was "a major lifeline to the Jews in Poland."[6] At the peak of its activity 700,000 Jews in the East were dependent on its largesse. In Austria-Hungary the JDC funneled its aid through the *Allianz Zu Wien* (Viennese coalition) which in turn supported 400,000 Jews from the war zone. When the United States entered the war some funds continued to be channeled to these organizations through Holland.

For Russian Jewry the Revolution and the subsequent civil war increased its difficulties. It produced an additional 200,000 Jewish casualties. Between 1918 and 1920 the JDC distributed an additional $27,000,-000 for relief of Russian Jewry. With experience their services grew more efficient and far-reaching. Special child care trains and soup kitchens were utilized to feed the Jewish population. A program to rebuild damaged Jewish educational and cultural institutions was begun. The agency's far-flung operations were administered by a staff of trained field workers, two of whom, Rabbi Bernard Canto and Professor Israel Friedlander, were killed by marauding guerrillas.

In 1921 the Soviet authorities, recognizing the value of the agency, requested that it embark on new kinds of programs. Together with the Jewish Colonization Society, it embarked on a massive program to reshape Soviet Jewry. It established credit unions and built cooperatives to help those Jews willing to resettle on the soil to become farmers. Over a period of five years, $60,000,000 were spent on this program. In 1924 the agency received a mandate from the Soviet authorities to help in the rebuilding of the Jewish community. The government would supply free land, seed, and machinery for the resettlement of Jews in agricultural colonies in the Crimea. Working through its own agency, Agro-Joint, an additional $16,000,000 was expended for that purpose. Paradoxically, it may have been precisely this close cooperation with the Soviet authorities during the twenties which aroused Stalin's suspicion of the agency's activities during the Cold War. During that period it was several times accused at show trials and in propaganda broadcasts of being an arm of American intelligence. It figured prominently in the coerced confessions in the satellite countries during the "Black Years," between 1948 and 1952.

In February, 1906, shortly after the full extent of the depredations of the Kishineff and the subsequent pogroms became known, sixty leading American Jews met in New York City and organized a new defense organization, the American Jewish Committee. In terms of the Jewish tradition the concern of Jews of high station with the protection of Jewish interests was not extraordinary. The defense function customarily was filled by the court Jew, the *shtadlan*, whose high position enabled him to intercede in behalf of Jewish interests. The organization of the American Jewish Committee merely institutionalized this customary role as had already been done in Britain (the British Board of Deputies) and France (the *Alliance Israelite*) as well as the original Board of Delegates of American Israelites. The *modus operandi* of these groups was to operate without a mass base. There was a fear of stirring up the rabble rousers. In the case of the founders of the AJC, there was expectation that if such an organization were not established, less controllable elements in the community would seize the initiative since "organization was in the air."[7]

The Kishineff pogrom brought home to the "uptown" philanthropists that the expenditure of money after the ravages had taken place was a wasteful and futile exercise. Much needless suffering could be avoided if something could be done to halt the depredations before they occurred. It was well known that the pogroms in Russia took place with the consent and often at the behest of the Tsarist regime. In this area at least government-to-government pressure might be employed. But single influential Jews could do little. Men like Jacob Schiff, Oscar Straus, and Cyrus L. Sulzberger who were engaged in these activities felt overburdened. Some broader organization to protect Jewish interests before the authorities was required. The American Jewish Committee (AJC) was conceived to fill this need.

The guiding spirit behind the American Jewish Committee was a fifty-year-old attorney, Syracuse-born Louis Marshall. Almost from the moment of his arrival in New York City in 1898 to join the law firm of Guggenheimer and Untermeyer, Marshall seemed destined to play a leading part in Jewish affairs. Although a member of the uptown clique—he was President of Temple Emanu-El, the flagship of Reform temples in New York—Marshall felt none of the disdain for the new Jewish immigrants so frequently to be noted among his "uptown" compatriots. He mastered Yiddish and even tried his hand at publishing a Yiddish newspaper, the *Jewish World*. He was instrumental in helping to form the Jewish Relief Committee, and its great successor organization, the JDC.

Above all, Marshall was a brilliant lawyer who used his talents to plead the causes of American Jewry before various administrations in Washington. Between 1906 and 1911 he waged a ceaseless struggle for the abrogation of the Commercial Treaty of 1832 with Russia. He was involved in virtually every cause close to the heart of the immigrant community. While President of the AJC between 1917 and 1929, he led the battle against the restrictive immigration laws then advocated by nativist elements and supported by some uptown Jews; he fought against the imposition of informal quotas for Jews at the nation's universities and when, during the period of the "Red Scare," the New York State legislature purged five socialist Assemblymen, Marshall was among the distinguished attorneys who drew up an *amicus curiae* brief to be presented to the Judiciary Committee.

Marshall was no more a Zionist than he was a socialist, but this did not prevent him from seeing when an injustice had been done or a momentary harmony of interest existed. He was, for example, instrumental in helping to organize the non-Zionist segment of the Jewish Agency which served as the principal government administrative agency in Palestine. During the critical turn-of-the-century years Marshall was one of the few leading personalities in American Jewry able to serve as a bridge between its proud preexisting community and the needy new arrivals who, many felt, threatened its interest. Without such a bridge the history of American Jewry might have been far different.

The attempt to create a bridge is reflected in the organization of the AJC. Its constitution, adopted in November, 1906, called for an executive committee of five. All did not go smoothly, however, and there was constant pressure to broaden the base of the organization. Competing organizations such as B'nai B'rith and the Union of American Hebrew Congregations, who viewed themselves as filling a defense role, would have been happy had the new organization never made its debut at all. Only a skillful compromise stilled their fears about what these powerful *shtadlanim* would do to their organizational integrity. Some never reconciled themselves to the existence of the AJC but the majority watched contentedly as the AJC developed into the strongest defense organization of American Jewry.

Nevertheless, the problem of doing justice to all the competing interests in the American Jewish community was not easily solved. This was especially true of the interests of the new immigrants. Marshall, who had come a long way to meet the East European Jews on their own terms, nevertheless continued to be apprehensive regarding their tendency to think in terms of ethnic politics. "What I am trying to avoid more than anything else," he confided to a friend, "is the creation of a political organization, one which will be looked upon as indicative of a purpose on the part of the Jews to recognize that they have interests different from those of other American citizens."[8] The way to prevent the newcomers from developing such unacceptable practices was to make room for them within the AJC, to broaden its base so that it was truly representative of American Jewry. The old court Jew approach was bound to be ineffective because it would compel the East Jewish immigrants to develop their own organizations. Already there were signs of resentment among the leaders. Things could not forever be done for them and to them, but not with them. In the long run not even the steps suggested by Marshall proved sufficient to head off the establishment of new organizations based on concepts favored by East European Jews, ideas of mass representation and Jewish "peoplehood."

Not all agreed with Marshall on the need to broaden the base of the AJC. Some like Oscar Straus and Adolf Krauss were convinced that the organization would be more effective if it retained its small private character. "The suggestion that mere numbers can give rise to statesmanlike advice in matters affecting the Jewish people is unthinkable," maintained Sulzberger. He advised "crushing" the "know-nothing element" among the native Jews and the "arrogant assumptions" of the East Siders.[9] Straus was not so even-handed in his approach to the "rabble rousers." Judaism was a religion and nothing more; to consider it otherwise raised the specter of dual loyalties, an idea he felt should be anathema to all self-respecting American Jews.

Nevertheless, it was decided to proceed with Marshall's plan to make a place for representatives of the ghetto at the council table. "A new Jewry has arisen in the United States since 1881," observed Jacob Schiff,, "and their confidence is necessary for any general representative body."[10] Thirty-five additional members were to be enlisted for the executive committee of the AJC. Meyer Sulzberger became the new president while Julian Mack, a prominent Zionist, and Isidor Newman, a New Orleans merchant and banker, became vice presidents. Eventually, the addition of local advisory councils gave the AJC a more federated administration. In New York, the AJC broadened its base by coopting the entire leadership of the New York Kehillah Council which had been organized by Judah Magnes in 1908. The Council of the Kehillah was itself composed of members of many different organziations. In 1911 the AJC invited still other organizations to become members at large.

However, the efforts to broaden the base of the AJC were only partly successful. The Zionists and the socialists ignored the AJC's approaches. At one point the Federation of American Zionists sent an uncommitted delegate, but he was rejected by the AJC because he could not speak for his organization. Sometimes, too, alliances of convenience developed. Thus, the socialist-minded leadership of the United Hebrew Trades had no scruples about working with the AJC when their common distaste for the Zionists was involved. In the words of Nahum Syrkin, the leader of Poale Zion, they formed an "unholy alliance between Hester Street and Wall Street."[11]

Several events in 1914 made it essential that the issues which divided American Jewry be settled promptly. The war had not only created havoc in the Jewish communities of Eastern Europe, it had also brought an unexpected opportunity to realize the Zionist program for reestablishing a Jewish homeland in Palestine. The dissolution of Turkey, "the Sick Man of Europe," would leave Syria and the Middle Eastern segments of the Ottoman Empire up for grabs. Undoubtedly these provinces would fall into British hands and if that occurred Zionist leaders like Chaim Weizmann expected a national home eventually to be granted to the Jewish settlers in Palestine.

Further enhancing Zionist hopes at home was the spurt of organizational energy which accompanied the successful recruitment of Louis Brandeis. There now existed a Zionist counterpart of the AJC and the war itself had rushed certain crucial questions to the fore. There would be need for a Jewish delegation to the peace conference and that in turn would require some *modus vivendi* in the Jewish community. The issue was joined when a group of little-known Zionists pressed an effort to establish yet another national Jewish organization, to be organized on the principle of Jewish "peoplehood" and mass democratic participation. Ignored by the AJC, the group turned to B'nai B'rith to gain leverage and when that too failed, it turned to the "National Workingmen's Committee on Jewish Rights," a defense organization taking shape on the left side of the Jewish political spectrum. The new group's maneuvering between the major organizations lasted for two years. The sparks which flew from the intrusion of these "illustrious obscure" were white hot. Tackling the issue of representation meant direct confrontation.

Judah Magnes, the charismatic leader of the New York Kehillah, resigned from the group in disgust when he sensed that its organizational principles would exacerbate the divisions within the community. Especially nettlesome was the question of dual loyalties. Some "uptown" Zionists had come to believe that Zionism could legitimately be grafted onto the existing organizational structure. "I never had the slightest fear," observed Judge Julian Mack, "that any of those [Zionist] ideas will make the Jews of this country any less good Americans, or that there is such a conception as a political nation within the American nation."[12] But for others the very idea of a specific Jewish political interest was anathema.

In March, 1915, a provisional committee headed by Louis Brandeis began in earnest to lay the groundwork for the new national organization. It would be known as the American Jewish Congress and when Brandeis was condemned for lending his good name to an organization which could only lead to further fragmentation of American Jewry, he retorted that "unity means not oneness in opinion but oneness in action"[13] For a moment such oneness in action proved possible.

A year later, in March, 1916, 367 representatives of various organizations met in Philadelphia to charter a course for the newly founded organization. The organizational principle was stated best by Stephen Wise, who moved the delegates by reminding them that what the group wanted was "not relief but redress, not palliation but prevention, not charity but justice. . . ."[14] It was an eloquent paraphrasing of the primary grievance of the East Siders. Beyond the issues of whether the organization should call itself Conference or Congress, was the question of finding a place and a role in Jewish life in America. The AJC, convinced that it could do little to prevent the new group from coming into existence, sought to limit its jurisdiction and longevity. It would concern itself with the postwar problems of Jewry to be discussed at the peace conference. When that task was done the organization would be disbanded. The American Jewish Congress, as viewed by the leadership of the AJC, merely represented a temporary coming together for limited ends, but even such a compromise was opposed by those who were convinced that Zionism would ultimately subvert the foundations of American Jewry.

But AJC leaders like Jacob Schiff and Louis Marshall, if they had not reconciled themselves to the idea of a new Jewish political commonwealth, could support the idea of a vital Jewish cultural center in the Holy Land. It was this view that made possible a compromise program for the new organization. It was accepted in July, 1916, and included a dual approach to the Jewish problems in Europe: It would urge the protection of minorities in the various new nations to be created by the Treaty on the basis of the formula of national self-determination. For those Jews who wanted to leave Europe to live in a Jewish national homeland, that too would be urged by the Jewish delegation. A conference to include delegates from all national Jewish organizations and a special election within the Jewish community to achieve a better consensus of the desires of the community were scheduled.

Accordingly, in June, 1918, the American public was treated to the remarkable spectacle of watching one of its many hyphenate groups conducting an internal election which would, in a sense, determine its future course. Over thirty organizations participated and ballots were cast. But just as the dream of unity seemed to be realized a new discordant note was heard. The National Workingman's Committee on Jewish Rights, representing the socialist segment of the community, convinced that the socialism then being implemented in the Soviet Union meant that the solution to the Jewish problem was at hand, withdrew from the American Jewish Congress. That would be a view held by thousands in the following decades.

The antagonism between Zionists and non- or anti-Zionists was intensified by the issuance of the Balfour Declaration by the British Foreign Office on November 2, 1917. The declaration contained a qualified promise that a Jewish national homeland would be created in Palestine. On April 10, 1918, the AJC issued a bland response to the declaration. Those who wanted to settle in Palestine "attracted by religious or historic association" were welcome to do so. If the Committee had to think of Palestine at all, it preferred to envisage a center "for the stimulation of our faith, for the pursuit and development of literature and science" and for other cultural activities. It could hardly envisage an independent Jewish sovereignty and it reminded its members of the strong reservations in the declaration regarding the Arabs living in the area.

It was not until December, 1918, almost four years after the idea had first been broached and barely a month before the nations were scheduled to meet at Versailles, that the call went out for the first convention of the American Jewish Congress to meet in Philadelphia. Some 400 delegates, a quarter of whom represented organizations, met and chose Julian Mack president by acclamation, Louis Marshall was elected as one of the twelve vice-presidents called for by the organization's charter. Jacob Schiff was elected to his customary post of treasurer.

The new organization had little time to waste. A delegation to the peace conference was selected but instructing it would prove difficult. The reason was that the question of cooperation with those representatives of the world Zionist movement, who would also be at Versailles, to urge the legal recognition of Palestine Jewry as a separate entity, was bound to come up. The delegates were eventually instructed to cooperate with delegates of the world Zionist Organization in order to ensure the development of Palestine into a Jewish commonwealth. At the same time the delegation would also work toward wringing a guarantee for the security and civil rights of minority groups, Jews and others, who would find themselves within the domain of the newly-formed or re-shaped nations—Poland, Czechoslovakia, Yugoslavia, Rumania, Hungary, and Austria, which would be created by the treaty. The position was summed up in a memorial presented to President Wilson on March 2, 1919. It urged Wilson to support the Balfour Declaration.

But the much desired unity continued to elude American Jewry. Three days after the memorial had been presented to Wilson the *New York Times* featured a parallel anti-Zionist memorial. Among its signatories was Adolph Ochs, publisher of the *Times*, and many other members of the outspokenly anti-Zionist faction of the AJC. "We raise our voice in warning and protest," read the memorial, "against the demand of the Zionists for reorganization of the Jews, and a national unit to whom ... territorial sovereignty in Palestine shall be committed ..."[15] It was a dissenting voice that would not be stilled until the Nazi threat of the thirties made clear the full logic of the Zionist position on "territorial sovereignty."

In the first round of confrontation with the anti-Zionists, the Zionists won a nominal victory. It was reflected in the rise in the membership ranks of the various Zionist organizations. By the summer of 1919 membership had reached the remarkable figure of 149,013. But membership figures were only part of the story. The movement continued to be plagued by internal conflict which had been simmering since 1917. The issue came to a head at the Cleveland Convention in 1921. After the dust cleared the original Brandeis leadership group had been replaced by the Eastern-Europe oriented faction who looked toward Chaim Weizmann and the world Zionist movement for its direction. True to its word, the American Jewish Congress adjourned *sine die* on May 30, 1920, after completing its work at Versailles. Even here a faction led by Rabbi Stephen Wise strove to keep the organizing principle and the name of Congress alive.

Related to the foregoing events, and at the same time distinct from them, was New York Jewry's remarkable experiment in ethnic self-government. Called Kehillah to conjure up visions of the most successful attempt at community self-government in sixteenth-, seventeenth-, and eighteenth-century Russia and Poland, the New York Kehillah never remotely approached its historical namesake in scope and effectiveness. Nevertheless, its organization marked a distinct departure in the history of American Jewry and therefore deserves our special attention.

The Kehillah's life span from 1908 to 1922 was relatively short, but it corresponded in time to that period in American Jewish history when the basic organization outlines the community would assume were being fashioned. Naturally it was also affected by the heated ideological conflicts which wracked American Jewry during that period. Moreover, although confined to New York City, it was more than simply a local phenomenon. New York Jewry served as the organization and cultural hub of American Jewry and its programs not only affected a considerable portion of American Jews directly but also were viewed as models by the community at large.

The movement to establish a Kehillah was triggered by the appearance of an article authored by Theodore A. Bingham, New York's Police Commissioner, in the prestigious *North American Review*. The Commissioner charged New York's Jewry, which composed only one fifth of the city's population, with producing fifty percent of its crime. Such accusations were fairly common among a certain breed of Progressive reformers who preferred to find in the mass influx of the "new" immigration the source of the nation's ills, especially as it was reflected in municipal corruption. Nevertheless, emanating from an official source, Bingham's charge carried a special sting. The immigrant community, its racial pride already adversely affected by the problems attending a particularly difficult accommodation, and perhaps remotely aware that there was an element of truth in the Commissioner's charges, could not lightly cast them off.

The strident cries for the Commissioner's political scalp which rose from the Lower East Side were predictable. Bingham was compelled to retract his statement and apologize. Even so his charge continued to nettle. There was a feeling that the Jewish community was too vulnerable to such charges, and that there was no one to defend it. What was needed, according to Judah Magnes, the thirty-one-year-old associate rabbi of Temple Emanu-El, was "to define [Jewish] rights and liberties and also [to] cope with the problem of criminality...."[16] Some order had to be brought to the organizational chaos which left Jews open to such charges and prey to the agents of vice.

For Judah Magnes the obvious solution was to form a strong central community organization which would be responsible for bringing order to the community. If the moment in Jewish history when the local kehillahs ruled supreme could not be completely recaptured, it was nevertheless possible to create some degree of structure around which the various elements of the community might voluntarily coalesce. Magnes seemed ideally suited to bring the disparate components of New York Jewry together.

Like his brother-in-law, Louis Marshall, he seemed equally at home in the "uptown" and "downtown" milieu. He was a rabbi of the leading Reform congregation in the nation ministering to the spiritual needs of the Schiffs, Warburgs, and Seligmans. But occasionally he liked to pray in the small *shtiblach* of the Orthodox. In addition he was an ardent Zionist and, after 1905, served as the secretary of the American Zionist Federation. The "downtown" worthies viewed their prize with pride. "The advent of a reform rabbi in our ranks," wrote the Zionist leader, Louis Lipsky, "was the occasion for general rejoicing: it meant a break had been made in the enemy citadel."[17] That may have been an over-statement, but Magnes's growing disenchantment with the Reform movement which led to his resignation from the pulpit of Emanu-El, served to endear him to Orthodox Jews as well. The Kehillah, whose presidency Magnes assumed in 1909, became an extension of his personality so that when his interest waned in 1917, so did the Kehillah.

The movement to establish a Kehillah is viewed best in the context of the general thrust to coordinate Jewish organizational life at the turn of the century. Affiliations and mergers were occurring on the religious and labor fronts, in the Zionist movement and among the *landsmannschaften* and philanthropic agencies. The movement for an American Jewish Congress based on the principle of mass participation offered, in effect, an alternate method to circumvent the shoals of organizational disunity. But in 1908 no single organization existed to fill the need of dealing with the social and economic problems faced by Jews on the grass-roots level. The Kehillah was conceived primarily to meet this need. The source of the conception, interestingly enough, was not exclusively Jewish. It is possible to see in the desire for efficient community organization and the priority given to "cleaning up" vice and crime in the ghetto, glimmerings of the general Progressive spirit then sweeping the land.

A meeting of the steering committee held at Clinton Hall on October 11, 1908, issued a "clarion call" to the various organizations to send delegates to the organizing conference. Soon a representative community council composed of twenty-five community leaders, a disproportionate number of them Orthodox Jews, took shape. Finally on February 27, 1909, a meeting of 300 delegates representing 222 organizations was convened. Included were 74 synagogues, 18 charitable organizations, 42 mutual benefit societies, 40 lodges, 12 educational institutions, 9 Zionist societies, 9 philanthropic groups, and 9 sundry religious societies. Conspicuously absent were delegates from the United Hebrew Trades.[18]

Elected temporary chairman, Magnes was charged with the responsibility of "democratizing" the community and "wip[ing] out the insidious distinctions between the East Europeans and West Europeans,

foreigners and natives, uptown and downtown Jews, rich and poor."
He was to make the Jews "realize that [they] are one people with a
common history and common hopes."[19] It was an ambitious goal and
there was precious little power in the Kehillah to realize it. From the
outset voices were raised in opposition to the kehillah idea. Louis
Marshall, although instrumental in gaining the support of the AJC, was
convinced that it was impossible to organize Jewry along the lines envisaged by Magnes. "When one considers the many elements of which
the Jewish community consists," he informed Magnes, "it is idle to
believe that any organization can ever come into being based on the
idea of pure democracy."[20] Time would prove that Marshall's prognosis
was accurate but Magnes, anxious above all to "heal" the ailments of
the Jewish community, swept aside such warnings. Energetically he
began to build an organization "that shall derive its authority from the
people, and that shall give expression to the will of the people."

The shoals of disunity which Marshall had warned about almost
immediately buffeted the fragile new organization. For practical reasons,
Magnes innocently agreed to establish a direct link between the Kehillah
and the AJC. His decision was motivated partly by the desire to further
the AJC's policy of broadening its popular base. He also realized that
the Kehillah's funding problem could be solved by such a liaison. In
his mind there was no conflict of interest in such a close relationship
since he did not question the sincerity of his brother-in-law Marshall
who assured him that the AJC had no desire to capture the Kehillah.[21]
But the entangling alliance did, in fact, have unfortunate consequences.

Suspicions were aroused when it became apparent that the AJC was
gaining a stronger voice in the affairs of the Kehillah. This was due
partly to the composition of its governing board and partly to the dependence of the Kehillah on "uptown" for its operating expenses. Thus
when the AJC formally coopted the twenty-five member executive board
of the Kehillah as its New York chapter, the die was cast. There would
always be the suspicion that the Kehillah was merely an ill-concealed
attempt by "the insidious influence of philanthropy" to control "downtown" affairs. There was, in fact, some truth in Louis Lipsky's contention
that in the normal course of things the moneyed piper called the tune.[22]
The Kehillah would be simply another arena in which the "uptown"-
"downtown" rivalry was played out. Rather than enhancing unity it
would become a victim of the Jewish community's endemic disunity.

That conflict, however, did not at first noticeably interfere with the
Kehillah's effectiveness. Its organization into bureaus, each designed to
focus on a particular problem, seemed to be eminently suitable. The
Bureau of Religious Affairs (Vaad Harabonim) was created in 1909 to

bring order into the chaotic situation which had developed around the problem of certifying kosher foods. In addition, the problem of marriage and divorce regulations, which vexed the Orthodox community, would be handled by committees of conciliation. All in all its functions were reminiscent of the traditional *Beth Din* (rabbinic courts of law) which played an important role in the Jewish communities of Europe.

In 1910, Israel Friedlander and Henrietta Szold recruited Dr. Samson Benderly, a noted Palestinian-born educator who had created a model educational system in Baltimore, to head the Kehillah's Bureau of Education. Endowed with uncommon energy and talent, Benderly set out to professionalize the training of Hebrew teachers and to establish several model Jewish religious schools. His plan called for the training of one hundred American-born teachers annually. These, he felt, would be better able to deal with American students than the Old-World Jewish scholars to whom the teacher's role often fell by default. A new curriculum was planned for the growing number of *Talmud Torahs* (afternoon religious schools) which were springing up in Jewish neighborhoods. Modern teaching techniques were introduced.

Under Benderly's leadership the Bureau of Education was markedly effective in implementing its plans. By 1916 the consolidated Jewish educational enterprise had 200 schools, 600 teachers, and 35,000 students. His appetite whetted by success, Benderly proceeded to make more grandiose plans for which ever larger sums of money were required. By 1914 the Bureau's deficit had surpassed $32,000 and a year later it had climbed to $73,000.[23] Benderly was compelled to cut back on his activities. Moreover, he was coming under pressure to alter his curricular priorities by Jacob Schiff, who alone contributed $35,000 annually to the Bureau's budget. Schiff, perhaps vexed at Benderly's ardent Zionism and miffed at Magnes's "intense Jewish nationalism," suspected that the Kehillah and especially its education operation were a "grave danger to many things we need hold dear."[24]

Men like Schiff insisted on "Americanization" as a prime educational goal. But for East European Jews that word had become a euphemism for the attempt to make them over into an acceptable "uptown" type. It was a threat to their ethnic identity. The problem was partly solved by arranging a broader base for the Bureau's financing. In 1917 it began to receive funds from the Federation of Jewish Philanthropic Societies. In a sense that signified that the community at large had taken responsibility for Jewish education, but that too would soon entail demands for certain priorities. Money rather than principles appeared to have the largest say in the course the Jewish community would take. Nevertheless, the Bureau of Education endured beyond the life of the Kehillah itself.

It was absorbed by the Jewish Education Committee in 1939. In retrospect it would probably be considered the Kehillah's most conspicuous success.

The Kehillah grew steadily in influence and stature during the first eight years of its existence. An annual statistical inventory, the *Jewish Communal Register*, was begun in 1911. It proved to be an invaluable statistical compilation on which to base long-range community planning. New York Jewry became the only ethnic community to possess a complete and accurate picture of itself. In 1917, the year when the *Communal Register* published its first report, an employment bureau was also established. It was not an ordinary employment agency since it also offered supplementary facilities for training and placement of handicapped workers. Ultimately, the Kehillah's labor bureau furnished machinery for the settlement of the many labor disputes which plagued the community. The actual use of the Kehillah's good offices to mediate labor disputes began before the establishment of the Bureau. It played an important role in resolving the strike in the fur industry in 1912 and the conflict in the men's clothing industry in 1913.

The principal task of the Kehillah was the suppression of ghetto vice. Its organization, it will be recalled, was triggered by the charge of widespread vice in the ghetto. Magnes was anxious, not only to protect the Jewish community from such charges, but to eliminate any illegal activity which might serve to substantiate them. One of the Kehillah's moderately successful programs was directed to this end.

In August, 1912, a Bureau of Social Morals was established. Working quietly behind the scenes, a small group of men began to tackle the vice problem. First it was necessary to determine precisely how much vice there was in the ghetto and who was responsible for its organization. This was no simple task since the vice lords worked behind the scenes and a veritable battle of statistics had effectively beclouded the actual vice scene. Working through their own informal intelligence network, the group was able to obtain the needed inside information which served as the basis for an anti-vice campaign.

By January, 1913, the campaign was beginning to show results. The information obtained by the intelligence network was transmitted to Mayor Gaynor's office for official action. There followed police raids, revocation of liquor licenses, break-up of prostitution rings, and the indictment of several extortioners and other assorted vice lords. Particularly noteworthy was the arrest of Yuski Nigger, "king of the horse poisoners," which brought to an end a six-year reign of terror on the Lower East Side.

The information on which the arrests were made usually proved uncannily accurate. Sometimes a mere warning from Kehillah authorities proved sufficient to curb vice. But much depended on the active cooperation of the municipal authorities, especially the police. When the administration of John Purroy Mitchell came to office the anti-vice activities of the Bureau of Social Morals lost momentum. The Mitchell administration was averse to availing itself of the information of the Bureau's "secret service." In 1917 the Bureau was reorganized, but lack of funds and the diminishing of the more visible manifestations of vice caused a loss of public interest. A final evaluation of the Bureau's activities might show that while it succeeded in reducing the surface manifestations of ghetto vice it was less successful in grappling with its root causes.

On the surface the Kehillah appeared to be still operating effectively in 1918. That year's annual convention was attended by 840 delegates, an impressive number. It was addressed in hopeful terms by the "big guns" of the Jewish community, Schiff, Marshall, and Friedlander. But below the surface all was not well. The 1918 annual convention was destined to be the last great governing meeting of the Kehillah. As Louis Marshall had predicted, the problem of ethnic governance appeared not to be amenable to easy solution. The idea of a mass-based American Jewish Congress movement appeared to be gaining the initiative. Magnes, sensing that the Congress movement was pushing the Kehillah into the historical wastebasket, grew to distrust its founders. He felt that they were merely contributing further to the divisiveness which compromised all efforts at effective action.

An attempt by the Kehillah to stave off decline by decentralizing into eighteen sub-districts did not succeed. A lessening of energy and the pull of powerful vested interests made the implementation of existing programs difficult. By 1922 only the outer organizational shell of the Kehillah remained; the moving spirit no longer existed. By the end of that year the shell had collapsed as well.

Its demise had some interesting lessons for those interested in a more effective community. The endemic fragmentation in the community could not be magically healed by imposing organization from the top. Class as well as the cultural and political divisions were too deep for that. Even at its high-water mark the Kehillah attracted only 10 to 15 percent of the community's organization. Most of the major organizations were included, but some smaller groups were not. The socialist-minded labor group around the UHT and the group of young intellectuals who met at the Educational Alliance, for example, studiously avoided the Kehillah. Nor did the organization succeed in reaching out to that growing section of the Jewish population whose rapid secularization ruled out any contact with organized Jewry.

But most basic to its eventual failure was the very lack of cohesiveness which it was designed to ameliorate. Political, ideological, and cultural conflicts were so intense among Jews that at times it appeared as if the notion of the existence of a single Jewish community was a figment of the imagination. In practice there was little in the way of common interest or enterprise, or even common experience, which might support unity in the community. Almost from the outset the Kehillah was caught in the cross-fire of organizational strife. Each organization attempted to use the Kehillah for its own design. Rather than superseding them, the Kehillah became an arena for community strife.

The AJC wanted to broaden its popular base while at the same time maintaining control over the "demagogic" downtown leaders. By the same token, when the socialists did attend the annual convention, it was paradoxically to form a temporary alliance with their uptown antagonists better to thwart the thrust of the Zionists. For Zionists, on the other hand, the Kehillah's platform was viewed as an ideal instrument to further their own goals. They were anxious to detach the Kehillah from the uptown moorings which Magnes had created. When they failed, they reverted to their isolation to wage their own bitter internal battles. None of the organizations seemed able to support the Kehillah for the sake of New York Jewry which was, after all, its principal objective.

Judah Magnes, who more than any other leader was credited with the creation of the Kehillah, was also in some measure responsible for its decline. His radical pacifism during the war antagonized the "uptown" financial backers of the Kehillah who tended to be super-patriotic and loyal. Moreover, his outspoken Zionist sentiments tended naturally to estrange him from men like Jacob Schiff, but at the same time his opposition to Brandeis's appointment to the Supreme Court in 1916 and his distaste for the Congress movement failed to win him friends in that camp. Both parties were essential in supporting the Kehillah venture. Sensing his isolation, Magnes was ready to abandon his post by 1917. But various pressures, including the wish to see some of its programs to a successful conclusion, prevented him from doing so until 1922. Even then the Kehillah might have continued, but Magnes's most likely successor, Israel Friedlander, was killed in the Ukraine.

Even if it had been possible to overcome the problems within Jewry, which made its existence so difficult, there was still no guarantee that the Kehillah could ever have become a permanent feature of American Jewish life. Its basic conception was based on the premise that such a structure was necessary because of a hostile social environment. Bingham's slander was seen as a symptom of this antagonism. But the premise was seriously flawed. It was thought that America's attitude toward Jews did not differ substantially from that of the nations of Europe. It soon became clear that the parallel was hardly borne out by the facts. Despite an occasional manifestation of anti-Semitism, it was apparent to most Jews that they possessed reasonably good chances to avail themselves of the opportunity for economic betterment. Most had actually based their life strategies on that assumption rather than on fear of discrimination. The sense of insecurity, perhaps the most important ingredient for the maintaining of kehillahs in Eastern Europe, was not duplicated in America. The belief that it was, represented merely a carry-over of European norms. Actually, the reverse situation appeared to be more applicable. Sensing that it was permissible to enter into American life, many Jews were anxious to divest themselves of their old cultural baggage as rapidly as possible. In America it was the benevolence, rather than the hostility of the host-nation environment, which would form the primary threat to Jewish survival. The Kehillah, in short, was conceived to counteract a threat associated with a different historical time and place. It was not appropriate for the American environment, transcending as it did the limits of permissible ethnic mobilization within the host nation.

Nevertheless, the Kehillah experiment brought certain benefits to New York's Jews even while it proved unable to bridge the strong forces which divided them. It provided a cadre of professionals, especially in the education and social work fields, who were relatively immune from the strife which was always present in the community today. The momentum for professionalism carried over to other Jewish communities so that even though Jews failed to organize themselves in a political way, service in health care, education, family welfare, and general philanthropy were remarkably complete.

Organizing American Jewry in the first decades of the century appears to have taken on all the aspects of a seasonal sport. It was never achieved and led merely to an ever-growing number of organizations in the field. We will see that once their bureaucracies hardened into permanent shape rather than becoming building blocks out of which unity might come, they were the cause of deeper division.

CHAPTER XV

The New American Jewish Political Profile

WHEN A GROUP CASTS ITS BALLOTS, SELECTS ITS LEADERS, FORMS ITS organizations, and agitates over issues important to its members, it makes a statement about itself. Political behavior identifies a group much as a fingerprint identifies a person. This chapter examines the emerging political identity of American Jewry as it was reflected in its posture on certain domestic and foreign issues. Understanding the emerging Jewish political personality is a formidable task because its contours did not resemble those of other minority groups. Only rarely in their history had Jews been permitted fully to identify themselves politically. One of those rare opportunities came in America, and the Jewish political identity that was revealed added a unique ingredient to the American political scene.

One would assume that the intense ideological convictions which were the bane of American Jewish organizational life would also be reflected in its secular political behavior. But that was not the case in the early years of the century. Indifference and revulsion combined to minimize the Jewish impact on local politics. The political leverage to which their growing numbers entitled them was not reflected by a proportional increase in the number of Jewish office holders. As late as 1923 only six of the thirty-six district leaderships in New York City, which possessed one of the highest concentrations of Jews in the world, were Jewish. The city did not elect a Jewish mayor until 1973. The predominantly Jewish Eighth Assembly District registered the lowest proportion of voters in the city in 1912.[1]

This seeming indifference to local politics can be traced to many factors. Like all new arrivals, Jews had language and other acculturation problems which required time to overcome. More important were the unique priorities which the group assumed. Primary energy was devoted to economic betterment. As long as economic mobility was accessible, the need for good government was felt to be of secondary importance. "The Jews were regarded as so completely taken up with their economic adjustment to their new country," commented one

[228]

observer, "that their frequently mentioned absence from the political machinery was accepted as entirely explainable."[2] Accustomed to being estranged from a government which they experienced in malignant form in Russia, Jews were happy to be left alone. Naturally, they relied primarily on their diligence rather than on government largesse to raise themselves from the ranks of the downtrodden. To view political activity as a means of group aggrandizement, as did the Irish, was totally alien to them. As the turn of the century Jews were barely represented in the municipal civil service partly because they did not seek such employment.[3] Local politics, especially ethnic ticket balancing, seemed strange to them, unaccustomed as they were to participation in government on any level.

The political style which Jews brought with them from Eastern Europe seemed anomalous. In the autocratic anti-Semitic atmosphere of Tsarist Russia Jews rarely had the opporunity to exercise power. They were uncorrupted by its use. That was the other side of the highly idealistic approach they brought to government and politics. Their innocence made it difficult to fathom the practical *quid pro quos,* the earthiness of local machine politics. Jews would be required to learn the game of American politics from scratch.

In sharp contrast, the Irish, who were rapidly gaining control of the municipal political machines in the 1880's, appeared to possess a natural instinct for such politics. The Irish concentration in urban areas, their church-fashioned ethnic cohesiveness, their familiarity with the language and their early arrival, were readily translatable into political power beyond what their numbers warranted. Once in control of local politics, they were naturally reluctant to share their power with the newcomers, especially with Jews. The two groups, with some distinct exceptions, were usually found on opposite ends of the political spectrum. Many Jews, for example, supported a movement for municipal reform in the late 1880's as it was personified by Henry George in the mayoralty campaign of 1886. But the Irish establishment would have none of it. Father Ed McGlynn's Anti-Poverty Society, which shared the Jewish preference, was quickly squelched by Archbishop Corrigan, and the Irish moved on to consolidate their hold on Tammany and fatten on its spoils. Subsequently Jews were repelled by the tactics used to defeat George and many recoiled from politics. Earlier, when Tammany offered the mayoralty nomination to Nathan Straus in 1884 in order to garner the Jewish vote, he would not accept it. It was tainted.

In a sense the confusion felt by Jewish voters was understandable. For years they had dreamed of democracy, but once they saw it in practice they could not account for the mediocre types which seemed everywhere to rise to the surface. How could democracy spew forth such corruption when human nature was basically good? "I was pained by the ease with which corrupt politicians were able to persuade our uneducated Jews to sell their votes," Cahan relates sadly in his diary. "There were no elections in the country from which we had fled. The ballot box and all it represented was the sacred hope for which many of our socialist comrades in Russia had martyred their lives."[4] Yet when Jews were elected, it was a Jewish barkeep like "Silver Dollar Smith," a type not distinctly different from his non-Jewish Tammany cronies, who came to office. Such politicians grew wealthy granting small favors to the hapless immigrant population. For overlooking the Sunday Law they were allowed to plunder the public purse.

If Jews experienced difficulty in understanding the political practices of the Irish, that group was equally puzzled about Jewish political attitudes. The Jewish voter, they came to understand, took politics seriously. He was probably the best-informed voter in the city. Political issues were an endless source of debate in the Jewish community. Yet, although Jews had a popular base from which they could make their power felt, they did not build a political machine to mobilize it. Tammany learned that normal *quid pro quos* and even outright purchasing of votes could not garner the Jewish vote. Cahan's observation notwithstanding, the influence of the vote buyer, the bane of poor neighborhoods, had relatively little impact in Jewish wards during the turn of the century.[5] "There does not exist a more unpromising field for the political tricksters than the Jewish quarter of the city," wrote a reporter in the *Forum* in April 1893; "their quiet critical analysis of political nostrums is most disheartening to the district leaders of Tammany."[6] The Jewish voter was different; he could be mobilized on the basis of ideas. That meant that the Jewish voter would be a maverick, a tendency that became fully discernible in later decades.

In the early years after his arrival, his purist approach to politics and his reformist instincts gave the impression of a Jewish version of a reformer type, a Russian Jewish "mugwump." Jews were intensely issue-oriented. "No audience in the city is quicker to grasp the question at issue," reported one observer.[7] He might have added that no voter was quicker to make an issue of the question. The Jewish voter injected a moralistic tone into the local political scene which was barely comprehensible to the local ward heelers. One could grow accustomed to the ascetic streak of moralism so often noted as charactertistic of the patrician Progressive. But the Jews were not Progressives, in the American sense of the word. Nor were they by any stretch of the imagination patrician. Their moralism stemmed partly from the strong influence of socialism and more remotely, from the well-springs of prophetic Judaism. Their Marxism, such as it was, was tempered by Isaiah. As socialists they were passionately committed to improving the human condition. They based their strategies on long-range theories regarding societal development which prepared them to go further than the limited amelioration proposed by the Progressive reformers. What Jewish reformers lacked was an understanding of the game of politics as it was played in America. What their socialist theory did not provide is an understanding of how to obtain and hold power. That was in the province of the less ethereal local ward heeler.[8]

Nevertheless, the socialist-oriented civic consciousness of the downtown Jews occasionally mixed well when combined with the Progressive orientation of the uptowners. The synthesis produced reformers like Stephen Wise, Henry and Belle Moskowitz, Joel and Arthur Spingarn, Edward Seligman, Pauline Goldmark, Manuel Nathan, and Louis Brandeis, who were variously in the forefront of the movement for women's rights, racial equality, the need for juvenile courts, municipal government reform and regulation of trusts.

For East European Jews the liaison with the reform movement posed certain problems. It did not take long to discover that many Progressives held the immigrant in disdain and desired nothing so much as to remold him into an acceptable type. Moreover, the Progressive reformer's zeal for what the Jewish immigrant considered as merely ameliorative measures rather than as needed structural changes exacerbated the sharp contrasts in temper and mores and tended to keep them apart. Christian reformers were suspected of desiring to proselytize among Jewish immigrants. "To the untutored eye missionaries were indistinguishable from reformers," commented one observer.[9]

Despite these hurdles many Jews did find their way to the Progressive movement. The Citizens' Union, founded in 1897, boasted a number of Jews among its founding members. It subsequently proved attractive as an outlet for the Jewish reformist impulse. That impulse was already perceptible in the mayoralty campaign of 1886, when Henry George, who placed second, garnered 15,000 of his 68,000 votes in the predominantly Jewish seventh, tenth, and thirteenth wards. The Jewish Workers' Alliance, a special organization established by Cahan, Miller, and Hillquit, campaigned strenuously for George. Together with the vote for Theodore Roosevelt, also a strong favorite among Jews, they cast 128,545 ballots for the candidates they preferred. Abraham Hewitt, a wealthy iron manufacturer, won by a plurality of 90,552. In 1897 Jews again were responsive to the reformist campaign for the office of Mayor waged by James B. Reynolds, director of an East-Side settlement house.

Reynolds, however, lost the election and went on to become the Roosevelt Administration's informal liaison to the Lower East Side. It appeared as if the Jews would circumvent the local political club and use the settlement house as a substitute.

At times a direct Jewish interest was paramount in determining how the Jewish vote went. Thus William R. Hearst was preferred over reform candidates because his newspaper featured passionate appeals for social justice and racial tolerance, sentiments close to the heart of the average Jewish voter. Moreover, the Hearst press presented detailed accounts of the Kishineff pogrom, combining them with earnest appeals for aid to the Russian Jews. For Hearst such concern may have had an ulterior purpose of mobilizing the Jewish vote. In 1904 he went so far as to publish a Yiddish paper, the *Yiddisher Amerikaner*, in an unsuccessful effort to win the mayoralty election. But for the Jewish voters, who may have understood that Hearst's sentimentality was designed to win their votes, the experience of being wooed had delights all its own. It gave them an unaccustomed feeling of importance.

Moreover, the attempted seduction by one suitor often tended to increase the attention of others. In 1906, Hearst, running on the Tammany ticket for New York's governorship, was one of the factors which prompted the Republican Roosevelt to appoint Oscar Straus to the post of Secretary of Commerce. Ostensibly the popular President wanted "to show Russia what we think of Jews in this country," but subsequent events revealed that he was anxious to prevent Hearst from winning the election and had requested Jacob Schiff to submit likely Jewish candidates for the post. He then selected Straus, insisting that he had appointed on the basis of "merit and merit alone."[10] Willy-nilly the Jews were being drawn into the maelstrom of ethnic politics. The Lower East Side became an important campaign stop for all candidates anxious to hold political office. Immigration policy, relations with Russia and Rumania, good government, all issues important to Jews, received a higher priority on the political agenda.

It was issues and the candidates who advocated them, rather than party, which earned the loyalty of the Jewish voter. On the national level they customarily found the candidates of the Republican Party preferable. But when idealistic intellectual types like Woodrow Wilson were proffered by the Democrats, Jews changed their preference. Such a switch could prove difficult for some who followed the voting pattern of the older German Jewish community or felt a special debt to the Republican Party. "After all, Theodore Roosevelt's name was on the immigration papers which let us in," explained one Jewish voter.[11] Stemming from the authoritarian milieu of Eastern Europe, Jews naturally attributed such generosity to the head of state.

Above and beyond this, Roosevelt had created a reservoir of good will among Jewish voters. In 1895 he assigned an all-Jewish police detail to protect Pastor Herman Ahlwardt, a German preacher known for the stridency of his anti-Semitism. (The same was done by Fiorello La Guardia, the irrepressible mayor of New York, when he assigned a Jewish police detail to protect the harassed German consulate in New York.) Theodore Roosevelt also took care to observe other niceties of ethnic politics. He invited the Rabbinic Council of America to the White House and twice ventured to predict that at some point in the distant future, a Jew would be President. Few occasions were missed to praise the fine character of the new Jewish citizens and how beneficial they were for the development of the nation. In 1902 he appointed his Secretary of Commerce, Oscar Straus, to succeed ex-President Benjamin Harrison on the Hague Court. Such measures helped to cement Jewish loyalty to the Republican Party on the national level. The ties were not fully broken until another Roosevelt discovered a means to attract the Jewish vote.

One suspects that the Jewish voter was as much pushed away from the Democratic Party by the fact of Irish dominance as he was pulled toward the Republicans by such tactics. Nor did loyalty to the Republican Party apply to all Jews. Many Jews had been won by the local Democratic machine because of its practical help to immigrants as well as by a peculiar class loyalty. The local machine took care to turn out the Jewish vote. Jews of "De Ate" customarily gave a narrow majority to the Tammany candidates in local and national elections. Moreover, Tammany was always "right" on the most crucial issue for Jews, immigration policy. That was not true of the Republican Party and led the Jewish barkeep politician, "Silver Dollar Smith," to switch to Tammany in 1892. Moreover, while Jews never won full representation in Tammany, some Jews were able to make their political mark through Tammany conduits. Henry Goldfogle, Tammany's Jewish spokesman for the Lower East Side, was elected to Congress in 1900 and the next year Jacob Cantor became borough president of Manhattan while Aaron Levy became Democratic leader of the State Assembly.

If direct group interest could gain the Jewish vote for candidates like Hearst, reform candidates like Seth Low, the former President of Columbia University who ran for the mayor's office in 1901, proved to be no less attractive. Low gained a sizable segment of the "uptown" and "downtown" Jewish vote as did William T. Jerome, the anti-Tammany candidate for the office of district attorney. The 1901 campaign indicated how important the support of the Jewish voter had become. The Lower East Side was flooded with campaign literature written in Yiddish and special efforts were made to reach the Jewish voter through his spiritual and organizational leaders.

The growth of the Jewish population had given the community an importance in local politics which, if properly organized, might give Jews a decisive voice. By 1910, 13 percent of the eligible voters of Manhattan were Jewish and with a more educated second generation on the way, the percentage of actual voters would rise. At the same time the exodus of Jews from the Lower East Side to the "better" neighborhoods of Brooklyn and the Bronx meant that Jewish influence would be citywide rather than confined to a few districts in Lower Manhattan.

Paradoxically, the development of a Jewish voting bloc concerned with advancing its group interests was a source of apprehension for established "uptown" Jews. The idea of ethnic loyalty and the open recognition of a specific group interest were abhorrent to them. It meant being less American. A "warning note" was carried by the *American Hebrew* from Rabbi Philipson: "There has been a tendency in a number of communities to regard the Jewish vote as a solid vote and there have been efforts put forth to control it. Every manifestation of this is ruinous. . . . It is unjewish, it is un-American."[12]

But such warnings fell on deaf ears. The new immigrants did not yet share the apprehension about the way in which they appeared as Americans. In the ghetto it seemed as if every one was Jewish; they were only dimly aware of the "outside." The ethnic impulse seemed a natural one to follow. They openly rejoiced when Jews such as Oscar Straus, Henry Morgenthau, Louis Brandeis, and Bernard Baruch were appointed to high political office. Although such Jews were far removed from their ken, they understood instinctively that the surest recognition of their Americanism was to be rewarded their share of political power. It was a far cry from the way things had been in Eastern Europe and they were grateful.

Their natural impulse led them to use the ballot to reward their friends and punish their enemies. That pattern was especially discernible when there was no controversy about where the Jewish interest lay. The immigration issue was one such. When James M. Curley ran for mayor of Boston in 1913 he received 85 percent of the Jewish vote. He was known to be a jealous guard of the Irish prerogative in Boston, but he was also a strong proponent of a liberal immigration policy. By the same token, Wilson's veto of the literacy test bill went far to endear him to Jewish voters. Ethnic interest existed and one could not simply ignore it. Indeed, by 1904 the *American Hebrew* sounded a different note on the issue of ethnic interests. Philip Cowen urged the support of Roosevelt for a second term because he "had indisputably done things that entitle him to the good will of our people."[13]

The game of ethnic politics could also entail conflict for the Jewish voter. When, for example, Oscar Straus was pitted against Tammany's William Sulzer in the Bull Moose gubernatorial election, it created perplexing problems for the Jewish voter. Ethnic loyalty dictated a vote for Straus, but Sulzer was leading the fight from his position as Chairman of the House Foreign Affairs Committee to abrogate the Russo-American Commercial Treaty of 1832. In the end the pull of ethnic loyalties proved superior, Sulzer won the election but Straus ran ahead of him in Jewish districts and in fact polled a higher number of votes than Roosevelt, who headed the ticket. The campaign of 1912 posed a greater quandary for the Jewish voter on the national level because all four candidates had come out strongly against immigration restriction. The problem was solved by ticket splitting; a sizable proportion of the Jewish vote went to Wilson and to Eugene Debs, the candidate of the Socialist Party.

Socialism also acted as a magnetic force on a portion of the Jewish community. Naturally when the ideological and ethnic were combined in one candidate, as they were in the case of Meyer London, he was virtually unbeatable. Daniel De Leon, the nominal Curaçao Jew, who headed one branch of the Socialist Party, consistently received over 30 percent of the Jewish vote when he ran for assemblyman.

In some measure the rise of the Socialist Party vote from a mere 25,000 in 1905 to 118,000 in 1912 is partly attributable to the support of the new Jewish voter. But the advent of war, which found most of the Socialists opting for a pacifist or international disarmament position, considerably muted public support for the Socialists. The Jewish pacifist Socialist, Meyer London, was elected handily to Congress in 1914 and 1916, but in 1917 the Socialist vote had receded to 80,000.[14] Undoubtedly many Jewish voters went along with the general patriotic sentiment triggered by the war and after Russia deposed its Tsar the way seemed clear for wholehearted support of the Allied cause. Nevertheless, in 1917 the Socialists of New York still boasted considerable strength. They had in office ten assemblymen, seven aldermen, and one municipal court justice.

The enthusiasm socialism generated among immigrant Jews never dominated the entire community. Of the eleven Jews elected to the New York State Senate in 1914, two were Republicans and nine were Democrats. There were five Jewish Republicans and two Socialists in the Assembly that year. The peculiar inability of Socialists to present one truth to the Jewish voting public tended to undermine their strength.

Even on the crucial question of the war, the Socialists found themselves divided. Internal strife was particularly rife in the Jewish sections of the Socialist party. The Jewish voter might well wonder why Socialists who claimed to possess a knowledge of the immutable laws which govern society, never seemed able to discover laws to govern themselves.

Like his American counterpart in the election of 1920, the so-called "solemn referendum," the Jewish voter was ready to come down from the idealistic "high" generated by the Wilson administration and the war itself. To be sure the high-flown idealism of the Fourteen Points and especially the fourteenth point, the League of Nations, as well as preliminary signals that Wilson would support the Balfour Declaration, momentarily strengthened Jewish links to the Democratic Party.

However, the newly developed enthusiasm proved not to be transferable to James Cox, the compromise nominee of the Democrats. Nor did the magic of the Roosevelt name extend to young Franklin Roosevelt, Cox's running mate. Undoubtedly some Jewish voters vaguely recalled that Harding had at one time been accused of anti-Semitism by the Ohio State Democratic Committee and many were aware that he had opposed granting a seat on the Supreme Court to Louis Brandeis in 1916. The election of 1920 increased Jewish representation in Congress from six to eleven. All were Republicans except for Henry Goldfogle of Tammany, Adolph Sabbath, a Chicago Democrat, and Meyer London, the Socialist representative of the Lower East Side, whose lonely pacifism during the war would be vindicated by the drift of public opinion during the twenties.

Generally, however, it is difficult to determine a clear Jewish political preference during the critical postwar years. Although Harding supported the restrictive Reed Johnson Immigration Act, he received a respectable number of Jewish votes, and Coolidge, his Republican successor, received a higher percentage of Jewish votes than John W. Davis, the Democratic candidate for president in 1924. In that election, too, it became clear that liberal-socialist support was a constant in the Jewish political profile. In some Jewish districts the candidate of the newly formed Progressive Party ran first. The advent of the New Deal in 1933 would show this preference more clearly. If Jews generally mustered little enthusiasm for local politics, their interest in foreign affairs exceeded that of the average American. We need not seek far afield for an explanation of this reversal of normal group interests. There was among American Jews a traditional nostalgia for their link to K'lal Yisrael, the community of Israel, which had a global and spiritual dimension beyond any particular geographic location. That feeling was supported by the natural interest immigrants felt for the home they had left. Their relatives and friends continued to experience the very adversities which had compelled the immigrant to uproot himself. In fact, it seemed as if there were always Jews somewhere who were in dire need of help. Lest he forget, the immigrant's memory was prodded by word of mouth and by the Anglo-Jewish and Yiddish press. The pattern seemed clear. The interest in their brethren overseas was responsible for a general interest in foreign affairs and for a specific strategy to succor their coreligionists abroad by pressuring for diplomatic intercession by the American government.

We must briefly return to the nineteenth century to see how this precedent developed. The first opportunity of American Jewry to make their influence felt was in 1840 when an accusation of blood libel against the Jews of Damascus occurred. Accusations that Jews murdered non-Jewish children for the purpose of the ritual of making Matzohs for Passover were heard periodically since the Middle Ages. The Damascus case, classic in its outlines, was actually the fifteenth case of its kind since the beginning of the century. In February, 1840, the blood libel charge was slightly different since it concerned the death of a Moslem child, but the charge was supported by Franciscan monks. It led to the arrest of thirteen prominent Jews and sixty children, all of whom were tortured for the purpose of wringing confessions from them. The confessions were subsequently repudiated, but at the insistence of the French consul the ritual murder charge was retained. The Damascus Blood Libel case became enmeshed in the international rivalries for dominance in Syria.

The intrusion of the American government into the affair was all the more remarkable because it was actually based on good will. A mass protest rally held in London on July 3, 1840, served to inform John Forsythe, Van Buren's Secretary of State, that the dispatches of the American consular agent in Damascus, Chasseaud, were false. Chasseaud expressed the government's concern to the Egyptian authorities: "The President," read the note, "fully participates in the public feeling and he cannot refrain from expressing surprise and pain, that in this advanced age, such unnatural practices should be ascribed to any portion of the religious world. . . ." In a similar message sent to David Potter, the American Minister in Turkey, the President expressed "lively satisfaction" at the actions taken by other Christian governments to "suppress and mitigate these horrors."[15] The unsolicited message represented a projection of American religious tolerance. It assumed that in Europe, Jews were considered to be part of the accepted "religious world" as they were in America, rather than the near pariahs they actually were.

Also noteworthy is the response of American Jewry. A resolution from a group of Jews meeting at a mass rally in New York City was received by the Van Buren administration after the aforementioned note had been sent. Once begun the mass protest ritual soon spread to other Jewish centers: Philadelphia on August 27, 1840, Charleston on August 29, Cincinnati on August 31, Savannah on September 3 and Richmond on September 4. For the first time in American Jewish history the community organized a concerted nationwide action.

How effective such government intercession was in practice is difficult to determine. Ultimately the Jewish prisoners of Damascus were released and the libel repudiated. But that did not happen until four Jews had died and a rash of similar accusations had swept Europe. Perhaps the true significance of the event lies in the evidence of growing American Jewish cohesiveness. In Philadelphia, for example, a Committee of Correspondence under the leadership of Isaac Leeser was organized for the express purpose of establishing contact with other Jewish communities. But Leeser's desire to use the momentum created by the Damascus incident to establish a national organization was not to be fulfilled until the last decades of the century, and then only nominally.

Eighteen years after the Damascus case, the infamous Mortara kidnapping once again roused American Jewry to action. The case concerned the forced seizure, by Papal troops, of a seven-year-old Jewish child, Edgar Mortara, who had ostensibly been secretly baptized by his nurse when he was an infant. That baptism was cause enough for the Holy Office to insist that the child be reared by some Catholic institution. No amount of pleading with Pius IX succeeded in having the child restored to his parents. Moved by the poignancy of the case, American Jewry requested Lewis Cass, Buchanan's Secretary of State, to intercede. But the Buchanan administration rejected the idea on the ground that "it is the settled policy of the United States to abstain from all interference . . . as they expect other nations to abstain from all interference in the internal affairs of our country."[16] At one stroke the precedent established by the Van Buren administration in 1840 was reversed.

Things had changed considerably since 1840. The Irish-Americans took some interest in the Mortara case and closeness to the Democratic Party gave that group some leverage. The *New York Tablet*, an Irish Catholic organ, insisted that once baptized the child was Christian and "deserved" a Christian upbringing. Why, asked the *Tablet*, was there no similar outcry when the abolitionists abducted slaves from the South? A good many Protestant newspapers, many with a strong Know-Nothing flavor, endorsed the Jewish cause, if only for the fact that the Catholics favored the other side.

Nor did the Mortara case bring a higher level of Jewish unity in its wake. Again as in 1840 there were numerous protest rallies and requests for action by prominent Jewish leaders, but the efforts of men like Isaac Leeser to establish a permanent organization proved of little avail. The Rabbinical Council, formed in 1855, showed few signs of life by 1858, when the Mortara case became news. Twenty-five organizations responded to a call to establish a new organization to be called the Board of Delegates of American Israelites. It was modeled on the British Board. In 1863 the new organization requested Secretary of State William H. Seward to intercede on behalf of the Jews of Morocco, where the situation had become critical. Seward instructed the American consul "to exert all proper influence to prevent repetition of the barbarous cruelties to which Israelites . . . have been subject."[17] The Lincoln administration thus reversed the policy of the preceding Democratic administration.

The Board of Delegates remained in existence until 1887, bringing a tenuous unity to American Jewry. Beneath the surface simmered the conflict between the Reformers headed by Isaac Wise and the traditionalists, led by Isaac Leeser.

In the final decades of the nineteenth century and the first decade and a half of the twentieth, the attention of American Jewry focused increasingly on the mistreatment of its religious brethren in Tsarist Russia. The Russian policy of discrimination against and extrusion of Jews involved America in several ways. It was, we have seen, primarily responsible for bringing millions of Jewish immigrants to American shores. When some immigrants, armed with their newly acquired American citizenship, returned to Russia to do business, an additional dilemma was created for American authorities when they fell afoul of discriminatory regulations. Naturally these returnees claimed the protection of the American government under the guarantee of equal protection of the laws. Most important, the existence of an aroused community with a growing ability to make its political weight felt could not forever be ignored by policy makers. The problem of Russia's treatment of Jews was thus bound to become a concern in Russo-American relations.

The discriminatory treatment of American Jewish citizens doing business in Russia came to the fore in 1879 when Herman Rosenstraus purchased real estate in Kharkov only to be denied title to his property. Russian law forbade Jews to own urban real estate. Could these laws be applied to Jews who were American citizens? The Hayes administration was in a dilemma. It had complied with the request of the Board of Delegates of American Israelites for diplomatic intercession "as will best accord with the . . . liberal sentiment of the American people."[18] But it did not take long for Jewish leaders to discover that the problem was imbedded in the Commercial Treaty of 1832 with Russia which contained a clause guaranteeing the rights of American citizens only "on condition of submitting to the laws and ordinances there prevailing." The problem of nonprotection of American Jewish citizens was inherent in the treaty itself which meant Jewish leaders had to agitate for its abrogation. It was not long before James G. Blaine, Secretary of State in the Garfield administration, informed St. Petersburg that the Commercial Treaty would not be renewed if discrimination against Jews continued.

Untoward incidents, however, continued to complicate Russo-American relations. In January, 1882, an American Jew found himself in St. Petersburg working as a stable director for a visiting circus. When the Russian authorities discovered his religion they ordered him out of the city even though, according to the dispatch of the American Minister, he was "not one of those Talmud Jews." Eventually the Russian authorities relented and the Jewish stable director was permitted to continue his work. But as the number of Jews returning to Russia increased, the authorities began making arrests indiscriminately on the charge that these former Russian citizens had avoided their military obligation. At the time Russia maintained selective rather than universal conscription. The practice led Representative Irvin Dungan to introduce a Congressional resolution which proposed that relations with Russia be severed until "such time as that Government shall cease discrimination against the Hebrews . . . and remove the arbitrary and brutal restrictions now imposed upon them against the protest of the civilized world."[19]

In 1892 a Supreme Court decision in the Geofroy vs. Riggs case, which specifically extended the "equal treatment under law" clause to treaties, made it difficult for the State Department to ignore open discrimination against American citizens abroad. When the Russian consul in New York refused to issue a visa on religious grounds, the Department hastily informed the Russian government that the American government could not be "expected to acquiesce in the assumption of a religious inquisitorial function within our borders by a foreign agency. . . ."[20] The Department discontinued its practice of automatically rejecting passport applications for former Russian Jews because in effect that meant that it was implementing a policy of discrimination against American citizens.

The issue came to a head in 1897 when the Russians refused to visa the passport of a wealthy Californian Jew, Adolph Kutner, who wanted to visit Russia. In May, 1897, Senator Perkins of California introduced a resolution requesting intercession by the government. Nothing came of the matter, but there was a noticeable increase in Jewish pressure on the Administration. John Hay, Roosevelt's Secretary of State, complained five years later that the *American Israelite* has "been beating us black and blue for our tactics in not going to Russia." He instructed Alvey Adee, who actually administered the State Department, to compose yet another note to St. Petersburg. "Even if Russia does nothing," thought the politically sensitive Hay, "we shall have a good note to print next winter."[21] But before Adee could fulfill the Secretary's instructions, news of the Kishineff pogrom altered the situation. Russia's anti-Jewish depredations would now become a matter of critical concern in the relations between the two countries.

The American involvement with Russia over its anti-Jewish physical depredations goes back to the early 1880's. In May, 1881, the Garfield administration received reports that Russian mobs "debauched with liquor and plunder" were murdering Jews in Elisavetgrad. Blaine, the Secreary of State, turned to Whitehall to investigate the possibility of joint action. His dispatch drew a parallel with the situation in fifteenth-century Spain: "Then as now in Russia, the Hebrews fared better in business than his neighbor, then as now, his economy and patient industry bred capital, and capital bred envy and envy persecution and persecution disaffection and special separation. . . . The Jews are made a people apart from other peoples, not of their volition, but because they have been repressed and ostracized in the communities in which they mixed."[22] Such a philosemitic analysis of the Jewish situation was probably unheard-of in diplomatic exchanges. Predictably, its eloquence did not convince the British Foreign Office that a joint démarche was called for.

The fact that the inflow of Jewish immigrants was directly related to anti-Semitic actions in Russia and Rumania set the groundwork for eventual government intercession. But the issue was a complex one involving American commercial interests. Nevertheless, when the number of pogroms increased in 1890, Blaine did not hesitate to relate immigration to Russian policy. His note protested the depredations on the grounds that the huge outflow of destitute Jews settling in America was sparked by the "oppressive measures" of the Russian government and that the "hospitality of a nation should not be turned into a burden."[23] President Harrison personally pointed out that "the banishment . . . of so large a number of men and women is not a local question. A decree to leave one country is in the nature of things an order to enter another. . . ."[24] There was some suspicion, however, that the President was not so much "moved by philanthropy . . . but his unwillingness to have expelled Hebrews come to this country."[25] The relation of the depredations to the massive inflow of immigrants would be a continuing concern to the Washington authorities. In 1902 Hay sent a note to all signatories of the Berlin Treaty, which brought independence to Rumania, in which he pointed out that that nation's refusal to adhere to Article 44 of its constitution, the article protecting minorities, forced these hapless Jews "spurned by their native land . . . upon the charity of the United States."[26]

It was not long before Jews themselves learned to use the fear of immigration to gain government intercession. In January, 1913, at the end of the Second Balkan War, Louis Marshall requested Taft to place the question of the treatment of Jews before the peace conference. He strengthened his case by pointing out that the alternative to improved treatment would be an ever greater number of Rumanian Jews seeking havens in America.[27] Intercession for improved treatment of Jews was clearly not simply a question of Christian charity, as it had been for the Van Buren administration during the Damascus Blood Libel. It had become a matter of national interest.

By the 1880's, moreover, the composition of American Jewry was undergoing a rapid change. An increasing number of American Jews were of East European derivation and therefore more directly aroused by the atrocities. Often they had experienced them firsthand. New techniques were developed to focus pressure on the Washington policy makers. After new outbreaks occurred on Christmas Day of 1882 a proclamation to be delivered to the Garfield administration was circulated among non-Jewish political leaders. It was signed by former President Ulysses Grant, Karl Schurz, Oliver Harriman, Whitelaw Reid, and Leland Stanford. The fear that the anti-Jewish pogroms would adversely effect Russo-American relations was transmittted to St. Petersburg through the American Minister, William Henry Hart. It was Hart who had composed a detailed memorandum, "Condition of Public Affairs in Russia and of the Jews in the Empire," for the department's edification.

But Hart soon found ample reason to question the effectiveness of diplomatic intercession. Apparently it had no effect whatsoever in convincing Russian officialdom to mend its ways. The Russian Foreign Minister, De Gries, denied that the American model of peaceful ethnic mixture, which Hart had used in making his case, was applicable to Russia, whose Jews, according to the Foreign Minister, were "altogether unfitted for more liberty than they now possess." The truth was, of course, that Russian authorities were not unhappy to see the Jews leaving Russia. That such a population movement directly concerned the United States was not officially acknowledged.

By the turn of the century it was clear that effective American action such as the abrogation of the Commercial Treaty of 1832 required greater pressure on the Washington policy makers. That in turn depended on the dramatic deterioration of the condition of Jews in Russia and the emergence of the United States as a world power. In the years which followed both conditions came to pass. Ultimately the United States was compelled to take that drastic step. But to their chagrin, Jews discovered that even strong diplomatic intercession could not assure good treatment to their religious brethren. In their desperation to do something they had assigned too great a task to diplomacy. Having never possessed sovereign power, they tended to overestimate its capacity.

CHAPTER XVI

Jews and American Foreign Affairs, 1900-1920

MORE THAN ANYTHING ELSE, THE KISHINEFF POGROM, WHICH OCCURRED between April 19 and 21, 1903, helped to bring the Jewish question in Russo-American relations to the fore. The massacre had an electrifying effect on American Jewry. In a short period of time Jews held seventy-seven public meetings in fifty population centers in twenty-seven states. "The scenes at the mass meetings transcended description," wrote Louis Lipsky, "the sacrifices of the poor, the giving of jewels, the weeping that attended the simplest accounts of the riots, the passion in the giving all."[1] Lipsky saw it as a great turning point in American Jewish history. Jews turned naturally to the Roosevelt administration for succor. They wanted redress for the victims and all possible influence to be used to prevent recurrence.

The cry for diplomatic intercession posed several problems. Jews, we have seen, tended to place inordinate faith in diplomatic interventions and insisted on having an ever-greater number of them. The realistic Roosevelt, on the other hand, had nothing but disdain for diplomatic gestures not backed by power. In a more practical sphere, the American Ambassador to St. Petersburg was far from sympathetic to the plight of Russia's Jews. When aid to the victims was offered by American Jewry, he denied that it was needed. It was Straus who requested John W. Biddle, formerly his legation secretary in Constantinople and then secretary of the American Embassy in St. Petersburg, to expose the whole story of the Kishineff pogrom. Later Straus was instrumental in getting a more sympathetic ambassador appointed to the St. Petersburg post.[2]

That solved one problem but the increasing pressure on the Roosevelt administration for action was not so easily disposed of. When a delegation of American Jews visited the White House, Roosevelt was sympathetic. He explained that he felt it was fitting for the nation to make the most concerned protest. That was the least the nation could do to "acknowledge the debt due to the Jewish race."[3] But personally he doubted the efficacy of such notes if there was no intention of going

[244]

beyond words. That was the gist of what he told Oscar Straus whom he had come to consider a kind of unofficial representative of the Jewish community: "You know I am prepared to do anything that I can for all our citizens ... but unless we mean to do something further than simply protest it would look like an effort to catch votes."[4] Hay made a similar point to the more adamant Jacob Schiff. The Secretary went as far as contributing $500 to the Jewish Relief Committee as a visible manifestation of his sympathy.

It was not that the Roosevelt administration held such normal political inanities in complete contempt. Barely a year before the State Department had in fact composed a protest note to the Bucharest government concerning a series of repressive apprenticeship laws which it was felt would drive Rumanian Jews to American shores. Straus and other Jewish leaders were undoubtedly aware that the note would do little to change the situation. Nevertheless Straus expressed public admiration for the compelling "logic and force" of the note even though it was obviously designed primarily for domestic consumption.[5] Adee, who was responsible for composing these elevated sentiments, received word from Hay that "the President is greatly pleased ... and the Hebrews—poor dears! all over the country think we are bully boys."[6] But there was a point beyond which the Roosevelt administration was unwilling to go to garner the Jewish vote. Besides, such things had a way of backfiring. Rabbi Joseph Krauskopf, of Philadelphia's Knesseth Israel, for example, was not alone in viewing such notes as deliberate deceptions by the Administration. But his suggestion for American military intervention went far beyond the Administration's desire.

Like the succeeding administration of William H. Taft, Roosevelt reached a point when he refused to permit his diplomatic posture to be influenced by ethnic pressure at home. When fear of pogroms during the Easter season of 1905 again prompted leading Jews to request intercession, Roosevelt, annoyed at the incessant pressure, lumped the request with demands for intervention on the part of Armenians, Finns, Poles, and Congolese.[7] Although the President's economic sensibilities were less well developed than his sense of *realpolitik*, he realized that there was little point in exacerbating economic relations with the Russian empire. Thus when a new delegation came to see him on June 15, 1903, with a long petition to be forwarded to St. Petersburg through official diplomatic channels, Roosevelt and Hay, with the connivance of Straus, conceived of a way of deflecting the initiative while still getting publicity for the contents of the petition. True to Hay's prediction the Russian Ambassador refused to accept the petition. Disinclined to press the case further, Hay hit upon the face-saving device of placing the unread petition in the Department's archives and drafting a diplomatic note in its place which, while it would never be read by the Tsar, would be read before many Hebrew congregations. Coming as it did shortly before the election, it would have the desired political effect.

Considering that there were over three hundred pogroms between 1903 and 1906 which continually aroused the emotions of American Jews, it was surprising that they had not moved in the direction of economic retaliation sooner. There were two ways in which such economic pressure could be brought to bear: a threat to the continuance of the Commercial Treaty of 1832 which governed all commercial relations between the two nations and gave Russia access to the American market, and withholding of such investment capital as was in the hands of Jewish bankers. Both were extremely difficult to impose.

Pressure to revoke the commercial treaty began in earnest in July, 1904, when a House resolution to that effect was introduced. It urged the President to open up the question of the treaty so that equality of treatment might be assured to all American citizens. It was hoped by this means to force the Russian authorities to extend a degree of religious freedom to Jews which it had recently granted to other dissident religious sects in Russia. Rather than satisfaction, however, Jewish leadership watched in horror as the Russian authorities skillfully deflected the popular anger generated by Russia's ignominious defeat in the Russo-Japanese war by a series of new pogroms against the Jews. Jacob Schiff and Lord Rothschild's effort to withhold investment capital from Russia came to naught when French banking houses stepped into the breach. Kuhn, Loeb's financial assistance to the Japanese side during the Russo-Japanese war did not noticeably strengthen the financially hard-pressed Japanese at the negotiations in Portsmouth.

But the negotiations did present an opportunity for a delegation of Jewish leaders to discuss the Jewish problem with Serge Witte and Baron Rosen, the Russian Foreign Minister and Ambassador respectively. The delegation which was composed of Adolf Kraus, President of B'nai B'rith, Schiff, Seligman, Lewisohn, and Straus, did not receive much satisfaction. Witte, who was hardly representative of official opinion in St. Petersburg, admitted the worst of the depredations and even promised to use his influence to halt the pogroms. But he cautioned the leaders to go slow in trying to wring complete civil rights for Russian Jewry because he was convinced that any precipitous action would provoke even greater outrage by Russia's peasant masses.

Witte's visit to the Lower East Side hardly assuaged the aroused emotions of the Jewish masses. On June 22, 1906, another Congressional resolution stating that "the people of the United States are horrified by the report of massacre of the Hebrews in Russia," was introduced.[8] It was an example of the growing ability of Jewish leaders to bring pressure to bear. At the same time the newly formed American Jewish Committee succeeded in having a pledge inserted in both party platforms being readied for the election of 1908. It favored abrogation of the Commercial Treaty of 1832. Surely such a pledge would bring action.

It did not. Instead, Elihu Root, Hay's successor to the post of Secretary of State, reverted to the original policy of allowing the Department to serve as an administrative arm of the Russian government by withholding passports to Jews wishing to visit Russia. The Department would grant passports only to those who had received permission from the Russian Embassy. Moreover, the new policy, which was implemented in May, 1907, cast some doubt on the sincerity of the later Republican platform pledge to abrogate the commercial treaty with Russia. Root went further. He sent a circular letter to former Russian Jews contemplating a return trip to inform them of the Department's policy. For a period the Jewish leadership was preoccupied with regaining what they had won with great difficulty three decades earlier.

The Commercial Treaty itself continued to remain inviolable. A May, 1908, request by Mayer Sulzberger, President of the American Jewish Committee, urging Roosevelt to give notice to the Russians of the government's intention to abrogate the treaty, was referred back to Root for final disposition. Meanwhile the Russians, while not surrendering the basic principle of their right to discriminate, actually relented somewhat in practice. In 1909 they offered automatically to visa all passports granted to Jews provided they traveled on Russian steamers.

Taft entered office in 1909 committed "to continue to make every endeavour to secure the solution of such distinctions which in our eyes are both needless and opprobrious."[9] But when a delegation of Jewish leaders met with William Rockhill, Taft's designee for the St. Petersburg post, it was readily apparent that Taft did not take the commitment seriously. It was merely political rhetoric to garner the Jewish vote. That was confirmed when a delegation from the AJC visited the White House in February, 1910. Taft was reminded of his pre-election pledge. He was informed that France, Austria, and Germany had already wrung promises of better treatment of their Jewish nationals from St. Petersburg. Why could not American Jews enjoy similar protection and concern from their government?

Three months later, on May 25, 1910, a full-scale meeting on the Jewish question took place in the White House. The meeting was an explosive one and Jacob Schiff, angered at Taft's refusal to acknowledge that legally the Jews were entitled to such protection, walked out of the meeting. At the same time Jewish organizations redoubled their agitation on the question. A new Congressional resolution, introduced by Representative Herbert Parsons and Senator Charles Culbertson, called for immediate termination of the commercial treaty with Russia. Throughout 1911 the House Foreign Affairs Committee, chaired by William Sulzer, held well-publicized hearings on the resolution. Many prominent Jews testified. Men like Louis Marshall stressed that discrimination against American citizens abroad was not a Jewish problem but an American one. The hearings culminated when the Senate passed the resolution unanimously and the House by a vote of 300 to 1.

The Taft administration, now aware that its hand might be forced on the question of the commercial treaty, cautioned St. Petersburg to soften its position. But Sazonoff, the new Russian Foreign Minister, remained adamant regarding Russia's right to discriminate. Meanwhile political pressure was increased. Since 1912 was an election year, all three party platforms dutifully renounced the commercial treaty. Ultimately, in the face of Russian intransigence and rising agitation at home, the process of abrogation was begun. Taft, along with many others, continued to believe that Jewish demands for American standards of civil rights were unreasonable when applied to American Jews residing in Russia and hurt American commercial interests. Nevertheless, in August, 1913, Russian wood, pulp, and paper products, which formed the bulk of her trade with the United States, were removed from the "most favored nation" list by the Treasury Department. The Commercial Treaty of 1832 had finally been abrogated.

But 1913 was not a good year to celebrate such victories. The American economy turned sharply downward and when it finally did recover its vitality it would be directly attributable to war orders from the Allies, of which Tsarist Russia was one. That year, too, Russia presented more evidence of the depth of her anti-Jewish animus. The Mendele Beilis blood libel case presented American Jewry with a new *cause célèbre*. It added fuel to the anti-Tsarist emotions among Jews and dampened their enthusiasm for the Allied side in the war. How could one fight "to make the world safe for democracy," if the world's most autocratic regime was on the same side?

The war also signaled the end of years of agitation over the treatment of Jews in Rumania and the less well-known cases of Morocco and Persia. As in the case of Russia, the quest for intercession was only partly successful. But in the process of mobilizing their strength some important lessons were learned. It taught Jews what could be achieved by effective organization and public pressure. Many, like Marshall, came to believe that it was the best way to rectify an injustice. American

Jews subsequently placed a great deal of confidence in government-to-government action on behalf of their co-religionists overseas. That was the thrust of the American Zionist effort to influence the Wilson administration to support its goals in the Middle East.

The growth of Zionist sentiment among American Jews meant that an interest in a specific foreign problem, the establishment of a Jewish national homeland in Palestine, would henceforth occupy a high place on the American Jewish agenda. More than ever, the eyes of American Jews would be turned outward. The American government, as a matter of course, would be viewed as an instrument to help realize Zionist goals.

If the war created an opportunity to realize Zionist objectives, it also posed a quandary for the world Zionist movement. In the years when the battle between the Allies and the Central powers seemed drawn a great deal depended on choosing the right side or at least not placing all the Zionist eggs in one basket. Jews were fighting and dying on both sides. Russia's Jewry, in which the most militant sentiments for actual migration to Palestine were anchored, was at first totally cut off by the war and after the Revolution faced a regime basically hostile to the Zionist program. Some Zionist leaders, like Shmaryahu Levin, were inclined to favor the German side while others, best represented by Chaim Weizmann, cast their lot with the British. There were, in addition, some Zionist leaders like Judah Magnes who were repelled by the thought that a blood bath, as the war of attrition had become, would serve as the cradle for the birth of a Jewish homeland. The war had physically split the world Zionist movement and might yet count it as one of its casualties.

Ultimately several factors pulled the Zionist movement toward the Allied side. Included among them were the traditionally hostile attitude of the Turks toward the small Jewish settlement in the area, the determined wooing of Jewish public opinion by the British, the pro-British attitude of key Zionist leaders in the United States, and the fortunes of the war itself which, after the entrance of the United States, seemed clearly to favor the Allied side.

For American Zionists the choice was less difficult. As early as 1893, Turkey had reluctantly granted the right of Jews to buy land in Palestine and some American Jews had done so. But as Oscar Straus discovered during his tenure as Minister in Constantinople, the Turkish authorities were not anxious to promote Jewish settlement in the area and had at times prohibited visits to the area or severely restricted them in time. The tradition followed by elderly Jews of settling in the Holy Land to await death and burial, was frequently interfered with. Such practices did not endear the Ottoman Empire to the Jews. As in the case of Russia, the Turkish authorities made invidious distinctions between Jews and others desiring to settle in Palestine. Thus when Turkish authorities began deporting Zionist leaders of the Palestinian community, the die was cast. "We do not want Palestine from the Turkish assassinocracy," said Stephen Wise, the leader of the Congress movement.[10] Over a period of generations a proprietary interest toward the 85,000 Jews of Palestine had developed among American Jewry. Now at one blow the Turkish authorities threatened to dissolve it. Still, Stephen Wise notwithstanding, had the Turks offered Palestine, the Zionists would undoubtedly have accepted it with alacrity. It would have lightened their task in the ensuing years.

In 1914, the Yishuv (Jewish community in Palestine) was largely dependent on overseas philanthropy. The war had the effect of cutting these funds from Central Europe. Even in Allied countries such philanthropy was in any case at a low ebb and had largely been redirected to the Jewish population centers of Eastern Europe where the war had created a dire need. The thin line of pioneering settlements, so laboriously created, were threatened with extinction and with it one of the principal legitimizers of Zionist claims to the Holy Land. Yet the renewed Turkish hostility was not totally without foundation. They were aware that Zionist leaders like Chaim Weizmann had freely contributed their talents to the Allied war effort and that a Jewish legion comprised of three battalions and led by the militant revisionist Zionist leader, Lev Jabotinsky, was actively assisting the British cause. Particularly the legion, whose complement had been recruited among Jews in the United States and Canada, and whose leaders served as part of the mule corps in the ill-fated Gallipoli campaign, nettled the Turks.[11]

In 1915 Palestinian Jews had been given the option of becoming Turkish citizens or leaving the country. Six thousand Jews were expelled from the Jaffa district and shipped to Alexandria and scores of Zionist leaders who resided in Palestine were placed under arrest. These actions disturbed the equanimity of American Jewish leaders who feared that after the Turks liquidated the Armenians, they would "solve" their Jewish problem along similar lines. A timely intercession by Wilson which requested the Turkish government to protect Jewish life and property in the Holy Land, coupled with the stationing of two warships, the *Tennessee* and the *North Carolina*, in Turkish waters, prevented the situation from deteriorating. For the time being Jewish as well as American-sponsored Christian missionary interests in the area were secure.

Before 1917, the fact of American neutrality placed the major responsibility for relief and protection of Palestinian Jewry in the hands of American Jewry. They were apprised of the critical situation in Palestine by a series of cables from Henry Morgenthau, the American Ambassador to Turkey. To avoid catastrophe at least $50,000 would have to be raised immediately. Within a matter of weeks the necessary money was raised by the AJC and the Federation of American Zionists, for once acting in tandem. It would be distributed by Otis Glazebrook, the American Consul in Jerusalem.

After Palestine was successfully occupied by the British, a thirty-three-man medical unit was sent to Palestine. At the height of the crisis an American collier arrived in Jaffa, a cargo of nine hundred tons of potatoes in its hold to stave off starvation which threatened the community. But in its early stages the question of relief for Palestinian Jewry was complicated by the strict British blockade regulations. The situation was not fully stabilized until the United States severed relations with Turkey in April, 1917.

The rescue of the Jewish community in Palestine was essential if Zionism was to achieve its long-range goal, the establishment of a Jewish national homeland in the area. That would be brought about chiefly by political means in which American Jewry would perforce play a key role. The signal for American Zionist leaders to mobilize came when the British authorities, perhaps motivated by an exaggerated impression of the importance of Jewish public opinion on the world stage, issued the Balfour Declaration on November 2, 1917.

The first fruit of the collaboration of Zionist leaders with British leaders, the Declaration was in many ways the fulfillment of an age-old Zionist dream. It would serve as the legal basis for the Jewish commonwealth, and British dominance of the area made the promise of the Declaration realizable. "His Majesty's government view with favor the establishment in Palestine of a national home of the Jewish people," read the Declaration. The jubilant mood of the Zionists often prevented them from reading the full statement which was in fact carefully hedged. It also stated that the "civil and religious rights of existing non-Jewish communities in Palestine, or the rights and political status enjoyed by Jews in any other country," would be safeguarded.

It was these "existing non-Jewish communities," especially the majority Arab community, which would prove most troublesome to the Zionist settlers in later years. Arabs and Christians living in the Holy Land could also look to the Balfour Declaration for protection. An attempt to conciliate all factions involved in the area resulted in a document which would become the source of endless wrangling.

Even so the Balfour Declaration was the product of years of effort in which the American Zionist movement played an important part. The weight of the American government was essential in the delicate balancing game Zionist leaders were required to play to win such a declaration. Louis Brandeis and Stephen Wise, both fairly close to the Wilson administration, set out to gain the President's support for the Declaration.

In Britain, government support had largely been won by Chaim Weizmann, whose work at the University of Manchester had led to the development of a new cheap means of producing explosives. By 1916 Weizmann's reputation had reached an all-time high and he had ready access to British power holders whom he convinced of the justice of the Zionist cause. It was felt that Weizmann's unique combination of charm and commitment might work a similar magic on Wilson. At the subsequent meeting between the two leaders that feeling proved to be well-founded. Wilson was taken by Weizmann's near religious zeal for Zionism and the welfare of his people. Soon after the meeting word was received of Wilson's approval of the Balfour Declaration.

In the early months of 1918 the newly formed American Jewish Congress was informed that Wilson "was persuaded that the Allied nations with the fullest concurrence of our government and people are agreed that in Palestine there shall be laid the foundations of a Jewish Commonwealth."[12] Wilson even accepted the suggestion made by Zionist leaders that the phrase "national home for the Jew," in the Declaration should be changed to the more dignified "Jewish people." But in the inadvertent use of the term "commonwealth" rather than national home, the Wilson administration had gone further than the Declaration. The implication that an independent sovereignty was intended would raise a storm of opposition among American missionaries as well as anti-Zionist Jews.

In October, 1918, the Wilson administration moved further to implement its policy. Colonel House, assisted by Frank Cobb and Walter Lippmann, prepared a semi-official interpretation of the Fourteen Points, upon which the peace negotiations would ostensibly be based. The memorandum favored Britain as a mandatory power in the area and further recommended recognition of Palestine as a Jewish state "as soon as it is a Jewish state in fact."[13]

It was not Wilson's way to do anyone's bidding if it interfered with some dearly held objective like the restoration of peace. Before Wilson had come to support the Balfour Declaration he had attempted to use the Palestine question to bring peace closer. Sensing an opportunity to detach Turkey from the Central Powers, he sent Henry Morgenthau and Professor Felix Frankfurter to Palestine to determine if some *modus vivendi* could be found to allow Turkey to remain at least nominally present in the area. Camouflaged as a mission for ameliorating the condition of the hard-pressed Jewish community in Palestine, the arrival of the two representatives of the Administration proved extremely disturbing to the Zionist leadership. For them it was clear that Turkey must lose the war so that Zionism might attain its goal. Wih the help of the British Zionists, who had access to government communication facilities, the Morgenthau-Frankfurter mission was successfully deflected. Morgenthau became convinced that the mission could not be achieved and might hurt his political career.

More important in Wilson's thinking on Palestine was the opposition of the missionary movement. Never satisfied with the rule of the Turks in the area, missionaries were nevertheless even more skeptical regarding a possible Jewish hegemony. As the son of a Protestant minister, Wilson was naturally sensitive to their argument that government support of Zionism would, by antagonizing the Turks, endanger the missionary enterprise. It was that reason which led Wilson to delay declaring war against Turkey. Efforts to detach Turkey continued even after the two nations were at war. In the winter of 1917 rumors that the United States was on the verge of concluding a separate peace with Turkey were rife. In 1917, to appease the missionaries Wilson dispatched a special fact-finding mission composed of Henry King and Charles C. Crane to Palestine. Predictably the King-Crane commission recommended that the Wilson administration's support of the Balfour Declaration be modified. The inhabitants of the area were equally opposed to living under the administration of Turkey or Britain, according to the commission's report. It suggested that the government make clear that its support of a Jewish national home in Palestine did not mean that it supported the idea of Jewish political sovereignty in the area or that it intended to neglect the national aspirations of other groups.

The missionaries, who also opposed French dominance of Syria, actually felt that their interests would be furthered best by an extension of American influence in the area. That goal was also supported by highranking naval officers like Admiral Mark Bristol, commander of American naval forces in the Mediterranean and former High Commissioner in Turkey. Basing his ideas on a model reminiscent of Admiral Mahan, Bristol favored an American mandate over the entire Ottoman Empire and viewed the American missionary effort in that area as the natural handmaiden of American commerce.

These conflicting forces would come together for a final round of battle at the forthcoming Versailles Peace Conference. American Jewish leaders geared themselves for the struggle. After years of strife, agreement had finally been reached in October, 1916, when the American Jewish Congress was established for the purpose of representing American

Jewish interests at Versailles. The new organization did not get under way until December, 1918, barely a month before the conference was scheduled to begin. The delegation was composed of Julian Mack, who served as its chairman, Louis Marshall, Stephen Wise, Nahum Syrkin, Joseph Barondess, and Jacob De Haas. Its secretary was Bernard Richards, one of the founders of the Congress movement. Together the members of the delegation represented a careful balancing of the various interests of which American Jewry was composed.

The arrival of an American Jewish delegation at Versailles from a new and vigorous world power and representing a vital new Jewish community may be viewed as the beginning of American Jewish dominance of world Jewish affairs. After the Bolshevik seizure of power the large community of Russian Jews would gradually be cut off from world Jewry and within a decade the Jews of Central and Western Europe would be hard pressed by new forces whose ideological mainstay was the most virulent type of anti-Semitism.

Not until March 2, 1919, more than six weeks after the conference began, did Wilson receive the delegation. He expressed general agreement with their objectives. But in the wings the opposition was gathering momentum. Much would depend on London's continued need to use Zionism to balance Arab nationalism. Arab opposition to Zionist designs on Palestine had already made itself felt through a series of riots and attacks on the pioneer settlements.

The American Jewish delegation joined forces with the *Comité des Delégations Juives auprés de la Conférence Paix*, the umbrella organization representing Jewish interests at Versailles. But the divisions within American Jewry persisted and were reflected in a divergence of opinion within the delegation. There were Zionist-minded delegates who were primarily concerned about establishing a Jewish homeland in Palestine. Not necessarily opposed to that idea, other delegates gave higher priority to plans to protect Jewish minorities by legal means in the countries where they resided. Only Louis Marshall's gifts as a great conciliator prevented an open break from developing. Ultimately, a *modus vivendi* was achieved. It left the representation of the Zionist interest to the World Zionist Organization, while the minority rights approach became the province of the *Comité*.

Predictably, the minority Zionist view ran into difficulties. The Zionist strategy of having Britain assigned as the mandatory power in Palestine and then to have the Balfour Declaration incorporated into the treaty was opposed by Britain's traditional rival in the area, France. To the adamant opposition of the Arabs and the French, was added the dissent of the Holy See and the American Protestant missionary groups. Anti-

Zionist agitation within American Jewry, aroused by the imminence of a Zionist breakthrough, again made its voice heard. While officially the AJC welcomed the Balfour Declaration, it now called attention to the reservations it contained. In May, 1919, a more extreme anti-Zionist group of Reform rabbis reminded the American delegation and the Jewish public of its fear regarding the question of dual loyalty. An investigatory commission was sent to Palestine and predictably returned with an unfavorable report.

The conference itself postponed consideration of the Palestine question and watched as the situation in the area deteriorated. In April and May, 1920, Arab riots broke out in Jerusalem and Jaffa. Numbers of Jews were killed. A coup which proclaimed Feisal, a leading Arab chieftain, as king of Syria and Palestine forced the hands of the European powers interested in the area. In August, 1919, Wilson received a second unfavorable report by Henry King. Undeterred, and despite his tragic involvement in a needless battle to have the Senate ratify the Treaty of Versailles, Wilson and other American leaders remained true to their pledge to Zionist leaders. They sent cables to San Remo, where the Supreme Allied Council was conferring on the Palestine question, to urge support of the Zionist aspirations in the area. When the results of the San Remo conference were made public it showed that the Zionist effort had not been in vain. The Balfour Declaration would be incorporated into the peace treaty with Turkey, while Britain would be the mandatory power in Palestine. There were to be additional years of frustration before a Jewish commonwealth was finally established.

Not itself a signatory of the San Remo Declaration, the United States insisted upon equal rights and privileges in the area. The Harding administration, which succeeded Wilson, viewed this conception as a kind of informal extension of the Open Door concept to the Middle East. Britain, however, was reluctant to go along with the American contention. Only under the persistent pressure of the Harding administration, itself continually prodded by missionary interests, did Whitehall relent. An Anglo-American convention regarding Palestine was signed in 1922. Article VII of that convention gave the United States a legal basis for interest in the area. No changes would be made without consulting American interests.

Meanwhile the American Zionists continued to push their cause. In April, 1922, the House Foreign Affairs Committee passed a resolution which favored giving "to the House of Israel its long-denied opportunity to reestablish a truthful Jewish life and culture in the ancient Jewish land." Introduced by Senator Lodge and Representative Gillette, the resolution had little effect on the indifferent Harding administration

Rather, it reflected the ability of the American Zionist movement, in the midst of disarray bordering on disintegration, to push resolutions devoid of meaning through Congress. In September, 1922, there followed the Joint Fish-Lodge resolution which paraphrased the Balfour Declaration. It was reluctantly signed by Harding, thereby fulfilling the Zionist objective of wringing a formal commitment from the American government.

Such actions, while heartening to the American Zionists, could not counteract the movement's loss of forward momentum. Partly, this was attributable to that, now familiar, bane of all Jewish organizations, lack of internal cohesion. The purge of the Brandeis faction left the American Zionist movement momentarily weak and without direction. It would have to be reenergized before the final goal of establishing a Jewish commonwealth could be achieved.

Those of the *Comité* who were primarily interested in having a minority rights clause inserted into the various peace treaties fared little better than the Zionists at Versailles. Jews generally tended to place great confidence in such forms of legal protection. The idea of guaranteeing minority rights had wide support among the Jews of Eastern Europe, who possessed a firsthand knowledge of the situation there. But what kind of rights? Eastern Jews, familiar primarily with the compartmentalized ethnic organization of Russia and Poland, viewed minority rights as consisting not only of the legal civil rights guaranteed to all citizens, but also of the right to have a degree of cultural autonomy, which might include their own school system where they could learn their own language. American Jews, accustomed to the idea of amalgamation and integration of ethnic minorities, were hard pressed to understand the need for separate cultural autonomy. To the non-Zionists it smacked of a "state within a state." Instead they favored the American idea—full civil rights and complete access to the opportunities for economic betterment. They could not fathom the fact that historical circumstances had, in fact, produced a separate Jewish nation in the East. It had been the restlessness of the suppressed minorities in the Austro-Hungarian empire which had helped bring on the war.

Nor had the war contributed to a solution of the minorities problem. Bloody pogroms continued to take place in Poland and in the Soviet Union, although in the case of the former, Paderewski, leader of the newly independent Polish state, denied that persecution of Jews continued on a large scale. When the two commissions which had been dispatched to investigate the charge issued their report in December, 1919, they affirmed what East European Jews knew only too well. Strong anti-Jewish feelings which led frequently to physical attacks persisted in the area. Some form of legal protection of minorities in these areas was imperative. The treaties with Poland, Austria, Rumania, and other newly constituted nations included provisions to write minority protection clauses into their constitutions. These clauses contained not only normal guarantees of citizenship rights but the right to a degree of cultural autonomy desired by the Jewish minority.

The faith of men like Louis Marshall, whose prodigious efforts helped make the minority clauses a reality, was to be short-lived. Foisted on resentful new nations, they would prove to be no stronger than the League of Nations which guaranteed them. Poland and Rumania disregarded them almost immediately. The League proved too weak to withstand the xenophobic reaction which was behind much of the nationalism of the new nations. Legal clauses notwithstanding, European nations reverted to their customary practice of persecuting vulnerable minorities.

The pattern became fully manifest in the thirties and forties, when Germany, with the collaboration of nations like Rumania and Poland, chose to solve their "Jewish problem" by liquidation. It was to be the establishment of a sovereign Jewish nation rather than the legal guarantees of their rights which would prove a more certain way to guarantee Jewish security. But the discovery that it would take more than legal clauses to change the hearts of men came too late to save millions of European Jews.

CHAPTER XVII

The Twenties and the Thirties:
Accommodation, Exclusion and Crisis

HAD AMERICAN JEWRY FOLLOWED A NORMAL DEVELOPMENT DURING THE following three decades, its history would have been relatively easy to relate. It would have been an account of a particularly successful ethnic group personifying the American dream. Included in the story would have been its successful acculturation and a special emphasis on its astounding economic mobility, its rising educational level, and its growing affluence. These are, in fact, important parts of our story. But the decades of the thirties and forties were cataclysmic ones in Jewish history which culminated in the destruction of one-third of the world's Jews. That traumatic event profoundly affected the course of Jewish history, especially that of American Jewry, which after the destruction of Europe's Jews, emerged as its largest and most viable component.

The ascendancy of an acculturated generation of descendants of East European Jewish immigrants in the twenties marks an important juncture in American Jewish history. Gradually the distinctive cultural profile of Eastern Jewry was ground down. Its language was abandoned in favor of the native tongue. Between 1917 and 1927, the Yiddish press lost more than 200,000 readers. The 1930 census indicated that only one in four Jews declared Yiddish as their mother tongue. The sharp ethnic subdivisions, Russian, Rumanian, Hungarian, Lithuanian, Galician, and German, which had been a traditional source of rancor, were becoming merely a source of humor as "intermarriage" between the groups occurred with increasing frequency. An undifferentiated American secular culture was gradually replacing the East European religio-ethnic culture the immigrants had brought with them.

Sometimes the manifestations of the change were easily visible. In the Old World, for example, Jews had been indifferent to physical sport, but in America love of sports and admiration for athletes became a near mania among the young. Hundreds of ghetto youngsters aspired to careers as boxers and baseball players and when Hakoah, the all-Jewish

[258]

soccer club of Vienna, visited New York in 1927 they were greeted by throngs of enthusiastic Jewish fans.

The process of cultural homogenization did not eliminate differences between Jews all at once. The division between "uptown" and "downtown" Jews persisted, although the roles between German and East European Jews were now frequently interchanged. Upwardly mobile, acculturated products of immigrant homes began to take their place among the "uptowners." In most cases the wealth of these *arrivistes* did not yet match that of the children of the original German-Jewish settlers, but the fact that so many were able within a short time to amass some wealth changed the terms of the relationship. If in earlier years the original Jewish settlers feared that the immigrants would remain dependent and would never acculturate, now one often heard complaints about their "pushiness" and their *nouveau riche* vulgarity.

There was little manifestation of blind mimicry of the model set by the older Jewish settlers. East European Jews and their descendants continued to possess a greater preference for big city life. They concentrated in urban communities of 100,000 or larger in the Northeast. Not until the thirties did a sizable number follow their German-Jewish brethren, and incidentally the general American pattern, of settling in the South and the West. Their reluctance to move to the interior, however, did not stem from a loyalty to territory and region so characteristic of other immigrant groups. They were in fact prone to do a considerable amount of moving around within their urban confines. A drive out of the ghettos to "better" neighborhoods led by 1927 to a decline in the Jewish concentration in Manhattan and to a growth of new Jewish communities in the Crown Heights, Borough Park, and Flatbush sections of Brooklyn, the Grand Concourse area of the Bronx, and the bare beginnings of isolated Jewish pockets in Queens and Long Island. The movement reflected not only growing Jewish prosperity but the development of New York City's mass transportation system.

Demographic changes would also have a profound impact on American Jewish development. After it had reached its peak of 3.7 percent of the general population in 1937, a proportional decline of the Jewish population occurred. The proportional increase in the number of Jews between 1877 and 1926 was thus reversed by the effect of the restrictive immigration laws of the twenties, later marriages, and generally smaller family units. By 1967 the Jewish proportion of the population had declined to 2.92 percent and all indications are that it will continue to decline, albeit at a slower rate. Like their Sephardic and German-Jewish counterparts, contemporary American Jewry appears destined, at least in terms of population, to be a relatively inconspicuous group.

Even as their proportion of the population declined, Jews played a disproportionately important role in the economy. Clues to their remarkable economic success might be found in the increase in philanthropic giving among the sons of immigrants. Or one could glance at the business opportunity columns in the Yiddish press to realize that in the free atmosphere of America Jews had finally found an outlet worthy of their talents and business acumen.

Like their German Jewish forerunners, the new immigrants and their descendants tried their hand at banking and finance. The pompously named Bank of the United States was a source of pride to "downtowners" because its founders, Joseph Marcus and Saul Singer, were living proof that Eastern Jews could also excel in finance. At its peak the bank provided for the needs of 400,000 East-Siders and numerous Jewish institutions. In 1927 it boasted a capitalization of $45,779,225. Disillusionment set in during December, 1930, when, without warning, the bank failed. Thousands of Jewish depositors lost their life savings and when an investigation showed that slip-shod banking practices were partly responsible for the failure, their confidence in banks was shaken.

At the same time the twenties saw a change in the character of the older German Jewish banking houses. The war had brought in its wake a change from debtor to creditor status which meant that one of the major roles for Jewish banking houses, the attraction of investment capital from European Jewish bankers, would have to be reversed. At the same time these older banking houses became independent of family connection and their links to the Jewish community. A major banking house like Kuhn-Loeb, which controlled about 2.8 percent of the nation's banking business at the turn of the century, was by the twenties no longer distinguishable as a Jewish banking house. Its employees were not conspicuously Jewish and its owners had long since abandoned the tell-tale signs of their Jewishness. But the growth of Jewish representation in gentile banks continued to be restricted, and more particularly in the crucial insurance business which had become an important source of investment capital. The picture varied, however. Of the 1,375 members of the New York Stock Exchange, 18 percent were of Jewish origin.[1] It is ironic that just as the phenomenon of a specifically Jewish banking interest dating from the late nineteenth century began to decline, there should have arisen the charge of an international Jewish banking conspiracy from men like Henry Ford.

By the nineteen-thirties a distinct Jewish economic profile was discernible. In basic industry such as metallurgy, mining, the petrochemical industry and transportation there was virtually no Jewish representation. But they could be found in by-product industries such as junk and scrap metal. The latter business according to the authoritative *Fortune* study was 90 percent Jewish.[2] Jewish business was most often concentrated where manufacturing and merchandising converge; they were the jobbers, wholesalers, and general merchandisers. Even in these areas Jewish preponderance was more apparent than real. Jews could frequently be found in mass retailing in the urban areas of the Northeast but their number tended to thin out in the interior of the country. Even in areas where Jews had pioneered, such as mail-order merchandising and retail chains, Jews were not represented in disproportionate numbers. The growth of chain stores could in fact appear to be an ominous development to the thousands of small independent Jewish retailers who squeezed out a living in this way.

Yet despite their low demographic profile and their economic marginality, Jews somehow had high visibility in the economy. Some of that may have been in the eyes of the beholders who were often wont to imagine Jewish dominance even where it did not exist. More likely the explanation is that Jews tended to concentrate in those areas where pioneering Jewish businessmen had made a breakthrough. "What is remarkable about the Jews in America," observed the editors of *Fortune*, "is not their industrial power, but their curious distribution, their tendency to crowd together in particular squares of the checkerboard."[3]

Paradoxically, while Jewish predominance in certain areas of the economy was viewed by anti-Semitic elements as evidence of a Jewish conspiracy to dominate business and commerce, it was in fact a symptom that certain sections of the economy were still "off-limits" to Jews. Talk of Jewish dominance was more often based on illusion than reality. That was especially true in the film industry in which many Jews pioneered. But by the 1930's much of the control had been stripped from these capital-starved pioneers and given to the bankers. Only three of the major studios had a sizable representation of Jewish capital.

Actually, it was clear by the thirties that the professions would easily rival and perhaps eventually overtake a business career as the favored choice of third-generation offspring. Subtle recognition of this career pattern came from the professional schools which began to employ numerous devices to limit their Jewish enrollment in the twenties. An anomalous situation was thus created. By erecting barriers against Jewish candidates, the professional schools were actually assuring that those Jews who were selected and did succeed in becoming doctors, lawyers, and engineers, were, because of the keen competition for place, superior to their gentile counterparts in the same fields. Restrictions, moreover, did not cease upon earning a professional degree. Prestigious Wall Street and Washington law firms were rarely accessible to Jewish attorneys. These customarily turned to the riskier and less remunerative trial work as an outlet for their talents. Behind the stereotype of the shrewd, conniving Jewish lawyer there may have lurked an unhappy professional, overqualified for his position. Jewish professionals remained underrepresented in the medical societies, bar associations, and among administrators of universities, from among whose members many of the top-echelon government administrators were recruited. In short, restriction in professional schools meant that other worlds, like government administration, would remain closed to Jews.

We have seen that labor organization offered a good opportunity for a certain kind of Jewish intellectual. The weakening of the Jewish labor movement in the twenties affected these people as well as the rank and file members whom the union proved unable to protect from the vagaries of the cycle. The unions' militancy was lessened by the influx of a new generation of workers who had not undergone the soul-searing experience inherent in the struggle to organize. The twenties witnessed a counterattack by organized employers who capitalized on the prevailing xenophobia of the decade. They argued that organized labor was inimical to the "American system."

In addition, the Jewish labor movement was faced with a threat from the other side of the political spectrum. The newly organized Communist Party employed the Trojan-horse tactics advocated by the Secretary General of the Comintern, George Dimitrov, to gain control of the Jewish labor movement by boring from within. Much of the labor movement's energy and resources were expended in fighting this threat to its independence. In 1922 the Workmen's Circle Fraternal Order, a central pillar of the Jewish labor movement, which had been singled out for penetration, adopted a resolution which condemned the activities of the would-be infiltrators. Nevertheless, for a time several lodges appeared to be more loyal to the Party line than to the Order.

Once having gained control, Communists used the organizations for their own purpose. In the general strike of 1926, for example, $800,000 of an emergency unemployment fund was misappropriated during a hopeless strike which was not settled until the Executive Board of ILGWU took over and brought peace to the industry.[4] The original UHT group was usually able to withstand Communist-inspired infiltration attempts which were centered in the Trade Union Educational League (TUEL). But some locals were left in total disarray and others were lost entirely. Both sides resorted to goon squads, a practice which had characterized the initial struggle to organize. By 1929 the worst of the "red threat" had passed its peak. Strong opposition from within the labor movement guided by a timely split within the Communist

Party and the general ameliorative thrust of the New Deal muted the threat. Membership in traditionally Jewish unions rose from a low of 50,000 in 1933 to 200,000 a year later.[5]

The invigorated Jewish labor movement of the thirties could not, of course, produce employment during the Depression, from whose adverse effects the Jewish worker was hardly exempt. The increase in applications for assistance received by Jewish welfare agencies which grew by 42.8 percent in New York City by August, 1931, and at almost double that rate in cities like Baltimore and Minneapolis, bears mute testimony to the devastating impact of the Depression on Jews. Undoubtedly the Jews who turned to public welfare were fewer in number than other segments of the population. The result was a serious straining of the resources of voluntary philanthropy. In turn this had a negative effect on the crucial role American Jewish philanthropy was called on to play abroad during the critical decade of the thirties. By 1932, for example, the American Palestine Appeal was able to raise only half its normal sum. Collection for the AJDC and other agencies showed a similar decline.

The twenties in American history were the scene of the final round of battle between the values of nineteenth-century ruralism and the new urban America to which American Jewry was so firmly linked. The fall-out from that often bitter conflict was destined to affect the Jews in a special way.

Yet Prohibition, which might be viewed as a manifestation of the Protestant fundamentalism prevalent in rural America, barely affected Jews, among whom alcoholism was almost unknown. The imbibing of spirits among Jews was associated with sacramental purposes and joyous occasions and, except for the holy day of Purim, was always strongly regulated. The Volstead Act generously exempted sacramental drinking from government regulation. Undoubtedly some Jews had little difficulty in stretching the merely sacramental to the joyous. The drinking of a "schnapps" for some Jews befitted almost any occasion. The moderate abuse became serious enough in 1922 for the indefatigable Louis Marshall to assure D. H. Blair, the Commissioner of Internal Revenue, "that the Jews of this country are practically unanimous in frowning down any attempt that may be made to evade the law."[6]

Jews were less successful in evading one of the primary products of the unpopular prohibition law, the growth of organized crime which thrived on filling the demands for alcohol not available through legal channels. Some of the distilleries from which the illegal liquor was supplied were owned by Canadian Jews, as were some of the rum runners who delivered it to American markets. The Jewish community also produced its own Al Capones and criminal gangs, such as Brownsville's "Murder Incorporated." Once on the scene, criminal elements infiltrated into the garment industry and the kosher meat business. In the former, the turbulent struggles to organize created a unique demand for thugs as Jewish unions and employers resorted to strong-arm methods, resulting in a spiral of violence. Both sides soon had cause to regret the use of such tactics, for once criminals found their way onto the payroll it proved nigh impossible to remove them. Many a sound business was sucked dry by these criminal elements. Yet crime itself never became a way of life among American Jews. Its existence rather reflected the extent to which American Jewry had become part of the American scene in the twenties, gangsters and all.

If prohibitionism and its entourage of unwholesome consequences affected Jews only peripherally, the nativism and xenophobic reaction against radicalism were bound to have a more direct impact. Jews, after all, could claim precisely such types in disproportionate numbers. A. Mitchell Palmer, the Attorney General, who initiated the practice of anti-radical raids, predictably caught many Jews in his net. His model, moreover, was slavishly copied on the state and local level. In New York State, for example, five legally elected Socialist Assemblymen were expelled from that body. Two of them were Jewish. Two organs of the refurbished Ku Klux Klan, the *Searchlight* and the *Fiery Cross*, saw in the establishment of the Comintern in 1919 the beginnings of a world conspiracy, and linked the threat to Jews, maintaining a continuous clamor that Jews would bring revolution and chaos to America as they had already done in Russia.[7] The Greater Iowa Association, convinced that Jewish peddlers flocking into that state were clandestinely disseminating Bolshevik propaganda, sounded the same alarm.[8]

It was primarily in the agitation for immigration restriction that Jews felt the impact of nativism. Jews generally possessed a sixth sense of what the theory of Nordic supremacy portended. It was a Jewish social worker, Nissim Behar, who organized the most effective counterattack to restrictionalism through the National Immigration League. Jews succeeded in winning an exemption from the restrictionist provision of the Literacy Test Act which was finally passed over Wilson's veto in 1917. Immigrants fleeing from religious persecution who were literate in their own language were exempt from the act.

Nevertheless, the movement to restrict immigration, buttressed by nativist passions, gained momentum in the postwar period. This occurred precisely at the juncture when events in Eastern Europe, the Civil War in Russia, and persecution of Jews in Poland and Rumania created a greater need than ever for a haven in America. Much of the agitation preceding the temporary immigration act of 1921 and the Reed Johnson Act of 1924 was clearly anti-Semitic in character. It was especially evident in the rush to pass the act of 1921. Restrictionists, aware that the 1920–1921 fiscal year had brought the record number of 119,000 East European Jews to America, were anxious to curtail the entrance of an even greater number during the next fiscal year. The hearings which preceded the passage of the Immigration Act of 1924 repeatedly cited the radicalism of the Jews of the Lower East Side as evidence that Jews were inherently un-American and would never become good citizens. The instrument of restriction was the national origins formula which established a quota system for each country and clearly favored immigrants from the nations of Western and Northern Europe over those from the East and the South. The relatively low quotas for East European countries meant in effect a limit on the number of Jews who might emigrate to America.

While immigration restriction was directed against foreigners, and only incidentally against Jews, there was ample evidence that a specific anti-Jewish animus was also part of the nativist sentiment of the twenties. As early as 1914 the lynching of Leo Frank, the Jewish manager of an Atlanta pencil factory, portended that urbanization of poorly prepared rural masses could spell disaster for middle-class Jewish outsiders.[9] In addition, the war contributed to a deterioration of the fragile civility which kept a modicum of peace in a disparate population. Predictably, Jews were a favorite target for slander. Despite the fact that immigrant Jews enlisted in the armed forces in disproportionately high numbers and sustained a high percentage of casualties, rumors began to circulate that Jews were draft dodgers and "combat shy." Jewish soldiers, many living among Christians for the first time in their lives, were subject to anti-Semitism in the army camps which dotted the nation. Government officials sometimes allowed their anti-Semitism to be reflected in their official attitudes. The Provost Marshal for selective service, for example, issued a "Manual of Instructions for Medical Advisory Boards" in which doctors were cautioned that "the foreign born, especially Jews, are more apt to malinger...."[10]

To those who measured the pulse of anti-Semitism in the nation it was apparent that the twenties were producing a new urban base for this hate phenomenon. It was no longer confined to rural groups, like the Populists, whose rare contact with Jews permitted their fantasies to roam freely. Rather than arguing that Jews were unproductive, the new group was wont to complain about the keen business competition Jews offered. Lewis Gamet, writing in the *Nation*, now thought that it was "the very rapidity with which the Jew adjusts himself to primary conditions of life in America [which] is his chief handicap."[11] There was thus little that was internally consistent about the anti-Semitism which emerged in the twenties. On the one hand, Jews were considered radical and poor human material for assimilation; on the other, they adjusted too well and too rapidly.

Anti-Semitism as a matter of course was reflected in restricted employment opportunities, especially in white-collar jobs. One study estimates that Jews in the twenties were excluded from 90 percent of the available white-collar employment in New York City. But while such restriction was a matter of concern for many Jews it was the restrictionist policy in institutions of higher learning which became a *cause célèbre* in the Jewish community. We have seen that Jews had discovered early that formal education offered a rapid means of mobility. Besides, there was the additional advantage of satisfying a historically conditioned appetite for learning. A professional calling naturally occupied a respected place among second- and third-generation Jewish immigrants.

That hunger was reflected in Jewish enrollment in colleges and professional training institutes. Between 1890 and 1925 Jewish enrollment in colleges grew at a rate five times faster than the general population and by 1919, 9.7 percent of the total number of students receiving professional training were Jewish. The preponderance of Jews in professional schools was particularly evident in the New York Metropolitan Area. The approximately 25 percent of the population which was Jewish produced 38.5 percent of the enrollment in professional schools. The disproportionate number of Jewish students was also in evidence in the local colleges. In 1918, 85 percent of the enrollment of C.C.N.Y., 27.5 percent of Brooklyn Polytechnic Institute, 18.7 percent of Columbia University, 28.7 percent of Hunter College and 20.9 percent of New York University, were Jewish.[12] Jewish attendance in the prestigious Ivy League schools also showed a sharp increase. The phenomenon did not pass without critical notice: "The Jew," one observer complained, "sends his children to college a generation or two sooner than other stocks, and as a result there are in fact more dirty Jews and tactless Jews in college than dirty and tactless Italians or Armenians or Slovaks."[13]

Jewish students showed a preference for careers in business and finance. Accounting attracted 25 percent while medicine, engineering, law, and dentistry followed in that order of preference. After negotiating the hurdle of acceptance the Jewish student often faced hostility from faculty and fellow students. Native students who were not compelled to undergo the keen competition for entrance into college tended to view their college days as a time for sowing their wild oats rather than a period of serious application. The earnestness of Jewish students and their unabashed competitiveness for grades won them the animosity, rather than the admiration, of their Christian fellow students. "History is full of examples where one race has displaced another by underliving and overworking," complained one Ivy League student.[14]

The intrusion of Jews into American higher education was not in fact a totally new phenomenon. We have already seen the Hebraic context of much of what passed for higher learning during the Colonial period. But then Jews served as trustees or officers and only rarely as students. As early as 1787, Reverend Gershon Seixas was elected as a trustee of King's College and Mordecai Noah was one of the prominent Jews who helped to found New York University in 1831. Barnard College was founded by a somewhat eccentric and strong-willed Jewess, Natalie Meyers. But while Jews might be identified as founders or contributors to endowment funds for educational institutions, their representation among the student body in conspicuous numbers did not occur until the sons of East European immigrants began to press for admission. All at once Jewish students became conspicuous, not only for their increasing numbers, but because their style and keen drive for scholarship was at variance with the standards of the existing student body. Rather than regarding higher education as a mobility instrument, the American university functioned as an adjunct to the social establishment for the training of future leaders. These ambitious Jewish students were unaware of what Thorstein Veblen called the "canons of genteel intercourse" which governed these institutions and were transmitted by them. Character, sportsmanship, and leadership ability ranked higher than scholarship and intellectualism. The governing class naturally possessed a sense of proprietorship in the older and more prestigious universities which their parents and sometimes grandparents had attended. Their resentment was expressed in a popular ditty sung by members of the established fraternities:

> Oh, Harvard's run by millionaires
> And Yale is run by booze,
> Cornell is run by farmer's sons,
> Columbia's run by Jews.
>
> So give a cheer for Baxter Street
> Another one for Pell
> And when the little sheenies die,
> Their souls will go to hell.[15]

The reaction against the admission of more Jewish students occurred in the early years of the twenties. Increasingly such devices as alumni screening committees, character tests which sought such factors as "public spirit" and sociability, and quotas based on geographic region, were employed to limit the enrollment of Jewish students. The decline of Columbia's Jewish enrollment from 40 percent in 1920 to 22 percent in 1922 indicates how effective such devices were.

But it was Harvard, rather than Columbia, which was the scene of the most celebrated *numerus clausus* case. It was triggered by the revelation that Harvard's Jewish enrollment, which had been only 10 percent in 1919, had risen to 15 percent in 1921. That aroused a fear that Harvard was on the verge of becoming a "new Jerusalem," a label assigned to a dormitory "reserved" for Jewish students. Using the pretext that a continued rise in Jewish enrollment would raise the anti-Semitic sentiment among the student population to a dangerously high level, President Lawrence Lowell prepared to reduce the proportion of Jewish students. It was not a lack of scholarship that nettled. "The idea that any shrewd boy can by cramming get by on written examinations," asserted the President of Brown University, and "must thereby automatically be admitted to college is anti-American."[16] It was that Jewish students were overcompetitive and for that reason perhaps disloyal.

But Lowell's plan to restrict Jews ran into surprising opposition because it neglected to take into account the Jewish constituency which was already in existence among Harvard alumni, students, and faculty. Harvard's prior liberal tradition of admission based solely on ability had been instrumental in creating this group and it was ready to fight for "its" Harvard. Also unforeseen was the fact that restrictionism would reawaken dormant "town and gown" antagonism. That meant that Catholic Irish politicians, who now governed the greater Boston area, would forego no opportunity to hit back at the citadel of Protestant Brahminism. Almost immediately the Boston City Council and the Massachusetts State Legislature threatened an investigation to discover if grounds existed for the removal of Harvard's tax exemption. Newspapers and political leaders spoke out against the university. Strangely, American Jewry, which had hardly reacted when N.Y.U. and Columbia University imposed quotas, was outspoken in its protest against Harvard's action. Harvard was considered as the pace-setter among Jews and its actions would determine the course of other universities: "If the Jew loses his fight to gain admission to the college campus, he is defeated in a far more significant battle, namely the right to entrance into higher spheres of the professions and commerce," noted one rabbi.[17] It was a view shared by many Jews.

The fight to keep Harvard open to Jews was led by Louis Marshall and Judge Julian Mack, the Zionist leader who happened also to be a member of the Harvard Board of Trustees. A complication occurred when President Lowell, unknowingly speaking to a former Jewish graduate of Harvard, asserted that the clannishness of Jewish students was partly to blame for the quota. Again the true nature of the Christian dilemma in regard to Jews in high places was starkly revealed. On the one hand, they were considered clannish, on the other, they assimilated too readily. For many Jews the outspoken anti-Semitism of the masses was infinitely preferable to such hypocrisy. At least then the Jews knew where they stood.

Marshall rejected outright Lowell's contention that he was merely trying to allay the growth of anti-Semitism among the student body. "The only tests that we can recognize [for admission], are those of character and scholarship," insisted Marshall.[18] He would not help the President achieve his "disgraceful purpose." On the face of it he won his battle against Harvard. In June, 1922, a special faculty committee repudiated Lowell's admission plan. But the victory was an empty one because it proved impossible to impose a new policy on the leadership clique who ran Harvard. New informal screening procedures gradually whittled down Harvard's Jewish enrollment. Not until the Cold War reminded the nation about the scarcity of talent did Harvard and other leading universities again give the highest priority for admission exclusively to academic ability. Today Harvard's Jewish enrollment is approximately 25 percent, Columbia's has returned to 40 percent and Princeton, whose Jewish quota was less than 2 percent in 1941, now accepts 15 percent.[19]

Harvard's attempt to reduce Jewish enrollment touched the interest of a relatively small number of Jews. Moreover, the reasoning behind the drive toward a Jewish quota would barely be considered a manifestation of the open anti-Semitism with which most Jews were acquainted. However, they were soon to experience the more virulent form to which they were not unaccustomed, through the antics of the great American folk hero, Henry Ford. His role as a principal spokesman of anti-Semitism is difficult to trace because he shared with Jews a mutual interest in bringing World War I to an end in 1916. Several Jews were involved in Ford's peace-ship project, a visionary private effort to bring peace.

It may have been the unwillingness of the money market to fund Ford's $75,000,000 internal debt which aroused Ford's fury against "Wall Street" and the money power. In his mind Ford reverted from the role of the millionaire industrial statesman, which he had assumed during the war, to that of a humble tinkerer who possessed a special genius for mass-producing automobiles. With the conversion, Ford's thinking took on a populist anti-Semitic coloration. Life was a contest between people like himself, who were creative and productive, and parasites like bankers and financiers who sat in their plush Wall Street offices and manipulated the world. Ford soon came to believe that these figures, who populated his fantasies, were Jews.

Beginning in May, 1920, the Ford-owned *Dearborn Independent* serialized the most scurrilous piece of anti-Semitic literature, *The Protocols of the Elders of Zion*. Its theme concerning a Jewish conspiracy to rule the world fitted nicely into Ford's paranoic imaginings. For the next seven years a steady flow of anti-Semitic propaganda emanated from the Ford-owned journal. The intervention of Arthur Brisbane, Ford's favorite Hearst columnist, President Taft, Woodrow Wilson heading a group of 119 distinguished Americans, and the Federal Council of Churches, could not convince Ford to abandon his anti-Semitic tirades. It had become his obsession.

Where argument and reasoning failed, a direct threat to Ford's pocketbook proved more successful. A million-dollar libel suit was filed against the cranky millionaire by a little-known Jewish attorney from Detroit. At the same time Jewish defense organizations, weary of pleading with Ford to relent, organized a consumer's boycott of Ford products. The campaign got underway in the final months of 1920 and it was not long before Ford's attorneys began secret negotiations with Louis Marshall. After much bickering the negotiations produced a formal apology by the mogul which was featured prominently in the nation's leading newspapers on July 8, 1927. Ford promised to make amends for the harm he had "unintentionally' committed. Louis Marshall accepted the apology for American Jewry "because essentially the spirit of forgiveness is a Jewish trait."[20] As in the case of Harvard the "victory" proved to be an empty one. Anti-Semitic literature backed by Ford money continued to enjoy wide circulation and reminders of his promise were ignored. Then as suddenly as it had started Ford seemingly was converted to philosemitism. In 1938 he issued a press release praising Jewish workers in his plant and in 1941 he offered his huge rubber plantations in Brazil, Fordlandia and others, as a resettlement haven for Jewish refugees.[21]

Compared to the ominous new wave of anti-Semitism in the thirties, Ford's activities in the twenties appeared like the idiosyncrasies of an eccentric. Abetted by the social tensions released by the Depression and supplemented and subsidized by the worldwide apparatus of the "New Order" in Germany, anti-Semites everywhere went on the offensive. Its spokesmen, George Sylvester Viereck and his Flanders publishing company, William Dudley Palley and his Silver Shirts, Father Charles

Coughlin and his Social Justice movement, Fritz Kuhn and the German-American Bund, and such lesser lights as Gerald K. Smith, John F. Cassidy, and Francis Moran, reached an immense audience with their message of hate. The effects were to superimpose a new type of anti-Semitism which included "buy Christian" campaigns, physical attacks on Jews, and the most violent propaganda advocating the traditional forms of economic discrimination and exclusion.

Jewish apprehension about the turn of events grew apace. "Faced with the unbelievable record of Nazi barbarities," stated the preface of the authoritative *Fortune* study on American Jewry, "leading members of the Jewish community... have been shocked into fear. The apprehensiveness of American Jewry has become one of the important influences in the social life of our time."[22] The study was sanguine about the actual impact of the new virulent anti-Semitism. It thought that the program was carried forward by a relatively small group of perhaps 15,000 activists, mostly of German-American origin. It did not, as many supposed, stem from the domestic crisis, the study concluded, but was actually a German import.[23] Americans continued to be largely indifferent to it.

If that was so, it was perhaps due to the fact American Jewry had become an elusive target for anti-Semitic propaganda. Entrepreneurial skills and competitiveness, which Jews were thought to possess in great abundance, were believed to be admirable characteristics in the American value system. They were in conflict with that other part of the anti-Semitic stereotype which saw Jews as radicals and un-American. The image projected by anti-Semitic propaganda lacked clarity. Even the populist imagination, which had been regenerated by the Depression, laid the blame for the failure of the system, not on Jews, but on caretakers of native stock such as Herbert Hoover, Samuel Insull, and Charles Mitchell.

Yet another factor augured badly for the proponents of anti-Semitism. The new political coalition on which the New Deal victory was based contained ethnic urban blocs and was thus marked by a rejection of the nativism of the twenties which was the seedbed of anti-Semitism. Jews as urban voters and liberals perforce played a sizable role in the New Deal coalition. They had entered the twenties still favoring Republican candidates but by 1924 Jewish voting behavior was undergoing a gradual change. In the election of 1924, Al Smith cut heavily into the normal Jewish vote for the Socialist, Norman Thomas, and the Republican, Theodore Roosevelt Jr., all candidates for the governorship of New York State. The contingent of Jewish congressmen shifted to the Democrats as a result of the same election. The ethnic-urban-liberal coalition on which F. D. Roosevelt capitalized, was first set into motion by Al Smith. Once part of the new alignment, Jewish voters proved more loyal than other ethnic groups whose commitment to Roosevelt began to decline after the election of 1936 when the second, and perhaps more radical, New Deal took shape. During the late thirties and early forties the Jewish "love affair" with Roosevelt was in full bloom. So strong was his hold on the Jewish voter that David Dubinsky, the spokesman for Jewish labor, was compelled to organize the American Labor Party in New York State so that the traditionally radical Jewish voter might have an opportunity to cast his ballot for the patrician Roosevelt on a "non-capitalist" ticket. In 1936 the new party polled 274,924 predominantly Jewish votes. Jews were by then so well integrated into the Democratic party, which had also won the hearts of a majority of American voters, that Roosevelt was reelected for no less than four times. In fact there was some feeling that Jews had become too well associated with Roosevelt and the New Deal. For some the New Deal became synonymous with the "Jew Deal."

By the thirties, too, Jewish defense organizations had gained some experience in counteracting the impact of anti-Semitism on public opinion. They developed an intellectual defense which made anti-Semitism appear to be part of a generally abnormal behavior pattern. Study after study proved beyond doubt that anti-Semitism was part of an unhealthy authoritarianism, while tolerance and liberalism were not only morally right but symptoms of good mental health.[24] "Cultural pluralism," a term suggesting the benefit of a degree of group particularity, became the new catch word. At the same time Jewish organizations established interfaith organizations like the National Conference of Christians and Jews in 1934. It served as an umbrella organization for the numerous interfaith groups springing up. That development also serves as additional evidence that by the thirties American Jewry had lost some of its particularity and self-consciousness. Jews had become, if not less Jewish, more American, and by that fact more difficult to isolate as a target for group hatred.

Withal, the exposed position Jews assumed on the issue of intervention gave to anti-Semites a strong weapon to promote their cause. It was on that issue that Jews diverged from general public opinion which continued to bask in the delusive tranquility of isolationism. It was not only sympathy for the tribulations of their co-religionists abroad which made American Jews prone to advocate a more active foreign policy. For various historical reasons Jews have always been more global-minded than their fellow Americans. Studies show that Jews more than other cohesive groups were better informed on foreign-policy problems, they were more likely to belong to organizations which were interested in such problems, and they tended to be more active in such organizations and were more likely to write to their legislative representatives concerning foreign problems.[25]

When the Nazi regime revealed its virulent anti-Semitism in the thirties, Jewish public opinion, which had been largely peace oriented and to some degree isolationist, rapidly assumed an interventionist point of view. With the exception of the Jewish Communists, all elements of the Jewish political and religious spectrum recognized in the Nazi movement a menace to Jewish survival. After *Kristallnacht*, few Jews could be found who were not convinced that Hitler and his regime must be stopped by physical force, if necessary.

But to Americans who were not directly linked to the beleaguered Jews of Germany, such a position smacked suspiciously of serving a specifically Jewish rather than the broader national interest. Anti-Semites spared no effort to associate the advocacy of interventionism with an exclusively Jewish interest. That was the theme of a speech delivered by Charles Lindbergh, the popular American folk hero, in Des Moines on September 11, 1941. Lindbergh warned that the Jews, the British, and Roosevelt were conspiring to bring the nation into a war against Germany and that such a war would prove catastrophic for America. It was a line echoed in the halls of Congress by Gerald Nye, Louis T. McFadden, William Borah, and other isolationist Congressmen. The linking of Jews to interventionism became a weapon in the isolationist arsenal.

On the grass roots level the association was found to aggravate the troubled relationship between Irish and Jewish Americans. With certain distinct exceptions, Irish-Americans were in the isolationist camp. Their continuing hatred for the British and, more important, a pronounced fear of the menace of Communism took clear precedence over Fascism which in the Mediterranean countries was associated with the protection of the Catholic Church. Even such opponents of anti-Semitism as Father James M. Gillis, editor of the *Catholic World*, deplored the fact that liberals paid less attention to the persecution of the Church under leftist regimes in Spain and Mexico than they did to the persecution of the Jews in Germany. His view was not far removed from the far less tolerant one of Father Francis Talbot, who was convinced that the nation's liberals were Catholic baiters determined to destroy the American Catholic Church. According to Patrick Scanlan, editor of the Jew-baiting *Brooklyn Tablet*, American liberals "hate the Church just as bitterly, just as ignorantly and unfairly as any klansman."[26]

That element of American Catholicism which revealed an anti-Semitic ideology is best personified by Father Charles Coughlin, who emerged early in the Depression as the silver-tongued orator of the air waves. Coughlin, who resonated the beliefs of small-town America, did not begin his public career as a spokesman of anti-Semitism. That developed later. In 1932 he supported Roosevelt's candidacy and became something of a spokesman for the welfare state. As late as 1936 he opposed American participation in the Olympics to protest Nazi treatment of Jews. Nor did the program of his newly-organized National Union Party reveal any overt signs of anti-Semitism. But after the outbreak of the Civil War in Spain Coughlin's views underwent a change. He reverted to visionary currency reform schemes, such as the abolition of the Federal Reserve System. Suspicions regarding currency are the telltale signs of the strident populist imagination.

His voice became more discordant when his radio oratory proved unable to wean away a sizable portion of the working-class vote from the New Deal and frustrated his political ambitions. It was then that talk of the existence of a Jewish conspiracy began to be heard. His *Social Justice* journal began to hint that Fascism was, after all, a legitimate response to "Godless" Communism. Because Jews opposed the former and were often to be found on the left side of the political spectrum, they were considered anathema. Jewish advocacy of intervention against Fascist aggression was viewed as an attempt to weaken that bulwark ideology in the struggle against Communism. It was circuitous reasoning, but as we have seen, it served to link anti-Semitism and isolationism. It was the same kind of reasoning which prompted Ambassador Joseph Kennedy to caution the film industry, which he believed was controlled by Jews, to avoid producing anti-Nazi films. Gerald Nye, the leader of the isolationist faction in the Senate, improved on Kennedy's ploy of merely giving helpful suggestions to the industry and simply accused Hollywood of trying to push the nation into a war with Germany.

The receptivity of Irish-Americans and other hyphenates to Coughlin's message may have been due more to resentment of the rapid economic advancement of American Jewry than to concern about foreign policy matters. The fact that Jews recovered faster from the effects of the Depression made it difficult for some Irish-Americans to understand the preoccupation of Jewish organizations with the problems of economic discrimination. Why were the Jews not concerned about economic discrimination against other groups, asked Father Scanlan in the *Brooklyn Tablet*. The Irish, he claimed "were fast being reduced to the most inconspicuous place" in the economic order.[27] The problem stemmed partly from the Irish preference for employment which offered security and pensions but held out only slow lock-step advancement—usually in the municipal civil service. The Jews, on the other hand, forced into the risky, but frequently more remunerative careers in small business, were sometimes able to leap over the Irish in the race for middle-class status. The resentment engendered a fertile field in which the seeds of anti-Semitism could blossom.

Nevertheless, measuring the degree to which such resentment contributed to Irish antagonism against Jews, or for that matter, to the antagonism of other ethnic groups like Germans, Italians, Poles, and Slovaks, poses certain problems. If Coughlin represented an archtypical political type who for a time had great drawing power among urban ethnics and small-town Americans, there were also leaders in the Catholic hierarchy, like Archbishop Stritch of Milwaukee, Coughlin's superior, Cardinal Mundelein of Chicago, Archbishop Rummel of New Orleans, and many others in the hierarchy and the laity who persistently spoke out against Coughlin and generally held more liberal views. Political leaders like Roosevelt also attempted to move the Catholic hierarchy to a less divisive position. Before Myron Taylor, Roosevelt's special emissary to the Vatican, left for Rome in 1940, the President instructed him to remind the Holy See of his concern about the continued anti-Jewish feeling and actions in such Catholic centers as Brooklyn, Baltimore, and Detroit.[28]

Predictably, as isolationism fell into disrepute its anti-Semitic element also lost its sting. *Kristallnacht*, the night of November 9, 1938, when Nazi gangs burned and looted Jewish stores and synagogues is, according to some historians, the best point in time to pinpoint the downturn of isolationist sentiment.[29] The incident earned such disapprobation among the American people that the German Ambassador, Hans Dieckhoff, cabled frantically to the Wilhelmstrasse that "even the most bitter anti-Semites are anxious to disassociate themselves from methods of this kind. . . . With few exceptions the respectable patriotic circles which are thoroughly anti-Communist and for the greater part, anti-Semitic in their outlook, also begin to turn away from us."[30] The dispatches of Herbert von Dirksen, German Ambassador in London, struck a similar note. The ambassadors did not exaggerate. Public opinion polls showed 88 percent of the American public disapproving of these depredations.[31]

Yet while public empathy toward Jews had a positive effect, as did the outbreak of war between the Axis and the United States, it did not magically erase the virus of anti-Semitism. The tensions released by the war heightened intergroup hostility. Polls taken in 1942 showed again the prominence of an anti-Semitic stereotype. Jews ranked consistently low on polls asking Americans to evaluate various groups on the quality of their citizenship. The Harlem riot of 1942 contained an ominous portent of things to come. It featured the looting of Jewish-owned stores and inflammatory anti-Semitic oratory by certain black leaders. Only in 1944, when the public began to sense that the war would draw to a victorious end, did anti-Semitic sentiment decline. By 1946 pollsters experienced difficulty locating any signs of it. It was the beginning of a new period of acceptance of Jews, one which would prove to be of fairly long duration.

Had the public goodwill toward Jews occurred five years earlier, it might have changed one of the most tragic pages of Jewish history. It was precisely in the midst of the war, and the few years preceding it, that Jews desperately needed the goodwill of the American people and their government. They required a slight alteration in the restrictive immigration law so that thousands of refugees who had been uprooted by Hitler could find a haven in America. But while many Americans sympathized with the plight of the refugees, they remained unalterably opposed to admitting them. Indeed, as the crisis heightened in intensity the American public actually hardened its anti-refugee stand.[32] Not even Jewish refugee children were exempt from the public opposition to raising quotas. It was partly the Roosevelt administration's sensitivity to the public's opposition to a more generous refugee policy which limited its activities on behalf of the beleaguered Jews of Europe.[33] There were, of course, other factors involved in that tragic inaction, not the least of which was the condition of American Jewry.

CHAPTER XVIII

The Roosevelt Administration, American Jewry and the Holocaust

HAD IT NOT BEEN FOR THE CATASTROPHE WHICH BEFELL THE JEWS OF Europe the Roosevelt years might have been inscribed as a golden age in the history of American Jewry. Instead, the holocaust, a term used to denote the liquidation of European Jewry, revealed the limits to which the Roosevelt administration was willing to extend itself on behalf of the unfortunates caught in the Nazi net. Serious internal weaknesses within the ranks of American Jewry which interfered with their ability to act during the crisis came to the surface. American Jews have been tormented by their failure ever since and much of their subsequent behavior toward Israel, where many of the survivors of the holocaust have settled, can be explained by their feeling of culpability regarding their wartime role.

Those who were called upon to take up the cudgels for their European brethren were divided and insecure. Rather than promoting unity, the crisis tended to divide them further and to intensify their insecurity. One by one the fragile bridges which had been painfully erected to bind American Jews together gave way and they stood helpless in the face of the threat.

Yet the community was rich in organizational resources. In the 1920's it boasted eighty-two national organizations with a membership of about 1,150,196. The national organizations were supplemented by hundreds of local ones composed largely of religious congregations. Such mass participation in the community's organizational life would, under ordinary circumstances, be considered the surest sign of the community's vitality. But in reality the organizations provided merely an artificial blush of health. When the crisis was upon them, American Jewish organizations displayed an inability to speak with one voice.

At the root of Jewish disunity there were deep-seated religio-cultural differences. The problem was compounded by the voluntarism of organizational and congregational life and the continuing impact of secularism. The rancor which characterized the relationship between the

[277]

three religious branches of American Judaism had hardly diminished with time. Yet from outward appearances all three religious communities appeared to be thriving. By 1926, 3,118 congregations were in existence, a remarkable growth of 96.2 percent since 1906.[1] In the next decade an additional 610 congregations were established. The increase in the number of congregations was matched by an increase in membership and wealth. That was especially true of the Reform and Conservative branches.

"Politics" continued to produce the sharpest strife within American Jewry. In reality this term is insufficient to describe the struggle within the community. The growth of Zionist strength appeared to make the possibility of unity even more remote. Having proved unable to reconcile themselves to the existence of the Orthodox camp, the Socialists seemed even less able to accept the Zionist movement. There was also no peace between "downtown" socialists and "uptown" reformers; furthermore, neither faction had much use for Zionists. Soon enough differences hardened into "matters of principle." The Socialists were convinced that a solution of the Jewish problem lay in the establishment of a socialist society. Anti-Semitism was viewed as being a product of a sick capitalist society which pits one man against his brother. Such exploitation and the antagonism it breeds would cease only when the capitalist order itself was replaced by a socialist one. While Socialist-Labor-Zionists agreed with the socialist analysis, they leaned toward a religio-ethnic solution—socialism within a separate Jewish political context. For them Jewishness was itself worthy of preservation. The solution proposed by the pure socialists was not only unworkable, it proposed to solve the Jewish problem by dissolving the distinctive Jewish culture which most Jews wished to retain.

An interior world of its own complete with complex splits and schisms —that was the world of Jewish socialism. The successful revolution in Russia served to regenerate antagonisms which had for years lain dormant. Under Lenin's leadership the new society had made a promising beginning in ridding Russia of the scourge of anti-Semitism. Attempts to "normalize" Jewish class structure and to solve the Jewish problem within a socialist context were begun. The Communist Party had approved massive agricultural experiments in the Crimea where it planned with the help of outside financing to resettle thousands of Jews. Subsequently there would be a Soviet experiment in creating an autonomous Jewish republic in Soviet Asia in the near empty lands between the Biro and Bidzahn Rivers. Never before had a Russian regime appeared so anxious to utilize the special managerial talents possessed by Russian Jews. Thousands of Jews moved to the larger cities to obtain a university education. Others filled the vacuum in administration left by the disintegration of the Tsarist government. What more could be asked for? Many Jews became convinced that a solution to their problem had been found and showed their gratitude by joining the Communist Party. By 1927 Jews formed the third largest national group in the Communist Party.[2] The same conviction undoubtedly accounts for the growth of Jewish membership in the Communist Party of the United States.

Strangely enough, the Joint Distribution Committee, financed largely by money from wealthy Jews, proved susceptible to communist charms. Influenced in part by their opposition to the objectives of political Zionism, and aware of the great improvement in the condition of Russian Jewry, the leaders of the JDC poured millions of dollars into Soviet-sponsored agricultural resettlement schemes in the Crimea and the Ukraine. The funding agency for this venture was the Joint Reconstruction Foundation which was established jointly with the Jewish Colonization Society (ICA). But the "strange alliance" between uptown philanthropy and the Soviet government, who matched those contributions with land and other necessities, did not survive the decade. Ultimately these groups, too, learned to look at the events in the Soviet Union with more discernment. By the time of the Cold War, history had come full cycle. The JDC was repeatedly cited in show trials behind the Iron Curtain as a Western espionage agency.

But the events in the Soviet Union did contribute to a realignment of forces on the left side of the Jewish political spectrum. When the dust settled on the American-Jewish scene, one could observe a new, well-organized communist wing with its own Yiddish journals, the virtual disappearance of what had formerly been known as anarchism, and a middle-of-the-road social-democratic movement which had muted its anti-Zionism enough to play some role in establishing the Histadrut, the Zionist-oriented labor federation in Palestine.

The world of American Zionism in the twenties and thirties formed a separate world which contained the full political spectrum, from the Zionist revisionists on the right to the relatively small Hashomer Hatzair youth movement, on the extreme left. After the Cleveland Convention of 1921, during which control of the movement was wrested from the Brandeis leadership, the fortunes of the movement appeared to ebb. The toppling of Brandeis predictably widened the rift within the movement. Dissatisfaction with the priorities established by the World Zionist Organization and with poor management persisted. Such issues, however, were merely surface manifestations of deeper differences. The practical social engineering necessary to the development of Palestine which the Brandeis faction preferred was, in one sense, merely an extension of the philosophy of Progressivism which set a high priority on operational efficiency as well as on the achievement of social justice. Its unemotional approach to the building of Zion was a reflection of the fact that Brandeis, as well as many of the new generation of American Jews, had no direct experience with the murderous anti-Semitism which served as the seedbed of Zionism in Eastern Europe. Nor had the original American Jewish community experienced the feeling of being alien in the land, a common anxiety among the Jews of the East where pogroms and deterioration of the Jewish economic condition had had a devastating effect.

The East European brand of folk Zionism, associated with the name of Chaim Weizmann, grew directly out of Jewish suffering in that area. Their concept of Zionism perforce was designed to serve as much more than merely a spur to the economic development of Palestine. It was first and foremost an instrument to achieve the cultural regeneration of East European Jewry. Having seen American Zionism as represented by Brandeis, Weizmann suspected "that there is no bridge between Washington and Pinsk."[3] Brandeis had to be removed, not only because his approach to Zionism would make the World Zionist Organization merely "a technical bureau with doubtful authority," it would also impose a passionless stamp on the whole Zionist venture which depended for zeal, no less than for settlers, on the Jews of East Europe.

After some shifting back and forth, Weizmann and his American lieutenants, Louis Lipsky and Emanuel Neumann, won their battle for control of the American Zionist movement, which, in any case, was composed largely of "downtown" elements. But in one sense it was a pyrrhic victory, for it removed the movement from its American tracks and transmuted it into a kind of service agency for the world Zionist movement. Brandeis and his group remained active in American Zionism, but the movement was never again to attract leaders of Brandeis's caliber.

By 1929 it appeared as if the conflict between Zionist and non-Zionist American Jews would be resolved amicably. In that year the long-simmering dispute over the composition of the Jewish Agency, the intended governing agency for Palestinian Jewry, was resolved at the 16th Zionist Congress held in Zürich. Louis Marshall, president of the American Jewish Committee, was invited to join the Jewish agency. It was a bold stroke because the involvement of a non-Zionist leader like Marshall enabled the Weizmann group to attract non-Zionist talent for the Zionist cause and at the same time to fulfill the legal requirements of the mandate. Connection with "uptown," moreover, would hopefully prove to be an asset to the Zionist movement in more concrete ways. However, the connection was not destined to thrive. With the waning of Weizmann's influence in the movement, the non-Zionist members of the Jewish Agency were progressively rendered powerless and overshadowed by the Zionist members. After the death of Marshall in August, 1929, non-Zionists began to abandon the Agency, although they continued to be active in such philanthropic projects as the American Friends of the Hebrew University.

The crisis faced by world Jewry in the thirties created a new opportunity for vitalization in the all but dormant American Zionist movement. For many Jews the Hitler menace served as evidence that the Zionist insistence on the need for a Jewish national home had all along been well founded. Had such a homeland existed, it might have been a haven for the thousand of Jewish refugees which Nazi racial machinations produced. German Jewry might never have become victims of a deranged tyrant. The need for Jewish leaders compelled to appear before the governments of the Western world, hats in hand, begging for refuge for their co-religionists, might have been avoided.

By the mid-thirties the membership of the various Zionist organizations was once again climbing. By 1935 they claimed 807,000 members; six years later the figure stood at 1,085,000, and by 1945 it had reached 1,436,000. The thirties thus witnessed the establishment of a virtual Zionist consensus which has characterized American Jewry ever since. Major non-Zionist organizations were compelled to take cognizance of the new mood and to mute their anti-Zionist stand. Those that did not bend with the wind, like the American Council for Judaism, found themselves virtually bereft of membership after the founding of the Jewish state in 1948. The internal political scene assumed a new shape to accommodate to the growing strength of Zionism.

In the center and moving slightly to the left was the refurbished American Jewish Congress. Its program gave strong support to the welfare state as well as to Zionism. Also in the center, but trailing off to the right, was the wealthier, more prestigious, defense-minded American Jewish Committee. Under its president, Cyrus Adler, it maintained a relatively conservative complexion. Like the mass organization B'nai B'rith it drew its support from the more Americanized elements in the Jewish community and those descendants of the German Jews who had remained in the fold. Linked to it were elements associated with the Reform movement, many of whom proved unable to reconcile their Americanism and Zionism. It was this group which later split off from the AJC to establish the vitriolically anti-Zionist American Council for Judaism. The left side of the political spectrum was occupied by several groups who placed themselves under the umbrella organization, the Jewish Labor Committee, in 1934. Under the leadership of Adolph Held, it drew its support from the non-communist socialist left which was associated with the still energetic Jewish labor movement. Still further left there existed a potpourri of smaller organizations which faithfully followed the lead of the Communist Party and whose membership base was found in those union locals who had been successfully penetrated in the twenties and thirties. Their posture was also strongly anti-Zionist.

Rather than bringing unity to the divided Jewish community, the Zionist thrust of the thirties tended to stiffen the lines of confrontation. Thinking in terms of its popularity, the Zionist leadership sought to impose its program on non-Zionist organizations. The results were catastrophic. Organizations like the American Jewish Committee, with vested interests of its own to safeguard, would not surrender their organizational integrity. The result was that organizational unity, absolutely essential for effective action during the holocaust, was never achieved.

In the absence of overall coordination each organization developed its own program to deal with the crisis. Separate delegations were dispatched to Washington to plead the case of rescue. Even separate planning for the postwar condition was undertaken in the supreme confidence that there would be a postwar Jewry to plan for. In September, 1943, Henry Monsky, who as president of B'nai B'rith possessed a good vantage from which to view the ineffectiveness of the organizations, called together thirty-two of the major Jewish organizations to meet in Pittsburgh. The object of the meeting was to achieve some kind of limited unity through the organization of an overall agency to be called the American Jewish Conference. From its inception, however, the unity established by the new organization was incomplete and threatening to fall apart.

Predictably, one of its major difficulties was the new Zionist militancy. A meeting of the Zionist Emergency Council at the Biltmore Hotel in May, 1942, had led to a resolution calling for the establishment of a Jewish commonwealth in Palestine. It was the position favored by the more militant labor Zionist wing led by David Ben Gurion in Palestine. When the 45th convention of the Zionist Organization of America adopted the Biltmore Program, in effect it threw down the gauntlet to those non-Zionist organizations who were willing to support philanthropic projects in Palestine, but continued to find political Zionism abhorrent. An attempt to tone down the resolution at subsequent meetings failed. Abba Hillel Silver, Ben Gurion's choice to mobilize the Zionist movement in America, introduced the commonwealth resolution to the conference, which approved it overwhelmingly. But in doing so,

Silver broke a prior pledge given to the leadership of the American Jewish Committee not to push the resolution. The exit of the Committee from the American Jewish Conference was predictable as were the loud recriminations which followed.

The house of Israel in America was thus a divided one, its walls barely supporting its roof, and its foundations weak. Friends and enemies within the Roosevelt administration soon became aware of the strife within the community. Undersecretary of State Sumner Welles, considered a friend of American Jewry, early observed that "Jewish opinion in the United States is widely and bitterly divided over the desirability of an independent Palestine."[4] Assistant Secretary of State Breckinridge Long, the bitterest foe within the Administration of all efforts to rescue the Jews of Europe, gleefully made a similar observation in his diary: "The Jewish organizations are all divided and in controversies of their own.... There is no adhesion nor any sympathetic collaboration—rather rivalry, jealousy and antagonism...."[5] Even Roosevelt, on more than one occasion, rued the fact that the Jews did not have a Pope with whom he might deal directly. American Jewry seemed unable to focus direct pressure on the Roosevelt administration. It made the task easier for those within the Administration, who were opposed to a more active rescue effort, to limit the slaughter.

The conflict over the boycott of German goods and mass protest rallies within the community serves to illustrate the difficulty in developing a unified strategy to counter the Nazis. The tactic of mass protest rallies and ultimately a boycott of German goods was initially favored by the more emotionally-committed Jews, first and second-generation immigrants, Orthodox or Zionist, who maintained a link with the Jews of Europe. The more established elements of the community frowned on such "emotional" displays. They considered them embarrassing and ineffective. The American Jewish Committee preferred quiet behind-the-scenes activity and after its leaders met with Cordell Hull in 1933, they were more than ever convinced that everything "within diplomatic usage" would be done by the State Department to help the Jews. So the new Secretary of State assured them and they could think of no reason why the Secretary would mislead them. After all, he had a Jewish wife and had always been well disposed toward Jews.

But the advocates of "emotional" displays possessed no such confidence. They understood that diplomatic intercession could accomplish little in the way of amelioration against government sponsored anti-Semitic actions. Some may have recalled that in 1920 when the newly established Polish government turned on its Jewish minority, Jews had responded with a largely ineffective boycott of Polish goods.[6]

The boycott movement began spontaneously in April, 1933, as a response to Julius Streicher's boycott of Jewish storekeepers in Germany. Soon there were a number of ad hoc committees in the field. Joseph Tenenbaum, President of the American Federation of Polish Jews, gave direction to the early boycott movement. After some hesitation the American Jewish Congress threw its organizational support behind the movement and organized its own boycott committee. Samuel Unter-meyer, a well-known government attorney, then organized the non-sectarian anti-Nazi League which together with the Joint Boycott Council of the American Jewish Congress and the effort of the Jewish Labor Committee became the core of a nationwide boycott campaign. A year later the ban on purchasing German-made goods was organized on an international basis.

Even while the movement to block the sale of German goods was gaining momentum its opponents were chagrined at the unseemly emotionalism of the Jewish lower classes. Massive protest rallies, such as the one held at Madison Square Garden on March 27, 1933, and dozens of smaller rallies held in remoter localities received press cover-age but how far did they go in improving the situation of German Jewry? Opponents of the boycott argued that such tactics actually worsened the position of helpless Jews in the Nazi grip. Moreover, such conspicuous special-interest pleading, they believed, tended to feed anti-Semitism which was on the rise throughout the thirties.

Like many other Americans at the time, Jewish boycott opponents tended to underestimate the strength of the Nazi movement. They be-lieved that what was occurring in the Reich was a temporary aberration. Beneath the surface there was after all the Germany which could be reasoned with, the Germany of Goethe, Heine, and Schiller. Jews traditionally associated Germany with the Emancipation and Enlighten-ment. Such thinking served to fortify the wait-and-see attitude of "uptown" Jewry.

It was reinforced by practical reservations regarding the effectiveness of the ban on German goods. Boycotts, they learned, were a two-way street which could boomerang on their organizers. Jews who had been employed by the German-American press had been fired. German-American organizations had banded themselves together in the Deutsch-Amerikanischer Wirtschaft Auschuss (DAWA) (German-American Eco-nomic League) to counter the boycott. In German and Irish enclaves of the city Jewish merchants were subjected to harassment as Jewish merchants were in Germany itself. The boycott, if allowed to develop unchecked, threatened to open up a Pandora's box of intergroup con-flict. For those like Cordell Hull, who placed great stock in the healing qualities of a free flow of goods, the ban represented a different type of threat. It would, feared Hull, do damage to German-American commercial relations and eventually hurt the recovery of the American economy. "The impression is growing in some American circles," observed the *Literary Digest* in a similar vein, "that protests are hurting German Jews and American relations."[7]

The most telling argument of the opponents of the boycott related to the inner inconsistency of its Jewish advocates. While American Jewry was being mobilized to boycott German goods, the financial agencies representing Palestinian Jewry had established a mutually profitable transfer agreement (*Ha'avara*) with the Reich. It permitted German Jewish immigrants to Palestine to take with them £1,000 in cash and the balance of their assets in the form of goods for which they would be paid in pounds sterling when they arrived in Palestine. The immigrant was actually acting as a salesman for the forced sale of German goods and while the German economy was earning no foreign exchange by the transfer, it was able to raise its sales volume and gained an advantage in penetrating a new market. So disturbed were the members of the World Jewish Congress by the lack of consistency in Jewish behavior that they earnestly urged the Jewish community "to find a solution to the problem of Jewish emigration . . . which will be in conformity with the general boycott movement of world Jewry."[8]

Beyond the welter of arguments, pro and con, it was clear that it would be the effectiveness of the boycott which would become the basic determinant of whether it should be continued. Boycott enthusiasts were convinced that they were hurting the German economy. They pointed out that Germany's precarious exchange situation on which the future of Goering's four-year rearmament program depended, would force the Nazi authorities to choose between the luxury of emotional anti-Jewish excesses or achieving its rearmament goal. Noted German economists like Hjalmar Schacht had already warned the leaders of the regime that for the first two years of their tenure, exports had dropped much more rapidly than the rate of other nations. By 1934 German exports to the United States had in fact been cut in half. The German economic experts suspected the boycott had played some role in creating this situation. Between 1934 and 1936 Nazi leaders, like Rudolf Hess, were convinced that they had broken the back of the boycott movement. Nazi optimism proved to be premature. In 1938 the economic agencies of the German government reported mournfully of a "strong contraction of trade . . . caused by the increasing difficulty of selling goods in the U.S.A. due to the devaluation of the dollar as well as the anti-German boycott."[9] A further decline was caused by *Kristallnacht* even while the foreign commerce of other trading nations increased. By January, 1939, boycott advocates could proudly point to Hitler's admission before a nationwide audience that "Germany must export or die."

Boycott advocates had turned a weapon, which was perhaps more intended to lift their own fallen spirits, into an effective economic lever, something that might succeed in wringing better treatment for the brethren living under the Nazi yoke. Indeed, that is precisely what occurred. The remarkable negotiations between George Rublee, an old Roosevelt crony from Groton days, and Schacht, President of the Reichsbank, which took place in the early months of 1939, produced a plan for bloodless solution of the so-called Jewish problem in Germany by means of a device not unlike the transfer agreement with Palestinian Jewry. Undoubtedly, the plan was motivated partly by the German government's need for relief from the growing effectiveness of the boycott.

In the long run, however, unilateral Jewish efforts to wring better treatment for the Jews of Germany could not hope to succeed. Jews were too weak and the Nazi government was especially immune to public pressure on the Jewish question. To relieve the trying situation in which German Jewry, and soon the Jews of Austria and Czechoslovakia, found themselves, government-to-government pressure would be required. The Jewish question had to become part of the agenda of outstanding problems which required the attention of the nations of the world. Some way had to be found to enlist the influence of the Roosevelt administration to bring this about.

Roosevelt rarely took a direct hand in the refugee-rescue problem. The hope for favorable action to shelter the refugees produced by Nazi racial policies rested with Congress where strong restrictionist sentiment prevailed. It ruled out any possibility of changing the immigration law to permit Jewish refugees to enter. Other activities, such as diplomatic intercession and liberal visa regulations, fell within the purview of the State Department. Much of the substance of German-American relations in the thirties revolved around questions of commerce. But as the stridency of Nazi anti-Semitism increased, the "Jewish question" came gradually to occupy the center of the diplomatic stage. Outspoken anti-Nazi statements made by such liberal politicians as Fiorello La Guardia could cause a flurry of diplomatic exchanges. So did the case of the German liner *Bremen* which was boarded by an unidentified group while docked at a New York pier and had its "black flag of piracy," the swastika emblem, removed. More troublesome for the State Department was the decision by the Secretary of the Treasury to apply increased countervailing duties on German imports and the Department of Interior's decision to refuse to sell helium to the Reich.

For American Jewry such evidence of government disapproval was a source of satisfaction, but they would have been still more delighted had these actions been accompanied by some generous gesture on the refugee front. They had hoped that when the private refugee agencies banded together in the National Refugee Service in 1938, at the government's behest, some action which would permit a distinction between immigrants and involuntary refugees would be forthcoming. The nation boasted a tradition of welcoming the latter group. Refugee advocates were encouraged by the early signs that Roosevelt sympathized with these unfortunate victims. Nor were they mistaken in this view. Frances Perkins, the Secretary of Labor, observed that "there was fierce indignation in him [Roosevelt] at the forces perpetrating these horrors upon orderly, useful, well-behaved human beings."[10] In 1935 the President requested the "most humane treatment under the law" for refugees. The special executive order issued by Herbert Hoover in 1930 ordering the consuls strictly to enforce the "likely to become a public charge" (LPC) provision of the immigration law was rescinded.

When on March 25, 1938, the President announced to startled reporters his plans to convene an international conference on the refugee problem, Jews and other refugee advocates had reason to hope that the Administration was heeding their pleas for action. It was not noticed that the invitation to thirty-two nations to meet at Evian-les-Bains in July was actually carefully hedged. The invited nations were assured that they would not be requested to alter their immigration statutes. It was a foregone conclusion that they would not do so in any case. Predictably little was achieved at the Evian conference in this respect. More hope was attached to negotiating a solution to the refugee crisis at its source in Nazi Germany through the newly-established Intergovernmental Committee on Political Refugees. Its first director, George Rublee, did in fact enter such negotiations in the early months of 1939. The result was the aforementioned agreement for a phased release of the Jews of Germany which bore some resemblance to the Ha'avara transfer arrangement with Palestine.

Despite Roosevelt's oft-repeated professions of good intentions it was apparent that at the grass roots level, where the Department of State reigned supreme, an increasingly stringent anti-refugee policy was being implemented. Refugees were experiencing ever greater difficulties in obtaining life-saving visas and even existing quotas remained underissued throughout the crisis. The source of much of the problem lay with the Department's consular service which legally possessed the final authority to determine who was to be admitted.

Among some of the consuls there existed a strong restrictionist sentiment which in many cases was supplemented by a specific antipathy toward Jewish refugees. The Department's administration of the immigration law went far beyond the requirements of the law. A deliberate policy of recalcitrance and delay was recommended by Breckinridge Long, the Assistant Secretary most directly involved with the refugee issue. He explained his policy in this way in June, 1940: "We can delay and effectively stop for a temporary period of indefinite length, the number of immigrants into the United States. We could do this by simply advising our consuls to put every obstacle in the way and to resort to various administrative advices which would postpone and postpone the granting of visas."[11] It serves as a good description of the anti-refugee policy followed by the Department. All manner of "administrative advices" were found that would deny visas to the refugees. Chief among these was a screening procedure designed to filter out the spies which German authorities had supposedly infiltrated into the refugee stream. By mid-1940 it had grown so stringent that it could be said, without fear of exaggeration, that a "paper wall" had been erected which effectively blocked refugees from reaching these shores.[12] Despite his reputation as a humanitarian, Roosevelt rarely interceded with the State Department in favor of the refugee cause. Rather he seemed to use the State Department as a foil to deflect the rancor of these refugee advocates and liberals. Paradoxically, these usually staunch supporters of his administration complied by reserving their rancor for the Department rather than for the President who, after all, was responsible for the actions of his administration.

The State Department was aware that it was acting in consonance with public opinion. It was reflected in the strength of Congressional restrictionists who tended to be more heartless than the Department. A bill to bring 10,000 refugee children to the United States outside the quota system (Wagner-Rogers) was rejected in 1939 and a similar proposal was turned down in 1940. Yet when it came to the admission of non-Jewish British refugee children, victims of the "blitz," congressional generosity was manifest. Behind the restrictionists in Congress were patriotic and professional organizations who feared that the nation would be inundated with refugees during a period of unemployment. Professionals, for example, were apprehensive lest the many qualified people in the refugee pool compete for the limited number of positions. "Before we welcome professional men from Europe," stated the President of the Medical Society of New York, "let us make sure that the professional standards meet our requirements, that codes of ethics are high and that before they begin practice they become citizens."[13] "Charity begins at home," cried the leader of an organization of war widows. Speaking about the prospects of admitting thousands of refugee children, Mrs. James Houghteling, wife of the Commissioner of Immigration, regretted "that 20,000 children would all too soon grow up into 20,000 ugly adults."[14] Many of the refugee children were thus never given the opportunity to grow to adulthood.

The events of *Kristallnacht* created a momentary surge of sympathy for the refugees which was reflected in Roosevelt's order permitting those refugees already in the country on visitors' visas to extend their stay. The President also temporarily recalled Hugh Wilson, his Ambassador in Berlin, as an official reaction against the excesses occurring in Germany. But six months later, to the dismay of some Jewish leaders, Roosevelt accepted the "Statement of Agreement" which contained plans for a phased extrusion of German Jewry under circumstances that bore some resemblance to a ransom scheme. The President seemed more disturbed that the so-called Rublee Plan concerned itself only with Jews. Like many Nazi officials he fell easily into the notion that there existed among Jews untold wealth, which could be used to bail out German Jewry. But Jewish leaders hesitated to accept the proposal. Many shared the fear of Judge Samuel Rosenman that if the Nazi regime succeeded in this scheme of extortion, the governments of Poland and Rumania would quickly follow suit and try to "sell" their Jews.[15]

The central problem throughout the crisis, a problem without an apparent solution, was to find a haven where European Jewry might be resettled. Not only were such places of refuge not available, Jewish philanthropy which might have met the cost of rescuing the refugees was at a low ebb because of the Depression. German Jewry, and to some extent the Jews of Europe generally, were, moreover, culturally and demographically ill-suited for pioneering resettlement which the Roosevelt administration had begun to advocate as a solution to the problem. The Jews of Germany, for example, were among the most highly urbanized group in Europe. One out of five held a university degree and 17.5 percent were professionals while fully 61.3 percent had been involved in business and commerce. Moreover 73.7 percent were over the age of forty. Had Hitler been more patient, natural attrition and intermarriage would have solved the "Jewish problem" in the Reich by the end of the century.

Nevertheless, despite the many roadblocks placed in their paths, thousands of refugees did succeed in settling in the United States, 52 percent of them in New York City and its environs. The treatment they received at the hands of their fellow Jews was correct, if not always cordial. Many Jews, not unlike others, did not favor the admission of Jewish refugees. The upper West Side of Manhattan and eventually Washington

Heights, where many found living quarters, was soon dubbed the "Fourth Reich." After being so intimately involved in German culture, the adjustment to the new society posed serious problems. Many of these status-conscious refugees experienced a precipitous decline in their position. Some were reluctant to begin the arduous climb to regain what they had lost through no fault of their own. Some may have expected the Jewish community to restore them to their former stations, or at least treat them with the deference to which they were accustomed. On the other hand, the sons and daughters of East European Jews who now frequently occupied positions of responsibility in the community, retained some of their parents' resentment toward the assimilationist Jews of Germany. They often suspected that German Jews were anxious to deflect Nazi racialism against East European Jews living in Germany. Ironically, the new arrivals really had more in common with the educated descendants of the Eastern Jews than the "uptowners" who had all but forgotten their German roots.[16]

There were pervasive differences too. The German Jewish refugees were not voluntary immigrants. They frequently derived from those classes that were least likely to emigrate. Understandably they suffered terrible longing for what formerly had been theirs. Most of them ultimately made the difficult adjustment to the new style of life. But there were some like Stefan Zweig, the noted author, and Ernst Toller, Bavarian revolutionist and erstwhile playwright, who could not adjust and eventually took their lives. Many others lived out the remainder of their days in limbo between two cultures.

It was not until after the war that Americans received some inkling of what a remarkable group these German Jewish refugees were. A good many of the scientists associated with the Manhattan project which developed the atomic bomb were Jewish refugees from Central Europe. A deeper search might have revealed that a sizable portion of the cultural and technological boom which marked America's postwar years rested on imported intellectual capital brought to America by the refugees. Europe's loss turned out to be America's gain. Had the Roosevelt administration been aware of the remarkable human resources in this group a greater rescue effort might have been mounted on their behalf.

If the search for havens for the Jews of Europe was the major preoccupation of Jewish leadership in the thirties, it was the Zionist movement which possessed the surest claim to having found one in Palestine. There Jewish pioneers had demonstrated the possibility of making that desolate land bloom again. But despite the fact that the pioneering effort had gained the kudos of the world's political leaders, this natural haven was denied to Jews. In May, 1939, after it seemed that Arab-Jewish reconciliation was a vain hope, the British government, anxious to buttress its position in the Arab world, issued a White Paper (a policy statement) which curtailed immigration and the purchase of land in the Holy Land. Jewish immigration would be restricted to ten thousand persons per year while 35,000 additional immigrants might be admitted at the discretion of the High Commissioner. Finally, it was intended that in 1944, after five years of restricted immigration, no Jews would be allowed to settle in Palestine. Thus, at one stroke the generous policy proclaimed by the Balfour Declaration, which held out the hope of eventually establishing a Jewish national homeland, was reversed. It was the White Paper, more than anything else, which radicalized the world Zionist movement. To undo the death sentence placed upon it by British policy, the Zionist movement was forced to embark on a desperate course.

Roosevelt was counted among the world leaders who had periodically expressed admiration for the Zionist pioneering effort in Palestine. But during the refugee crisis, his objections to the White Paper notwithstanding, he hesitated to intrude in what his foreign policy advisors insisted was a British sphere of interest.[17] Unwilling to abandon their goal without a struggle, American Zionist leaders, among others, undertook a massive campaign of agitation to convince the Administration to act. The agency through which they sought to mobilize Jewish and general public opinion was the Emergency Committee for Zionist Affairs which had been organized in 1938. Under its auspices hundreds of public demonstrations were held, and February 4, 1939, the anniversary of the signing of the Balfour Declaration, was declared a day of national prayer. Fifty-nine Senators, 194 Representatives, and thirty Governors were enlisted to voice their opposition to the White Paper.[18] Forty state legislatures adopted pro-Zionist resolutions and 1,500 Christian leaders, led by Senator Robert Wagner, were organized into the American-Palestine Committee. Another 2,500 Christian clergymen joined the Christian Council for Palestine. In May, 1942, the Emergency Committee itself demonstrated its defiance of British policy by pushing for the adoption of the Biltmore Program. The effect of the White Paper on American Jewry was thus to bring them firmly in support of Zionist aspirations.

At the same time the crisis revealed serious deficiencies in the leadership and organization of the American Zionist movement. Rabbi Stephen Wise, the leader of American Zionism, was sixty-eight years old in 1942 and his energies were channeled into innumerable liberal causes in addition to his primary Zionist interest. Many felt that under his leadership the Zionist Commission for Emergency Affairs was not functioning as well as it might. In 1943 the name of the Commission was changed to the American Zionist Emergency Committee (AZEC) and Rabbi Abba Hillel Silver, a younger man who supported Senator Robert Taft, was appointed to lead it. Wise and Lipsky, who had been "running" American Zionism, bitterly resented Silver's appointment. Unlike Wise, Silver's faith in the goodwill of President Roosevelt was not strong. Moreover, he was a stauncher supporter of the Biltmore Program and was instrumental in gaining its adoption. For a time Silver's assumption of leadership caused strife within the movement for Wise did not move gracefully from the center of the stage. "I shall show my fellow Zionists now," he informed Nahum Goldmann, "that I am not to be shelved, I am not to be displaced...."[19]

Despite such protestations the new leadership breathed life into the flagging Zionist effort. Armed with a budget of over half a million dollars, AZEC established a permanent bureau in Washington which acted as a focal point to direct the efforts of a growing network of local emergency committees. A magazine called *Palestine* and Walter C. Lowdermilk's prize-winning book, *Palestine, Land of Promise*, were published. Radio time for a weekly program, *Palestine Speaks*, was purchased. Dozens of mass rallies were organized at which such show-business personalities as Edward G. Robinson and Eddie Cantor sometimes appeared. At the same time a deluge of various kinds of pro-Zionist resolutions were passed by state and municipal legislative bodies. The campaign culminated with the adoption of commonwealth planks in both the Democratic and Republican campaign platforms of 1944.

Under Silver's leadership AZEC seems to have been most successful in molding Jewish public opinion in a Zionist direction. A Roper poll taken in 1945 which showed that 60.1 percent of American Jews were now in favor of the establishment of a Jewish commonwealth, reflected AZEC's effectiveness.[20] It became even more apparent in 1948 when AZEC played a key role in preparing the ground swell of public opinion in favor of American recognition of the state of Israel.

During the war the State Department was concerned lest the intense agitation by the Zionists disrupt the Anglo-American alliance. Department officers like Wallace Murray, who headed the Middle Eastern desk, opposed Zionist goals on both practical and ideological grounds. The importance of keeping the Arab world on the Allied side, or at least neutral, so that supplies could be funneled through Iran to the Soviet Union, was uppermost in their strategic considerations. It was supplemented by the persistence of a general antipathy to Zionist objectives

in the area, some of which may have originated with the strong missionary influence which traditionally made its weight felt in the Department.
The practical argument was reinforced by the opposition of the Joint
Chiefs of Staff, whose major concern was for an uninterrupted flow of
oil to keep the Allied war machine lubricated. Thus throughout the war
the State Department predictably clung to the line first laid down by
Charles E. Hughes, Warren Harding's Secretary of State: The Middle
East was a British sphere of interest in which the United States ought
not to interfere.

In April, 1943, after news of the Final Solution was known for six
months, Roosevelt dispatched Lt. Colonel Hoskins to the Middle East
to determine how peace and stability might be maintained in the area.
Hoskins, who was educated in the American University in Beirut, issued
a report recommending what amounted to a freeze of the situation for
the duration of the war. That in effect was the policy the Roosevelt administration followed. Palestine, which might have played a crucial role
in the rescue of Europe's Jews, was instead taken out of the picture.
Roosevelt resorted to a policy of gestures. Frequently he talked one way
to Jews and another way to Arabs. According to one author, every time
Roosevelt assured the Zionists of his support, the State Department
automatically sent contrary assurances to Arab leaders.[21] As the war's
end approached and agitation grew more intense, both sides were informed that no decision regarding Palestine would be made until after
the war and that both parties would then be consulted.

In the meantime the Roosevelt administration devised a strategy to
appease the Jewish community while not disturbing the tenets of the
policy it had decided upon. Part of that strategy entailed a search for
what Sumner Welles had called a "supplemental national home," areas
where masses of Jews might be resettled outside Palestine. To aid the
Administration in the search, Morgenthau enlisted the aid of the nation's
best-known resettlement expert, Isaiah Bowman.

There followed an examination of the possibility of resettlement in
dozens of areas: Alaska, Mindanao, British Guiana, Lower California,
Costa Rica, Brazil, Ecuador, Angola, Rhodesia, and many others. When
the Dominican Resettlement Association finally succeeded in settling a
handful of Jews in that country, the Administration touted the venture
to the heavens. Much effort, albeit almost completely unsuccessful, was
expended in trying to convince the Latin American republics to accept
such ventures. At one point in 1939, Roosevelt became fascinated with
the idea of settling Jews on the Orinoco plateau. Usually, however,
Roosevelt's enthusiasm increased in direct proportion to the distance
the projected havens were from the western hemisphere. In 1940 Roose-

velt became convinced of the practicality of a "big idea," to form a new republic to be known as the "United States of Africa." It would be composed of sections of Tanganyika and Northern Rhodesia and, failing that, of Angola. Morgenthau was asked to prepare a list of the thousand richest Jews to finance the project to which the President would graciously lend his name, the "Roosevelt Plan."[22] During that year, too, the President made the search for resettlement areas a permanent feature of his administration. He secretly appointed Henry Field, a noted anthropologist, to work on the idea of resettlement. Before the project was terminated Field had examined 666 likely resettlement areas.

But no substitute for the haven which Palestine might have become was ever found by the Roosevelt administration. Even if such a place of refuge had materialized, there remained nigh insurmountable difficulties in resettling the millions of Jews who required a new home. Instead, these people were compelled to become refugees seeking to infiltrate into existing national communities. After the United States entered the war the situation of European Jewry took an ominous turn for the worse. In January, 1942, after months of experimentation with various techniques of mass murder behind the Eastern front, the Nazi leadership formally decided on the "final solution" to the Jewish problem. It was planned systematically to exterminate the Jews of Europe. In the months which followed, the incredible scheme was actually put into practice in specially designed death camps, Auschwitz, Chelmno, Treblinka, Belzek, Majdanek, and Sobibor. Those Jews fortunate enough to escape the gas chambers, where Zyklon B gas was employed, were frequently subject to mass starvation in ghettos or were worked to death in the labor camps which dotted the map of occupied Europe.

When the refugee problem was augmented by the problem of rescue after 1942, predictably Jewish pressure on the Administration for action intensified. But this did not occur immediately because the mass murder operation beggared the imagination so that the would-be rescuers, no less than the victims, could not believe what fate had in store. It was here that the role played by the State Department was particularly heinous. It suppressed the news it received from World Jewish Congress sources in Switzerland which gave details of the actual operation of the "final solution" and thereby contributed to the "curtain of silence" which surrounded the activities in the mass murder factories. The ploy worked successfully for a few months, but ultimately news did leak out since it proved impossible to conceal the disappearance of millions of people. When the news did break in the early months of 1943 protest and demands for action reached new levels of intensity.

It is in the context of this renewed agitation that the idea of convening a new refugee conference on the inaccessible island of Bermuda was propounded. The idea originated in London and was eagerly accepted by the State Department. But implementing a program meant only to create good public relations while an actual mass murder scheme was in operation proved to be a serious blunder, as Breckinridge Long and his British counterparts soon discovered. Rather than dealing with the question of how to save those who faced liquidation in the death camps, the conferees confined themselves to discussing the disposition of those refugees in such areas as Spain and Portugal, who had, in fact, already found a precarious safety there. The response of rescue advocates was one of undisguised fury. Representative Emanuel Celler, who represented a heavily Jewish Congressional district of Brooklyn, labeled the conference a "diplomatic mockery" and a "betrayal of human instincts and ideals." He perceived the purpose of the conference as a "gesture to silence the clamor of the democratic peoples who demand an end to the European horror and tragedy."[23]

For some time rescue groups had recommended that a special government agency armed with sufficient power was required for an effective rescue program. In August, 1943, a House resolution proposing the creation of such a rescue commission was introduced. Long, sensing that such a proposal reflected directly on his handling of the refugee program, testified against the resolution in November. Flustered and rattled and suffering as usual from emotional tension, Long began with a flattering recitation of all the Department had done for the rescue of Jews. But he grossly exaggerated the number of refugees actually admitted into the country. The untruthful testimony backfired and served to identify him as the official whose personal distaste for Jews had led him to set up roadblocks against their admission to this country. Much of what he had done was opposed to the publicly proclaimed intentions of the Roosevelt administration.[24] In January, 1944, Long was removed from all Department activity concerning the rescue of Jews. It was an essential step if a more active government rescue effort was to be undertaken.

The major role in the establishment of the rescue commission, which was implemented on executive rather than Congressional initiative, fell to officials in the Treasury Department. That Department had been aware for some time of the State Department's reluctance to move on the rescue question. In the course of monitoring certain joint activities, Treasury officials had discovered evidence of the State Department's suppression of news of the "final solution." That, and other evidence of State Department sabotage, convinced Morgenthau, a neighbor and close friend of the President, that he should be alerted. Randolph Paul, one of Morgenthau's assistants, prepared a file, "Report to the Secretary on the Acquiescence of this Government in the Murder of the Jews." On January 16, 1944, Morgenthau and his assistant, John Pehle, after having softened the title of the prepared file, related its contents to the President. They also carried with them the text of a special executive order creating a War Refugee Board which proposed to place the responsibility for a coordinated government rescue program jointly under the State, Treasury, and War Departments. When the President signed the order, a new phase in America's effort to rescue the Jews was inaugurated.[25]

John Pehle, who from his Treasury post had good vantage from which to view the State Department's sabotage of the rescue effort, was appointed to direct the War Refugee Board (WRB). A million dollars from the President's emergency fund launched the new agency. Almost before the WRB could firmly establish itself it was faced with a new rescue crisis. Sensing that the war was lost, Nazi authorities had become doubly anxious to destroy the near one million Jews of Hungary before the demise of the Reich. The WRB initiated an energetic effort to prevent the deportation of the Jews of Hungary. Appropriate diplomatic posts were alerted to cooperate with the agents of the WRB, funds were channeled through the underground to aid small rescue schemes, and efforts were made to get food packages to the concentration camps. Most important, psychological warfare techniques were utilized to try to convince the Hungarian populace not to cooperate with the Eichmann Kommando, the special SS killer unit organizing the deportations. At the same time, new energy was breathed into the indifferent efforts of other agencies involved in rescue, among whom were the International Committee of the Red Cross, the Vatican, and various diplomatic missions of the neutral nations. They were encouraged to follow the American example. In April, 1944, even the restrictive immigration law was, symbolically at least, circumvented when the Administration accepted the so-called "temporary havens" plan to allow a number of refugees to settle in Oswego outside the law. Nine hundred and eighty-seven refugees were eventually temporarily settled in Oswego and other "free ports" were established in Italy and North Africa.

The attempt to save Hungarian Jewry demonstrated how difficult it was to save lives given the determination of the Nazi regime to extinguish them. Despite the efforts of the Roosevelt administration, over half of Hungary's Jews were liquidated. It became clear that many more thousands might have been saved had more energetic steps been taken earlier. This might have convinced Nazi leaders that the Allies did not, after all, condone the mass murder of Jews. Men like Goebbels believed that this was the case. Nevertheless, those Jews who did survive in Hungary, mostly those living in Budapest, owe their lives partly to the activities of the WRB and other agencies actively involved in the rescue effort.

In the midst of the WRB activities on behalf of surviving European Jews, dissension within the ranks of American Jews reached new heights. At its roots was the activities of a small nucleus of revisionist Zionists, led by Hillel Kook (alias Peter Bergson) who began a loud clamor in the press for more effective rescue action, even if it entailed temporarily abandoning Zionist objectives. The group was particularly harsh in its criticism of the American Zionist leadership whom they accused of holding lucrative jobs while doing nothing. The Zionist establishment responded in kind and the American reading public was treated to the spectacle of Jewish organizations fighting out their internal conflicts in the public press.[26]

At the same time, American Zionists, seemingly focusing more on the implementation of the Biltmore Program than rescue, succeeded in having an appropriate resolution (Wright-Compton) introduced in January, 1944. But the Administration was apprehensive lest the resolution disrupt plans to build an oil pipeline in Saudi Arabia, and succeeded in having it tabled. Silver's fears regarding Roosevelt's duplicity were confirmed as Sam Rayburn, Speaker of the House and close to the President, masterminded the Administration's spoiling strategy.[27] The Roosevelt administration preferred not to have its diplomatic hand forced.

Nor did Zionist hopes regarding favorable action at the Yalta Conference materialize. On his return trip, the already-ill Roosevelt invited Ibn Saud aboard the U.S.S. *Quincy*. At a previous time Roosevelt had thought that he could charm, and perhaps even bribe, Saud to cooperate with the Zionist goal in Palestine. But now Saud impressed him with his firm opposition to the Zionist endeavor. Instead the Arab monarch suggested getting rid of the vanquished Germans and giving their land to the Jews. It was a sure sign that the Arabs had no intention of paying for German atrocities.

As the battlefronts moved into the German heartland, it became apparent that, far from exaggerating the Jewish death toll, the enormity of the catastrophe had been underestimated. Hitler did not succeed in destroying world Jewry but he had delivered a death blow to those Jewish communities of Eastern Europe who traditionally compensated for the low birth rate of the remainder of world Jewry and additionally preserved the Jewish culture which guaranteed its future. The disappearance of these communities has left a demographic and cultural gap whose full effect on Jewish continuance only time can reveal. It was apparent that American Jewry which was reluctantly compelled to accept the mantle of leadership ensconced for centuries in Europe did not appear to possess enough vitality to compensate fully for the loss of much of European Jewry. Understandably, the years between the end of the war, when the extent of the loss gradually became clear, and 1948, when the state of Israel was established, were gloomy ones for Jews concerned with group survival.

CHAPTER XIX

The American Jewish Condition Today

AT THE HEART OF CONTEMPORARY AMERICAN JEWRY'S CONSCIOUSNESS IS concern about its continued ability to survive as a distinct group in America. Survival anxiety can be noted in virtually all the current preoccupations of the community which are examined in this chapter. It was evident in the sixties when community spokesmen overreacted to the anti-Semitic utterances of a handful of black militants. It is manifest in the community's continued concern about the rising rate of intermarriage. It again came to the fore in the reaction of Jewish leaders to "Key '73," the massive effort by certain Christian church organizations to revitalize their faith. Many Jewish spokesmen feared that the campaign was merely a cover for a massive effort to convert American Jews. Most recently it was manifest in the anxious perusal of the latest public opinion poll data to determine whether the energy crisis had indeed led to the anti-Semitic or at least anti-Israel reaction which some community leaders had predicted.

Those that would yield to the temptation of dismissing these reactions and the preoccupation with the survival of Israel, which is an integral part of it, to group paranoia do not adequately fathom the Jewish experience in the twentieth century. It was a century which first reneged on its promise of emancipation and civic equality for Jews and culminated with the ruthless annihilation of every third Jew during World War II. The holocaust, as that episode in Jewish history has become known, is the touchstone of all contemporary Jewish sensibility. Without understanding its effects there can be no understanding of Jewish group behavior. What appears to the detached observer as overreaction or paranoia is on closer perusal the normal reaction of a community that suffered grievous human losses while the world looked on indifferently. Jews who feel that the world conspires against them do not necessarily perceive a twisted reality. From one point of view that may in fact be a fairly accurate reading of the modern Jewish historical experience. Jews have not forgotten their past nor are they inclined to deny themselves the lesson they think it holds for them. They have developed a

[299]

catastrophe perspective which acts like an early warning system to alert them to every real or imagined threat. Had the Jews of Europe possessed such a perspective in the thirties the catastrophe which befell them might have been avoided.

Out of the holocaust experience has come American Jewry's almost unanimous desire to nurture the small and continually beleaguered Jewish community of Israel which offered a haven for the remnants of European Jewry. Today one rarely hears talk of dual loyalty, so common-place in prewar decades. Rather a new feeling of interrelatedness with Jews the world over permits an open espousal of Israel. The holocaust has produced what decades of American Zionist effort never succeeded in achieving, the Zionization of American Jewry. That sentiment has been reinforced by the series of "David and Goliath" struggles in 1948, 1956, 1967 and 1973 which created an image of the Israeli as a fighting Jew, far more comforting to American Jews than the saintly, civilized, but perennial victim which was the image of the prewar European Jew. In Israel American Jewry finally found the modern secular achieving society with which it could identify fully. The result was an unstinted outpouring of political and economic support for Israel. Huge sums of money, which the community was rarely able to collect to support its own institutions, are either directly contributed or invested to nurture the Israeli economy and social welfare programs. An American political leader with Jewish constituents does not need to be reminded that a key to the support of the Jewish voter is his position on Israel. Behind much of that unstinting support is the visceral knowledge that the survival of Israel is at the very heart of the Jewish survival as a community.

Yet American Jewry's strong support of Israel is not precisely identical with the support of political Zionism. As Americans, Jews understood little of the complex European cultural and ideological background which helped shape modern Zionism. Having never experienced the murderous anti-Semitism which European society produced in such abundance, they could not entirely fathom the yearning for Zion. Few American Jews feel called upon to settle in Israel. From 1948 to 1967 between 600 and 1,200 American Jews chose yearly to remove themselves to Israel, an infinitesimal proportion. The four years following the June War saw the number rise to perhaps 29,000 but the percentage choosing this course remains insignificant.[1] Many of these ultimately found life in Israel untenable and returned to the United States, there to be joined by a growing number of *Yordim* (Israelis who have emigrated, literally descended, from Israel). Many of the American *Ohlim* (literally, im-migrants who have chosen to ascend to Israel) are motivated by a strong desire to live a more Jewish life which they feel is possible only in Israel. Recently the small trickle of American immigrants to Israel has been supplemented by engineers and technicians seeking better employment opportunities and by those seeking to escape the seeming disintegration of urban life in America. There has also developed a small constituency composed of older, more established Jews, straddling both worlds by traveling back and forth yearly. If American Jewish immigration to Israel should increase, it will probably be drawn from this group. Conceivably too, Israel might receive the American *Ohlim* it so much desires if there is an increase in Jewish insecurity in the United States and concomitantly, an increase in prosperity and security in Israel.

One of the hidden costs of the most recent round of fighting in the Middle East may be a curtailment of immigration from America and other western nations. Potential immigrants have undoubtedly learned from the Yom Kippur war and the subsequent negotiations that peace and prosperity in Israel are at best uncertain. Nevertheless strong support for Israel continues to be the *sine qua non* of American Jewry even while it is given at a distance. The customary outpouring of financial and political support was manifest throughout the October crisis.

Yet, if American Jewry's support of Israel in the foreseeable future is a constant, some changes in the nature and perhaps in the depth of the commitment are also likely. The amazing outpouring of funds during the October war, for example, was contributed by roughly the same group which did so during the June war in 1967. They simply gave more but the number so committed, according to UJA spokesmen, did not increase. In a sense this group, which is composed of a relatively small handful of wealthy Jews, has gone as far as it is able to go. Nevertheless the Yom Kippur war, despite the ultimately good showing of Israeli arms, again proved indecisive. It has become clear that peace in the Middle East cannot be established by either side through force of arms. The October war demonstrated not only a new fighting élan among the Arabs. They were also able for the first time to bring their oil weapon to bear and to show considerable skill in the use of diplomacy and the mobilization of world public opinion for their cause. At the same time the war demonstrated Israel's utter dependence on the United States. It is for this and other reasons that American Jewry may in the future show more readiness to seek some other road to peace in the Middle East. There may develop a divergence of opinion between American Jewry and Israel on how best to assure Israel's continued existence.

As Americans, Jews can only experience the physical threat to Israel vicariously. The grueling war in Southeast Asia, which Jews especially opposed, has strengthened their pacifist sentiment especially among the idealistic university educated youth. They cannot fathom the reality of Israel's security dilemma and are repelled by the portrayal of the Arab-Israeli war in terms of the realpolitik of the discredited Cold War. Moreover they are Americans receptive to all the influences to which American public opinion is subject. Should there be some slippage in American support for Israel it would undoubtedly be reflected in Jewish public opinion as well.

Other divergences may stem from the fact while Israelis and American Jews share a common faith they are in fact members of separate communities with independent interests which may at some future time conflict. Moreover Israel is a separate sovereignty which must perforce deal with problems specific to nation states. A personality differentiation is already discernible. The brash, cocky confident posture of the *Sabra* (a Jew born in Israel) is the product of a small society where Jews are the majority. It does not necessarily sit well with Jews who have been brought up in communities where they are a minority which has learned to revere humility and quiet competence. Such personality conflicts may be exacerbated by the concern of the still powerful liberal secular elements among American Jews with Israel's seeming inability decisively to separate State from Church affairs, especially in the area of marriage and divorce laws. Even more nettlesome is the growth of an underclass composed of Arabs and non-European Jews in Israel. That development has been grist in the mill for a small group of radical universalists in Israel and America.

While Arab hostility is a fact of life for Israelis a spirit of virulent anti-Semitism which might have served as an equivalent threat and sensitized American Jewry has been conspicuously absent from the postwar American scene. The anti-Semitic spirit which was present during the Depression and holocaust years and partly accounts for the indifferent showing of the Roosevelt administration in rescuing Jews declined precipitously and was replaced by a positive affinity for Jews and things Jewish. It may be that the holocaust has created a "conscious inhibition" against anti-Semitism in the American public mind.[2] It has been reinforced by the steady diminution of Jewish ethnic particularity so that it becomes increasingly difficult to single out Jews as a target for hostility. Only 15 percent of American Jewry is still foreign born, and conspicuous geographic concentrations like the Lower East Side ghetto of the turn of the century have been partly dispersed by the movement to suburbia in which Jews were well represented. McCarthyism, the first xenophobic reaction to the stresses of the Cold War, did not contain the strong undercurrent of anti-Semitism which Jewish leaders have come to expect during such periods. A decade later George Wallace's contemporary populism carefully avoided an open attack on the Jewish community. In turn, the Jewish population of Montgomery gave him 25 percent of its vote. Wallace has received strong support from Mayer Perloff, a prominent Jewish political leader from Mobile.[3]

An exception to the dormant condition of American anti-Semitism can be found in the agitational rhetoric of a small group of black activists. It is not representative of the black community and stems from conditions specific to the relationship between Jews and blacks in the urban setting. Black militants speak incessantly of Jewish slumlords, gouging storekeepers, insensitive teachers, and numerous other Jewish "exploiters." Unfortunately the confrontation between black radicals and Jews has not been confined to the sphere of name-calling. It has been given substance by a clash of group interests symbolized best by the school decentralization issue. The outlines of the dispute became clear in the Ocean Hill-Brownsville district of New York City in 1968. In that school district the career and security interests of a largely Jewish group of teachers associated with the United Federation of Teachers were pitted against those of a local group of black activists who wanted control of the district which had been chosen for an experiment in decentralization.

The bitter emotions released by the Ocean Hill conflict were intensified by a subsequent clash over the validity of the civil service merit system. Most Jews strongly favored the merit system, not only because it produced what they believed to be the best results but also because of Jewish group self-interest. It had served many Jews as a practical vehicle to attain middle-class status. Feeling that they had earned these civil service positions by dint of their qualifications and test performances, Jews felt that to be compelled to surrender their positions because they were of a certain color or belonged to a certain group was unfair to them and a betrayal of basic principles. On their part, black and Puerto Rican activists have argued that merit simply does not apply to certain positions. They have been impatient with the general unwillingness of other groups to give them "a piece of the action." The result has been a deterioration of group relations, marked by anti-Semitic fallout among a minority of blacks and a racist backlash among some Jews. A growing number of issues, such as the problem posed by scattersite housing in middle-class neighborhoods, open admissions at City University, and distribution of poverty funds, feeds the conflict. Some Jews have become convinced that a beleaguered "Wasp" establishment, represented by politicians such as John Lindsay, former Mayor of New York City, and powerful foundations, are prepared to purchase civil peace, if not social justice, at the expense of Jewish community interests. Less extreme is the growing conviction that the postwar taboo against anti-Semitism is waning.[4]

The majority of American Jews, however, do not appear to feel that the overt hostility, often tactically employed by a relatively small group of blacks, represents a major threat to the Jewish community. New York City, where much of the strife has centered, is no longer as much the pacesetter for American Jewry as it once was. The great number of younger Jews who now live in suburbia are naturally more concerned with the problems in their local communities. They are often aware that the more serious threat to Jewish survival emanates from the continued openness of American society which seeks to absorb all religious and ethnic groups. The embourgoisement of American Jewry has created a greater potential for such absorption. There are now approximately 5,900,000 Jews in America; of these 77.8 percent reside in and around the nation's ten major population centers in the Northeast and Far West. The predominant urban configuration of American Jewry remains intact, but beneath the demographic statistics there are some factors which bode badly for Jewish survival as a distinct and recognizable group.

The attainment of middle-class status has in some ways proved to be a mixed blessing. It means that Jews follow, indeed lead, the middle-class family pattern of marrying later and having fewer children. Jews are America's most efficient family planners. According to one study conducted in 1957, the cumulative fertility rate of Jewish women aged forty-five and older was 19 percent below that of Protestants and 27 percent below that of Catholics.[5] In the early years of the century much of this natural loss was compensated by the immigration of masses of Jews from Eastern Europe but after the mid-sixties only 39,000 Jewish immigrants have entered the country under the provisions of the Immigration Law of 1966; this forms only 2.3 percent of the total. The new immigration law, unlike the restrictive law of 1924, is not seeking to weed out Jewish immigrants. The great population reservoir of Eastern Europe from which Jews were traditionally drawn, with the exception of Soviet Jewry, no longer exists. In short, by eliminating the Jews of Eastern Europe, the holocaust has had the belated effect of creating a demographic gap in the American Jewish population curve which impinges directly on its ability to survive. The absence of outside supplementary population sources contributes in part to the continuing decline of the Jewish proportion of the population. In 1937 Jews composed 3.7 percent of the general population. Today they are down to 2.9 percent.

That proportionate decline may serve as an appropriate background for the growing community concern regarding interfaith marriages.

Such marriages are a source of continuing strife between a portion of the Reform rabbinate and the more traditional-minded Conservative and Orthodox branches. When the growing intermarriage rate is viewed in conjunction with the declining American-Jewish birth rate, the problem of the sheer physical survival of the community comes into sharper perspective. Orthodox and Conservative rabbis, because they adhere to Jewish law, refuse to officiate at such marriages. Most Orthodox rabbis continue to discourage conversion to the Jewish faith and will not, except under the most extreme circumstances, offer the necessary religious training for such conversions. But, arguing that non-performance of such marriages will not only fail to bring about a lowering in the rate of intermarriage but will additionally serve to sever completely the already tenuous link of young people to Judaism, 40 percent of the Reform rabbinate perform such marriages. Reform and some Conservative rabbis also offer less discouragement to potential converts.

Panic about intermarriage is partly fostered by the fact that its prevalence can only be estimated. Only two states, Iowa and Indiana, both with unrepresentative Jewish populations, require the stating of one's religion to obtain a marriage license. The fear of intermarriage which is partly based on the possiblility that the critical Jewish population mass would become so diminished that the community would not be able to regenerate itself, has been present since the Colonial period.[6] At that time intermarriage made such deep inroads that only the timely arrival of German Jews assured the continuation of American Jewry. The same role may have been played by East European Jewry in the final decades of the nineteenth century. Today rapid assimilation as reflected in intermarriage coupled with the low birth rate and the continuing impact of secularization have again raised the question of survival. To many the issue is more critical today than before since there is no Jewish community on the world scene which might offer the necessary population transfusion from its own overproduction to assure continuance. In the long run it is the demographic problem, which in turn is related to the quality of Jewish family life and education, which is at the heart of the American Jewish survival dilemma.

Estimates of the rate of intermarriage range from a high of 42.2 percent, reached in Iowa between 1953 and 1959, to a low of 10 percent, reached in some urban Jewish population centers. In themselves such figures tell little because in-marriage, in which the non-Jewish partner converts, is not revealed. Neither do we learn anything regarding the faith in which the children of such marriages are raised. There are some indications that Jews do well in both categories so that the actual loss attributable to intermarriage may be negligible.[7] Part of the reason why the non-Jewish partner is likely to convert and raise the children in the Jewish faith is that it has been the Jewish male who is more prone to marry outside his faith and he is also more likely to insist on conversion of his mate. But to Orthodox Jews who trace Judaism through the female line, a non-convert or an improperly converted gentile female cannot produce a Jewish child. It is that factor which has made the inter-marriage question an incredibly difficult one to solve both in the American Jewish community and in Israel. Many of these marriages are, in fact, totally secular and therefore an actual, if not statistical loss, to all religious communities.

Perhaps more important for Jewish group survival is the effect the growing rate of intermarriage is bound to have on the dilution of the cultural and religious content of American Judaism. Intermarriage clearly often reflects a preexisting decline of group particularity. It is also a cause of further dilution of those characteristics which make any subgroup distinctive because conversion does not affect the uncles, aunts, and parents of the converted partner who naturally serve as models for the offspring of such marriages. The threat to Jewish sur-vival is not a statistical one at all but rather revolves about the question of how much in-marriage a particular subgroup can abide before an irreversible trend toward cultural dilution, which in turn generates more intermarriage, is set in motion.

The rise of the intermarriage rate tells a great deal about the condition of American Jewry *vis-à-vis* the general American community. It indi-cates that the process of Americanization and the secularization which it entails have progressed to a point where Jews are almost fully accept-able as marriage partners. The ethos on which American marriage is often grounded, namely, that young people ought to be free to marry those to whom they are drawn by romantic love, virtually assures that intermarriage between all groups will increase, particularly so among Jewish youth. Almost 90 percent of Jewish youth spend the critical years when they are likely to "fall in love" at college or university, often lo-cated a considerable distance from home. These institutions of learning have also traditionally served as a vast nesting ground and they are the most mixed and secular institutions in the nation.

At the heart of the survival dilemma is the quality of Jewish life in America. Those who come in daily contact with the Jewish young have become aware of their disaffection with Jewish life. Novelists like Philip Roth and Bruce Jay Friedman, although their descriptions often take the form of unfavorable caricatures, have nevertheless been more sensitive to the troubled state of Jewish life than social scientists. Oddly, the statistics of membership in Jewish organizations and religious congregations do not reflect this situation. They attract a relatively high proportion of Jews. A recent study of the Jewish community of Providence shows 75 percent of the Jewish population belonging to at least one Jewish organization and 17 percent belonging to four or more. Less than 25 percent are totally unaffiliated.[8]

Membership in religious congregations shows a similar glow of health. Sixty percent, approximately 3,000,000 Jews are affiliated with some branch of Judaism. Conservatism, which now boasts approximately 800 affiliated congregations, appears to be developing the most acceptable religious synthesis. The Reform movement, with approximately 600 congregations, and the Orthodox branch with approximately 1,600 congregations, albeit of a smaller transient variety, follow closely behind the Conservative lead.[9] Rather than fading from the picture, Orthodoxy shows new signs of vitality, while the Reform movement, once thought to be "the wave of the future," barely holds its own.

Yet when one peers behind these impressive statistics one cannot help but note a loss of vitality in American Judaism. Jewish secular and religious organizations no longer seem to encompass the whole of Jewish life in America. Conspicuously absent from these organizations, is the most vital element of the Jewish population, its college-trained youth. The backbone of these secular organizations is a disproportionate number of older members, especially women, without whose contribution of energy and commitment, one suspects, Jewish organizational life would collapse. In the suburbs, the fastest-growing area of Jewish settlement, membership in Jewish secular organizations is falling off.[10] These younger Jewish women prefer to join non-denominational general civic organizations such as the League of Women Voters or the local PTA and, more recently, the spate of peace organizations and women's liberation groups. Withal, the fires of organizational conflict have been banked, but the commitment to Jewish community life has declined as well.

On the congregational front, the construction of elaborate religious edifices appears to be inversely proportionate to the degree of religious commitment. Attendance at religious services on a daily or even weekly basis in these new suburban temples is confined to a small handful. The grandfathers, who worshiped in dimly lighted *shtiblach* (small rooms) with few of the amenities, possessed a deeper commitment to their faith and certainly a greater appreciation of its tenets. Expensive weddings and Bar Mitzvahs, services performed by mellifluent cantors, paid lecturers to speak at the temple, and dances have proven to be a poor substitute for faith and barely conceal the vacuity of much of what passes for Jewish religious life in America today. There is, in short, an absence of the religious passion which has always been a hallmark of

Judaism. Modernism has substituted rationalism and a bland middle-class ceremonialism which demand nothing and offend no one.

It is this absence of genuine religious commitment and the preference for empty ceremonialism which go far to explain the disaffection of some of the best and most sincere elements of the younger generation. One young Jew described the suburban congregation to which his family belonged as "simply an appendage to middle-class suburban culture that arose out of the assimilationist needs of a previous generation."[11] Many well-educated Jews prefer to live their adult lives in a cultural limbo rather than to be associated with what they conceive as the hypocrisy of institutional religion. Others fulfill their still strong need for moral commitment by participating in all manner of religious crazes, from Zen Buddhism to the Hare Krishna movement.

Undoubtedly the most interesting development to grow out of this search for authenticity by younger Jews has been the movement to band together in *Havurot*. The term was first used in the second century B.C. to describe the communities of Jewish pietists who maintained strict standards of ethical and religious purity apart from organized society. The contemporary *Havurots* are usually associated with some university campus and bear a resemblance to the secular communes which have attracted some disaffected young people. They are, however, less collective-minded and isolated from the mainstream. Usually the people involved possess a strong commitment to Judaism and do not hesitate to experiment with new ritual forms and the reviving of ancient ones. Their purpose is to reinvest Jewish religious life with beauty and meaning for contemporary living. But the *Havurot* movement has remained numerically insignificant and is virtually unknown among the masses of uncommitted Jewish college students on the campus. Whether it can produce an acceptable life style that offers traditional spiritual values to the mass of alienated Jewish young remains to be seen.

Interestingly, Orthodoxy, which showed few signs of being able to find a practical accommodation at the turn of the century, is today revealing many signs of vitality. At least part of the reversal can be attributed to the infusion of new blood from holocaust survivors, many of whom consider themselves a "saving remnant" of true Judaism and willingly assume a personal obligation to carry Orthodoxy forward. A solution to the problem of living a highly prescriptive life demanded by adherence to Orthodox tenets, in an intensely permissive secular society, has come to the surface. Many Orthodox Jews are today economically upwardly mobile while remaining strictly Orthodox. There appears to be much truth in the observation of Rabbi Emanuel Jacobowitz, the former spiritual leader of the nation's foremost Orthodox congregation, the Fifth Avenue Synagogue: "You no longer have to live on the Lower East Side in squalor to be a strictly traditional Jew."[12]

For Orthodoxy the dividends of the accommodation to modernism are already manifest. Orthodoxy has become competitive in the crucial area of fund-raising which serves as a certain sign of vitality in the Jewish community. Wealthy Orthodox Jews have proven generous in their philanthropic contributions to Orthodox institutions like Yeshiva University. Nor has the traditional conflict between religion and science proved to be an insurmountable hurdle. There exists today an association of Orthodox scientists consisting of some 500 members. Nevertheless, it is still too early to determine whether Orthodoxy has successfully halted the erosion which marked its early development in the United States, or merely slowed it down.

Like the Conservative branch, Orthodoxy has spawned an offshoot. More accurately, a formerly independent and often rival branch of religious Judaism has been grafted onto its stock. It is the Chasidei Chabad, the surviving remnants of Europe's prewar Hasidic movement. In the Old World, traditional Orthodoxy and Hasidism had little love for one another but in the post-holocaust period the conflict between the two groups has waned to be replaced, if not by a marriage of love, then by one of convenience. Far removed from the religious mysticism and ecstasy which is the hallmark of Hasidism, American Jews view the movement with some detachment, if not distaste, even while the religious "high" characteristic of the movement has attracted a small number of young deracinated American Jews.

In their life style, especially their distinctive manner of dress and their daily routines, the hasidim have, for the most part, withstood the impact of modernism. Like the Amish and the Mennonites and other pietist sects, they find it necessary to segregate themselves from the American scene. They maintain their own school system and places of worship and eschew the use of such modern communication instruments as television. They adhere strictly to their own standards of social behavior within their own communities. Recently they have gone so far as to furnish their own transportation to those who work in the city so that they might better comply with the strict rules regarding segregation of the sexes. Their communities are organized along hierarchical lines resembling nothing so much as the medieval court which serves as its prototype. The "Rebbe," who serves as spiritual as well as temporal leader, is an object of reverence. Often tales are spun concerning his great wisdom or miracle-working prowess. He is assigned virtually absolute power over his court and may, on occasion, intrude deeply into the personal lives of his flock. For modern American Jews, where the rabbi serves at the behest of the congregation, this lack of democracy and the assigning of divine powers to the "Rebbe," is viewed with some consternation. But despite the fact that the practices of Hasidism appear to be in direct conflict with the practices of modernism which have had such an impact on American Jewry, the religious zeal and the organizational energy of the Chabad movement have gained the respect of the other branches of religious Judaism. It is clear that the Hasidic movement flourishes without the benefits of organizational democracy. The admiration and popularity of Rabbi Joseph Schneersohn, spiritual leader of the most innovative of the Chabad sects, the Lubavitcher group located in the Crown Heights section of Brooklyn, is manifest in most conventional religious circles.

The reinvigoration of Orthodoxy has brought in its wake an increase in the number of Jewish Day Schools. In 1945 there were 69 such schools with about 10,000 students. Today the National Orthodox Day School Movement, *Torah Umesorah*, reports 401 such schools in 140 communities which educate from 75,000 to 80,000 students.[13] These schools customarily maintain a strict division between secular and religious education. Many are established on a financial shoestring, and once established the schools quickly develop an independent appetite for funds. To the dismay of other organizations dependent on community largesse, they compete vigorously for the philanthropic dollar. Funding the Orthodox as well as other Jewish day schools (the Conservative branch boasts 44 day schools, including five high schools) has become a source of bitter controversy within the local Federations which have been petitioned to underwrite their growth and development.

The desperate need for funds has also compelled the supporters of these schools to turn to the Federal and state government for aid, much like the supporters of the Catholic school system. Secular-minded Jews are bound to view this quest for the government dollar as a threat to the public school system which is considered sacrosanct because for many American Jews it continues to serve as a principal instrument of social mobility. In requesting government financial aid, moreover, the Orthodox supporters of the Jewish day school have broken a cardinal tenet of liberal secular ideology which holds that separation of church and state is a major ideological citadel of Jewish security in America. Small wonder then that many Jewish secular leaders have found the activity of the Orthodox Jews in the area of education a bitter pill to swallow. The feeling is that they have sought to impose their own priorities on the Jewish community by creating their own school system to transmit their special view of Judaism while insisting that the venture should be funded by the Jewish community at large.

As the deterioration of the public school system in the major cities becomes more evident, the Jewish day school is potentially in a position to take up the slack. It offers the possibility of delivering a Jewish education to thousands of Jewish children who stem from largely secular homes. Yet this has not come to pass. While the number of such schools has risen appreciably in the last decade (there are now 372 day schools as compared to 237 in 1960) there has not occurred a parallel increase in proportionate number of students attending them. Outside of New York City about 8 percent of the Jewish student population is enrolled in such schools but in the metropolitan area, which alone accounts for 7 percent of the total enrollment, there has actually occurred a drop of 3.6 percent in registration in all types of Jewish educational institutions (afternoon, Sunday morning, congregational schools and yeshivoth) according to statistics compiled by the Board of Jewish Education for the year 1971–1972.[14] At least part of the proportional decline is attributable to the drop in the birth rate from its postwar high and to the exodus from the ten major urban areas which formerly accounted for 90 percent of the enrollment in such schools.

There may be other factors which account for the relatively poor showing. American Jews may as yet not be prepared to abandon the public school system which served them so well. The ability of many comparatively affluent Jewish families to move to those areas in the city or suburbs where they believe the schools are still viable or to send their children to secular private schools has permitted a postponement of a critical community decision on what course of action to pursue should public school systems become wholly unsuitable. Virtually unchallenged thus far is the notion that such day schools can by themselves generate a greater commitment to Judaism or even that such is the motivation of parents enrolling their children in them. Both assumptions are questionable. Recent studies indicate that graduates of the farflung Catholic school system are no more committed to Catholicism than Catholic students who attended secular schools and in a good many cases they are less so. Nor would greater success for the Jewish day school necessarily reflect a reversal of the trend toward secularism or a sensitivity to Jewish community survival. Rather it might demonstrate a continued understanding of the relationship between quality education and mobility, which has always been characteristic of the Jewish middle class.

Whereas American Jewish youth has shown little inclination to support Jewish religious and secular institutions whose existence is necessary for the formal continuance of the community, they have been drawn in disproportionate numbers to programs and groups who advocate radical solutions to deep-seated economic and social problems. They are motivated by the same idealistic universalism which traditionally has evoked a deep response in the Jewish community. According to one observer as much as 50 to 75 percent of the participants in radical activities on the campus in the late 1960's stemmed from Jewish homes.[15]

Whether this disproportionate number of radical activists is a symptom of a deep-seated malaise or merely additional evidence that idealistic universalism continues to exercise a strong influence on the most intelligent of Jewish youth, depends on the particular vantage from which the phenomenon is viewed. Those less secure and apprehensive lest the conspicuous Jewish presence in the radical movements affect their own security, shudder every time names of well-known Jewish radicals are mentioned by the media. But on the other side of the political spectrum, radical Jews of the "old left" viewed the activities of the campus activists, whose parents they often were, with unconcealed pride.

We have seen that radicalism and a well-developed social conscience were present in good measure among the immigrants of the ghetto. Contemporary young Jewish radicals are part of this continuing tradition. But there is also something new in contemporary American Jewish radicalism. It has middle rather than working-class roots and rather than concerning itself with the problems of Europe or the coming revolution in Russia, it is almost exclusively preoccupied with American problems. It is being nurtured in an American incubator.

Most likely, the liberal-radical perspective of the current generation of Jewish students is related to the truly outstanding level of education they have achieved. University education tends to reinforce the left-wing social-democratic tendencies which have strong traditional roots in the Jewish community. The prophetic impulse may have motivated the grandparents who were closer to the Jewish tradition and whose politics followed logically from their circumstances. But for the young Jewish radical today, whose background is middle-class and secular, the radical style is at once more vicarious and visionary and less dogmatic. Their radicalism was reinforced by a particularly tragic war in Southeast Asia and perhaps by the residual effects of the holocaust, which, according to one observer, has left a "pool of anxiety" about war and racism in their collective psyche.[16]

Whatever the source, a small group of disaffected, radicalized, nominally Jewish youth has been in the vanguard of the politics of confrontation of the late sixties and in the development of the so-called "counter culture" of the early seventies. There is little that is recognizably Jewish about them, save that their approach to politics, which in the last analysis deals with power, is that of religious fervor and innocence. They are what Jews have always been, great believers. Only in that is their radicalism reminiscent of the religious spirit which motivated their ancestors.[17]

The American system, about which so many Jewish young people are in despair, has actually worked well for American Jewry. Paradoxically, young radical Jews are likely to be the offspring of a remarkably successful parent generation. Jewish annual income is consistently higher than that of other subgroups and often equals that of the high-status Episcopalians. The same pattern of success is discernible in Jewish occupational distribution. They possess the highest representation in the business and professional categories and even when they are blue-collar workers, their incomes are greater than those of their Christian fellow workers. The proportion of business proprietors and managers among Jews is three to four times as high as that of the general population and the number of professionals in the Jewish population far exceeds the normal distribution.[18] Jewish economic achievement personifies the American dream of success. It is the same dream about which so many of their offspring have become critical.

A vast improvement over the prewar economic position, when the Jewish base in business was narrow, and the attainment of professional goals difficult, has occurred. The traditional entrepreneurial daring, so characteristic of American Jewry, has been allowed full play. Jews have played pioneering roles in the new electronics, plastics, computers, frozen foods, and advertising industries as well as in the establishment of think tanks and the field of consulting. They form a sizable segment of the class of new "egghead millionaires" who make their fortunes by combining some proficiency in a technical field and business acumen. At the same time the traditional concentration of Jews in merchandising and light industry persists as does their underrepresentation on the executive boards of the five hundred largest American corporations.[19] Apparently Jews are avoided and avoid large bureaucratic organizations where promotion is slow and frequently determined by factors other than skill and talent. A similar motivation may lie behind the popularity of the independent professions among Jews. Medicine, dentistry, law, and accounting may all be practiced independently, allow the combination of business and professional skills, and do not require the support of large bureaucracies for success.

If small business was the most important channel to success for the first generation, in the succeeding ones it has become formal education and professional training. The education level of American Jewry far exceeds that of the general population. Recent surveys estimate that

85 to 91 percent of Jewish youth is enrolled in some institution of higher learning. The number of Jewish students completing college is almost twice as high as the national average and they are twice as likely to go on to graduate school. The higher income level of Jews correlates with their higher level of education. The massive Jewish infusion into higher education is also responsible for the remarkable increase in Jewish representation on college faculties. It is now over three times their proportion of the population and in the first-rank universities and the professional faculties in law, medicine, and the social sciences the figure is even higher, 17 percent and 33 percent respectively.[20]

If the increased level of secular education opens new prospects for Jewish youth, it also creates some problems, especially for Orthodox Jews. Secular education, they feel, tends to challenge their traditional value system and confuse the process of religious identification of the young. The problem is viewed with such concern that Rabbi Bernard Berzon, former head of the Rabbinical Council of America, has recommended the establishment of ten new colleges under Orthodor auspices for the purpose of arresting the corrosive effects of secular education on the religious convictions and identity of Jewish students.[21]

The disproportionate number of Jewish students on the campus has meant that Jewish youngsters have experienced to a greater degree the general disorders which have swept the nation's colleges in the last years. One recent study estimates that an astounding seventy to eighty percent of Jewish students have experimented with drugs. By itself this figure does not tell us much, nor does it indicate whether such experimentation involves "hard" or the more innocent "soft" drugs. But the fact that there may be as many as 50,000 Jewish heroin users, some to be found even among the ultra-orthodox Hassidic community, gives some pause for thought.[22] When one considers that among the immigrant generation which experienced great stress, alcoholism was virtually unknown, such figures, even if exaggerated, indicate that a great transformation of traditional Jewish values has occurred.

The seemingly secure economic position of American Jewry also contains trouble spots which may loom large in the future. Jewish occupational preferences, for example, are customarily geared to the city where most Jews prefer to live. They are prominent in small-scale urban manufacturing and retailing, the municipal civil service, especially teaching, and in the independent professions. As the quality of American urban life declines, these Jews are bound to be disproportionately affected.

The limiting of employment opportunities for teachers and educational administrators which comes in the wake of the partial abandonment of the merit system in favor of ethnic quotas, has caused a deterioration of morale for those already in the system and a wariness about entering this once favorite profession among Jews, on a permanent basis. Teaching has declined as a choice of profession among Jewish college graduates.[23] Of course that may also be a reflection of the higher class position Jews now occupy. Teaching is customarily a favorite choice among the offspring of lower-middle and working-class families. As the quota system spreads to other areas of the municipal civil service, it is the Jews from this stratum of the population that feel themselves particularly hard-pressed.

The accelerated changes in the economy and technology are bound to cause displacement. Skills which took a lifetime to master and businesses which have been lovingly nursed from infancy, become obsolete overnight. No more secure are the sizable number of Jewish merchants who, because of advanced age or low level of vocational skill, find themselves trapped in deteriorating neighborhoods of the city. In many sections of the city, life has simply become too insecure for the small merchant to continue in business. That lesson has been brought home most sharply to those Jewish merchants who have the misfortune to be located in formerly Jewish neighborhoods which have become black ghettos.

A new dimension is added to the picture by the recent discovery that the much-vaunted story of Jewish economic success is far less uniform than was imagined. Not only has the rapidity of the climb up the economic ladder given rise to problems among the offspring of the newly affluent, it has exacerbated the condition of those who for several reasons were not able to share in the general prosperity. They are the aged, the infirm, the socially marginal, and the "special circumstance" Jews, those who are physically or psychologically disabled by some trauma. Recent estimates indicate that there may be as many as 800,000 Jews living below the poverty line, 400,000 of them in New York City alone. The prideful touting of Jewish economic success has made these poor more invisible than most.[24]

Because much of the Jewish poverty problem is linked to the abnormal age distribution in the community, it does not lend itself to normal solution such as finding jobs for the unemployed. As the Jewish birthrate has declined, the number of aged has naturally shown a relative increase. A further fact to consider is that Jews live slightly longer than other groups. That contributes to the fact that geriatric problems, of which poverty is one of the most prevalent, will become particularly acute in the Jewish community. Moreover, the problem of the Jewish poor can be linked directly to the prosperity of the children. It has encouraged the movement of the young married set to the suburbs. This trend has left the older generation, which formerly might have found some function in an extended family pattern, isolated and often purposeless. A poverty of spirit overlies the poverty of the pocketbook. Jewish poor are people who have been cut off from the mainstream of life in more than one sense. The elaborate Jewish philanthropic infrastructure, which is fully alerted to the problem, is nevertheless hard-pressed to find a solution since demographic trends and population movements are not easily reversed.

The Jewish movement to suburbia reveals some interesting characteristics of the new generation of American Jews. Rather than dispersing Jews, it has frequently brought even more conspicuous Jewish population concentrations in its wake. "Golden ghettos," like Larchmont, Great Neck, Shaker Heights, and Newton can be found around many major American cities. They combine some of the characteristics of ghetto life with those of suburbia. They feature a mass of Jews often held together by the temple congregation. But rather than being of the working class and living in congested apartments, they are middle-class and live in private homes. Like suburbia in general, the aged are conspicuously absent from such communities, while children are present in great number.

It is difficult to imagine that after generations of preference for city life, the new generation of Jews was able precipitously to abandon the city without looking back. There are some indications that this is hardly the case. Jewish suburbanites appear to devote much energy to duplicating the urban cultural nexus in the suburbs. They are active in bringing theater, art shows, extension courses, and "good" restaurants to the suburbs. There is also some indication that as the children, cited by many as the original cause for leaving the city, reach their majority, the city once again begins to exercise its magic charms especially for those who recall their younger days in the city and view it through a romantic haze. They miss not only the "high" culture of city life, but more specifically "street culture," the tempo of activity and happenings on the street. When the children have left the roost, the streets of suburbia tend to be completely empty. One recent study of a largely Jewish suburb near Philadelphia shows that a sizable number of Jews have in their later years either chosen to move back to a small flat in the city or moved into the newly-developed suburban high-rise apartment houses, where one does not have to worry about the care of a large house and where the tempo of life is more suitable for middle-aged people still desiring to be active.

One could link such a preference to Jewish history. Having never experienced an authentic peasant stage in their historical development, Jews have been reluctant to develop what ethologists have identified in the animal kingdom as a "territorial imperative" and what sociologists might identify as an appreciation of property in land. The rapid economic mobility which makes it possible to change geographic location almost at will, tends to reinforce this historical pattern. The consequences of the absence of an appreciation for the non-commercial benefits of land development, according to one sociologist, reflected in their ability to abandon the neighborhoods of their youth in favor of a "better" area. Thus Jewish neighborhoods are more likely to dissolve when faced with a real or imagined threat, while other ethnic enclaves remain remarkably stable over several generations. Their residents "dig in" in the face of outside threats. This inability to commit oneself to the "turf" of the neighborhood gives full reign to what Marshall Sklare has called "avoidance behavior"—the willingness to abandon a threatened neighborhood.[25] The tendency to move rather than to fight has compounded the problem of the Jewish poor who do not possess the financial resources to move to a better neighborhood. They can most frequently be found living out their isolated existence in "changed" neighborhoods.

Strangely enough, while Jewish economic achievement has profoundly affected virtually every aspect of Jewish life in America, its influence is barely discernible in the area where one might expect it to be most conspicuous, namely, on the political scene. Jews do not vote their pocketbooks. Not only do Jews residing in better neighborhoods and affluent suburbs customarily retain their loyalty to the liberal wing of the Democratic party, but it seems likely that their commitment to liberal egalitarianism actually increases with their wealth. In the election of 1968 only 17 percent of the Jewish vote was cast for Nixon as compared to 49 percent of the general population. If Jews had complied with the political preference normally associated with their income level, 70 percent would have voted for Nixon.

Numerically, the Jewish vote is not significant, and as its proportion of the population declines, it will become less so. But that is only statistically true. In the atmosphere of grass-roots politics the conventional wisdom has it that few elections can be won without the "Jewish vote." The contradiction between the theoretical and the practical can be explained in several ways. Jewish voter turnout is 84 percent compared to 62.8 percent for the general population. Moreover, the Jewish vote is located largely in the major pivotal states, New York, Illinois, Pennsylvania, and, increasingly, California. Then, too, Jews are customarily better informed and more politically active than the general population.[26] They frequently play the role of opinion elites which gives them an influence beyond their declining numerical proportion. They have also begun to play an important role in financing campaigns which because of its critical importance amplifies the Jewish political voice. Specific Jewish political interests, such as the continued security of Israel and, to a lesser extent, the release of Soviet Jewry, receive disproportionate attention from ambitious politicians.

Basically, Jewish political preferences continue to fall into what has been loosely called the liberal camp. That proclivity was given great impetus by the Jewish voter's "love affair" with Roosevelt's New Deal. It carried over to support of Truman and Stevenson during the fifties. Jewish commitment to Roosevelt, which remains the wellspring of much of its contemporary liberalism, was itself a reflection of a pre-existing attraction of Jewish voters to a more active role of government in the economy. It was the welfare-state aspect of the New Deal, rather than Roosevelt's foreign policy, which attracted the Jewish voter. The war and the holocaust tended to reinforce the left-wing political sentiments of many Jewish voters. It was, after all, a rightist ideology—fascism—which generated the most murderous threat to the survival of the Jewish people in the twentieth century. On the other hand, it was the Soviet Union which bled the Nazi war machine to death. Predictably Jews experienced an afterglow of goodwill for the Soviet Union which was only dissipated by the treatment of their brethren in Russia during the so-called "black years" of Soviet Jewry. That was the period between 1948 and 1953 when Stalinist paranoia regarding the subversive influence of Jews caused Jewish cultural life to be crushed and many Jewish artists and writers to be liquidated. Today the attainment of the right of those Soviet Jews who so desire to emigrate to Israel, is a major plank in the Jewish political program.

Despite American Jewry's disenchantment with the Soviet system they proved to be indifferent raw material for Cold War polemics. Jews were far less avid than the general population in favoring the denial of civil rights to domestic communists.[27] The civil libertarian tradition, which had proven so essential to their own security, was not abandoned so lightly.

The election of 1948 offers important clues to the American Jewish political posture in the first decade of the postwar period. The Democratic ticket was split three ways. Former Vice President Henry Wallace led the left-wing elements of the former New Deal coalition and advocated an extension of the welfare-state program at home and reconciliation with the Soviet Union abroad. The program seemed made to order for the liberal Jewish voter. Predictably, in some heavily Jewish election districts in the Bronx and other parts of the nation Wallace sometimes received as much as 20 to 27 percent of the Jewish vote. (However, the more normal percentage of the Jewish voting preference for Wallace was less than half of that.) The Jewish vote for Wallace was heavier than any other ethnic group and might have risen higher if not for Truman's timely recognition of Israel in May, 1948. Basically, Jews continued to hold to their New Deal stance. That is best seen by tabulating the combined vote for Truman and Wallace which is about equal to that given to Roosevelt in the previous election of 1944. The momentum of Jewish support for the New Deal was still discernible in the elections of 1952 and 1956. While most of the nation "like(d) Ike" the typical Jewish voter was "madly for Adlai."

It comes as no surprise to find American Jews opposed to the domestic machinations of Joseph McCarthy. A Gallup poll taken in June, 1954, near the end of McCarthy's influence. showed 65 percent of the Jewish respondents disapproving of that political symbol of Cold War hysteria. That was more than twice as high as the rest of the nation.[28] It made no difference that McCarthy never attacked Jews directly and that two of his aides, Roy Cohn and David Schine, were Jewish. McCarthy had attacked what had become a kind of secular religion for many Jews, a mixture of liberalism and civil libertarianism at home with reconciliation abroad.

That political pattern continued in muted form into the 1960's. Jews as a group were particularly taken with John Kennedy's "New Frontier" and gave him a greater percentage of their vote than did his natural ethnic constituency, the American Irish. It appears that for the Jewish voter adherence to the liberal-progressive tenets outweighs the ethnic factor. They consistently vote for the more committed liberal over the identifiable Jew. In 1961, 63 percent of the Jewish vote in the New York City primary election for mayor went to Robert Wagner, who inherited impeccable credentials as a liberal from his father. Arthur Levitt, his opponent, was Jewish, but he could not boast even an indirect connection with Roosevelt, who served as a kind of secular messiah for the liberal Jewish voter. In the mayoralty election of 1964 Jews, especially the younger, more educated, and more affluent, who resided in Manhattan, preferred the Republican liberal, John Lindsay, over the Jewish machine Democrat, Abraham Beame. Party label and religious affiliation counted for less with the Jewish voter than the candidates' liberalism.[29]

But things had changed considerably by 1972. So polarized has the Jewish vote become that it is difficult to speak of a unified Jewish political thrust. While affluent, educated, younger and more American-ized Jews retain their allegiance to the secular ideology of liberalism, less educated, less mobile, and more ethnic Jews show some signs of abandoning it. In place of the marked social conscience of the old Jewish voter, one can now often find a sense of beleagueredness and some racial backlash. The new impulse is strong in the city where disintegration of services, deterioration of the school system, and grow-ing physical insecurity have generated what might be classified as a politics of resentment. The new trend is apparent in the returns from Jewish districts in the election of 1972. George McGovern, who under normal circumstances, might have expected from 85 to 90 percent of the Jewish vote, received only from 60 to 70 percent in most Jewish districts. Nixon, the Republican candidate, on the other hand, more than doubled the normal Republican vote, receiving between 30 and 40 percent.

Yet predictions of a permanent change in the Jewish political posture may be premature. Jews did not switch as heavily to the Republican candidate as other voting blocs and they probably will revert to the Democratic Party in subsequent local elections. McGovern, moreover, continued to do well with the aforementioned more affluent, more educated Jews. These Jews play an opinion-leader role and may actually serve as better indicators of the trend of Jewish political preference. The continuing high education and mobility level indicates that this group is being continually fed by new Jewish voters. One need only observe the continuing strong liberal-radical cast of the Jewish college students to realize that the hold of the ideologies of humanistic universal-ism remains largely in fact. In 1972 the Jewish voter arrived at a cross-roads which is partly reflected in the greater number of Jewish voters who chose not to vote at all.[30] Nor should one forget that the majority, albeit less overwhelmingly so than in prior elections, still cast their ballots for the liberal Democratic candidate. The most important de-velopment on the Jewish political horizon may, in fact, relate to the aging of the Jewish population. Idealism and hope are partly functions of youth. The increasing age of the Jewish voter may create changes in Jewish political behavior which the conservative vision has failed to achieve.

There is in the American Jewish condition today cause for both hope and despair. It is undeniable that the process of embourgeoisement in America is not only altering the distinctive Jewish group personality but also weakening the ties that hold Jews together. Yet it is also apparent that the will to survive as a community is still strong. Jews are not as far on the road to total absorption as other ethnic groups in America. Moreover the Americanization process has stamped a uniform face on the variegated tribe which was once American Israel thereby eliminating the basis for the endemic strife within the community. Differences based on class and national origins are gradually disappearing. There is emerging a secular, well-educated, middle class citizen who can identify with all of American Jewry even while feeling secure as an American. The link to Judaism, while often tenuous, remains at least in a secular sense. That is what the outpouring of good will during the 1967 and 1973 wars between Arabs and Jews means.

But while survivalists are heartened by the American Jewish reaction to these crises they have perhaps made too much of them. Whether a purely secular tie to Judaism will prove sufficient to halt erosion is questionable. The great secret of Judaism's remarkable survival can be found partly in the fact that Judaism has offered its adherents an entire civilization. It has never been merely another ethnic group. When the religious layer was peeled away, one found beneath it a strong folk tradition with its own institutions, language and culture. That extra insurance against erosion seems to be waning in America. We find the descendants of East European Jews to be coming full circle to the position formerly occupied by their Iberian and Central European predecessors. Like them they have proven to be remarkably successful in their commercial and professional undertakings. Like them they are talented adapters and accommodators. And like them they are on the road to becoming an inconspicuous undifferentiated minority. The completion of the analogy has ominous implications for survivalists for their successful adaption proved also their undoing as a distinct community in America. We find barely a trace of these once vital groups today. Can American Jewry find elements of vitality within itself strong enough to halt the full repetition of the historical cycle? That is the crucial question faced by American Jewry today.

Notes and References

CHAPTER I

1. Quoted by George L. Berlin, "The Brandeis Weizmann Dispute," in the *American Jewish Historical Society Publications* (hereafter, *PAJHS*), LX (September, 1970), 39.

2. Marranos or New Christians became the term applied to those Jews who accommodated themselves to the new situation especially after 1391, by conversion to Christianity. The term means "damned" or "swine."

3. M. Kayserling, *Christopher Columbus and the Participation of the Jews in the Spanish and Portuguese Discoveries* (New York, 1894), 31.

4. Arnold Wiznitzer, "Crypto Jews in Mexico During the Sixteenth Century," *PAJHS*, I (March, 1962; June, 1962), 168–214, 222–68. Sixteen percent of the crimes of heresy before the Mexican Inquisition concerned the crime of Judaizing. Of the 2,281 records of the Holy Office of the Mexican Inquisition examined by the author, 351 involved Marranos.

5. Solomon Grayzel, *A History of the Jews: From the Babylonian Exile to the Establishment of Israel* (Philadelphia, 1965), 496. See also S. Broches, *Jews in New England*, Part I: *Historical Study of the Jews in Massachusetts*, 1650–1750 (New York, 1942), 4. Anita L. Lebeson, *Jewish Pioneers in America, 1742–1848* (New York, 1931), 21. Puritans entertained a similar belief and a missionary issued an appeal to London to help Indians in 1650. Another named Thorowgood published *Jews in America* in which he explores the possible relationship between Jews and Indians. Cotton Mather and William Penn also were preoccupied with the subject. Actually the theme was not Jewish in origin, having been entertained by Catholic missionaries such as Bartolóme de las Casas a century before.

6. Details can be gleaned from Samuel E. Morison, *Admiral of the Ocean Sea: A Life of Christopher Columbus* (Boston, 1942), 148–49.

7. See for example Seymour M. Lipset and Aldo Solari (eds.) *Elites in Latin America* (New York, 1967), 24–29, for the Jewish and Protestant origins of the most productive elites in Latin America today. Also David McClelland, *The Achieving Society* (New York, 1961), 365–66. The opinion of the constructive role played by Jews in colonial Latin America is not universally shared. Salvador de Madariaga, a Spanish scholar, holds Jews partly responsible for the ultimate fall of the Spanish empire because of their ability to corrupt the Spanish character. They "became the most dangerous, pertinacious and intelligent enemies of the Spanish Empire," observed Madariaga. Salvador de Madariaga, *The Fall of the Spanish Empire* (New York, 1947).

8. Hyman B. Grinstein, *The Rise of the Jewish Community of New York, 1654–1860* (Philadelphia, 1945), 72.

9. Joshua Trachtenberg, *Consider the Years: The Story of the Jewish Community of Easton, 1752–1942* (Easton, Pennsylvania, 1944), 23.

10. Edward A. Synan, *The Popes and the Jews in the Middle Ages* (New York, 1965), 76.

11. Jacob R. Marcus, *Early American Jewry*, Vol. I: *The Jews of New York, New England and Canada, 1649–1794* (Philadelphia, 1953), 4.

12. For an interesting description of this environment see, Mark Zborowski and Elizabeth Herzog, *Life is With People: The Culture of the Shtetl* (New York, 1967).

13. Lloyd P. Gartner, *The Jewish Immigrant in England, 1870–1914* (London, 1960), 16.

14. Marcus, *Early American Jewry*, II, 530.

15. Henri Pirenne, *Medieval Cities*, trans. Frank D. Halsey (New York, 1925), 11–13, 75–91; Israel Abrahams, *Jewish Life in the Middle Ages* (New York, 1958), 211–29.

16. Abrahams, *Jewish Life*, 211–12.

17. Max J. Kohler, "Jewish Activity in American Colonial Commerce," *PAJHS*, X (1902), 56; Cecil Roth, *The Jewish Contribution to Civilization* (Cincinnati, 1940), 275.

18. Miriam K. Freund, *Jewish Merchants in Colonial America* (New York, 1939), 30, quoting observation by Joseph Addison made in 1712.

19. Roth, *Jewish Contribution*, 266–77. Roth dismisses the thesis promulgated by the German political economist Werner Sombart attributing much of the rise of capitalism to Jews who he felt possessed a mysterious Levantine instinct which made them prone to such activity.

20. Kayserling, *Christopher Columbus*, 13–14, 45, 72.

21. Quoted by Kohler, "Jewish Activity . . . ," 52, from Herbert B. Adams, *Columbus and His Discovery of America*, p. 386.

22. More difficult to dismiss are the Hebrew letters *beth* and *hai* which appear in letters to his son but not in letters to the queen. These letters ostensibly stand for the Hebrew phrase *Baruch Hashem*, blessed is the name, frequently used by professing Jews. There is also the puzzling boast occasionally made by Columbus that he was a descendant of the house of David of the "blood royal of Jerusalem." Undoubtedly Marranos proud of the ancient lineage were wont to make such boasts. The proposition is examined in some detail by Lee M. Friedman, *Jewish Pioneers and Patriots* (New York, 1955), 63. It is supported by Salvador de Madariaga, a Spanish biographer of Columbus. Samuel E. Morison who wrote the definitive English biography of Columbus rejects the idea of his Jewish ancestry (*Admiral of the Ocean Sea*, 206), as does the late dean of Jewish history, Cecil Roth.

23. Kayserling, *Christopher Columbus*, 2–4.

24. Roderigo Sanchez was the Queen's inspector, Marco was surgeon, Mastre Bernal was the physician strongly suspect of Judaizing, Rodrigo de Triana was the first crew member to sight land, Luis de Torres was the interpreter who spoke Hebrew, Chaldaic, Arabic aside from Spanish, and Alfonso de la Calle was an ordinary crew member. (La Calle is the traditional term for Jew street.)

25. Roth, *Jewish Contribution*, 78.

26. Kayserling, *Christopher Columbus*, 15.

27. Lipset and Solar, *Elites in Latin America*, 24–29; Kohler, "Jewish Activity . . . ," 53.

28. Roth, *Jewish Contribution*, 251–91; Kohler, "Jewish Activity . . . ," 54 ff.

29. Roth, *Jewish Contribution*, 273. See also Violet Barbour, *Capitalism in Amsterdam in the 17th century* (Ann Arbor, 1966), p. 25.

30. Morris U. Schappes, *A Documentary History of Jews in the United States, 1654–1875* (New York, 1950), 4–5, April 26, 1655.

31. *Ibid.*, 2–3.

32. Abram V. Goodman, *American Overture: Jewish Rights in Colonial Times* (Philadelphia, 1947), 8.

CHAPTER II

1. The estimate belongs to Goodman, *Overture*, 3. In New York City the proportion of Jews to the general population declined from a high of 2.5 percent in 1695 to 1.2 percent in 1794. Grinstein, *Jewish Community*, 464.

2. Abraham V. Goodman, "A German Mercenary Observes American Jews During the Revolution," *PAJHS*, LIX (December, 1969), 227.

3. Marcus, *Early American Jewry*, II, 494–95, 503. In the eighteenth century, for example, it is probable that every Jew who settled in Connecticut (probably less than a dozen) married outside of the faith. See also Malcolm H. Stern, "Jewish Marriage and Intermarriage in the Federal Period, 1776–1840," *AJA*, November 19, 1967, 120–23.

4. Louis B. Wright, *The Cultural Life of the American Colonies, 1607–1763* (New York, 1957), 72; William L. Sperry, *Religion in America* (Boston, 1963), 29.

5. Marcus, *Early American Jewry*, II, 498.

6. Anson P. Stokes and Leo Pfeffer, "The Background of American Religious Freedom," in *The Politics of Religion in America*, ed. Fred Krinsky (Beverly Hills, 1968), 21–22.

7. Schappes, *Documentary History*, 1–2, September 22, 1654. (Extract from Letter of Peter Stuyvesant to the Amsterdam Chamber of the Dutch West India Co.)

8. Lee M. Friedman, *Early American Jews* (Cambridge, 1934), 52.

9. Schappes, *Documentary History*, 4, April 26, 1655.

10. Goodman, *Overture*, 82.

11. Wright, *Cultural Life*, 79.

12. Goodman, *Overture*, 14.

13. Quoted by David de Sola Pool, "Hebrew Learning Among the Puritans of New England Prior to 1700," *PAJHS*, XX (1911), 32.

14. *Ibid.*

15. *Ibid.*, 82.

16. Broches, *Jews in New England*, I, 4; William J. Chute, ed., *The American Scene, 1600–1860, Contemporary Views of Life and Society* (New York, 1964), 203.

17. Goodman, *Overture*, 168.

18. *Ibid.*, 168–72, 176–83; Leon Huhner, "The Jews of Georgia in Colonial Times," *PAJHS*, X, 65–96.

19. Stokes and Pfeffer, "The Background of American Religious Freedom," 32.

20. Wright, *Cultural Life*, 46. English stock were 60.9 percent, Scotch-Irish 14.3 percent, German 8.7 percent, Dutch, French and Swedish 5.4 percent, South Irish 3.7 percent, unassignable 7 percent.

21. For development of this theme see Will Herberg, *Protestant, Catholic, Jew: An Essay in American Religious Sociology* (New York, 1955).

22. For a development of this point see Daniel J. Boorstin, *The Americans*, Vol. I, *The Colonial Experience* (New York, 1958), 18.

23. Sperry, *Religion*, 36.

24. *Ibid.*, 38.

25. Wright, *Cultural Life*, 77; Stokes and Pfeffer, "The Background of American Religious Freedom," 25.

26. Sperry, *Religion*, 58.

CHAPTER III

1. Boorstin, *Colonial Experience*, I, 193; T. Harry Williams, Richard N. Current, Frank Freidel, *A History of the United States to 1877* (New York, 1969), 66.

2. Alexis de Tocqueville, *Democracy in America* ed., Phillips Bradley (New York, 1945), II, 166.

3. Schappes, *Documentary History*, 5, April 26, 1655.

4. *Ibid.*, 11, June 14, 1655.

5. Freund, *Jewish Merchants*, 41–42.

6. Schappes, *Documentary History*, 6, November 11, 1655.

7. *Ibid.*, 12–13, April 20, 1655.

8. Lebeson, *Jewish Pioneers*, 111–15.

9. Goodman, *Overture*, 41.

10. *Ibid.*, 25.

11. Freund, *Jewish Merchants*, 50.

12. Anita L. Lebeson, *Jewish Pioneers in America, 1742–1848* (New York, 1931), 86; Freund, *Jewish Merchants*, p. 56. Some of these like Isaac Touro were refugees from the Lisbon earthquake of 1755.

13. Lebeson, *Jewish Pioneers*, 56 ff.

14. Schappes, *Documentary History*, 20, January 12, 1733.

15. Morris A. Gutstein, *The Story of the Jews of Newport: Two and a Half Centuries of Judaism, 1658–1908* (New York, 1936), 166.

16. Joseph L. Blau and Salo W. Baron, eds., *The Jews of the United States, 1790–1840, A Documentary History* (New York, 1963), I, 97. See also Richard Pares, *Yankees and Creoles, The Trade Between North America and the West Indies before the American Revolution* (Cambridge, 1956).

17. Max J. Kohler, "Jews of Newport," *PAJHS*, V, 195, Max J. Kohler, "Jewish Activity in American Colonial Commerce," *PAJHS*, X (1902), 47–64.

18. Gutstein, *Jews of Newport*, 23, 463.

19. John H. Franklin, *From Slavery to Freedom: A History of Negro Americans* (New York, 1967), 104; Goodman, *Overture*, 50.

20. Kohler, "Jewish Activity in American Colonial Commerce," 61.

21. Schappes, *Documentary History*, 37, October 29, 1762 (Instructions to a ship's captain).

22. Gutstein, *Jews of Newport,* 164–65.

23. Franklin, *Slavery,* 45.

24. Goodman, *Overture,* 8.

25. Freund, *Jewish Merchants,* 103.

26. *Ibid.,* 106.

27. *Ibid.,* 103.

28. Alfred D. Chandler, Jr., Stuart Bruchey, Louis Galambos, eds. *The Changing Economic Order: Readings in American Business and Economic History* (New York, 1968), 3.

29. Schappes, *Documentary History,* 32 (Michael Gratz to Barnard Gratz in London, July 6, 1770).

30. Trachtenberg, *Easton,* 1, 23.

31. Edwin Wolf II, *The History of the Jews of Philadelphia from Colonial Times to the Age of Jackson* (Philadelphia, 1957), 66–67. In a petition by "the suffering traders of 1754" to London compensation was requested. They were awarded a grant of land in what is today West Virginia. See also Lebeson, *Jewish Pioneers,* 109.

32. Goodman, *Overture,* 150.

33. Leon Huhner, "The Jews of Georgia in Colonial Times," *PAJHS,* X, 65–96. [79–108]

34. Samuel Oppenheim, "The Jewish Signers of the Non Importation Agreement of 1765," *PAJHS,* XXVI (1918), 236.

35. Schappes, *Documentary History,* 95, August 11, 1800 (A Letter to the Printers Gazette of the United States. . . .")

36. Marcus, *Early American Jewry,* II, 527.

37. Schappes, *Documentary History,* 578–79.

38. See especially Cecil Roth, "Some Jewish Loyalists in the War of American Independence," *PAJHS,* XXXVIII (September, 1948), 81–107.

39. Lebeson, *Pilgrim's People,* 125.

40. *Ibid.,* 111.

41. Goodman, "German Mercenary Observes American Jews," 222.

42. Grinstein, *Jewish Community,* 69.

43. Schappes, *Documentary History,* 501–51.

44. Marcus, *Early American Jewry,* II, 531.

45. *Ibid.,* 528–29. Quoted from the South Carolina *Gazette and General Advertiser,* August 30, 1783.

CHAPTER IV

1. A. T. Steele, *The American People and China* (New York, 1966), 8.

2. Blau and Baron, *Documenary History,* I, 142.

3. *Ibid.,* 98.

4. *Ibid.,* 143.

5. *Ibid.,* II, 318, 320.

6. *Ibid.,* 306–307.

7. *Ibid.,* I, 134.

8. Hirschler, *Jews from Germany,* 60.

9. Blau and Baron, *Documentary History,* I, 3.

10. Korn, *Jews and Negro Slavery,* 37.

11. *Ibid.,* 41–42.

12. Jacob R. Marcus, *Memoirs of American Jews*, Vol. I (Philadelphia, 1955), 183–84.

13. Korn, *Jews and Negro Slavery*, 26.

14. Blau and Baron, *Documentary History*, I, 176–77.

15. See Winthrop Jordan, *White over Black*, and Kenneth Stampp, *The Peculiar Institution* (New York, 1963), 78–80, 136–37.

16. Korn, *Jews and Negro Slavery*, 48.

17. Blau and Baron, *Documentary History*, I, 206–207.

18. Joel Williamson, *After Slavery, The Negro in South Carolina During Reconstruction, 1861–1877* (Chapel Hill, 1965), 145–46.

19. Korn, *Jews and Negro Slavery*, 48; Blau and Baron, *Documentary History*, II, 551.

20. Korn, *Jews and Negro Slavery*, 30.

21. Schappes, *Documentary History*, 99–101.

22. Korn, *Jews and Negro Slavery*, 35–36.

23. Berg, "Founders and Fur Traders," *Commentary*, 77.

24. Barry E. Supple, "A Business Elite: German-Jewish Financiers in Nineteenth-Century New York," *The Business History Review*, XXI, (1957), 176. In the early 1890's Jacob Schiff, head of Kuhn, Loeb & Co., helped organize the Union-Pacific R.R. Cyrus Adler, *Jacob Schiff, His Life and Letters* (New York, 1929), I, 15.

25. Blau and Baron, *Documentary History*, III, 817. September 15, 1836.

26. *Ibid.*, I, 130.

27. Louis Berg, "Peddlers in Eldorado," *Commentary*, 40 (July, 1965), 66–67.

28. Schappes, *Documentary History*, Petition of Zeire Hazon. Blau and Baron, *Documentary History*, III, 906.

29. *Ibid.*, III, 894.

30. *Ibid.*, III, 901. See also Isaac Goldberg, *Major Noah: American Jewish Pioneer* (Philadelphia, 1936), 139–42.

31. See also Selig Adler, *From Ararat to Suburbia: The History of the Jewish Community of Buffalo* (Philadelphia, 1960), 6–9.

CHAPTER V

1. Eric E. Hirschler, ed., *Jews From Germany in the United States* (New York), 1955), 42, and Rudolf Glanz, "Jews in Relation to the Cultural Media of the Germans in America," *Yivo Bleter*, XXV, No. 1 and 2, pp. 70–95. For the indistinguishability from German immigrants, see Oscar Handlin, "American Views of the Jew at the Opening of the Twentieth Century," *PAJHS*, XL (1951), 325–26.

2. Louis Berg, "Founders and Fur Traders," *Commentary*, 51 (May, 1971), 79.

3. U. Z. Engelman, "Jewish Statistics in the United States Census of Religious Bodies, 1855–1936, *Jewish Social Studies*, IX (April, 1947), 129–31. In 1850 the monetary valuation of these congregations stood at $415,600 and boasted a seating capacity of 17,688.

4. Mark Wischnitzer, *To Dwell in Safety: The Story of Jewish Migration Since 1800* (Philadelphia, 1948), 5.

5. Blau and Baron, *Documentary History*, III, 804. Quoted in *Allgemeine Zeitung des Juedentums*, September 28, 1839.

6. *Ibid.*

7. Bertram W. Korn, "Jewish 48'ers in America," *American Jewish Archives*, II, 5. Korn found only 28 names of Jewish immigrants who might qualify as 48'ers.

8. Guido Kish, "The Revolution of 1848 and the Jewish 'On to America' movement," *PAJHS*, XXVII (March, 1949), 188.

9. Wischnitzer, *To Dwell*, 18–19.

10. Schappes, *Documentary History*, 159.

11. Hirschler, *Jews From Germany*, 34; Wischnitzer, *To Dwell*, 6.

12. Blau and Baron, *Documentary History*, III, 887–88.

13. Schappes, *Documentary History*, 158.

14. *Ibid.*, 141.

15. Blau and Baron, *Documentary History*, I, 418.

16. Schappes, *Documentary History*, 198. Circular addressed to the Jews of New York, September 3, 1837.

17. Isaac M. Wise, *Reminiscences*, trans. and ed. by David Philipson, (New York, 1901), 21.

18. Anita L. Lebeson, *Pilgrims People* (New York, 1950), 171.

19. Grinstein, *Jewish Community*, 167.

20. Blau and Baron, *Documentary History*, I, 213–14; Hirschler, *Jews From Germany*, 22; Grinstein, *Jewish Community*, 40.

21. Stephen Birmingham, *The Grandees: America's Sephardic Elite* (New York, 1971), 263.

22. Hirschler, *Jews From Germany*, 9. Quoted from the *Life and Letters of Francis Lieber*, New York, 1881.

23. Trachtenberg, *Easton*, 125.

24. Wise, *Reminiscences*, 38.

25. *Ibid.*

26. Trachtenberg, *Easton*, 125.

27. Blau and Baron, *Documentary History*, I, 56.

28. Abraham V. Goodman, "A Jewish Peddler's Diary," *American Jewish Archives*, III, June, 1951, 104.

29. Hirschler, *Jews From Germany*, 45–46. Excerpted from Abraham Cohn's diary, 1842–1843. Tfilim are put on every morning by an observant Jew.

30. Berg, *Peddlers in Eldorado*, 66.

31. Floyd S. Fierman, *Some Early Jewish Settlers on the Southwestern Frontier* (El Paso, 1960), 8–10.

32. See Stephen Birmingham, *Our Crowd, The Great Jewish Families of New York* (New York, 1967).

33. Supple, "German Jewish Financiers . . . ," 144–45.

34. See especially William Miller, *Men in Business: Essays in Entrepreneurship* (Cambridge, 1952).

35. Supple, "German Jewish Financiers . . . ," 144–45.

36. Birmingham, *Crowd*, 96.

37. Supple, "German Jewish Financiers . . . ," 170.

38. *Ibid.*, 176.

39. Moses Rischin, *The Promised City: New York's Jews, 1870–1914* (New York, 1970), 52–53.

Chapter VI

1. Blau and Baron, *Documentary History*, I, 48–49.
2. Irving Katz, *August Belmont: A Political Biography* (New York, 1968), vii.
3. Schappes, *Documentary History*, 185–86.
4. Cited by Rudolf Glanz, *Jew and Irish, Historic Group Relations and Immigration* (New York, 1966), 55–56.
5. *Ibid.*
6. C. W. Jordan, *White over Black: American Attitude Toward the Negro, 1550–1812* (Baltimore, 1969), 36–37; see also Schappes, *Documentary History*, 405–18, "Bible View of Slavery," A Discourse by Rabbi Morris Jacob Raphall, January 4, 1861.
7. Bertram W. Korn, *American Jewry and the Civil War* (New York, 1961), 19.
8. *Ibid.*, 21.
9. Suhl Yuri, *Eloquent Crusader: Ernestine Rose* (New York, 1970).
10. *Ibid.*, 15; Schappes, *Documentary History*, 332.
11. Bertram W. Korn, *Jews and Negro Slavery in the Old South, 1789–1865* (Elkins Park, 1961), 61.
12. Korn, *Civil War*, 27.
13. Korn, *Jews and Negro Slavery*, 25–27.
14. See Louis Ruchames, "Jewish Radicalism in the United States," in Peter I. Rose, ed., *The Ghetto and Beyond: Essays on Jewish Life in America* (New York, 1969); 231. See also Louis Ruchames, "The Abolitionists and the Jews," *PAJHS*, LX (June, 1971), 325–43.
15. Korn, *Civil War*, 189.
16. Jonathan Waxman, "Arnold Fischel: 'Unsung Hero' in American Israel," *PAJHS*, LX, June, 1971, 325–43.
17. Korn, *Civil War*, 107.
18. *Ibid.*, 122.
19. Schappes, *Documentary History*, 472.
20. *Ibid.*
21. Korn, *Civil War*, 43–44.

Chapter VII

1. Schappes, *Documentary History*, 342.
2. *Ibid.*, 346.
3. Blau and Baron, *Documentary History*, II, 676.
4. *Ibid.*, I, 171–72.
5. David Philipson, *The Reform Movement in Judaism* (New York, 1931), 334.
6. *Ibid.*, 343.
7. Blau and Baron, *Documentary History*, II, 560.
8. *Ibid.*, II, 563. Discourse, November 21, 1825.
9. Edward E. Grusd, *B'nai B'rith: The Story of a Covenant* (New York, 1966), 13.

10. Wise, *Reminiscences*, 210–11.
11. Blau and Baron, *Documentary History*, III, 710.
12. *Ibid.*, 704.
13. Goodman, "A Jewish Peddler's Diary . . . ," 109.
14. Wise, *Reminiscences*, 302.
15. *Ibid.*, 41–44.
16. Blau and Baron, *Documentary History*, III, 669.
17. Lebeson, *Pilgrims People*, 236.
18. Schappes, *Documentary History*, 179. See also Bertram W. Korn, *The Early Jews of New Orleans* (Waltham, 1969), 196–97.
19. Schappes, *Documentary History*, 177–78.
20. Wise, *Reminiscences*, 57.
21. *Ibid.*, 79.
22. *Ibid.*, 71–72.
23. Adler, *Ararat to Suburbia*, 69.
24. Blau and Baron, *Documentary History*, II, 535–39.
25. *Ibid.*, II, 533–34.
26. Schappes, *Documentary History*, 171–77.
27. Nathan Glazer, *American Judaism* (Chicago, 1957), 39.
28. Philipson, *Reform Movement*, 356.

CHAPTER VIII

1. Samuel Joseph, *Jewish Immigration to the United States, 1860–1924* (New York, 1914), 142–43.
2. *Ibid.*, 42–48.
3. In Rumania, 20 percent of the artisans were Jewish and 88 percent lived in towns. In Austria-Hungary, primarily Galicia, the configuration differed slightly because of the surprisingly high percentage involved in some aspect of agriculture (18 percent). Most of these were probably in the category of estate or farm managers. There too 29 percent of the Jewish population was involved in commerce, primarily petty trade.
4. Salo Baron, *Modern Nationalism and Religion* (New York, 1960), 22.
5. Rischin, *Promised City*, 28.
6. For an analysis of the socioeconomic context of the rise of secular ideologies, see Ezra Mendelsohn, *Class Struggle in the Pale, the Formative Years of the Jewish Workers' Movement in Czarist Russia* (Cambridge, 1970).
7. Elias Tcherikower, *The Early Jewish Labor Movement in the United States* (New York, 1961).
8. B. D. Weinryb, "East European Immigration to the United States," *Jewish Quarterly Review*, XLV (April, 1955), 497–528.
9. Wischnitzer, *To Dwell*, 67.
10. Joel S. Geffen, "Whither: To Palestine or to America in the Pages of the Russian Hebrew Press *Ha-Melitz* and *Hayom* (1880–1890). Annotated Documentary," *PAJHS*, LIX (December, 1969), 179–200.
11. Abraham Cahan, *The Education of Abraham Cahan*, trans. Leon Stein, Abraham P. Conana, Lynn Davison from *Bleter Fun Mein Leben*, vols. I & II (Philadelphia, 1969), 186–87, 198.
12. S. P. Rudens, "A Half Century of Community Service: The Educational

Alliance," *AJYB*, 46, p. 74; Joseph, *Jewish Immigration*, 91; Rischin, *Promised City*, 270.

13. Joseph, *Jewish Immigration*, 91, 105–108, 109–112; Rischin, *Promised City*, 270.

14. Tcherikower, *Early Jewish Labor*, 73.

15. Wischnitzer, *To Dwell*, 44.

16. Joseph, *Jewish Immigration*, 133–34; Tcherikower, *Early Jewish Labor*, 125; Zosa Szajkowski, "The Attitude of American Jews to East European Jewish Immigration (1881–1893)," *PAJHS*, XL (March, 1951), 243–44.

17. Mary Antin, *The Promised Land* (Boston, 1912), 174.

18. Cahan, *Education of . . .*, 212.

19. Cited by Tcherikower, *Early Jewish Labor*, 115.

20. Cahan, *Education of . . .*, 217.

21. Harold U. Ribalow, ed., *Autobiographies of American Jews* (Philadelphia, 1965), 169.

22. Anzia Yezierska, *How I Found America* (New York, 1920), 265.

23. Tcherikower, *Early Jewish Labor*, 124.

24. Irving A. Mandel, "The Attitude of the American Jewish Community Toward East European Immigration As Reflected in the Anglo-Jewish Press," *American Jewish Archives* III (June, 1950), 18–20.

25. Cahan, *Education of . . .*, 218–19.

26. Szajkowski, "Attitude of American Jews . . .," 225–26.

27. Wischnitzer, *To Dwell*, 121.

28. *Ibid.*, 3.

29. Szajkowski, "Attitude of American Jews . . .," 233.

30. C. Morris Horowitz and Laurence J. Kaplan, *The Jewish Population of New York Area, 1900–1925* (New York, 1959), 13–15.

CHAPTER IX

1. Louis Wirth, *The Ghetto* (Chicago, 1928).

2. Irving Howe, "The Lower East Side: Symbol and Fact," in *The Lower East Side: Portal to American Life*, ed., Allon Schoener (New York, 1966), 14.

3. *New York Times*, January 18, 1895 (Schoener).

4. Henry James, *The American Scene* (New York, 1967), 130–39.

5. Rischin, *Promised City*, 272; Arthur A. Goren, *New York Jews and the Quest for Community, The Kehillah Experiment, 1908–1922* (New York, 1970), 18.

6. Quoted in Tcherikower, *Early Jewish Labor*, 122–23.

7. Howe, "Lower East Side," 14.

8. *Evening Post*, June 17, 1899.

9. Milton Hindus, ed., *The Old East Side* (Philadelphia, 1969), 102.

10. *New York Tribune*, August 16, 1903.

11. Tcherikower, *Early Jewish Labor*, 140; Nathaniel Weyl, *The Jew in American Politics* (New York, 1969), 79.

12. See for example Morris Cohen, *A Dreamer's Journey* (New York, 1949).

13. Antin, *Promised Land*, 198.

14. Jacob A. Riis, *How the other Half Lives* (New York, 1902), 114.

15. *Evening Post*, January 10, 1903.

16. *Ibid.*, October 3, 1903.

17. *Ibid.*, January 10, 1903.

18. Cahan, *Education of . . .*, 400–401.

19. Melech Epstein, *Jewish Labor in U.S.A.: An Industrial, Political and Cultural History of the Jewish Labor Movement, 1882–1914* (New York, 1950), I, 356.

20. *New York Tribune*, August 16, 1903.

21. Quoted by Hindus, *Old East Side*, 59, from *Impressions and Experiences*.

22. Rischin, *Promised City*, 91; Bernheimer, *Russian Jews*, 55, 341.

23. Antin, *Promised Land*, 194.

24. Egal Feldman, "Prostitution, the Alien Woman and the Progressive Imagination, 1910–1915," *American Quarterly*, XIX, No. 2 (1967), 192–206.

25. Goren, *Kehillah Experiment*, 157.

26. Daniel Bell, *The End of Ideology* (New York, 1962), 129, 141, 149–50.

27. Tcherikower, *Early Jewish Labor*, 109.

CHAPTER X

1. John Higham, *Strangers in the Land, Patterns of American Nativism, 1860–1925* (New York, 1968), 92.

2. The full story is well told by Leonard Dinnerstein, *The Leo Frank Case* (New York, 1968).

3. Brandes, *Immigrants*, 177.

4. *New York Times*, July 30, 1893.

5. Rudolf Glanz, *Jew and Irish, Historic Group Relations and Immigration* (New York, 1966), 44–46.

6. Higham, *Strangers in the Land*, 182.

7. Oscar Handlin, "American Views of the Jew at the Opening of the Twentieth Century," *PAJHS*, XL (June, 1951), 339.

8. Lincoln Steffens, *Autobiography* (New York, 1931).

9. Handlin, "American Views of the Jew . . . ," 325–26.

10. Robert Rockaway, "Ethnic Conflict in an Urban Environment: The German and Russian Jews in Detroit, 1881–1914," *PAJHS*, LX (December, 1970), 135.

11. Szajkowski, "Attitude of American Jews . . . ," 231.

12. Goren, *Kehillah Experiment*, 14.

13. Rockaway, "Ethnic Conflict . . . ," 146.

14. Rischin, *Promised City*, 239.

15. Rockaway, "Ethnic Conflict . . . ," 135, quoting from *Jewish American*, November 22, 1901, 4.

16. S. P. Rudens, "A Half Century of Community Service, The Educational Alliance," *AJYB*, XLVI (1944–1945), 75.

17. *Ibid.*, 74.

18. Rockaway, "Ethnic Conflict . . . ," 142.

19. Wischnitzer, *To Dwell*, 126.

20. Gebriel Davidson, *Our Jewish Farmers and the Story of the Jewish Agriculture Society* (New York, 1943), 33.

21. Cited by Tcherikower, *Early Jewish Labor*, 121.

22. Gabriel Davidson, "The Jew in Agriculture in the United States,"

AJYB, XXXVII (1935), 103; Joseph Brandes in association with Martin Douglas, *Immigrants to Freedom: Jewish Communities in Rural New Jersey Since 1882* (Philadelphia, 1971).

23. Davidson, *Our Jewish Farmers* . . . , 33–34.

CHAPTER XI

1. See for example Tcherikower, *Early Jewish Labor*, 175; Morris Hill-quit, *Loose Leaves from a Busy Life* (New York, 1934), 20–36.

2. Esther L. Panitz, "The Polarity of American Jewish Attitudes Towards Immigration, 1870–1891," *PAJHS*, LIII (December, 1963), 120.

3. B. D. Weinryb, "East European Immigration to the United States," *Jewish Quarterly Review*, XLV (April, 1955), 497–528.

4. Quoted in Milton Hindus (ed.), *The Old East Side, An Anthology* (Philadelphia, 1969), 99.

5. Tcherikower, *Early Jewish Labor*, 337.

6. Hillquit, *Loose Leaves*, 20–36.

7. Hutchins Hapgood, *The Spirit of the Ghetto* (New York, 1968), 187–88.

8. Epstein, *Jewish Labor*, I, 212.

9. Ernest Poole in an article in *Outlook*, November 21, 1903, which appeared in Allon Schoener (ed.), *Portal to America, The Lower East Side, 1870–1925* (New York, 1967), 69–70.

10. *New York Times*, July 29, 1895.

11. See Chapter VI.

12. Wischnitzer, *To Dwell*, 44.

13. Nathan Reich, "The 'Americanization' of Jewish Unionism, A Two Way Process," *Jewish Quarterly Review*, XLV (April, 1955), 545–47.

14. Howe, "Lower East Side," 12.

15. Cahan, *Education of* . . . , 228.

16. Tcherikower, *Early Jewish Labor*, 286.

17. Will Herberg, "The Jewish Labor Movement in the United States," *AJYB*, LIII (1952), 15.

18. Epstein, *Jewish Labor*, I, 303–305.

19. Herberg, "Jewish Labor Movement," 17.

20. Epstein, *Jewish Labor*, I, 402.

CHAPTER XII

1. Quoted in Hindus, *Old East Side*, 46.

2. Uriah Z. Engelman, "Jewish Statistics in the United States, Census of Religious Bodies (1850–1936)," *Jewish Social Studies*, IX (April, 1947), 134–39.

3. Mordecai Waxman, *Tradition and Change* (New York, 1958), 7.

4. Marshall Sklare, *Conservative Judaism* (New York, 1972), 231–32. See also Moshe Davis, *The Emergence of Conservative Judaism* (Philadelphia, 1963), 280.

5. *Universal Jewish Encyclopedia*, VI, 244.

6. Cited in John J. Appel, "The *Trefa* Banquet," *Commentary* (February, 1966), XLI, 76.

7. Rockaway, "German and Russian Jews...," 145–46 (September 19, 1903).

8. Nathan Glazer, *American Judaism* (Chicago, 1963), 58.

9. Norman Bentwich, *Solomon Schechter: A Biography* (Philadelphia, 1938), 347–48.

10. Engelman, "Jewish Statistics...," 142.

11. Marshall Sklare, "Recent Developments in Conservative Judaism," *Midstream* (January, 1972), 3–7.

12. See Aaron Rothkopf, *Bernard Revel. Builder of American Jewish Orthodoxy* (Philadelphia, 1972).

13. *Universal Jewish Encyclopedia*, I, 240–41.

CHAPTER XIII

1. *Shulamit*, June 21, 1889.

2. Max J. Kohler, "Some Early American Zionist Projects," *PAJHS* (1900), 75.

3. Rudolf Glanz, *Jew and Mormon: Historic Group Relations and Religious Outlook* (New York, 1963), 41–43, 53 ff.

4. Marnin Feinstein, *American Zionism, 1884–1904* (New York, 1965), 13.

5. Cyrus Adler and Aaron Margalith, *With Firmness in the Right, American Diplomatic Action Affecting Jews, 1840–1945* (New York, 1946), 42. Feinstein, *American Zionism*, 56–57.

6. Feinstein, *ibid.*, 57.

7. Louis Lipsky, *Thirty Years of American Zionism* (New York, 1927), 87.

8. Arthur Ziegler, "Emma Lazarus and Pre-Herzlian Zionism," in *Early History of Zionism in America*, ed. Isadore Meyer (New York, 1958), 97–108.

9. Naomi W. Cohen, "The Reaction of Reform Judaism in America to Political Zionism (1897–1922)," *PAJHS*, XL (June, 1951), 372.

10. David Philipson, *The Reform Movement in Judaism* (New York, 1931), 72; see also *My Life as an American Jew* (Cincinnati, 1941).

11. Jonathan Shapiro, *Leadership of the American Zionist Organization, 1897–1930* (Urbana, 1970), 82.

12. Quoted by Feinstein, *American Zionism*, 184.

13. Ben Halpern, "Brandeis' Way to Zionism," *Midstream* (October, 1971), 313.

14. Melvin Urofsky, *A Mind of One Piece, Brandeis and American Reform* (New York, 1971), 95–115.

15. Shapiro, *Leadership...*, 61–70.

16. Jacob De Haas, *Louis D. Brandeis, A Biographical Sketch* (New York, 1929), 161.

17. *Ibid.*

18. *Ibid.*, 181.

19. *Ibid.*

CHAPTER XIV

1. Hyman B. Grinstein, "The Efforts of East European Jewry to Organize its Own Community in the United States," *PAJHS*, XLIX (December, 1959), 76.

2. In Jewish belief charity is obligatory rather than voluntary. The poor are considered the special wards of God, who is the source of all earthly wealth. The Jew who has become wealthy is merely a temporary custodian of God's wealth and is obliged to share it with those in need. *Shtetl* synagogues used this obligation to establish the *Kuppah*; a rotating fund maintained by the wealthier members of the congregation to help the less fortunate.

3. Harry L. Lurie, *The Jewish Federation Movement in America: A Heritage Affirmed* (Philadelphia, 1961), 83–84.

4. *Ibid.*, 34–58. For a summary description of the consolidation process in social services, see Charles S. Levy, "Jewish Communal Services: Health, Welfare, Recreational and Social," in *The American Jew: A Composite Portrait*, Oscar I. Janowsky, ed. (Philadelphia, 1964), 253–76.

5. Joseph J. Schwartz and Beatrice I. Vulcan, "Overseas Aid," in Janowsky, *American Jew*, 277–78.

6. *Ibid.*, 279–80.

7. Naomi W. Cohen, *Not Free to Desist, A History of the American Jewish Committee, 1906–1965* (Philadelphia, 1972), 9.

8. Louis Marshall, *Champion of Liberty, Selected Papers and Addresses*, Charles Reznikoff, ed. (Philadelphia, 1957), I, 22. Marshall to Dr. Joseph Stalz, January 12, 1906.

9. Cohen, *American Jewish Committee*, 15.

10. Quoted in Moses Rischin, "The Early Attitude of the American Jewish Community to Zionism (1906, 1922)," *PAJHS*, XLIX (March, 1960), 190.

11. Goren, *Kehillah Experiment*, 250.

12. Quoted in Rischin, "Early Attitude . . . ," 192.

13. Quoted in A. Leon Kubowitzki, *Unity in Dispersion, A History of the World Jewish Congress* (New York, 1948), 19.

14. *Challenging Years: The Autobiography of Stephen Wise* (New York, 1949), 203 ff.

15. *New York Times*, March 5, 1919, p. 7. (Cited in Rischin, "Early Attitude . . . ," 199.)

16. Norman Bentwich, "The Kehillah of New York, 1908–1922," article in *Mordecai Kaplan Jubilee Volume* (New York, 1953), 78.

17. Lipsky, *American Zionism*, 117.

18. Goren, *Kehillah Experiment*, 49.

19. Bentwich, "Kehillah," 80.

20. Reznikoff Marshall, *Champion of Liberty*, I, 34.

21. Goren, *Kehillah Experiment*, 53.

22. Lipsky, *American Zionism*, 213.

23. Goren, *Kehillah Experiment*, 102.

24. *Ibid.*, 107.

CHAPTER XV

1. Rischin, *Promised City*, 231.

2. Glanz, *Jew and Irish*, 83–84.

3. Charles Bernheimer, *The Russian Jews in the United States* (Philadelphia, 1905), 263–64.

4. Cahan, *Education of*, 291.

5. Bernheimer, *Russian Jews*, 133.

6. *Ibid.*, 269.

7. *Ibid.*, 261.

8. Hindus, *Old East Side*, 261; Tcherikower, *Jewish Labor Movement*, 127.

9. Rischin, *Promised City*, 199.

10. Fuchs, *Political Behavior*, 52.

11. *Ibid.*, 51.

12. Philipson, *Reform Movement*, 70–71.

13. Fuchs, *Political Behavior*, 53.

14. James Weinstein, *The Decline of Socialism in America, 1912–1925* (New York, 1969), 119–75.

15. Blau and Baron, *Documentary History*, III, 929; see also Cyrus Adler and Aaron Margalith, *With Firmness in the Right: American Diplomatic Action Affecting Jews, 1840–1945* (New York, 1946), 3–11.

16. Adler and Margalith, *Diplomatic Action*, xxvii.

17. *Ibid.*, 20.

18. Adler and Margalith, *With Firmness*, 178.

19. *Ibid.*, 234.

20. *Ibid.*, 235.

21. Kenton J. Clymer, "Anti-Semitism in the late Nineteenth Century, The Case of John Hay," *PAJHS*, LX, June, 1971, 351.

22. Adler and Margalith, *With Firmness*, 206.

23. Adler and Margalith, *With Firmness*, 219–20.

24. Joseph, *Jewish Immigration*, 199.

25. Szajkowski, "Attitude of American Jews . . . ," 234. (Quoted in the *New York Herald*.)

26. Oscar S. Straus, *Under Four Administrations* (New York, 1922), 166.

27. Once before, in July 1891, a committee which included Straus, Seligman, and Schiff, informed Benjamin Harrison that American interests were directly involved since Russian depredations and brutality resulted in casting hordes of destitute immigrants on American shores. Harrison responded by appointing a commission to investigate the causes of immigration. Naomi W. Cohen, *A Dual Heritage: The Public Career of Oscar S. Straus* (Philadelphia, 1969), 59–60.

CHAPTER XVI

1. Lipsky, *American Zionism*, 183.

2. Cohen, *Dual Heritage*, 128, 131.

3. Adler and Margalith, *With Firmness*, 264.

4. Straus, *Four Administrations*, 216.

5. Adler and Margalith, *With Firmness*, 126.

6. Clymer, "John Hay," 349.

7. Cohen, *Dual Heritage*, 135.

8. Adler and Margalith, *With Firmness*, 276.

9. *Ibid.*, 282. For an examination of the events leading up to the abrogation see Naomi W. Cohen, "The Abrogation of the Russo-American Treaty of 1882," *Jewish Social Studies*, XXV (January, 1963), 3–41.

10. Stephen S. Wise, *Challenging Years, The Autobiography of Stephen Wise* (New York, 1949), 184.

11. Joshua H. Neumann, "The Jewish Battalions and the Palestine Campaign," *AJYB 5680*, XXI, 120–40.

12. Adler and Margalith, *With Firmness*, 79.

13. Joseph Rappaport, "Zionism as a Factor in Allied-Central Power Controversy (1914–1918)," in *Early History of Zionism in America*, ed. Isadore Meyer (New York, 1958), 319.

Chapter XVII

1. "Jews in America," ed. *Fortune Magazine* (New York, 1936), 7 (bound reprint).

2. *Ibid.*

3. *Ibid.*, p. 15.

4. Benjamin Stolberg, *Tailor's Progress* (New York, 1944), 137.

5. Will Herberg, "The Jewish Labor Movement in the United States," *AJYB*, LIII (1952), p. 47.

6. "Report of the American Jewish Committee," *AJYB*, XXV (1923–24), 378–79.

7. Robert K. Murray, *Red Scare: A Study of National Hysteria, 1919–1920* (New York, 1964), 91–92.

8. John Higham, *Strangers in the Land, Patterns of American Nativism, 1860–1925* (New York, 1968), 279.

9. Leonard Dinnerstein, "Atlanta in the Progressive Era, A Dreyfus Affair in Georgia," in *Antisemitism in the United States*, ed. Leonard Dinnerstein (New York, 1971), 87–101.

10. *AJYB*, XXI (1919–1920), 633–34.

11. John Higham, "American Anti-Semitism Historically Reconsidered," in *Jews in the Mind of America*, ed. Charles H. Stember, 242.

12. *AJYB* (1917–1918), 407.

13. Stephen Steinberg, "How Jewish Quotas Began," *Commentary*, LII, (September, 1971), 69; see also Morton Rosenstock, *Louis Marshall, Defender of Jewish Rights* (Detroit, 1965), Chapter IX, for general background.

14. *Ibid.*, 70.

15. *Ibid.*, 71. For general background see also Stephen Steinberg, *The Academic Melting Pot, Catholics and Jews in American Higher Education* (New York, 1974).

16. Morton Rosenstock, "Are There Too Many Jews at Harvard," in *Antisemitism in the United States*, ed., Leonard Dinnerstein, *Antisemitism*, 103–104.

17. *Ibid.*, 105.

18. *Ibid.*, 106.

19. James Yaffee, *The American Jews, Portrait of a Split Personality* (New York, 1968), 52.

20. Quoted by Judd Teller, *Strangers and Natives: The Evolution of the American Jews from 1921 to the Present* (New York, 1968), 103. For a full background of the Ford episode see Rosenstock, *Louis Marshall*, 128–200.

21. *New York Times*, December 1, 1938, 12; James G. McDonald MSS, School of International Affairs, Columbia University, Confidential Memorandum of McDonald-Ford Negotiations in Dearborn, April 1, 1941.

22. *Fortune* (1936 study), 1.

23. Morton Keller, "Jews and the Character of American Life Since 1930," in *Jews in the Mind of America*, ed. Charles Stember, 259–66. See also Sander Diamond, *The Nazi Movement in the United States* (Ithaca, 1974).

24. See for example the dozens of such sociological studies listed and summarized in Melvin M. Tumin, *An Inventory and Appraisal of Research on American Anti-Semitism* (New York, 1961).

25. Alfred O. Hero, *Americans in World Affairs* (Boston, 1959), 72 ff.

26. David J. O'Brien, "American Catholics and Antisemitism in the 1930s," in Dinnerstein (ed.) *Antisemitism in the United States*, 110.

27. *Ibid.*, 115. See also David J. O'Brien, *American Catholics and Social Reform, The New Deal Years* (New York, 1968), 169–81.

28. Elliot Roosevelt, ed. *F.D.R.: His Personal Papers, 1928–1945* (New York, 1950), II, 997, February 13, 1940.

29. Arthur Link, *American Epoch: A History of the United States Since the 1890's* (New York, 1955), 473.

30. *Documents on German Foreign Policy, 1918–1945*, series D, V (Washington, 1951). Dieckhoff to Weizäcker, November 14, 1938, 639–41.

31. Stember, *Jews in the Mind*, 137.

32. *Fortune Quarterly Survey*, XVIII (July, 1938), 80; XX (April, 1939), 102.

33. David S. Wyman, *Paper Walls, America and the Refugee Crisis 1938–1941* (Amherst, 1968); and Henry L. Feingold, *The Politics of Rescue: The Roosevelt Administration and the Holocaust, 1938–1945* (New Brunswick, 1970).

Chapter XVIII

1. Uriah Z. Engleman, "Jewish Statistics in the United States. Census of Religious Bodies, 1850–1936," *Jewish Social Studies*, IX (April, 1947), 160.

2. A good account of this pattern is contained in Lionel Kochan, ed., *The Jews in Soviet Russia Since 1917* (New York, 1970), 66 ff.

3. George L. Berlin, "The Brandeis-Weizmann Dispute," *PAJHS*, LX, (September, 1970), 40.

4. Sumner Welles, *A Time for Decision* (New York, 1941), 266–67.

5. Fred L. Israel, ed., *The War Diary of Breckinridge Long, Selections from the Years 1939–1944* (Lincoln, 1966), 366, January 11, 1944.

6. *AJYB*, XXII (1920–1921), 141.

7. Quoted in Judd L. Teller's *Strangers and Natives: The Evolution of the American Jews from 1921 to the Present* (New York, 1968), 177.

8. A. L. Kubowitzki, *Unity in Dispersion. A History of the World Jewish Congress* (New York, 1948), 104–105.

9. H. G. Reissner, "The American Anti-Nazi Boycott," *Jubilee Volume*, Herbert A. Strauss and Hans G. Reissner, eds. (New York, 1969), 69.

10. Frances Perkins, *The Roosevelt I Knew* (New York, 1947), 348.

11. Long MSS, Manuscript Division, Library of Congress, Memorandum to Berle and Dunn, June 26, 1940.

12. See David S. Wyman, *Paper Walls, America and the Refugee Crisis 1938–1941* (Amherst, 1968).

13. *New York Times*, June 23, 1938, 13.

14. Pierrepont Moffat Diary, Houghton Library of Harvard University, May 25, 1939.

15. F. D. Roosevelt MSS, Hyde Park Library, President's Personal File #64, Samuel Rosenman to FDR, December 5, 1938.

16. Werner J. Cahnman, "Comments on the American Jewish Scene," in *Conference on Acculturation*, ed. H. A. Strauss, American Federation of Jews from Central Europe, May 16, 1965.

17. Cordell Hull, *Memoirs of Cordell Hull* (New York, 1948), II, 1529.

18. Samuel Halperin, *The Political World of American Zionism* (Detroit, 1961), 127.

19. Quoted by Doreen Bierbrier, "The American Zionist Emergency Council:—An Analysis of a Pressure Group " *PAJHS*, IX (September, 1970), 85.

20. Halperin, *American Zionism*, 38.

21. Bartley C. Crum, *Behind the Silken Curtain* (New York, 1947), 36–39.

22. J. M. Blum, *Roosevelt and Morgenthau, A Revision and Condensation of From the Morgenthau Diaries* (Boston, 1970), 519.

23. *Contemporary Jewish Record*, IV, no. 5 (October, 1943), 525.

24. The best description of Long's anti-refugee attitude is contained in Israel, *War Diary of Breckinridge Long*.

25. See Feingold, *The Politics of Rescue* and Blum, *Roosevelt and Morgenthau*, 531–33.

26. See for example the pamphlet "Washington Post, A Victim of British Intrigue" (Washington: Hebrew Committee of National Liberation, October, 1944).

27. Selig Adler, "Franklin D. Roosevelt and Zionism, The Wartime Record," *Judaism* (Summer, 1972), 265.

Chapter XIX

1. Gerald Engel, "North American Settlers in Israel," *AJYB*, 71 (1970), 185.

2. Stember, *Jews in the Mind of America*, 23.

3. Mark H. Elovitz, "Wallace and the Jews," *Congress Bi-Weekly*, 39 (June 30, 1972), 9–13.

4. *New York Times*, May 16, 1971, 55.

5. Marshall Sklare, *America's Jews* (New York, 1971), 41.

6. Malcolm H. Stern, "Jewish Marriage and Intermarriage in the Federal Period, 1776–1840," *American Jewish Archives* (November, 1967), 142–3.

7. Leonard J. Fein, "Some Consequences of Jewish Intermarriage." Mimeographed paper, Commission on Jewish Affairs, American Jewish Congress, 1970.

8. Sidney Goldstein and Calvin Goldschneider, *Jewish Americans, Three Generations in a Jewish Community* (Englewood Cliffs, 1968), 206.

9. Marshall Sklare, "Recent Developments in Conservative Judaism," *Midstream* (January, 1972), 3–4.

10. Goldstein and Goldschneider, *Jewish Americans*, 208.

11. *New York Times*, November 28, 1969, 28.

12. Jaffe, *American Jews*, 89.

13. Figures distributed by the Jewish Telegraphic Agency, "The Jewish Day School, 1963–1973."

14. *New York Times*, March 11, 1973, 49. See also footnote 13 and David Singer, "The Growth of the Day School Movement," *Commentary*, 56 (August, 1973), 53–57.

15. Stanley Rothman, "Student Activism," *Commentary*, 54 (July, 1972), 93.

16. Robert Liebert, *Radical and Militant Youth: A Psychoanalytic Inquiry* (New York, 1971), 233.

17. For an elaboration of this view see Henry L. Feingold, "The Jewish Radical in his American Habitat," *Judaism*, 22 (Winter, 1973), 92–105.

18. Sklare, *America's Jews*, 64–65. See also Gordon, *Assimilation in American Life*, 185.

19. *Ibid.* (Sklare), 65.

20. Steinberg, "Jewish Quotas," 67.

21. *New York Times*, May 2, 1971, 14.

22. "The Youth Scene," *Jewish Week*, 181, 18 Ilyar, p. 1.

23. *New York Times*, June 25, 1972, 31; Herbert Bienstock, "Professional and Job Prospects for Jews in the Seventies," *The Jewish Digest* (April, 1972), 29–34.

24. Dorothy Rabinowitz, "The Other Jews: Portraits in Poverty," American Jewish Committee, January, 1972.

25. Marshall Sklare, "Jews, Ethnics, and the American City," *Commentary*, 53 (April, 1972), 72–73.

26. Morris N. Kertzer, *Today's American Jews* (New York, 1967), 74. For a general observation of this phenomenon, see Alfred O. Hero, *Americans in World Affairs* (Boston, 1959).

27. Werner Cohn, "The Politics of American Jews," in *The Jews, Social Patterns of an American Group*, ed., Marshall Sklare (New York, 1958), 614–26.

28. *Ibid.*

29. Despite some evidence of a conservative trend in 1971 Jews were still the strongest proponents of integration. See Andrew M. Greeley and Paul B. Sheatsley, "Attitudes Toward Racial Integration," *Scientific American*, 225 (December, 1971), 13–19.

30. Milton Himmelfarb, "The Jewish Vote (Again)," *Commentary*, 55 (June, 1973), 81–85.

Selected Bibliography

The following works on American Jewish history represent only a partial listing of what is available in the field. Readers interested in a more complete listing should consult Moses Rischin, *An Inventory of American Jewish History* (Cambridge, 1954); Jacob R. Marcus, "A Selected Bibliography of American Jewish History," *PAJHS*, Vol. LI (December, 1961), 97–134, and *An Index to Scientific Articles on American Jewish History* (Cincinnati, 1971). These listings are kept up to date by Nathan Kaganoff, librarian-editor of the American Jewish Historical Society, in his "Judaica Americana" which appears almost every quarter in the *PAJHS*. Published original sources such as documents and correspondence, many used in this book, can best be gleaned in Joseph L. Blau and Salo W. Baron, eds., *The Jews in United States, 1790–1840. A Documentary History*, 3 vols. (Philadelphia, 1970), and Morris U. Schappes, ed., *A Documentary History of the Jews in the United States, 1654–1875*, 3rd ed. (New York, 1971). The most noteworthy monographic articles which are cited specifically in the footnotes appear in the *Publications of the American Jewish Historical Society (PAJHS)*. The best of these have been collected under one cover by Abraham J. Karp, ed., *The Jewish Experience in America: Selected Studies From the Publication of the American Jewish Historical Society*, 5 vols. (Waltham, 1969). Monographic articles also appear in *American Jewish Archives, Jewish Social Studies (JSS)* and the *American Jewish Yearbook (AJYB)*. A quick source of biographical data for Colonial Jewry is Joseph R. Rosenbloom's, *A Biographical Dictionary of Early American Jews, Colonial Times Through 1800* (Lexington, Ky., 1960). For the later period *Autobigraphies of American Jews*, Harold U. Ribalow, ed. (Philadelphia, 1965), and Harry Simonhoff's *Saga of American Jewry, 1865–1914, Links of an Endless Chain* (New York, 1959), are useful. There are in addition dozens of studies of Jewish life in specific local communities which are especially useful for information on the social and commercial activities of Jews. The best of these are Hyman B. Grinstein, *The Rise of the Jewish Community of New York, 1654–1860* (Philadelphia, 1945); Charles Reznikoff, *The Jews of Charleston, A History of an American Jewish Community* (Philadelphia, 1950); Bertram W. Korn, *The Early Jews of New Orleans* (Waltham, 1969); Joshua Trachtenberg, *Consider the Years, The Story of the Jewish Community of Easton, 1752–1942* (Easton, 1944); Louis J. Switchkow and Lloyd P. Gartner, *History of the Jews of Milwaukee* (Philadelphia, 1962); Morris A. Guttstein, *The Story of the Jews of Newport* (New York, 1936); Selig Adler, *From Ararat to Suburbia, The History of the Jewish Community of Buffalo* (Philadelphia, 1960); Edwin Wolf 2nd and Maxwell Whiteman, *The History of the Jews of Philadelphia From Colonial Times to the Age of Jackson* (Philadelphia, 1957).

The following list of books in the field is intended to be supplementary. Complete references to monographs and monographic articles used in this book are contained in the footnotes for each chapter.

I. Old World Beginnings, Colonial America, the Revolution, Federal Period

ABRAHAMS, ISRAEL. *Jewish Life in the Middle Ages* (New York, 1958).

BARBOUR, VIOLET. *Capitalism in Amsterdam in the 17th Century* (Ann Arbor, 1966).

BOORSTIN, DANIEL. *The Americans, The Colonial Experience* (New York, 1958). Vol. I.

DUBNOW, S. N. *History of the Jews in Russia and Poland*, trans. by I. Friedlander (Philadelphia, 1916–1920), 3 vols.

FRIEDMAN, L. M. *Early American Jews* (Cambridge, 1934).

———. *Jewish Pioneers and Patriots* (Philadelphia, 1942).

HERSHKOWITZ, L., ed. *Wills of Early New York Jews, 1704–1799* (New York, 1967).

HYAMSON, A. M. *The Sephardim of England, A History of the Spanish-Portuguese Jewish Community, 1492–1959* (London, 1952).

KAYSERLING, M. *Christopher Columbus and the Participation of the Jews in the Spanish and Portuguese Discoveries*, trans. by Charles Gross (New York, 1894).

LEBESON, A. L. *Pilgrims People* (New York, 1950).

MADARIAGA, SALVADOR DE. *The Fall of the Spanish Empire* (New York, 1947).

MARCUS, J. R. *The Colonial American Jew, 1492–1776* (Detroit, 1970), 3 vols.

———. *Early American Jewry* (Philadelphia, 1953), 2 vols.

MORISON, S. E. *Admiral of the Ocean Sea, A Life of Christopher Columbus* (Boston, 1942).

ROTH, C. *The Jewish Contribution to Civilization* (Cincinnati, 1940).

SAMUEL, W. S. *A Review of the Jewish Colonists in Barbados in 1680* (London, 1936).

SOLA POOL, D. DE. *Portraits Etched in Stone: Early Jewish Settlers, 1681–1831* (New York, 1952).

WIZNITZER, ARNOLD. *Jews in Colonial Brazil* (New York, 1960).

II. Culture, Religion, Commerce (Ante Bellum Period)

AHLSTROM, S. E. *A Religious History of the American People* (New Haven, 1972).

BAILYN, B. *New England Merchants in the 17th Century* (Cambridge, 1955).

BIRMINGHAM, S. *Our Crowd* (New York, 1967).

BLOOM, H. I. *The Economic Activities of the Jews of Amsterdam in the 17th and 18th Century* (Williamsport, Pa., 1937).

CHYET, S. F. *Lopez of Newport, Colonial American Merchant Prince* (Detroit, 1970).

EMMANUEL, I. S. *Precious Stones of the Jews of Curaçao* (New York, 1957).

FREUND, M. K. *Jewish Merchants in Colonial America* (New York, 1939).

GLANZ, RUDOLF. *Jew and Mormon: Historic Group Relations and Religious Outlook* (New York, 1963).

————. *Studies in Judaica Americana* (New York, 1970).

GOODMAN, A. V. *American Overture, Jewish Rights in Colonial Times* (Philadelphia, 1947).

HARRINGTON, V. *The New York Merchant on the Eve of the Revolution* (New York, 1935).

HELLER, J. G. *Isaac M. Wise, His Life, Work and Thought* (New York, 1965).

HERBERG, W. *Protestant, Catholic, Jew, An Essay in American Religious Sociology* (New York, 1955).

HIRSCHLER, E. E., ed. *Jews from Germany in the United States* (New York, 1945).

KOHUT, G. A., ed. *Ezra Stiles and the Jews* (New York, 1902).

KISH, G. *In Search of Freedom. A History of American Jews From Czechoslovakia* (London, 1949).

KORN, B. W. *German-Jewish Intellectual Influences on American Life, 1824–1972* (B. G. Rudolph Lecture in Judaic Studies, 1972).

KRINSKY, F., ed. *The Politics of Religion in America* (Beverly Hills, 1968).

LEBESON, A. L. *Jewish Pioneers in America, 1492–1848* (New York, 1931).

PARES, R. *Yankee and Creoles: The Trade Between North America and the West Indies Before the American Revolution* (Cambridge, 1956).

PHILIPSON, D. *The Reform Movement in Judaism* (New York, 1931).

PLAUT, G. *The Rise of Reform Judaism, A Sourcebook of its European Origins* (New York, 1963).

PORTER, G. and H. C. LIVESAY. *Merchants and Manufacturers, Studies in the Changing Structure of 19th Century Marketing* (Baltimore, 1971).

SCHLESINGER, A. M., SR. *The Colonial Merchants and the American Revolution, 1763–1766* (New York, 1939).

SCHUMANN, A. S. *No Peddlers Allowed* (Appleton, Wis., 1948).

SPERRY, W. L. *Religion in America* (Boston, 1963).

UCHILL, I. *Pioneers, Peddlers and Tsadikim* (Denver, 1957).

WISCHNITZER, M. *To Dwell in Safety, The Story of Jewish Migration Since 1900* (Philadelphia, 1948).

WISE, I. M. *Reminiscences*, trans. and ed., by D. Philipson (New York, 1901).

WRIGHT, L. B. *The Cultural Life of the American Colonies, 1607–1763* (New York, 1957).

III. Political Behavior (Ante Bellum)

DINNERSTEIN, L. and M. D. PALSTON, eds. *Jews in the South* (Baton Rouge, 1973).

FUCHS, L. H. *The Political Behavior of American Jews* (Glencoe, 1956).

GOLDBERG, I. *Major Noah, American Jewish Pioneer* (Philadelphia, 1936).

JORDAN, C. W. *White Over Black, American Attitudes Toward the Negro, 1550–1812* (Baltimore, 1969).

KATZ, I. *August Belmont, A Political Biography* (New York, 1968).

KORN, B. W. *Jews and Negro in the Old South, 1789–1865* (Elkins Park, 1961).

————. *American Jewry and the Civil War* (New York, 1961).

MEADE, R. D. *Judah P. Benjamin* (New York, 1943).

MEYER, I., ed. *Early History of Zionism in America* (New York, 1958).

SUHL, Y. *Eloquent Crusader, Ernestine Rose* (New York, 1970).

WILLIAMSON, J. *After Slavery, The Negro in South Carolina During Reconstruction, 1861–1877* (Chapel Hill, 1965).

IV.   East European Immigration, the Ghetto, the Jewish Labor Movement

ANTIN, M. *The Promised Land* (Boston, 1917).

BERNHEIMER, C. *The Russian Jews in the United States* (Philadelphia, 1905).

BRANDES, J. *Immigrants to Freedom, Jewish Communities in Rural New Jersey Since 1882* (Philadelphia, 1971).

CAHAN, A. *The Education of Abraham Cahan*, trans. L. Stein, et al. (Philadelphia, 1969).

––––––. *The Rise of David Levinsky* (New York, 1917).

COHEN, M. *A Dreamer's Journey* (Boston, 1949).

COWEN, P. *Memories of an American Jew* (New York, 1932).

DAVIDSON, G. *Our Jewish Farmers and the Story of the Jewish Agricultural Society* (New York, 1943).

DUBOFSKY, M. *When Workers Organize, New York City During the Progressive Era* (Amherst, 1968).

EPSTEIN, M. *Jewish Labor in the U.S.A., An Industrial, Political and Cultural History of the Jewish Labor Movement, 1882–1914*, 2 vols. (New York, 1950–1953).

GARTNER, L. P. *The Jewish Immigration in England, 1870–1914* (London, 1960).

GLANZ, R. *Jew and Italian, Historic Group Relations and the New Immigration, 1881–1924* (New York, 1971).

GOLD, M. *Jews Without Money* (New York, 1930).

HANSEN, M. L. *The Atlantic Migration* (Cambridge, 1940).

HAPGOOD, H. *The Spirit of the Ghetto* (New York, 1965).

HILLQUIT, MORRIS. *Loose Leaves From a Busy Life* (New York, 1934).

HINDUS, M., ed. *The Old East Side* (Philadelphia, 1967).

HOURWICH, I. A. *Immigration and Labor* (New York, 1912).

HOWELLS, W. D. *Impressions and Experiences* (New York, 1896).

HURWITZ, M. *The Workmen's Circle, Its History, Ideals, Organization and Institutions* (New York, 1936).

JOSEPH, S. *Jewish Immigration to the United States* (New York, 1914).

––––––. *The History of the Baron de Hirsch Fund, The Americanization of the Jewish Immigrant* (New York, 1935).

LIPSKY, L. *Thirty Years of American Zionism* (New York, 1927).

MANNERS, A. *Poor Cousins* (New York, 1972).

MENDELSOHN, E. *Class Struggle in the Pale, The Formative Years of the Jewish Workers Movement in Czarist Russia* (Cambridge, 1970).

METZKER, I., ed. *A Bintel Brief* (New York, 1971).

RISCHIN, M. *The Promised City, New York's Jews, 1870–1914* (Cambridge, 1962).

ROSE, P. I., ed. *The Ghetto and Beyond, Essays on Jewish Life in America* (New York, 1969).

ROSKOLENKO, H. *The Time That Was Then, The Lower East Side 1900–1914, An Intimate Chronicle* (New York, 1971).

SANDERS, R. *The Downtown Jews, Portrait of an Immigrant Generation* (New York, 1969).

SCHOENER, A., ed. *Portal to America, The Lower East Side, 1870–1915* (New York, 1967).

SEIDMAN, J. *The Needle Trades* (New York, 1942).

STEFFENS, L. *Autobiography* (New York, 1931).

SHAPIRO, J. *The Friendly Society, The History of the Workmen's Circle* (New York, 1971).

STOLLBERG, B. *Tailor's Progress* (New York, 1944).

TCHERIKOWER, E. *The Early Jewish Labor Movement in the United States* (New York, 1961).

WIRTH, L. *The Ghetto* (Chicago, 1928).

V. Religious, Philanthropic and Organizational Developments

ADLER, C. *I Have Considered the Days* (Philadelphia, 1941).

BENTWICH, N. *For Zion's Sake, A Biography of Judah Magnes* (Philadelphia, 1954).

————. *Solomon Schechter, A Biography* (Philadelphia, 1938).

COHEN, N. *Not Free to Desist* (Philadelphia, 1972).

DAVIS, M. *The Emergence of Conservative Judaism* (Philadelphia, 1963).

FEINSTEIN, M. *American Zionism, 1884–1904* (New York, 1965).

GOREN, A. *New York Jews and the Quest for Community, The Kehillah Experiment, 1908–1922* (New York, 1970).

HALPERIN, S. *The Political World of American Zionism* (Detroit, 1961).

KARPF, M. J. *Jewish Community Organization in the United States* (New York, 1938).

LEVITAN, T. *Islands of Compassion: A History of Jewish Hospitals in New York* (New York, 1961).

LURIE, H. L. *The Jewish Federation Movement in America: A Heritage Affirmed* (Philadelphia, 1961).

MASON, A. T. *Brandeis* (New Yorrk, 1946).

PHILIPSON, D. *My Life as an American Jew* (Cincinnati, 1941).

RABINOWITZ, B. *The Young Men's Hebrew Association* (New York, 1948).

REZNIKOFF, C., ed. *Louis Marshall, Champion of Liberty* (Philadelphia, 1957), 2 vols.

ROSENBLATT, S. *The History of the Mizrachi Movement* (New York, 1951).

ROSENSTOCK, M. *Louis Marshall, Defender of Jewish Rights* (Detroit, 1965).

SCHACHNER, N. *The Price of Liberty* (New York, 1948).

SHAPIRO, Y. *Leadership of the American Zionist Organization, 1897–1930* (Detroit, 1971).

SKLARE, M. *Conservative Judaism, An American Religious Movement* (Glencoe, 1955).

VI. Anti-Semitism

ADORNO, T. W., et al. *The Authoritarian Personality* (New York, 1950).

DINNERSTEIN, L. *Antisemitism in the United States* (New York, 1971).

GOLDEN, H. *A Little Girl is Dead* (New York, 1967).

HIGHAM, J. *Strangers in the Land: Patterns of American Nativism, 1860–1925* (New York, 1968).

HOFSTADTER, R. *Anti-intellectualism in American Life* (New York, 1962).

STEMBER, C. H., et al. *Jews in the Mind of America* (New York, 1966).
STRONG, D. S. *Organized Anti-Semitism in America* (Washington, 1941).

VII.   Jews in Foreign Affairs

ADLER, C. and A. MARGALITH. *With Firmness in the Right: American Diplo-matic Action Affecting Jews, 1840–1945* (New York, 1946).
ADLER, S. *The Isolationist Impulse* (New York, 1961).
COHEN, N. W. *A Dual Heritage: The Public Career of Oscar S. Straus* (Philadelphia, 1969).
DAVIE, M. R. *Refugee in America* (New York, 1947).
FEINGOLD, H. L. *The Politics of Rescue, The Roosevelt Administration and the Holocaust, 1938–1945* (New Brunswick, 1970).
The Autobiography of Nahum Goldmann, Sixty Years of Jewish Life, trans. by H. Sebba (New York, 1969).
HERO, A. O. *Americans in World Affairs* (Boston, 1959).
MORGENTHAU, HENRY. *All in a Lifetime* (New York, 1922).
MORSE, A. *While Six Million Died* (New York, 1968).
PROSKAUER, J. M. *A Segment of My Time* (New York, 1950).
SAFRAN, N. *The United States and Israel* (Cambridge, 1963).
STRAUS, O. *Under Four Administrations* (New York, 1922).
TARTAKOWER, A. and K. GROSSMAN. *The Jewish Refugees* (New York, 1944).
WISCHNITZER, M. *Visas to Freedom, The History of HIAS* (New York, 1956).
WISE, S. S. *Challenging Years* (New York, 1949).
WOLF, S. *The Presidents I Have Known from 1860 to 1918* (Washington, 1918).
WYMAN, G. *Paper Walls* (Amherst, 1969).

VIII.   Contemporary Condition

GOLDSTEIN, S. and C. GOLDSCHEIDER. *Jewish Americans: Three Generations in a Jewish Community* (Englewood Cliffs, 1968).
GORDON, M. I. *Assimilation in American Life: The Role of Race, Religion, and National Origins* (New York, 1964).
JANOWSKY, O. I., ed. *The American Jew: A Composite Portrait* (Philadelphia, 1964).
POLL, S. *The Hassidic Community in Williamsburg* (New York, 1962).
SHERMAN, C. B. *The Jews Within American Society* (New York, 1961).
SKLARE, M. and JOSEPH GREENBLUM. *Jewish Identity on the Suburban Frontier: A Study of Group Survival in the Open Society* (New York, 1967).
SKLARE, M., ed *The Jews: Social Patterns of an American Group* (New York, 1958).
————. *America's Jews* (New York, 1971).
SKLARE, M. and M. VOSK. *The Riverton Study* (New York, 1957).
TELLER, J. L. *Strangers and Natives, The Evolution of the American Jew From 1921 to the Present* (New York, 1968).

Index